Fuels Paradise

Fuels Paradise

*Seeking Energy Security in Europe, Japan,
and the United States*

John S. Duffield

Johns Hopkins University Press
Baltimore

© 2015 Johns Hopkins University Press
All rights reserved. Published 2015
Printed in the United States of America on acid-free paper
2 4 6 8 9 7 5 3 1

Johns Hopkins University Press
2715 North Charles Street
Baltimore, Maryland 21218-4363
www.press.jhu.edu

Library of Congress Cataloging-in-Publication Data

Duffield, John S.
Fuels paradise : seeking energy security in Europe, Japan, and the United States /
John S. Duffield.
pages cm
Includes bibliographical references and index.
ISBN 978-1-4214-1673-1 (pbk. : alk. paper) — ISBN 978-1-4214-1674-8
(electronic) — ISBN 1-4214-1673-5 (pbk. : alk. paper) — ISBN 1-4214-1674-3
(electronic) 1. Energy security—Europe. 2. Energy security—
Japan. 3. Energy security—United States. 4. Energy policy—
Europe. 5. Energy policy—Japan. 6. Energy policy—United States. I. Title.
HD9502.A2D84 2015
333.79—dc23   2014031361

A catalog record for this book is available from the British Library.

Special discounts are available for bulk purchases of this book.
For more information, please contact Special Sales at 410-516-6936 or
specialsales@press.jhu.edu.

Johns Hopkins University Press uses environmentally friendly book materials,
including recycled text paper that is composed of at least 30 percent
post-consumer waste, whenever possible.

To Cheryl, again and always

CONTENTS

Acknowledgments *ix*
List of Abbreviations *xi*

1 The Puzzle: *Diverse State Responses to Energy Insecurity* 1

PART ONE: ANALYTIC FRAMEWORK

2 What's the Problem? *Energy Security in the Developed Democracies* 19

3 What's a State to Do? *Potential Policy Responses to Energy Insecurity* 31

4 Explaining State Responses to Energy Insecurity 42

PART TWO: CASE STUDIES

5 Britain: *From Fossil Fuel Importer to Exporter—and Back* 67

6 France: *Nuclear Power and Its Discontents* 117

7 Germany: *From Dependence on Persian Gulf Oil to Russian Gas* 151

8 Japan: *Across-the-board Energy Insecurity* 195

9 The United States: Plus ça change . . . 240

10 The Quest for Energy Security: *Findings and Implications* 289

Notes *327*
References *335*
Index *365*

ACKNOWLEDGMENTS

Numerous individuals and organizations provided assistance that was essential to the completion of this project, and it is a pleasure to be able to acknowledge them here. I first wish to thank Georgia State University and the German Marshall Fund of the United States for generous financial support. The earliest incarnation of the project was supported by a GSU Research Initiation Grant. Then a substantial fellowship from the German Marshall Fund financed a semester free from teaching responsibilities and a summer of research in Europe in 2006. The College of Arts and Sciences at GSU granted me an additional semester leave, and departmental professional development funds paid for a return trip to Germany in 2007. A GSU Scholarly Support Grant made it possible for me to spend three weeks conducting interviews in Japan in 2010.

While overseas, I benefited from the generosity of a number of institutions. The German Marshall Fund office in Brussels granted me the use of an office and its many resources. The German Council on Foreign Relations in Berlin (DGAP) gave me access to its library. The Centre Américain at Sciences Po in Paris provided me with a desk and telephone. Chuo University in Tokyo extended an affiliation and an opportunity to present some of the arguments in this book. I am also indebted to the dozens of individuals in Europe and Japan who granted in-depth interviews, sometimes lasting more than an hour. In order to maintain confidentiality, I cannot name them here, but I can extend my deepest gratitude.

Along the way, a number of professional colleagues helped in a variety of ways, from sharing contacts in Europe and Japan to providing assistance with the design of research protocols to demystifying the logistics of doing fieldwork in five foreign countries. Among those to whom I am most grateful are Ed Morse, Friedemann Müller, Kim Reimann, Len Schoppa, Satoko Yasuno, and especially, Brian Woodall, who accompanied me during much of my time in Japan and provided invaluable assistance with interviews while serving as a peerless guide to Japanese politics, history, culture, and cuisine. In addition, Toby Bolsen, Peter Dombrowski, and Charles Hankla provided feedback on parts of the manuscript.

At Georgia State, I have been fortunate to have the help of a steady stream of capable research assistants: Katrina Boyko, Sean Ding, Karit Guerrero, Holly Lindamood, Raluca Miller, Sara Miller, Ilídio Nhantumbo, Jean-François Onivogui, Kris Sauriol, Ian Smith, and Camille Wolpe.

Parts of chapter 10 appeared in an earlier form in "The Return of Energy Insecurity in the Developed Democracies," *Contemporary Security Policy* 33, no. 1 (April 2012): 1–26.

I wish to thank my editor at Johns Hopkins University Press, Suzanne Flinchbaugh, who took an immediate interest in the project and who ensured an expeditious review of the manuscript. An anonymous reviewer provided a number of suggestions that helped to improve the final version. During the production process, Jack Rummel's careful copyediting made my life much simpler, and senior production editor Debby Bors ably guided me through the challenges of proofreading and indexing to the finish line.

Finally, I dedicate this book to my wife. Like every other major professional and personal project in my life, this one could not have been completed without her patience and tolerance as well as her love and support. She has put up with my long absences, whether overseas or in the basement office, and she has provided moral support and encouragement when the going was slow. Just by being there to share the all the excitement and frustration, joys and disappointments that inevitably accompany a big undertaking such as this, she makes it all worthwhile. Thank you, Cheryl!

AEE	Agence pour les économies d'énergie
AFME	Agence française pour la maîtrise de l'énergie
AGR	advanced gas-cooled reactor
ANRE	Agency for Natural Resources and Energy
ANWR	Arctic National Wildlife Refuge
ASEAN	Association of Southeast Asian Nations
ASN	Autorité de sûreté nucléaire (Nuclear Safety Authority)
bcm	billion cubic meters
BEP	Basic Energy Plan
BGS	British Geological Survey
BMU	Bundesministerium für Umwelt (Federal Ministry of the Environment)
BMWi	Bundesministerium für Wirtschaft (Federal Ministry of Economics)
BNOC	British National Oil Company
BRP	Bureau de recherches de pétrole
CAFE	Corporate Average Fuel Economy
CBM	coal-bed methane
CCL	Climate Change Levy
CCS	carbon capture and storage
CDF	Charbonnage de France
CDU	Christlich Demokratische Union Deutschlands
CEA	Commissariat à l'énergie atomique
CEGB	Central Electricity Generating Board
CENTCOM	U.S. Central Command
CERT	Carbon Emissions Reduction Target
CFP	Compagnie française des pétroles
CHP	combined heat and power
COET	crude oil equalization tax
CSU	Christlich-Soziale Union
DEMINEX	Deutsche Erdölversorgungsgesellschaft
DM	Deutsche mark
DOE	U.S. Department of Energy
EAS	East Asia Summit
EBV	Erdölbevorratungsverband

EC	European Community
EDF	Électricité de France
EEG	Erneuerbare-Energien-Gezetz (Renewable Energy Law)
EIA	U.S. Energy Information Administration
EISA	Energy Independence and Security Act (2007)
EMR	Electricity Market Reform
EPAA	Emergency Petroleum Allocation Act
EPACT	Energy Policy Act (2005)
EPCA	Energy Policy and Conservation Act (1975)
EPR	European pressurized water reactor
ERAP	Entreprise de recherches et d'activités pétrolières
ESS	Emergency Sharing System
ESSG	Energy Security Study Group
ETS	Emissions Trading Scheme
EU	European Union
EV	electric vehicle
FBR	fast breeder reactor
FDP	Freie Demokratische Partei
FF	French francs
GCR	gas-cooled reactor
GDA	Generic Design Assessment
GDF	Gaz de France
GDP	gross domestic product
GHG	greenhouse gas
GNP	gross national product
GW	gigawatt
IEA	International Energy Agency
IEEJ	Institute of Energy Economics of Japan
IEKP	Integriertes Energie- und Klimaprogramm
IMF	International Monetary Found
IPC	Infrastructure Planning Commission
IPCC	Intergovernmental Panel on Climate Change
IRENA	International Renewable Energy Agency
JBIC	Japan Bank for International Cooperation
JETRO	Japan External Trade Organization
JNOC	Japan National Oil Company
JOGMEC	Japan Oil, Gas, and Metals National Corporation
JPDC	Japan Petroleum Development Corporation

LCPD	Large Combustion Plant Directive
LCTP	Low-Carbon Transition Plan
LDV	light-duty vehicle
LNG	liquefied natural gas
LPG	liquefied petroleum gas
LPOPE	Loi de programme fixant les orientations de la politique énergétique (energy policy law)
LWR	light-water reactor
MBD	million barrels per day
METI	Ministry of Economics, Trade, and Industry
MITI	Ministry of International Trade and Industry
MOX	mixed plutonium-uranium oxide
mpg	miles per gallon
MSP	Minimum Safeguard Price
mtoe	million tonnes of oil equivalent
MW	megawatt
NATO	North Atlantic Treaty Organization
NCB	National Coal Board
NEDO	New Energy Development Organization
NEPDG	National Energy Policy Development Group
NEXI	Nippon Export and Investment Insurance
NNES	New National Energy Strategy
NPS	National Policy Statement
NUM	National Union of Mineworkers
ODA	official development assistance
OECD	Organisation for Economic Co-operation and Development
OPEC	Organization of the Petroleum Exporting Countries
OSCE	Organization for Security and Co-operation in Europe
PEC	primary energy consumption
PNLCC	National Program for Tackling Climate Change
PPI	Programmation pluriannuelle des investissements (multiyear investment program)
PRT	Petroleum Revenue Tax
PSPA	Petroleum and Submarine Pipelines Act
PV	photovoltaic
PWR	pressurized water reactor
RO	Renewables Obligation
RPS	renewable portfolio standard

RTFO	Renewable Transport Fuels Obligation
SFC	Synthetic Fuels Corporation
SGHWR	steam-generating heavy water reactor
SPD	Sozialdemokratische Partei Deutschlands (Social Democratic Party)
SPR	Strategic Petroleum Reserve
tcm	trillion cubic meters
TEPCO	Tokyo Electric Power Company
TRR	technically recoverable resources
TWh	terawatt hours
UAE	United Arab Emirates
UK	United Kingdom

CHAPTER ONE

The Puzzle

Diverse State Responses to Energy Insecurity

> The political theorists who work on security matters still tend to think of strategy as something pertaining mainly to military security, to defence policy and not to energy policy.
>
> —Susan Strange, *States and Markets*

> It has become clear that interruptions in the flow of critically needed resources can be as detrimental to the balance of international power—and hence national security—as more conventional confrontations.
>
> —Walter Carlsnaes, *Energy Vulnerability and National Security*

During the first decade of the twenty-first century, concerns about energy security reached levels not witnessed since the 1970s and early 1980s. And in large part because of such concerns, the major developed democracies—Britain, France, Germany, Japan, and the United States—undertook sweeping reviews of their energy policies and initiated significant policy changes. As in the 1970s, moreover, the decade of the 2000s also saw proposals for additional efforts at international cooperation to promote energy security, especially within the International Energy Agency (IEA), the North Atlantic Treaty Organization (NATO), and the European Union (EU). That, however, is where the similarities between the two periods largely end.

In contrast to the 1970s, when the principal sources of energy insecurity in virtually all developed countries were high oil prices and uncertainty about oil supplies, the energy security concerns of the early 2000s were much more diverse. The focus of U.S. policy, for example, continued to be on reducing the country's dependence on foreign oil. The primary source of concern in France was the country's aging nuclear power plants. In Britain, the problem was how to manage the transition from self-sufficiency in fossil fuels to being a net importer of oil and, especially, gas. And German energy security worries centered on the reliability of foreign natural gas supplies, especially those from Russia. Partly as a result of these differences, the central responses of these otherwise politically and economically similar countries were also quite varied. Despite common interests in energy efficiency and diversifying energy supplies, national policies were characterized by significant differences in emphasis on government intervention, market liberalization, nuclear power, renewable energy sources, and foreign policy initiatives, to list but several of the more prominent issues.

Even in the 1970s, the developed democracies responded to energy insecurity in notably different ways, employing distinct mixes of external and internal policy instruments to address their concerns. Significant variation existed in the degree to which governments sought to promote conservation and energy efficiency, especially with regard to the use of oil. Important differences also emerged in the development and promotion of alternatives to oil, such as nuclear power and natural gas. Thus, although total energy consumption in all five countries in 1985 stood roughly at the same levels as 12 years before, they had reduced their oil use by widely varying amounts. These different approaches at home were reflected in the limited degree of cooperation to promote energy security that took place among the advanced industrialized democracies under the auspices of the EU and the IEA, which was established in 1974 expressly for that purpose. They were also paralleled by contrasting stances toward the oil-exporting regions of the world, especially the Persian Gulf.

Objectives

In view of these puzzling past and more recent patterns, this book has three basic objectives. The first is to describe in comparative perspective how the major developed democracies have responded to heightened concerns about energy security, both following the oil shocks and during the first decade of the twenty-first century. What particular energy security problems have those countries faced? What policy options have they had at their disposal? What choices among those options have they made?

A second and closely related goal is to provide a theoretically informed explanation of state responses to energy insecurity, both across space and over time. Why have the major developed democracies made—and not made—particular choices? What factors best account for the principal similarities and differences in their approaches and policies? Of particular interest is understanding the reasons for the observed variations in state responses.

The third purpose is to explore the implications of these responses and their determinants, especially for international cooperation to promote energy security. What are the prospects for, and principal obstacles to, cooperation at the regional and global levels, especially among the major developed democracies? To what degree do they face common problems that lend themselves to joint approaches? In what ways could differences in their concerns and preferred policy responses limit their ability to work together? Clearly, the answers to these questions will depend on the underlying determinants of state responses to energy insecurity. And because energy insecurity is likely to remain a major concern for many states in the coming years, it will continue to be important to anticipate how major powers are likely to respond in order to manage and, where possible, prevent potential conflicts.

The Limited Literature on State Responses to Energy Insecurity

In pursuing these objectives, this book fills a substantial gap in the literature. The oil shocks of the 1970s precipitated an outpouring of scholarly works on the responses of oil-consuming states. Many focused on individual countries, especially the United States (e.g., Mancke 1976; Bohi and Russell 1978; Goodwin 1981; Temkin 1983; Bull-Berg 1987) and, secondarily, Japan (e.g., Wu 1977; Morse 1981c), while quite a few offered comparative analyses of how industrialized countries dealt with the oil shocks (e.g., SIPRI 1974; Vernon 1975; Menderhausen 1976; Lindberg 1977; Krapels 1980; Kohl 1982; Yergin and Hillenbrand 1982; Kemezis and Wilson 1984). Complementing these descriptive accounts were a number of primarily prescriptive works, although the bulk of these were directed in particular at U.S. energy policy (e.g., Teller et al. 1976; Conant and Gold 1978; Stobaugh and Yergin 1979; Deese and Nye 1981; Plummer 1982a). In addition, some scholars analyzed the creation of the IEA and Western cooperation to promote energy security more generally (e.g., Walton 1976; Willrich and Conant 1977; Keohane 1978 and 1984; Cowhey 1985), and as the IEA's limitations became evident, others sought to understand the obstacles to cooperation as well as its future prospects (e.g., Lieber 1983; Jentleson 1986; Kupchan 1987; Kapstein 1990).

Most of the literature spawned by the oil shocks was atheoretical in nature, however. With the principal exception of John Ikenberry's path-breaking research on the adjustment strategies pursued by industrialized countries (1986a; 1988), few works were informed by or drew on theories of comparative and international politics. Thus the literature contributed little to broader scholarly debates on the determinants of public policy and state behavior.

Although there has been a resurgence of interest in the subject of energy security in recent years (e.g., Marquina 2008; Moran and Russell 2008; Müller-Kraenner 2008; Pascual and Elkind 2009; Stokes and Raphael 2010; Bahgat 2011; Sovacool 2011; Brown and Sovacool 2012; Goldthau 2012), scholars have devoted little attention to analyzing and comparing specific state responses to the energy security concerns of the past decade. To be sure, much has been written on U.S. energy security. A number of recent works describe and explain America's dependence on foreign oil, in particular, and how it has shaped U.S. foreign and military policy, both in general and toward specific regions (e.g., Bahgat 2003; Pelletiere 2004; Klare 2004a; Rutledge 2005; Duffield 2008; Yetiv 2008). Paralleling these analyses are primarily prescriptive works on how to reduce U.S. energy insecurity (e.g., Kalicki and Goldwyn 2005; Yergin 2006; Sandalow 2007; Zubrin 2007; Doran 2008; Hakes 2008; Luft and Korin 2009a).

In contrast, scholars have produced virtually nothing so far on the recent concerns about and efforts to address energy insecurity in the other major advanced democracies. What does exist consists primarily of government reports and studies produced by analysts associated with think tanks (on Britain, see Helm 2005, 2007a; on Germany, see Götz 2005; Müller 2005, 2007; on Japan, see Evans 2006; Chrisstoffels 2007). Missing entirely is any theoretically informed comparative analysis of state responses to energy insecurity in the 2000s, and no work has attempted to compare the policies adopted in recent years with those of the 1970s.

This book, then, contributes to our understanding of state responses to energy insecurity in several ways. It brings the empirical record up to date to include the developments and events of the last decade. It examines systematically state responses in a comparative framework that is both cross-national and longitudinal. And it grounds the entire analysis in theories of state behavior. Along the way, the book aspires, however modestly, to contribute to broader debates about the determinants of state behavior and public policy. And by suggesting the types of energy policies that are more or less feasible and effective under different circumstances and the types of constraints that policymakers are likely to face as they seek to promote their countries' energy security, it may also be of some policy relevance. At a minimum, it should help to illuminate the opportunities for—and likely limits to—promoting international cooperation on energy issues.

Principal Arguments

The book makes four broad arguments. The first concerns the determinants of policy responses to energy insecurity. This book places particular emphasis on the strength of the state while offering an original way of conceptualizing it, or what I term the three "faces" of state strength. The second argument addresses the impact of earlier policy choices on later energy security concerns and policy decisions, or so-called policy legacies, noting the existence of a significant degree of path dependence. The third relates to the substantial obstacles to international cooperation to promote energy security. And the fourth argument regards the impact of recent developments in the production and distribution of energy, especially the "fracking revolution," on the prospects for achieving energy security.

The Importance of State Strength

Depending on the particular challenges that they face, states can take a potentially large number of actions to promote their energy security. At home, they may seek to reduce the consumption of insecure energy supplies, to increase domestic production of those same energy sources or substitutes, and to establish contingency plans and stockpiles for dealing with sudden shortages, among other things. Abroad, they may seek to increase the reliability of their access to existing foreign energy supplies or to develop alternative sources of supply.

Correspondingly, a large number of factors can shape the set of policies that states actually pursue. An obvious place to begin is with a state's domestic energy resource endowments, which vary substantially across major energy-consuming states. Another important determinant is likely to be the character of the corresponding society. It may be marked by broad dispositions to favor or oppose particular policies, for example, as rooted in a particular political culture (Duffield 1999). Or there may be powerful private actors and coalitions within society that lobby the government for policies that serve their particularist interests (Moravcsik 1997). This book, however, places emphasis on the characteristics of the state, especially state strength. It argues that many features of a country's responses to energy insecurity cannot be understood without reference to its particular forms of state strength and weakness.

The concept of state strength has been developed by students of comparative politics (e.g., Krasner 1978a; Nordlinger 1981; Skocpol 1985; Ikenberry 1988). Within the existing literature, one can distinguish between two principal components of state strength (Hollifield 1990; Chen and Dickson 2010). One is the decision-making autonomy of the state, or its ability to determine policy goals and strategies independently of the preferences of society as a whole or those of special interests. The other component concerns the ability or capacity of the state to mobilize and deploy domestic resources and, more generally, to control and direct socioeconomic and political forces in society so as to achieve policy goals. This second aspect of state strength will depend on the types of authority, policy instruments, administrative skills, and other resources available to the state.

Although the concept of state strength has been a highly productive one, the literature contains an important blind spot. Most studies that employ the concept focus on policies that seek to shape the domestic economy and society (again, a noteworthy exception is Ikenberry 1988). But, as noted above, policies pursued in response to concerns about energy security may have both internal and external dimensions. Thus to understand the choices states make within and across these two arenas, one must also consider a third component of state strength: the ability of the state to pursue and achieve its goals with respect to outside actors and structures. Like its internal counterpart, this international dimension of state capacity may have numerous sources, such as diplomatic skill, military power, economic and financial resources, and the authority to control access to national markets.

Thus, at least for the purposes of understanding state responses to energy insecurity, it is useful to conceptualize state strength as having three principal faces. The particular combination of domestic and international policies that a country pursues will depend considerably on its relative strength in each of these areas: policymaking autonomy, domestic capacity, and international capacity. And the five countries examined in this book have exhibited considerable variation along all three dimensions, both cross-nationally and over time.

For example, when it comes to domestic policy matters, the United States has been widely considered to have very limited decision-making autonomy and domestic capacity. With regard to external policy, however, the U.S. executive has often enjoyed considerable freedom of maneuver and powerful policy tools. In contrast, France has long been viewed as the exemplar of the strong state, with a highly insulated policymaking apparatus and the ability to play a large role in the economy and society. Nevertheless, the ability of the French state to unilaterally determine domestic outcomes has always been marked by important exceptions and may have eroded over time (e.g., Katzenstein 1976; Krasner 1978a; Skocpol 1985; Suleiman 1987; Hollifield 1990).

The Policy Legacies of State Responses: Path Dependence

The second argument of the book concerns the impact of earlier choices on later sources of energy insecurity and policy responses, or what have been called policy legacies. To a striking extent, the actions taken—or not taken—in response to the oil shocks of the 1970s determined the challenges the major advanced democracies have had to deal with during the last decade. Although the states faced a very similar set of energy security concerns in the earlier period, they have confronted a much more diverse set of challenges in the 2000s, in no small part because their previous responses differed in important respects.

The United States did the least to reduce its oil dependence and, as a result, its recent energy security concerns have been the most similar to those of the 1970s: the high price of oil and petroleum products and the country's dependence on oil imports. In contrast, France invested the most heavily in nuclear energy, which now accounts for more than 40 percent of its primary energy consumption. But as a result of this emphasis, France's primary concern of the 2000s has centered on the aging of—and the eventual need to replace—its nuclear power plants. Britain responded to the oil shocks in part by making sure that the recently discovered oil and natural gas resources of the North Sea were exploited to the fullest extent, but as production has declined in recent years, it has faced the challenges associated with once again finding itself a fossil fuel importer. And many of Germany's recent concerns stem from the fact that, in its efforts to diversify away from oil, it has become increasingly dependent on imported natural gas, much of which comes from Russia via fixed pipelines and cannot easily be replaced in the event of a supply disruption. Thus state responses to energy security have been characterized by a significant degree of path dependence.

Obstacles to International Cooperation to Promote Energy Security

Because of different policy preferences in the 1970s, the advanced democracies attained only a modest degree of cooperation to promote energy security in response to the oil shocks. The most notable achievement was the creation by members of the Organisation for Economic Co-operation and Development (OECD) of the IEA as a forum for coordinating their policies for dealing with oil supply disruptions and, in the longer term, reducing oil dependence. The IEA did quickly establish an arrangement for sharing oil supplies in the event of an emergency, but its members were unsuccessful at developing meaningful measures for limiting oil consumption and imports, and France initially refused to participate in the organization at all. Even the IEA's most important feature, the emergency oil sharing system, was revealed to have significant limitations when first put to the test during the second oil crisis. The system's mandatory demand restraint and reallocation of oil supplies would only be activated if one or more IEA members suffered a supply reduction of at least 7 percent. Yet it soon became clear that smaller reductions could have negative economic consequences, especially if they generated substantial price increases (Scott 1994, 84–86, 115–17).

The third argument of the book is that the prospects for significant multilateral cooperation to promote energy security are even more limited today than they were in the 1970s. As noted above, the recent reemergence of concerns about energy security spawned a number of proposals for collective action, many of which have concerned the IEA, NATO, and the EU. While some agreements may be reached, however, progress toward new cooperative arrangements has been slow and extremely limited. With the possible exception of the EU, divergent national energy security concerns and policy preferences have and will continue to place sharp limits on what can be accomplished and make meaningful collective responses difficult, if not impossible, to orchestrate. And even within the EU, substantial obstacles remain before that body can respond in a unified way to energy security challenges.

Fracking and Energy Security

Finally, the book begins to explore the implications of recent advances in the production, distribution, and use of energy for energy security. Of particular interest has been the widespread introduction in the United States of "fracking," which combines advances in seismic imaging, horizontal drilling, and hydraulic fracturing to release oil and natural gas from hitherto unexploited deposits of shale and other "tight" rock formations located deep underground. As a result, U.S. oil and gas production has experienced a sharp revival. Output of crude oil has reached levels not seen in two decades, and that of natural gas is at an all-time high and still rising. As a result, energy security has become much less salient an issue in the United States, although the country remains vulnerable to oil price shocks.

The energy security benefits of fracking will not be shared equally, however, either by the countries examined here or by many others around the world. Japan has almost no reserves of shale oil and gas. Germany and especially France have somewhat more potential, but so far, they have not allowed fracking on their soil. Only the British government has shown much enthusiasm for fracking, but public opposition remains strong.

To be sure, these countries will benefit indirectly from the use of fracking elsewhere. Fracking in other European countries, such as Poland, may ease the region's dependence on Russian gas. Likewise, Japan will benefit from the exploitation of shale gas in China, which would temper the latter's rapidly growing demand for gas imports. The rapid rise of U.S. natural gas production has already helped by obviating the need for imports of liquefied natural gas (LNG) and driving down the price of American coal, which has been substituted for gas to generate electricity in Europe. And expected future exports of LNG from the United States should help import-dependent states to diversify their sources of gas supplies. But fracking is unlikely to transform the energy security situation of other countries to the extent that it has that of the United States. Energy insecurity takes too many different forms to be addressed by a single technological breakthrough.

The Approach

To achieve its objectives, this book conducts a theoretically informed, comparative case study analysis of the responses to energy insecurity of the five largest advanced industrialized democracies—Britain, France, Germany, Japan, and the United States—during two time periods, the 1970s and the first decade of the twenty-first century. This choice of cases is based on both substantive and methodological considerations.

The five countries of concern have consistently been among the world's largest energy consumers. In 1973, at the time of the first oil shock, they all ranked among the top six oil users and among the top seven overall energy consumers, accounting for half of global energy use and some 54 percent of world oil consumption. Even as recently as 2000, their combined energy consumption still amounted to around 40 percent of the world's total, and they still numbered among the top nine energy users and represented four of the six or seven largest consumers of oil, natural gas, and nuclear power. Thus the policy choices of these countries have exerted some of the greatest influences on regional and world energy markets, and their participation has been and remains critical to the success of cooperative international schemes to promote energy security.

At the same time, these countries have shared a number of common characteristics. They all feature industrialized market economies and democratic political systems. Thus their governments operate under relatively similar, if not identical, societal constraints. Broadly speaking, moreover, they have all faced similar energy security concerns as importers of substantial amounts of fossil fuels. And they are roughly similar in size, especially in comparison with most other countries. Few states have matched them in terms of economic and other power resources. As a result of their overall size and resources, these five states have all enjoyed a relatively broad range of potential policy options, both domestically and internationally. They have not been entirely at the mercy of outside forces but have possessed the ability to influence the external environment to a significant extent. This high, if still limited, degree of comparability should facilitate the process of identifying the sources of variation in their policy responses.

Some might question whether it makes sense to study the policies of Britain, France, and Germany individually rather than the EU as a whole. Until the last decade, however, the EU has not had a distinct energy policy. To the contrary, energy policy has been one area in which the member states have guarded their national prerogatives with particular vigilance. Thus how and to what degree Britain, France, and Germany have sought to address their energy security concerns in the context of the EU has been an important aspect of their policy responses in recent years (Birchfield and Duffield 2011).

The time periods covered by this book are marked by important differences. The 1970s featured the two big oil shocks separated by just five years, while the first decade of the twenty-first century was characterized by a more diverse and sometimes more slowly developing set of concerns. But these two periods also represent the two episodes since World War II, other than the immediate postwar years, when concerns about energy security have been most acute. Both the 1970s, as a result of the oil shocks, and the first decade of the 2000s, for a wider variety of reasons, saw energy security move, at least temporarily, to the top of the policy agenda in each of these countries. In contrast, the years leading up to the first oil shock and then between the early 1980s and the late 1990s were generally characterized by a glut of oil supplies and low energy prices. Fears of supply shortages and a sharp rise in oil prices did occur during the 1990–91 Gulf War, but that crisis passed quickly and had little lasting impact on energy policies.

In many respects, the responses to the energy security concerns of the early twenty-first century are still unfolding. This book is limited, however, to examining policy developments through the end of the first decade. This cutoff, though somewhat arbitrary, can be justified on several grounds. By 2009 or 2010, the basic thrust of energy security policy in each country in response to the heightened energy security concerns of the decade had largely been set. In addition, worries about energy security had been overshadowed by concerns about climate change, the state of the economy following the global financial crisis and subsequent recession, and nuclear safety. Thus where important policy shifts occurred in subsequent years, they were not justified in terms of energy security. Finally, four of the five countries experienced changes of government in those two years, with the fifth (France) following in 2012. Nevertheless, evidence from more recent years is included where it sheds light on the effectiveness of each country's policy responses in promoting its energy security.

The scope of the analysis is restricted in at least three further respects. First, energy security concerns can result from developments and conditions located both inside and outside a country. This book, however, emphasizes those elements of insecurity that stem from a country's dependence on external sources of energy and from its efforts to reduce that dependence. It is these types of concerns that potentially lend themselves to the full range of policy responses, both domestic and international, that is of interest in this book. In addition, disruptions of foreign energy supplies are likely to affect multiple countries at the same time, increasing the likelihood that states will face similar energy security challenges and thus facilitating a comparison of their policies.

Second, the book focuses on responses intended to reduce energy insecurity over the medium to long term, not short-term measures such as temporary rationing or driving restrictions that might garner publicity but are difficult to sustain and do little to improve a country's overall energy security position. As energy policy expert Jay Hakes has noted in the American context, "It generally takes at least two to six years for positive effects of federal legislation to have much impact (and longer for investments in research and development)" (Hakes 2008, 70). Such a time frame may also allow the analysis to include not only changes in policy but the development of new policy instruments.

Third, the focus is limited to the policy responses of national central or federal governments to periods of heightened energy insecurity. In some countries, other levels of government may exercise important roles in the determination of energy policy. In addition, powerful private actors may respond in their own ways to the same conditions. But it is typically only the national government that can act with authority in both the domestic and international realms, and it typically possesses the greatest authority and the most extensive range of policy instruments. Thus the preferences and actions of other actors are treated as part of the environment to which the national government must respond.

The project employs the method of structured, focused comparison (George and Bennett 2004). This involves asking a set of standardized, general questions of each case to ensure the acquisition of comparable data across all the cases. Ideally, it would also use process tracing, which "attempts to identify the intervening causal process—the causal chain and causal mechanisms—between an independent variable (or variables) and the outcome of the dependent variable" (George and Bennett 2004, 206). Process tracing, however, is made difficult by the relatively large number of cases—five countries, two times periods—for a qualitative analysis and the complexity of each case. In practice, a state's overall response to energy insecurity may take the form of a large number of distinct policies. Indeed, a careful examination of any one of the 10 subcases could easily fill a single book, as exemplified by Ikenberry's study of U.S. adjustment policy following the oil shocks (1988).

Thus, in order to keep this project to a manageable size, it will not be possible to trace the development of any single policy in much detail. Instead, it will be necessary to condense what in some cases was a long and complicated series of actions influenced at different times by different factors into what is effectively a single set of policy choices. The goal is to provide an accurate overall summary of each state's response as well as of the principal determinants in each period, although each case will provide an overview of how the policy response was developed.

The complexity of each case, however, has the advantage of allowing for considerable within-case comparison. By systematically examining the full range of policies intended to promote energy security that are considered and adopted at roughly the same time within a single country, we are able to obtain greater explanatory leverage. To facilitate such a comparison, chapter 3 develops a comprehensive typology of possible policy responses to energy insecurity.

The method of data analysis, then, is straightforward. For each case, I first use the relevant data to develop a thorough description of the policies contemplated and adopted by the country in question during each particular time period. Second, I use the data to evaluate alternative explanations of those policy choices. The types of empirical sources used, however, differ substantially for the two periods. For the 1970s and early 1980s, the book draws heavily on secondary works. As noted above, a substantial scholarly literature already exists on the energy policies of the major industrialized democracies following the two oil shocks. Where useful, I supplement these works with primary sources, such as reports by the EU and the IEA. Here, the principal challenge is not finding data but integrating the available information into the analytic framework.

The more recent period represents a much greater challenge, given that little scholarly work has yet appeared on how states have responded to the energy security concerns of the past decade. Consequently, the book relies almost entirely on primary sources such as government documents and studies, statements by political leaders and public officials, analyses by independent experts, and press reports. In addition, I draw on interviews with scores of policymakers and government officials, policy experts in the academy and private sector, and other highly informed observers of national energy policies that were conducted over a total of four months of field research in Europe and Japan.

Organization

The remainder of the book is divided into two main parts and a conclusion. Part 1 presents the conceptual and theoretical framework, which consists of three chapters. The first chapter establishes the boundaries of the problem: energy security in the advanced democracies. It defines the concept of energy security as employed in the book and reviews the principal common threats to energy security that the major industrialized democracies have faced in the postwar era.

It pays particular attention to the oil shocks of the 1970s and the more diverse concerns of the first decade of the 2000s, when the issue of energy security once again moved to the top of the policy agenda in all five countries.

Chapter 3, the next chapter in part 1, presents a comprehensive typology of potential policy responses to concerns about energy insecurity. A necessary first step in comparing state behavior is to determine the possible range of variation of the phenomenon under investigation. Accordingly, the project seeks to identify and categorize in an analytically useful way the types of actions that major industrialized countries might take in response to energy insecurity, analogous to Ikenberry's insightful typology of adjustment strategies (Ikenberry 1988). As noted above, these responses can take both external and internal forms. At home, states may seek to reduce consumption of an insecure energy source, to promote production of that source and/or substitutes, and to make emergency preparations for possible future supply disruptions. Abroad, they may attempt to reduce the risk of foreign supply disruptions by securing existing sources of energy and transportation routes, to diversify their energy supplies by developing alternative sources, and to coordinate all of the above measures with other states that face similar threats. Within each of these broad categories may be a number of more specific policies and approaches.

How do states seeking to enhance their energy security choose from this wide range of options? Potential determinants of state responses to energy insecurity are the subject of chapter 4, the third chapter of part 1. Although no extant theory deals specifically with the question of state responses to energy insecurity, a number of existing approaches in the scholarly literature on international relations and comparative politics offer relevant insights. Consequently, the project draws on this literature to create an explanatory framework that organizes potentially important determinants of state responses in a logical fashion.

Obviously, much will depend on how the threat is defined, which is a function in turn of the country's current energy mix and where that energy comes from. Particular responses will also be constrained and facilitated, at least initially, by other energy-related policies. Traditionally, energy security has been but one of several goals that energy policy is intended to achieve (e.g., Griffin 2009). Also important have been ensuring the affordability of energy supplies and, increasingly, limiting the environmental impact of the production, transportation, and consumption of energy. In addition, energy policy has often been used to pursue social goals such as job creation and the economic development of particular regions. Perhaps needless to say, these other goals are often in tension with the promotion of energy security.

Beyond those initial conditions, the first place to look is at a state's material resources and technological endowments. What types of policy responses are physically possible? A second important set of determinants is likely to be found within the society in which the state is embedded, both in terms of broad cultural and ideological dispositions and the interests of particular, organized social groups. But as discussed above, this book places particular emphasis on the characteristics of the state itself, especially state strength, of which three "faces" stand out: decision-making autonomy, domestic capacity, and international capacity. Appropriately, the chapter devotes considerable attention to elaborating this multidimensional concept of state strength. A final section explores the question of path dependence and how the choice of policies at an earlier time period can shape future energy security concerns and condition future policy responses.

Part 2 provides a detailed analysis of the energy security policies of the major developed democracies in response to both the oil shocks and the concerns of more recent years. It contains five chapters, with one devoted to each country. To facilitate comparison, the chapters follow a parallel structure that consists of three main sections.

The first section examines the state's response to the oil shocks of the 1970s. It reviews

- the country's pattern of energy consumption and energy policies prior to the oil shocks
- the impact of the oil shocks and how the problem of energy security was defined at the time
- the overall thrust of the state's policy response, including the process by which policy was formulated
- specific domestic policy measures to promote energy security
- international actions taken to promote energy security
- the overall impact of the policy response: how and to what degree did it improve the country's energy security?

The second section in each chapter addresses the state's response to energy insecurity during the past decade. It follows a similar organizational scheme, with the principal difference being that it considers the broader range of energy security concerns that characterized the first decade of the 2000s, not just those pertaining to oil. In addition, given the recent nature of these events, its evaluation of the impact and effectiveness of these policy responses is necessarily more limited and speculative.

A third section seeks to explain the state's policy responses in terms of the analytic framework developed in part 1, paying particular attention to the influences of state strength and policy legacies. This step is necessarily somewhat more subjective and involves a significant element of judgment. But potential biases in the interpretation can be guarded against by using data from a variety of sources and looking for consistency across them. Thus in my field work I have sought to interview subjects from both inside and outside of government, both the executive and legislative branches of government, multiple ministries and agencies, and different political parties.

The conclusion begins by summarizing the findings of the individual country chapters in comparative perspective. It examines similarities and differences in the threats to energy security faced by the five countries, in their policy responses, and in the principal determinants of those responses. It establishes in particular in what ways and to what degree variations in state strength can account for the different choices that the countries have made as well as the role of path dependence in shaping their challenges and responses. The chapter then draws out the theoretical and practical implications of these findings. The latter focus on the prospects for international cooperation to promote energy security. The chapter explains the limits of the achievement of the 1970s and why collaborative efforts in recent years have faced even greater obstacles to their realization. Finally, the chapter examines the implications of advances in the production, distribution, and use of energy, especially fracking, for these and other countries.

PART ONE: ANALYTIC FRAMEWORK

What's the Problem?

Energy Security in the Developed Democracies

Energy security means different things to different countries based on their geographical location, their geological endowment, their international relations, their political system and their economic disposition.

—Gal Luft and Anne Korin, "Energy Security: In the Eyes of the Beholder"

What is energy security? And what have been the principal energy security concerns of the developed democracies? This chapter establishes the boundaries of the problem addressed in this book. It defines the concept of energy security as used here and then reviews the principal threats to energy security that the major advanced industrialized countries have faced in the postwar era. In practice, the main external energy security concerns have been the result of actual or potential disruptions in the supply of an imported or international traded energy source, which could result in either physical shortages or high and volatile prices. But even that commonality has left significant room for variation in the specific types of energy sources that are of concern (e.g., mainly oil, natural gas, and nuclear power) and especially in the potential causes of supply disruptions (e.g., intentional embargoes and production cutbacks, domestic upheavals in energy exporting countries, terrorist attacks, and international conflict). For all intents and purposes, the developed democracies faced a very similar set of concerns in the 1970s, which revolved around the availability of adequate quantities of oil from the Persian Gulf. In more recent years, however, their concerns have diverged, reflecting a greater diversity in the nature and sources of the energy they use.

What Is Energy Security (and Insecurity)?

Traditionally, the subject of energy security has not received much scholarly attention. One reason is that interest in the topic tends to be episodic. It waxes with each new energy crisis and then wanes as soon as the crisis has passed. Another reason is that the study of energy security has not been embraced by the field of security studies, which might be its natural home. As Stephen Walt once argued in an influential article, the focus of security studies has been—and should be—the phenomenon of war or, more generally, "the threat, use, and control of military force" (Walt 1991). Insofar as energy has not had a direct bearing on these admittedly important concerns, it has tended to be neglected by the field.

Some scholars have maintained, however, that such a focus is too narrow. Edward Kolodziej, for example, criticized Walt's failure to pose, let alone explore, alternative definitions of security studies (1992). He and others have called for more attention to nonmilitary aspects of security.

In this spirit, Richard Ullman has offered a broader conception of national security. "We are, of course, accustomed," he wrote, "to thinking of national security in terms of military threats arising from beyond the borders of one's own country." Instead, he proposed the following, "more useful" definition: "A threat to national security is an action or sequence of events that (1) threatens drastically and over a relatively brief span of time to degrade the quality of life for the inhabitants of a state, or (2) threatens significantly to narrow the range of policy choices available to the government of a state or to private, nongovernmental entities (persons, groups, corporations) within the state" (1983, 1).

This conception of national security promises to be particularly useful for thinking about the problem of energy security. Nevertheless, it can be difficult to develop generalizations about energy insecurity because it has so many potential sources and can take so many different forms. Each country relies on a unique mix of energy supplies obtained from a distinct set of sources. Thus in order to clarify the concept as used in this study, it is necessary to make two basic distinctions.

The first is that between energy-importing countries and energy exporters (see also Willrich 1975, 65). In the developed countries, energy insecurity often stems from the fact that few are entirely self-sufficient in energy. Many must import a substantial proportion of their energy supplies from other countries, and energy is one of the most traded commodities.[1] This interdependence creates two distinct sets of problems: importers want secure access to foreign energy sources, or security of supply, while exporters seek the assurance that their production will be purchased at a fair price over a long period, or security of demand (Willrich 1975, 94; Luft and Korin 2009b, 9). This study is focused on the former set of concerns.

The other basic distinction is that between security of supply concerns stemming from actions or events inside a country and those emanating from outside the country. Energy security can be threatened by a wide range of developments within a state's own borders. Some of these may be the result of natural events, such as when cold weather interfered with European coal production after World War II or when hurricanes disrupted oil production, imports, and refining in the

Gulf of Mexico in 2005. Others may have human causes, such as terrorist attacks on energy infrastructure or when a poorly designed electricity market led to blackouts in California in 2000. As noted in chapter 1, however, this study emphasizes state policy responses to external sources of energy insecurity, which will be identified in more detail below.

Key Dimensions of Energy Security

Over the years, scholars and other experts have put forward dozens of definitions of energy security.[2] Taken as a whole, these definitions distinguish among four important dimensions of energy security, which have been succinctly summarized by Daniel Yergin: "The objective of energy security is to assure adequate, reliable supplies of energy at reasonable prices and in ways that do not jeopardize major national values and objectives" (1988, 111).

It is well worth taking a moment to explore each of these dimensions in greater depth. The first dimension is adequacy or sufficiency: is the total volume of energy supplies enough to meet reasonable present and future needs? Willrich has defined sufficiency as permitting "the national economy to function in a politically acceptable manner" (1975, 67). To this should be added enough energy to satisfy the energy requirements of a state's military forces. The second dimension is reliability or certainty: are energy supplies potentially subject to disruptions and interruptions of a significant magnitude or duration? Here we see that energy security also includes an important element of risk.

The third dimension is economic affordability: are energy supplies available at reasonable prices? David Deese has defined prices as affordable "if they stop short of causing severe disruption of normal social and economic activity" (Deese 1979–80, 140). Even if supplies are adequate in volume and reliable, sufficiently high prices can eventually threaten a state's national security by undermining its economy. The challenge here is to distinguish such threats from more quotidian concerns about the effect of energy prices on the standard of living and economic competitiveness.

The fourth dimension is the most difficult to summarize but captures all the other ways in which dependence on external energy supplies might threaten a state's national security. Thus, for example, energy supplies must be adequate, reliable, and economically affordable without involving the acceptance of political conditions that might compromise a state's political independence and freedom of action. Increasingly, moreover, it may be necessary to factor in environmental considerations when it comes to obtaining energy supplies from various sources abroad or at home.

In sum, energy insecurity can be the result of deficits in any of these dimensions. And when it comes to measures a state may take to increase its energy security, there can be important trade-offs across them. For example, steps intended to increase the reliability of access to foreign energy sources may come with political strings attached, and the affordability of certain energy supplies may vary inversely with their abundance, since higher prices tend to bring forth additional supplies. In addition, it is clear that energy security overlaps to an irreducible degree with the other broad goals of energy policy—economic efficiency and, increasingly, environmental sustainability. Thus greater energy security must often be purchased at the cost of reduced efficiency and/or greater damage to the environment.

External Threats to Energy Security

What general forms can external threats to a state's energy security take? One important source of concern can simply be the failure of energy-exporting countries to make or allow sufficient investment in their energy production and/or transportation facilities to compensate for declining output or rising demand. As a result, energy consumers may find their energy supplies to be increasingly inadequate or may have to pay ever higher prices in order to obtain sufficient supplies. In some cases, depending on market conditions and trade arrangements, a producer may be able to raise unilaterally the price that it charges its customers.

More often than not, however, energy insecurity is the result of disruptions or interruptions in existing foreign energy supplies and trade.[3] These disruptions can take a wide variety of forms. Some may be intentional in nature, as when a producer sharply reduces the amount of energy that it exports or embargoes shipments to particular importing states, typically to apply political pressure. In the case of the use of the so-called "oil weapon," the effectiveness of such tactics have been the subject of considerable analysis and debate (e.g., Licklider 1988). But they are not limited to oil and, in any case, continue to raise concerns. Presumably, how effective politically motivated cutbacks can be will depend in no small part on how readily an importer can reduce its consumption and/or obtain alternative supplies from other sources.

Even when a producer has no intention of limiting production and exports, its output may be expressly targeted by third parties. Traditionally, this has been a tactic of other states, who may use it to put pressure on either the exporting or importing countries. For example, they may seek to attack production and export facilities or energy supplies in transit along vulnerable transportation routes. Or they may exploit the fact that critical transportation infrastructure, such as pipelines or shipping lanes, runs through their own national territory. In recent years, however, the intentional disruption of energy supplies has also come to be a favored tactic of terrorist groups. Examples include attacks on oil pipelines and export terminals following the U.S.-led invasion of Iraq in 2003 and the attempt by al Qaeda to damage the massive Abqaiq oil processing facility in Saudi Arabia in 2006.

To these dangers must be added unintentional disruptions of the production and transportation of energy supplies. Within producing countries, these may be the result of strikes, coups, civil wars, revolutions, and other forms of domestic unrest. Recent examples include strikes in Venezuela that reduced production by three-quarters in 2003 and chronic violence and theft in Nigeria. Unintended supply interruptions might also be the consequence of wars involving energy-exporting states that are initiated for other purposes but nevertheless end up involving the targeting of energy facilities, such as the Iran-Iraq War of the 1980s. A further danger is hostilities or disorder along critical energy transportation routes, ranging from regional conflicts to piracy.

How serious a threat a reduction in energy supplies, whether intended or not, will pose to any given consumer country will be a function of at least five factors: the size of the disruption, its duration, the degree to which the country depends on the affected source, the availability of alternative sources of supplies or substitutes, and the country's ability to reduce consumption of the relevant energy source (Krapels 1980, 21). The latter three factors in particular will vary from country to country.

Common Threats to Energy Security in the Developed Democracies

This final section reviews the common external threats to energy security that the developed democracies have faced since World War II. Prior to the 2000s, the main source of concern was oil supply disruptions, whether intentional or unintentional, especially those originating in the Persian Gulf. In more recent years, the potential threats and concerns have become more diverse, making it difficult to provide broad generalizations.

The Early Postwar Years

Immediately following World War II, the United States, Western Europe as a whole, and even Japan enjoyed a high degree of energy independence. Both the major European states and occupied Japan still relied primarily on coal, and most of that was produced domestically or could be imported from friendly countries. Oil was starting to rival coal as the leading energy source in the United States, but it remained a net exporter of oil until 1949.

Through much of the 1950s, this picture did not change dramatically. Oil imports, especially from the Persian Gulf, increased steadily. But oil remained a relatively small share of the total energy supply in Europe and Japan, and the world oil market was characterized by excess supply capacity as more and more cheap Middle East oil became available. Thus the nationalization of the concession of the Anglo-Iranian Oil Company (later British Petroleum) in Iran and the subsequent boycott of Iranian oil production by the major oil companies in the early 1950s had little or no impact on consumers. Although Iranian production reached some 6 percent of world output in 1950, the oil companies simply boosted production elsewhere in the Persian Gulf to compensate for the shortfall (Schneider 1983, 32; Yergin 1991, 464).

The closure of the Suez Canal and the Iraq Petroleum Company pipeline through Syria during the 1956 Suez crisis was potentially more consequential. Roughly three-quarters to four-fifths of Western Europe's oil then passed through the canal or pipelines bringing Middle Eastern oil to the Mediterranean. Oil from the Persian Gulf could be rerouted around Africa, but there was inadequate tanker capacity to maintain deliveries at previous levels through the much longer route. This time, however, Western Europe was able to turn to the Western Hemisphere for help. The United States alone boosted its oil shipments to Western Europe tenfold, to nearly half a million barrels per day, although not until after Britain and France had agreed to a cease-fire and to withdraw their forces from the canal zone. Together, U.S. and Venezuelan oil compensated for three-quarters of the decline in shipments from the Middle East, and total West European imports fell by an average of only 8 percent over the five-month crisis period (Madelin 1975, 39–40; Schneider 1983, 37–39 and 534–35; Yergin 1991, 479–98).

The final noteworthy threat to Western energy security prior to the first oil shock occurred in 1967. By then, the collective oil import dependence of the advanced industrialized democracies had reached significant proportions. Whereas oil had accounted for only 20 percent of energy use in Europe and even less in Japan in 1956, the proportion was now in the vicinity of 50 percent and still rising. Then, in response to the outbreak of the Arab-Israeli war in June of that year, the Arab oil producers attempted to impose an embargo on the United States, Britain, and West Germany. Because of concurrent domestic disturbances in several oil-exporting countries, Middle East oil production initially dropped by as much as 6 million barrels per day (MBD) before stabilizing at about 1.5 MBD below previous levels, equivalent to the amount of Arab oil that normally went to the three embargoed countries.

This first embargo is generally regarded as having been a failure, however. One reason is that the Arab states were unable to agree on overall production cutbacks. Moreover, most of the loss that did occur was quickly made up for by a surge in U.S. production and increased output by Venezuela, Iran, and Indonesia more than compensated for the rest. The available supplies were redistributed where needed, and within three months, the embargo had been lifted and Arab oil production had returned to previous or higher levels (Schneider 1983, 117–18; Yergin 1991, 555–57; Little 2002, 63–64; Pollack 2002, 82).

The First Oil Shock: 1973–74

Thus it was not until the 1970s that the advanced industrialized democracies first experienced a truly acute common degree of energy insecurity as a result of events beyond their borders. The initial occasion was the so-called "first oil shock" of 1973–74. By then, the world oil market had changed fundamentally. Since the 1967 war, several members of the Organization of the Petroleum Exporting Countries (OPEC) had nationalized their oil industries, while others had demanded— and received—a growing degree of participation in the private oil operations taking place on their territories. Meanwhile, booming demand was putting upward pressure on the posted price on which long-term contracts for internationally traded oil were based, which rose from just $1.80 per barrel in the late 1960s to nearly $3 per barrel by mid-1973 (Yergin 1991, 577–84).

The OPEC countries then exploited the occasion of the 1973 Arab-Israeli war to flex their growing power. Following the U.S. intervention in the war that October, OPEC unilaterally raised the posted price by some 70 percent, to $5.12 per barrel. Simultaneously, the Arab members of the organization agreed to reduce oil production by 5 percent per month until Israel withdrew its forces from Arab territories, and several embargoed all oil shipments to the United States and the Netherlands. As a result, by December 1973, Arab oil output had declined from 20.8 MBD to 15.8 MBD, or the equivalent nearly 10 percent of free world production (Beaubouef 2007, 16–17).

In contrast to 1956 or 1967, however, the United States and the other advanced industrialized countries could do little in response. By the early 1970s, U.S. domestic oil production was going all out, and there was no spare capacity on which to draw. At the same time, other non-OPEC oil producers were able to increase output by a mere 600,000 barrels per day. Thus the OPEC countries were able to make the higher price stick and, at the end of December, they raised it further to $11.65 per barrel, a nearly fourfold increase over early October. Although the Arab states refrained from making any further production cuts, they did not end the embargo and restore production to pre-October levels until March 1974, and the posted price remained at the new, much higher level (Krapels 1980, 21 and 23–25; Schneider 1983, 221–44; Yergin 1991, 588–632 passim).

The one bright spot in this episode was that the international oil companies were able to reroute oil shipments so that no single country suffered a severe shortfall of imports. Any local shortages were primarily the result of rigidities in domestic markets. Indeed, according to one of the most detailed accounts, "by the time the embargo ended its effects were hardly noticeable" (Schneider 1983, 244). In addition, although the much higher oil prices helped tip Western economies into recession, some economists have argued that inappropriate monetary policy responses must share at least part of the blame (e.g., Bohi 1989). Nevertheless, the initial fear of shortages and the unprecedented jump in oil prices came as a major psychological blow that would color the thinking of Western publics and decision makers for years to come.

The Second Oil Shock: 1978–79

A second oil shock followed in the late 1970s. By then, the oil market had stabilized and, because of inflation, the actual cost of dollar-denominated oil was slowly declining in real terms. Indeed, many oil companies and major users were drawing down their inventories in anticipation of lower prices and plentiful supplies.[4]

Thus the origins of the second oil crisis were completely different from those of the first. It was precipitated not by another war in the Middle East but when Iranian oil workers went on strike in October 1978 to protest the policies of the Shah. Up to that point, Iran had been the fourth largest oil producer, after the Soviet Union, the United States, and Saudi Arabia. By the end of the year, however, its production had dropped sharply, from approximately 6 MBD to just 500,000 barrels per day, and its exports had fallen from 4.5 MBD to nothing.

Nevertheless, the events in Iran alone might not have been enough to precipitate a major crisis. Other states increased their output in order to compensate for the decline. As a result, overall noncommunist oil production decreased by a total of only 2 MBD, or about 4 percent. Over the course of the crisis, the total loss to the market was less than 200 million barrels of oil, or about 4 days of consumption outside the communist bloc.

Rather, the roots of the crisis lay equally in the responses of consumers. The preceding draw down in commercial inventories had left them unprepared for shortages. Thus many oil companies, independent refiners, and governments responded by building up their stocks as quickly as possible. As a result, the net shortfall amounted to as much as 5 MBD, which was comparable in size to the previous oil shock. To make matters worse, Saudi Arabia, after raising its output from 8.3 MBD in September to 10.4 MBD in December, reduced production to 9.8 MBD during the first quarter of 1979 and then temporarily lowered it by another 1 MBD during the second quarter, generating additional fears of a shortage.

The panicked response caused prices on the increasingly important spot oil market to more than triple between October 1978 and November 1979, from $13 to a temporary high of $41 dollars per barrel, notwithstanding the fact that total global production was higher in 1979 than it had been the previous year. The higher spot prices in turn facilitated a steady ratcheting up of OPEC contract prices, which rose from under $14 at the end of 1978 to an average of nearly $29 a year later and eventually stabilized at more than $34 dollars per barrel in mid-1980. In absolute terms, this price hike was even greater than that of the first oil shock.

The overall economic impact was also comparable in magnitude. GDP growth slowed in all the major advanced industrialized countries and in some cases turned negative. In addition, inflation ticked up, into the double digits in some countries, and unemployment once again surged. The OECD put the total economic loss of its members at 5 percent of gross national product (GNP) in 1980, the first full year after the higher prices were in effect (Yergin and Hillebrand 1982, 377–78; Colglazier and Deese 1983, 416; Carlsnaes 1988, 3).

Subsequent Major Oil Supply Disruptions, 1980–2000

Throughout the final two decades of the twentieth century, the principal source of energy insecurity in the developed democracies remained largely the same: the prospect of a major interruption of Persian Gulf oil supplies. During this period, two more noteworthy disruptions occurred, but neither had nearly as great an impact as those of the 1970s.

The second oil crisis had hardly subsided when yet another shock rippled through the world oil markets with the outbreak of the Iran-Iraq War in September 1980. Each party to the conflict quickly targeted the other's oil production and export facilities in the Persian Gulf. In addition, Syria shut down the Iraqi pipeline through its territory, leaving Turkey as the only outlet for Iraq's oil exports. Altogether, the war temporarily removed as much as 4 MBD from the market, or some 8 percent of free world demand. In response, spot prices jumped as high as $42 dollars per barrel, and most OPEC countries raised their official contract prices to $36 per barrel.

Nevertheless, the impact on the advanced industrialized democracies was quite limited. The overall price increase was relatively small in comparison with the oil shocks of the 1970s. Saudi Arabia quickly stepped up its own output by nearly 1 MBD, and it initially refused to raise the posted price of its oil above $32 per barrel. In addition, demand in the industrialized countries was already dropping sharply as a result of the earlier price increases, and the substantial stocks that the oil companies had accumulated the previous year provided a significant buffer. Thus spot prices declined almost as quickly as they had risen, falling to $35.50 by the end of the year and then just $32.50 by mid-1981 (Colglazier and Deese 1983, 420; Keohane 1984, 235; Long 1985, 29; Ikenberry 1988, 100; Yergin 1991, 711–14).

Then, in the mid-1980s, the world price of oil collapsed and remained relatively low—usually below $20 per barrel—until the very end of the 1990s as a result of reduced global demand and increased production in non-OPEC areas. The principal exception to this extended period of a soft oil market was the price spike that followed Iraq's invasion of Kuwait in August 1990. The invasion and subsequent UN sanctions removed 4 to 5 MBD of Iraqi and Kuwaiti exports from the market, or roughly 7 percent of global production. In response, prices on the spot market doubled, from approximately $16.50 per barrel in July 1990 to nearly $33 per barrel in October of that year. Nevertheless, the crisis was short lived. Once again, Saudi Arabia quickly ramped up its output, this time by some 3 MBD, and other OPEC countries added another 1.2 MBD of production. By January 1991, when Operation Desert Storm began, prices had fallen back to prewar levels, and the crisis was effectively over (see OTA 1991, 7; Greene et al. 1998; Beaubouef 2007, 154).

Common Energy Security Concerns since 2000

In the 1970s, "the industrial importing nations faced ostensibly common international dilemmas. . . . These shared interests gave governments reason to declare similar energy security goals" (Ikenberry 1986a, 107). Since at least 2000, however, the picture has grown more complicated. As will be discussed in more detail in the country chapters, the specific energy security concerns of each of the major developed democracies have diverged to an important extent since the 1970s. Nevertheless, many of those concerns share two important background conditions: an increasingly tight world oil market and growing dependence on imports of natural gas.

During most of the 1990s, oil was a buyer's market, and prices generally fluctuated between $10 and $20 per barrel. At the very end of the decade, however, the market began to tighten and, with the exception of a brief period after September 11, 2001, prices maintained a generally upward course until 2008.

The underlying cause was a global imbalance between supply and demand. Consumption in the developed countries was roughly stagnant, but oil use in the developing world was growing rapidly. China alone, where oil consumption nearly doubled between 1998 and 2008, accounted for more than one-third of the growth. Because of the low price of oil in the 1990s, however, investment in new exploration and production facilities had lagged. As a result, the gap between consumption and the world's production potential steadily narrowed until by the mid-2000s spare production capacity had fallen to as little as 1 MBD, or just 1 percent of global demand (Beaubouef 2007, 247; Duffield 2008, 56).

This careful balance between supply and demand might have been tolerable if the oil market had been fundamentally stable. But during the first half of the decade, it was rocked by a series of disruptions that raised concerns about the future availability of adequate oil supplies. At the beginning of 2003, a strike in Venezuela caused production to fall there by more than 2 MBD for two months. Then civil unrest in Nigeria reduced that country's exports by nearly 1 MBD. And the U.S.-led invasion of Iraq led to an extended drop in that country's oil production and exports (Beaubouef 2007, 246–47; Duffield 2008, 52). For a variety of reasons, the potential for further supply disruptions in the Middle East and elsewhere seemed substantial.

The upshot of these developments was a steady rise in the cost of oil. The spot price passed the $40 mark in 2004, $60 in 2005, $80 in 2007, and $100 in 2008 before hitting an all-time high of nearly $150 per barrel in July 2008. Most of the price rise could be attributed to the tight balance between supply and demand, but a significant component, frequently estimated at between 15 and 20 dollars per barrel, represented a "risk premium" that reflected the danger of another oil shock. Although the price subsequently dropped even more precipitously, to as low as $30 in late 2008, it quickly returned to historically high levels for the remainder of the decade.[5]

The other principal common set of energy security concerns revolved around dependence on imports of natural gas. West Germany had started this trend in the 1970s, when it began to import increasing amounts from the Netherlands, Norway, and the Soviet Union. Japan soon followed, single-handedly constructing an LNG industry that could bring imports by sea from other parts of Asia. For many years, Britain had been largely self-sufficient in gas, thanks to production in the North Sea. But in 2000, domestic output began to decline rapidly, sending suppliers scrambling to find foreign alternatives. Even the United States, which had traditionally been able to supplement its domestic production with secure supplies from Canada, seemed poised to require imports from other countries in order to meet demand.

As demand for gas imports grew, moreover, consumers in the advanced industrialized democracies were forced to seek imports from ever more distant sources. Nigeria and Qatar, in particular, became major suppliers of LNG, and new pipelines were extended across the Mediterranean to North Africa. Some of these new suppliers, however, were potentially subject to the same types of unpredictable forces that threatened to disrupt world oil markets.

Conclusion

This chapter has sought to define the term *energy security* as it applies to the advanced industrialized democracies, emphasizing the sources of energy insecurity that lie outside their borders. It has also provided a brief history of the principal common threats to energy security that these countries have faced since World War II. Although these threats stemmed for many years primarily from oil supply disruptions in the Middle East, the potential sources of energy insecurity have become more diverse over time, especially since the beginning of the twenty-first century.

How have the developed democracies responded to the threats to energy security that they have faced? Before we can answer that question and explain similarities and differences in their policy responses, we must take two further steps. The first is to articulate the full range of possible responses in order to facilitate a more systematic comparison. The second is to identify some of the most promising determinants of state responses to energy insecurity. The next two chapters complete the process of developing this analytic framework.

CHAPTER THREE

What's a State to Do?

Potential Policy Responses to Energy Insecurity

This book seeks to compare the policy responses of five developed democracies during periods of heightened concern about energy security. In order to do so systematically, we first need an explicit framework for categorizing and measuring these responses. Only then will it be possible to articulate clearly and concisely which actions each state has taken—or not taken—and then compare them.

What are the possible policy responses to concerns about energy insecurity? What measures can states take to increase their energy security? This chapter develops and presents a comprehensive typology of state responses to energy insecurity. A central distinction is that between internal and externally directed policies. Within each of these two broad categories, however, usually a quite wide range of additional options exists.

Alternative Ways of Distinguishing among State Policy Responses

The analysis of state policy responses can be explored along at least three major dimensions, to which I shall refer as depth, form, and breadth.

Regarding the first dimension, depth, scholars of comparative public policy have put forth increasingly differentiated typologies that concern how deeply policy and policy change may reach. In one of the first comparative studies of foreign economic policy, Peter Katzenstein distinguished between the definition of policy objectives or the ends of policy, on the one hand, and the instruments or means of policy, on the other (1978, 16). Subsequently, Peter Hall put forth a more differentiated typology of policy change that consisted of three orders, or levels, of increasing depth (1993, 278; see also Schreurs 2002, 27):

1. changes in the levels of existing policy instruments
2. changes in the basic instruments or techniques used to achieve policy goals
3. changes in the goals that guide policy

A second dimension of comparison concerns the different functional forms that policies can take. One can identify at least four broad sets of policy instruments, each of which includes a number of more specific tools (adopted from IEA 1996):

1. economic and fiscal policies, including taxes and fees, tax exemptions (or tax expenditures), subsidies, and direct grants
2. credit instruments, such as loans, loan guarantees, interest rate subsidies, and other forms of financing
3. regulation and deregulation, including general market regulation, price and volume controls, and technical and environmental standards
4. direct government action, including state-owned or -controlled research, production, or transmission, government services such as information provision, and diplomacy and military activities

Each of these four sets of policy instruments can be applied to a wide variety of potential energy policy goals. In addition, many can have both domestic and international applications.

Both of these approaches for categorizing and comparing policy responses are of value, but the primary approach taken in this book will emphasize a third dimension: the breadth, or range, of issue areas covered by potential policy responses. As noted above, energy security is a complicated concept. It touches on the adequacy, reliability, and affordability of energy supplies. As such, it may comprehend a wide range of policy areas. Indeed, the range of potentially relevant policies may seem overwhelming at times. Thus we must attempt to organize them according to some logical scheme.

Following the oil shocks, several scholars attempted to develop comprehensive but simplifying typologies. One of the first to do so was Mason Willrich, in a sweeping 1975 study of energy and world politics. He identified a number of different measures that an energy-importing country might consider in order to enhance its energy security, which he assigned to three broad categories (ibid., 69–74):

1. measures to decrease damage from possible supply interruptions
2. measures to strengthen guarantees of foreign supply
3. measures to increase energy self-sufficiency

Then, in a 1984 book on what they termed the "energy policy explosion," Paul Kemezis and Ernest Wilson put forth an even more comprehensive framework, though theirs, too, consisted of three broad categories:

1. securing energy imports
2. enhancing domestic energy supplies
3. managing energy demand

A third notable, if less comprehensive, categorization was offered by Walter Carlsnaes in his 1988 analysis of Swedish energy security (1988, 14–18):

- maintaining emergency stockpiles
- promoting international energy allocation programs among importing countries
- reducing energy imports via conservation and substitution

Also of relevance are John Ikenberry's attempts to characterize the different national adjustment strategies pursued by several of the major developed democracies following the oil shocks. Although his concerns were somewhat broader, since they included macroeconomic policies to address inflation, deflation, balance of payments deficits, and industrial competitiveness, Ikenberry nevertheless made two important distinctions that are of relevance to this study. One concerned whether the policy was aimed at the domestic or external environment. The other concerned whether the policy sought to transform the relevant target or to preserve existing arrangements (Ikenberry 1986b, 101–16; Ikenberry 1988, 6–7 and 16–19).

Toward a Typology of State Policy Responses to Energy Insecurity

The remainder of this chapter is devoted to presenting a comprehensive original typology of potential policies for responding to energy insecurity (and promoting energy security) organized by policy area that draws on these works. These possible policies are summarized in table 3.1. Before proceeding, however, several clarifications are in order. One concerns the relationship between this dimension of policy and the other two described above, depth and form. It should be emphasized that they are not mutually exclusive. Thus when evaluating state responses within a given policy area, it may be useful to compare them in terms of the depth of policy change and the particular instruments that are employed.

A second issue concerns the relationship between state responses to energy insecurity and other energy policies a state may pursue. There are no clear boundaries between the traditional goals of energy policy: security, economic efficiency and competitiveness, and increasingly, environmental sustainability. Thus it may be hard to distinguish between policies that are motivated primarily by concerns about energy security and those that are not. Some measures taken to promote energy security may also serve to further other (economic and environmental) goals of energy policy. By the same token, some policies pursued primarily for

Table 3.1. Potential policy responses to energy insecurity

Internal policy responses
Emergency preparations
 Stand-by rationing and allocation plans
 Strategic stockpiles
 Fuel-switching capabilities
Reducing dependence on foreign sources of energy
 Increasing domestic production
 Reducing consumption
 Promoting substitution
 Supporting relevant research and development

External policy responses
Policies toward energy producers and transit countries
 Ensuring access to existing energy supplies and transit routes
 Diversifying foreign energy supplies and transit routes
Policies toward other energy-consuming and importing countries

---

other reasons may nevertheless contribute to or detract from a state's energy security.

A third issue concerns the particular forms of energy that may be at the source of energy security concerns. As the previous chapter makes clear, dependence on oil imports has been a major, if not the exclusive, root cause of energy insecurity for the advanced industrialized democracies. Nevertheless, the following typology of potential policy responses attempts to describe them in the most general terms and not with regard to any particular form of energy. In addition, some responses to insecurity generated by dependence on one type of energy source may involve the use and development of other forms of energy, given the potential for substitution among them.

Finally, it is worth noting that states are not limited to making a single, unidimensional response to any particular energy security concern. To the contrary, they may respond with a number of distinct policies simultaneously or spread out over time, although there will presumably be some logical relationship between the various components of the response. States typically, moreover, have a variety of options available to them. Thus what we are interested in are the different sets of choices that states make among these possible combinations of policies. How much emphasis do they place on each option? What trade-offs do states make among them?

In this regard, however, perhaps the most fundamental distinction among policy options concerns the targets or locations of a state's policy goals (see also Mastanduno et al. 1989). As noted in the previous chapter, this study focuses on states that are actually or potentially dependent on foreign energy supplies and their responses to energy security concerns that originate outside the territory of the state. Most prominent among these have been actual and potential disruptions to foreign energy supplies. As such, as a first cut, states have two general ways in which they can respond. They may direct their energies toward influencing conditions lying outside the state, such as the behavior of foreign energy suppliers. Or they may seek to alter domestic conditions in ways that enhance their energy security. In other words, state responses to energy security can have both external and internal components, and one of the central concerns of this study is the relative emphasis that states have placed on these broad alternative approaches as well as the various suboptions contained within them. It is to the task of distinguishing among these various choices that we now turn, starting with the internal and moving to the external components.

Internal Policy Responses

What basic options do states have at home for increasing their energy security? Potential domestic policy responses to energy insecurity fall into two broad categories: contingency or emergency measures designed to minimize the short-term costs imposed by possible external supply disruptions and measures intended to reduce the state's vulnerability to disruptions of foreign energy supplies over the longer term. We will look at each of these in turn.

Emergency Preparations

Especially in the short run, it may be difficult for a state to reduce the amount of energy that it acquires from external sources, but it can take action to reduce the impact that a possible disruption of foreign energy supplies may have. Perhaps the easiest measures to devise, at least technically, are plans and procedures for rationing and allocating physical supplies of energy in an emergency. Such measures may involve, for example, restricting consumption to certain high-priority users, such as military forces, or limiting the frequency with which or the extent to which most consumers can obtain additional supplies. Or they may simply involve imposing much higher prices on a scarce energy source on a temporary basis. How politically feasible the implementation of such potentially painful measures would be in an actual crisis, however, is more difficult to assess.

Consequently, wealthy states also often pursue another approach to reducing the short-term impact of a disruption in foreign energy supplies, which is to establish emergency stocks of the energy source in question. Governments may choose to create such strategic stockpiles by themselves, or they may require or incentivize private actors to do so. The case-study chapters contain a number of examples of such stockpiling efforts.

A third general approach is to promote the acquisition of fuel-switching capacity by energy users. The goal here is not to alter fundamentally a state's energy mix but to ensure that energy users have at least short-term alternatives in emergency situations. Thus, for example, electric power plants that normally burn natural gas might be designed to be able to use certain petroleum products. Once again, in states with free market economies, this approach may necessitate inducing or requiring private actors to make the necessary investments.

Increasing Domestic Production

Over the longer term, states may seek to reduce their dependence on foreign energy supplies and, more generally, their vulnerability to potential disruptions of those supplies on a more lasting basis. There are three basic ways in which this can be done:

1. increasing (where possible) domestic production of the problematic energy resource
2. reducing directly the consumption of the resource
3. substituting on a long-term basis other forms of energy for the resource in question

These three approaches are not mutually exclusive, and states may use some combination of all three in order to reduce their foreign energy dependence.

The first basic way to reduce dependence on foreign sources of energy is simply to increase domestic production of the energy form of concern. Note that this is not an option for all states. Some may simply lack the basic natural resource endowments required to produce a particular energy source, or at least in quantities sufficient to make a difference. Where increased domestic production is a possibility, however, the scope for state action is particularly wide.

At one end of the spectrum of possibilities, the state itself may engage directly in production-related activities. The state can establish special state-owned entities for the purpose, or it can obtain a controlling share in a public-private enterprise. Alternatively, a state may use a variety of instruments to encourage private companies to produce the type of energy in question. It may seek to support such companies directly through the use of tax breaks, government subsidies and grants, lending on favorable terms, or access to resource-rich land. A state can also stimulate production by requiring that utilities and other consumers, including the state itself, purchase the energy produced at a certain price or in certain minimum quantities.

Reducing Domestic Consumption

Reducing a country's imports of a potentially vulnerable foreign energy source, even to nothing, through increased domestic production is not a panacea, however. It may reduce spending on imports, but as long as that energy source can be traded more or less freely across a state's borders, the underlying price that must be paid for it will still be determined by overall supply and demand in the relevant regional or global market. Thus a major supply disruption elsewhere in the world could still result in a sudden jump in the cost of the energy source, even if none is imported. For the purpose of enhancing energy security, then, more important than reducing imports is limiting overall consumption of the energy source of concern. That way, the impact of a sudden price increase is reduced.

Here there are two basic options. The first approach is to reduce directly the level of domestic consumption. A state may simply place a cap on consumption or imports and allow domestic market forces to determine the allocation and price of the resource. More commonly, however, states may seek to discourage consumption by imposing taxes. These can apply to the energy source itself (whether imported or domestically produced), imports of that source, and/or its derivative products (i.e., petroleum products such as gasoline and diesel in the case of crude oil).

Alternatively, states may seek to promote the more efficient use of the energy source in question. This can be done in a number of ways, although in most cases, it requires altering the behavior of the private actors who are responsible for the vast majority of energy consumption in market economies. States can use taxes to discourage the production and purchase of inefficient energy-using equipment, machinery, and vehicles, such as gas-guzzling automobiles. Conversely, they can use tax credits and other incentives to encourage private actors to make or buy more efficient alternatives. States can establish regulations setting efficiency standards for energy-consuming devices. And where the state itself is a major energy user, it can invest in more efficient vehicles, machinery, and equipment for its own use. Indeed, one common justification for doing so is to help manufacturers of those items achieve economies of scale, thereby bringing down the cost to private purchasers.

Promoting Substitution

The other basic, but indirect approach to reducing consumption is through the promotion of the use of substitutes for the energy source of concern. The potential for substitution will vary depending on how the energy source is used, that is, as a transportation fuel, to generate electricity, to produce heat, or as a material input into industrial processes. But there is always likely to be some potential for substitution.

Here one can identify two basic strategies. One is to promote the production and use of alternative energy sources that can be directly substituted for the source of concern. Examples include the production of synthetic fuels or biofuels as substitutes for gasoline and diesel in internal combustion engines, or the substitution of coal for oil and later biomass for coal in boilers. The other basic strategy is to promote the development of new technologies that employ readily available alternative energy sources to perform functions similar to those performed by the source of concern. Examples include internal combustion engines that burn natural gas in lieu of gasoline, or the generation of electricity with renewable sources of energy rather than by burning fossil fuels. It is also possible to combine both strategies. An example would be the development of efficient fuel cell technology and methods for producing hydrogen in large quantities for use in fuel cells.

Once again, a wide range of alternative measures is available. Similar to efforts to promote domestic production of an energy source that would otherwise be imported, the state can play a direct role in the development and production of these alternative energy sources and technologies through state-owned or state-controlled enterprises. Or it can provide a range of incentives—and impose various requirements—on private actors to do so. These measures include alternative fuel standards, feed-in tariffs and price supports, loan guarantees, tax credits, subsidies, and other instruments.

Finally, it is worth noting one cross-cutting set of measures for reducing a state's vulnerability to disruptions in foreign energy supplies. This consists of state efforts to promote research and development of relevance to each of the above categories. Here, too, the state can conduct such activities itself in government laboratories, or it can incentivize private enterprises through the use of various fiscal, regulatory, and credit instruments.

External Policy Responses

As noted above, various domestic policies do not exhaust the range of potential responses to energy insecurity. States may also have at their disposal a number of externally oriented actions. These can further be subdivided into two broad categories: policies that are directed at actual and potential foreign energy suppliers and transit routes, and those aimed at other import-dependent consumer countries.

Policies toward Energy Producers and Transit Countries

In the face of energy insecurity, an obvious strategy is for a state to attempt to secure access to foreign energy supplies (see also Willrich 1975). One general approach is to try to reduce the risk that existing supplies will be disrupted. Another is to seek to diversify the potential sources of foreign energy supplies in order to reduce vulnerability to the interruption of energy exports by any particular supplier.

How a state seeks to ensure the continued and timely delivery of existing energy supplies will depend on the precise nature of the potential causes of disruptions. As discussed in chapter 2, one danger is that foreign producers may withhold needed energy supplies—or divert them to other consumers—for political or economic reasons. The classical example of this threat was the 1973 Arab production cuts and oil embargo. In response to such a threat, a state may seek to negotiate agreements with the supplier to provide certain amounts of the energy sources of concern, although in the absence of effective means of enforcement, such agreements are no guarantee that supplies will not be withheld.

A more general strategy in the face of this type of threat is to foster closer political and economic relationships with energy-producing countries, and possibly with other countries through which the energy supplies must pass. Such efforts can take a number of forms, depending on the needs and desires of the producer and the resources available to the consumer state. They might include political alliance ties, the provision of investment opportunities and access to the importer's domestic market, economic and technical assistance, and more general efforts to promote political and economic interdependence.

In this context, it is worth mentioning two other, more extreme strategies. One is the use of coercion, or threats of force, to convince an energy-producing or transit country not to withhold or block supplies. The other is direct military action to seize energy production facilities and transit routes. These strategies are unlikely to be available to all states and even to many of the developed democracies, and they may be difficult to pull off successfully, but they are nevertheless theoretically possible.

In other cases, as also discussed in chapter 2, an energy-producing state or transit country may wish to ensure the flow of energy supplies at existing levels, but may face threats to its ability to do so. Such threats can emanate from a number of sources. Within its territory, the state may face domestic unrest, internal conflict, or terrorist attacks, as exemplified by the strikes that brought Iranian production and exports to a standstill in late 1978. Alternatively, a state may become embroiled in a military conflict with a neighbor that disrupts its ability to produce or to ship energy supplies, as occurred during the Iran-Iraq War. Or a state may find itself subject to coercive threats by a powerful third party, as the United States feared the Soviet Union might engage in toward Persian Gulf oil producers following its occupation of Afghanistan.

In such circumstances, a concerned consumer state has a number of options for strengthening and providing protection to threatened producer and transit states. It can provide military assistance of various kinds, such as weaponry and training. It can extend security guarantees or alliance commitments. It can deploy military forces as a precautionary measure. And, if necessary, it can actively intervene militarily in an internal conflict or interstate hostilities involving the energy exporter or transit state.

Alternatively, if the risks and uncertainty surrounding existing energy imports cannot be reduced to an acceptable level through such measures, it may make sense for a consumer state instead to seek to diversify the sources of its foreign energy supplies. A state, especially one with the financial and technological means of the advanced industrialized democracies, can promote the development of alternative energy supplies in a number of ways. It can extend direct financial and economic assistance to foreign governments. It can provide political support for the operations of private energy companies seeking to operate abroad. It can even finance exploration and development activities by private companies or government-owned entities. These methods are also potentially relevant to the development of transportation infrastructure, such as pipelines, in transit countries where necessary.

Cooperation with Other Consumer/Importer Countries

Policies directed at energy-producing and transit states are logical means of promoting the security of foreign energy supplies. But they do not exhaust the external policy options for enhancing a state's energy security. A review of potential state responses to energy insecurity would not be complete without mention of the possibilities for cooperating with other consumer and energy import–dependent countries.

Such cooperative efforts can be intended to serve a variety of goals: preparing for and coordinating the execution of emergency responses to disruptions of common foreign energy supplies, developing means of reducing existing levels of energy consumption and imports or producing alternative energy sources, negotiating with energy-producing states, and even orchestrating joint military interventions to secure foreign energy supplies. Each of these measures can be seen as an extension of a potential unilateral policy response to energy insecurity. Such domestic responses, however, may be more effective when pursued collectively with other states that face similar energy security risks.

Conclusion

This chapter has sought to identify the principal ways in which states can respond to energy insecurity. At the most general level, it has distinguished between potential internal and external policy responses. Within each of these broad categories, however, exists a wide array of options.

How do states in fact choose among these many ways to promote their energy security? Put differently, what are the most important determinants of state responses? In the next chapter, we identify some of the more promising explanatory factors.

CHAPTER FOUR

Explaining State Responses to Energy Insecurity

It is clear that countries with different political traditions and structures are going to design different energy policies. The divergence among policies will be greater than in the past partly because there is no clearly preferred replacement for oil and partly because of the increasing politicization of the matter, which means that the diversity of European political institutions will have proportionally more effect than the homogeneity of the European technical predicament.

—N. J. D. Lucas, "The Influence of Existing Institutions
on the European Transition from Oil"

In the face of energy insecurity, states may have a wide—perhaps even a bewildering—variety of policy options. What determines the choices that states make—and don't make—among those options? What factors and conditions most strongly shape how states respond to energy insecurity?

This chapter presents a framework for organizing potential explanations of state responses to energy insecurity. To do so, it draws on the scholarly literature of comparative politics and international relations. This framework is not meant to be comprehensive, however. Rather, it includes only those factors that seem most promising for explaining state behavior in this realm.

While it considers a variety of factors, moreover, the framework places particular emphasis on the concept of the state, especially different dimensions of state strength. Policy is the prerogative of the state, and the state is necessarily at the center of the making and implementation of national public policies. But the state does not exist in a vacuum. What the state does and how it acts are subject to numerous pressures and constraints emanating both from within its territorial boundaries and beyond. Thus a focus on state strength will illuminate the degree to which the state is able to resist, overcome, or perhaps even exploit those pressures and constraints in order to put its own distinct imprint on policy.

A second prominent element of this framework is its emphasis on policy legacies and path dependence. In energy policy, as in many other areas of public policy, choices made during one period can do much to shape the problems to be faced and to constrain the options available for addressing those problems at later times. Thus it is important to consider such factors, especially in an analysis with a longitudinal dimension such as this one.

One challenge in putting together such a framework is the lack of models on which to draw. As noted in chapter 1, there have been few previous efforts to explain state responses to energy insecurity, and even fewer of a comparative nature. A number of often valuable comparative studies were written on responses to the oil shocks (Vernon 1975; Menderhausen 1976; Lindberg 1977; Evans 1979; Kohl 1982, Lucas 1985), but these had very limited theoretical aspirations and thus contained little generalizable theoretical content. In addition, this literature appeared before and thus was unable to take advantage of more recent theoretical advances in the study of public policy. The principal exception is John Ikenberry's theoretically pathbreaking work on adjustment policies (1986a; 1986b; 1988), on which the framework presented here will draw heavily.

Before proceeding, it is also important to point out the limited nature of the theoretical aspirations of this chapter and the project more generally. The goal of this book is not to develop and test a general theory of state responses to energy insecurity, but the more modest one of describing and seeking to understand the responses of the major advanced democracies within a general analytic framework. Accordingly, this chapter does not seek to present specific testable hypotheses about the determinants of state responses to energy insecurity but simply to suggest where one might most profitably look for useful explanations.

Preliminary Considerations

How a state will respond to energy insecurity will depend in the first instance on the nature and magnitude of the problems that it faces, or at least how those problems are defined. This point may seem obvious, but it is important to highlight, especially in such a comparative study. Not all states start from the same place in terms of energy security, and insofar as the nature and magnitude of their concerns differ, we should not expect similar responses.

Energy security concerns may vary for a number of reasons. States may use different types and amounts of energy, and the forms of energy that they consume may be more or less substitutable. States may use the same type of energy in different ways and thus be more or less sensitive to disruptions in the supply or price swings of that energy source. They may obtain similar types of energy from different sources, and the availability of alternative sources of a given type of energy may vary. Thus the vulnerability of states to disruptions of energy supplies from a given common source may not be the same.

Later in this chapter, I will explore in more detail some of the reasons why energy security concerns may vary cross-nationally, especially in countries that are so similar politically and economically. Of particular interest here are the phenomena of policy legacies and path dependence. In this case, different policy choices in the 1970s, made for understandable reasons in response to a highly similar set of problems, contributed to the existence of often very different concerns in the 2000s.

This chapter will not examine, however, any purely cognitive or perceptual sources of variation in concerns about energy security. One assumption guiding this study is that the dangers and risks to energy security inherent in a particular situation will be perceived by most actors in more or less the same way. Different individual and organizational actors may attach different values to those actual and potential costs, and they may prefer different ways of responding to them, but their overall assessments of the situation will be largely the same. Where significant perceptual differences are in fact observed in the following cases, they will be noted.

How a state responds to energy insecurity may be further shaped, at least in the short term, by other goals of energy policy and existing policies to achieve them. As noted in the previous chapter, it may be difficult to distinguish policies to promote energy security from other elements of energy policy. In addition to energy security, energy policy typically has a variety of economic, social, and environmental goals. Ceteris paribus, states seek to keep energy prices low in order to raise living standards and maximize economic competitiveness. They may use energy policy to generate employment or support particular geographical regions. And increasingly, energy policy in the developed democracies has taken into account environment protection and sustainability. The precise nature of these other goals and the amount of emphasis placed on them will alter the costs and benefits of alternative approaches to promoting energy security. In some cases, they may dictate that the state respond to energy insecurity in a particular way or that it remove certain policy options from consideration entirely. And, of course, these additional, policy-related pressures and constraints will vary from country to country and over time.

Material Factors: Resource, Technical, and Financial Endowments

Within the context of existing energy policies and the nature and magnitude of energy security concerns, what additional factors or circumstances are likely to have a bearing on state responses? Perhaps the most obvious place to begin such an examination is with material factors. Physical, technological, and even economic and financial endowments establish the outer bounds of possible policy responses. In contrast to many other types of public policies, the subject of energy policy has an irreducible material component. Energy supplies must be found or created, processed, and transported before they can be consumed. What additional opportunities and constraints for policy do such factors generate?

The most binding constraint on state responses is the location of the raw materials from which energy supplies are derived. Some states are well endowed with such natural resources. As a result, they have the option of initiating, if they have not done so already, or expanding the exploitation of those resources to meet their energy needs.

Other states may have few or no significant reserves of energy raw materials. But even those states may vary greatly in the proximity they enjoy to foreign energy supplies. Some will have easy and secure access to the supplies they need, which may be obtained from a stable neighbor or a reliable nearby ally. The examples of Canadian oil and Norwegian natural gas readily come to mind. Other states may depend on energy shipments from distant and troubled regions of the world to meet much of their energy needs, as exemplified by oil imports from the Persian Gulf.

In the energy field, the ability to exploit energy resources is closely bound up with technology. This is certainly the case for fossil fuels. Underground stocks and reservoirs that were uneconomical or simply impossible to tap at one time and place may be cost effectively exploited at another. Given the nature of the countries examined in this study, the level of cross-national variation in the relevant technologies is unlikely to be substantial. But we are likely to see significant variation across the two time periods considered here. Since the 1970s, advances in seismic imaging, horizontal drilling, hydraulic fracturing, and other technologies have revolutionized the production of oil and gas from shale and tar sands as well as in ever deeper depths offshore. Thus even where fossil fuel reserves are present, technology does much to determine how much can be produced and at what cost.

The same arguments hold true for the development of alternative forms of energy and means of using energy more efficiently. At any given time, not every state has enjoyed the same level of endowment in the scientific, technological, and engineering resources required to develop substitutes for fossil-fuel-based liquid fuels and electricity generation, such as nuclear power, biofuels, and other renewable energy sources, or to reduce the amount of energy needed to power an economy of a given size. Nor has the magnitude of those endowments stayed constant over time.

Of course, technology does not place the same degree of constraint on state responses to energy insecurity as do natural resource endowments. The availability of many particular technologies is at least partially endogenous; they can be created or improved through investment in research and development or through importation from abroad. Nevertheless, how states respond to concerns about energy security at a particular time will likely be determined to an important extent by what technologies are already available or appear to be attainable in the near term.

Finally, overall national economic and financial resources bear mentioning. How a state responds may be influenced on the margin by how wealthy or indebted a country is at the moment. But such considerations are likely to constrain only the most expensive or resource-intensive policies and projects.

Notwithstanding the importance of such material factors, they rarely if ever will fully determine state responses to energy insecurity. On the contrary, they will usually leave considerable scope for choice, even in the most resource-poor states. As Ikenberry has noted, "A particular set of resources makes possible a wide range of alternative and overlapping strategies" (1986a, 119). Thus we must consider additional potential explanations.

Societal Pressures and Constraints

Given this project's concern with the characteristics of the state, another promising place to look for determinants of state responses to energy insecurity is in the society that surrounds the institutional apparatus for policymaking and implementation. As Ikenberry has also noted, states are "enmeshed in a complex set of relationships with society" (1988, 35). Society may be a source of strong policy preferences, favoring certain choices and outcomes over others.

Within the literature on societal determinants of public policy are two general sets of approaches. Collectivist approaches emphasize broad societal dispositions rooted in such features as political culture. Pluralist approaches emphasize the policy preferences of particularist interest groups within society and, where these preferences diverge, the political, economic, informational, and other resources at the disposal of different groups.

Broad Societal Dispositions

Elsewhere I have developed at length the argument that broad societal, or national, predispositions may be important determinants of public policy (Duffield 1998;

Duffield 1999). Thus I will simply summarize the most relevant elements of the argument here.

Some societies can be said to have distinct predispositions that dispose them in favor of certain types of policies and against others. These predispositions often manifest themselves in public opinion or other expressions of public attitudes. An important source of such predispositions and thus of national policy, especially in its broad outlines and over the long term, may be a society's political culture. Political culture refers to the subjective and often unquestioned orientations toward and assumptions about the political world that characterize members of a particular society and that guide and inform their behavior.

Political cultures have three important characteristics. They are a property of collectivities rather than simply of the individuals of which they are made up. They are in principal distinctive from one society to another. And most of the time, political culture changes only very slowly, if at all.

Scholars have distinguished three basic components of political culture. The cognitive includes empirical and causal beliefs. The evaluative component consists of values, norms, and moral judgments. The expressive, or affective, component encompasses emotional attachments, patterns of identity and loyalty, and feelings of affinity, aversion, or indifference.

Political culture is most likely to shape energy policy in three general ways. At the deepest level, it conditions the types of options that are seen to exist. As a result, some alternatives may not even be conceived of. Next, it defines which measures are judged acceptable, appropriate, or legitimate within the broader set of those that are imaginable, thereby placing further limits on the types of the policies that can be proposed, defended, and pursued. As a result, certain options are excluded from further consideration. Finally, political culture can strongly influence the evaluation of the remaining options and thus the choices that are made among them. It both conditions understandings of the likely results of alternative courses of action and shapes assessments of the costs and benefits and thus the effectiveness of the various possible options. The overall effect of political culture is to predispose societies toward certain policies rather than others. It all but rules out some options while making others more or less likely to be chosen. Thus it can significantly narrow the range of actions likely to be adopted in any given set of circumstances. Some of the broad policy issues where the influence of political culture is likely to be most evident are the role of state in providing energy supplies, the acceptability of taxes and/or higher energy prices, the popularity of nuclear energy, and support for high-profile external activities such as military operations.

Despite its potential usefulness, political culture's ability to account for public policy may be highly limited or even nonexistent in some circumstances. First, it may be vague or incomplete and thus offer little or no clear guidance on certain issues or aspects of policy. Second, it may be internally inconsistent and thus push policy in conflicting directions. Finally, there may be no distinct, dominant political culture within a given society.

Pluralist Approaches

These limitations suggest the value of pluralist approaches to understanding public policy. Here the focus is not on society as a whole but individuals and privately constituted political, social, and economic groups within society. These approaches view "policy as the outcome of a competitive struggle among affected groups for influence over particular policy outcomes" (Ikenberry et al. 1988, 7). Pluralist approaches emphasize three factors (Ikenberry et al. 1988; Moravcsik 1997):

1. the organization or structure of society with regard to the issue of area of interest: what are the relevant groups?
2. the particular preferences of those groups: what policies does each group want?
3. the relative strength of those groups: what resources, such as votes, money, information, or authority, do they have at their disposal for promoting their policy preferences?

Pluralistic approaches promise to be useful for understanding the formulation of energy policy. First, the economic stakes are often high. The production, distribution, and sale of energy constitute a significant percentage of economic activity in all of the advanced industrialized countries. Energy production, processing, transportation, and consumption often involve large companies with substantial resources, and the firms operating within these sectors are often well organized. Over time, moreover, concerns have grown about the environmental impact of energy production, transportation, consumption, and waste disposal, so environmental interest groups have increasingly taken an interest in energy policy as well.

In some formulations of pluralist theory, the state hardly matters. In one extreme version, aptly summarized by Eric Nordlinger, "the state is taken to be a largely manipulated, dependent, constrained, and responsive entity, little more than an arena in which the 'representatives' of contending societal interests come together to hammer out their differences. . . . Policy formation is understood as a response to the expectations and demands of those who control the largest armory of effective resources" (1987, 354). More generally, from this perspective, "government institutions essentially provide an arena for group competition, and do not exert a significant impact on the decisions that emerge" (Ikenberry et al. 1988, 7).

Few analysts, however, go so far in minimizing the role of the state, given its central place in policymaking and implementation. Many pluralist scholars would acknowledge, as has Jeff Frieden, that "underlying socioeconomic interests are mediated through a set of political institutions that can alter their relative influence" (1988, 89). More generally, as Ikenberry, Mastanduno, and Lake have argued, "state actors and institutions can play a critical role in determining the manner and extent to which social forces can exert influence" on policy (Ikenberry et al. 1988, 8). Thus whether, when, and how interest groups matter in the formulation and implementation of policy may depend on the characteristics of the state itself, a subject to which we now turn.

State Characteristics: The Three Faces of State Strength

This book argues that characteristics of the state, especially state strength, are important determinants of how the advanced democracies have responded to concerns about energy insecurity. Before exploring the different dimensions of state strength, however, it is first important to define precisely what we mean by the term *state*.

What Is the State?

Over the years, scholars have offered a number of definitions of the state. At the most general level, in the words Peter Hall, "the state is broadly understood as the executive, legislative, and judicial apparatus of the nation" (Hall 1993, 275). Within that broad definition, one can further distinguish two general conceptions of the state (Skocpol 1985, 3; Ikenberry et al. 1988, 10; Hall 1993, 276). One is the state as an actor or set of actors. Thus, wrote Nordlinger, the state "refers to all those individuals who occupy offices that authorize them, and them alone, to make and apply decisions that are binding upon any and all segments of society. Quite simply, the state is made up of and limited to those individuals who are endowed with society-wide decisionmaking authority" (1981, 11; see also Nordlinger 1987, 362). More narrowly, Mastanduno, Lake, and Ikenberry have defined the state as the politicians and administrators in the executive branch of the government (1989, 458).

Alternatively, the state has been conceptualized as a structure. For example, Margaret Levi has described the state as "a complex apparatus of centralized and institutionalized power that concentrates violence, establishes property rights, and regulates society within a given territory . . . states contain but are distinct from their laws, bureaucracies, and governments" (2002, 40–41). Thus, in this view, the state is separate from the people who occupy the positions of power and authority.

Following Ikenberry, however, this study adopts a synthetic approach that embraces both the agentic and structural properties of the state. As Ikenberry has argued, "The state is an organization staffed by executive officials positioned to make . . . strategic choices. . . . The state is also a structure that fixes in place the channels of access to the society and the economy as well as the instruments and institutions of government. The state as *actor* and the state as *structure* are related" (1986, 105–6). Likewise, Gianfranco Poggi has noted that the state "is perhaps best seen as a complex set of institutional arrangements for rule operating through the continuous and regulated activities of individuals acting as occupants of offices" (1978, 1). Following Nordlinger, the approach used here expressly includes "all public officials—elected and appointed, at high and low levels—who are involved in the making of public policy" (Nordlinger 1981, 10).

Why the State Matters

A focus on the state is justified on several interrelated grounds. One is the unique authority of the state to make policy. As Hall and Ikenberry have noted, "The state monopolizes rule making within its territory" (1989, 1–2). Or, in the words of Poggi, the state "reserves to itself the business of rule over territorially bounded society; it monopolizes in law and as far as possible in fact, all faculties and facilities pertaining to that business" (Poggi 1978, 1).

Another reason is the "state's unique position at the intersection of the domestic and international political systems." As Mastanduno, Lake, and Ikenberry have observed, "Although the interactions of international and national policies take place at many levels, our view is that the activities and choices of state officials, situated between these domains, are particularly important" (Mastanduno et al. 1989, 458–59; see also Skocpol 1985, 8; Ikenberry 1986b, 54; Putnam 1988). A third reason is that the state is not reducible to other societal actors and structures. As Krasner has argued, it is "useful to conceive of the state as a set of roles and institutions having particular drives, compulsions, and aims of their own that are separate and distinct from those of any particular societal group" (1978a, 10). Likewise, Weir and Skocpol have noted that "both appointed and elected officials have organizational and career interests of their own, and they devise and work for policies that will further those interests, or at least not harm them" (1985, 118).

In sum, the state is distinct from society and purposive in character (Mastanduno et al. 1989, 459). More important, "the state has an important impact of its own on the nature of public policy and considerable independence from organized social interests and the electoral coalitions that might otherwise be able to drive policy" (Hall 1993, 275). Going further, Nordlinger has argued that "the preferences of the state are at least as important as those of civil society in accounting for what the democratic state does and does not do" (1981, 1).

Dimensions of State Strength

So far, we have shown that states can matter when it comes to determining public policy. But when and how do they matter? In particular, which features of the state are most critical in determining "the differential ability of states to assert control over political outcomes" (Ikenberry 1986, 106)?

The overall concept developed and employed in this study is "state strength." Peter Katzenstein was one of the first scholars to distinguish between strong and weak states characterized by state-centered and society-centered policy networks, respectively (1976). Likewise, Krasner argued that "the strength of a state in relation to its own society can be envisioned along a [single] continuum from weak to strong" where "the weakest kind of state is one that is completely permeated by pressure groups," while an extremely strong state "is able to change the society and culture in which it exists" (1978a, 55–56; see also 1978b, 57 and 60). This unidimensional conceptualization of state strength was highly influential and became widely repeated in the literature, even if different terms were sometimes used to describe the ends of the continuum (e.g., Weatherford and Fukui 1989, 588; Mastanduno 1989, 467–68).

As James Hollifield has noted, however, the use of the term *state strength* tended to obscure distinct dimensions: "We must be careful to distinguish between state autonomy and strength. Some theorists have alluded to this distinction, but few have pursued it with any vigor. By state autonomy I mean the ability of governments to make or formulate policies without being subject to the 'excessive' demands of special interests. . . . The real test of state strength (or capacity) comes at the level of policy implementation" (1990, 58–59). Continuing, Hollifield writes that "relative autonomy of a democratic state implies the independence of politicians and policymakers from special interests in formulating policy. State strength refers to the administrative capacity of the state and its ability to implement policy" (1990, 74).

In drawing this distinction between state autonomy and what I will call state capacity, Hollifield makes an important contribution to our understanding of state strength. But for the purposes of this study, however, he does not go far enough. As discussed in chapter 3, state responses to energy security may have both external and internal dimensions. Hence it is also necessary to distinguish between the ability of the state to implement different types of policies in both the international and domestic arenas. As a result, we must consider three distinct dimensions, or "faces," of state strength that may vary independently of one another.[1]

State Autonomy

We start with the assumption that actors within the state have distinct policy preferences. At this point, we are not concerned about what those preferences are or where they come from, as long as they are distinct from and not simply reflections of the preferences of particular interest groups within society. The challenge then is to determine under what circumstances and to what extent state actors can make sure that policy reflects their preferences rather than those of societal actors, especially where the preferences differ. To the degree that the state is able to translate its own preferences into authoritative actions, it can be said to be autonomous (Nordlinger 1987, 361; see also Skocpol 1985, 9; Atkinson and Coleman 1989; Doner 1992, 399).

This is not to argue that the state will always contain only a single preference. Insofar as the state consists of numerous individuals organized into different agencies with varying concerns, it may harbor multiple policy preferences. Indeed, strong differences in preferred policies within the state may be quite common, as emphasized by the government or bureaucratic politics model of decision making (Allison 1971; Halperin 1974). In such cases, the effective preference of the state will represent an amalgamation of those distinct individual preferences (Nordlinger 1988, 882; see also Nordlinger 1981, 20). What is of concern here, however, is the extent to which those preferences originate in the state itself rather than simply representing the preferences of some group or groups within society.

When the state enjoys policymaking autonomy, what determines what the state wants? There is no simple answer to the question of where state preferences come from. Some potential sources of state preferences are ideology, organizational and bureaucratic interests, and the idiosyncratic preferences of influential individuals. It may be possible to construct a theory of state policy preferences, but in this study, we will be content to try to identify them empirically.

Likewise, a number of factors may determine the degree of autonomy enjoyed by the state. Certainly important are institutional arrangements, especially the institutions of societal interest representation (Moravcsik 1997). As Hollifield has noted, "One could conceive of any number of institutional arrangements that might facilitate state autonomy, ranging from strong party government and parliamentary supremacy, such as in Britain, to a strong administrative state that is detached from the vagaries of electoral politics, as is (was) the case in France" (1990, 59). Likewise, Amanda Schreurs has emphasized the rules and laws regarding how societal actors relate to governmental systems. These present both barriers and opportunities, incentives and constraints, establishing the channels through which private groups can—and cannot—seek to obtain influence with actors within the state (2002, 23–25).

Other scholars have emphasized characteristics located within the state itself. For example, Hall has argued that state autonomy depends on the presence of policy paradigms. "Policy makers are likely to be in a stronger position to resist pressure from societal interests when they are armed with a coherent policy paradigm." Conversely, "when such a paradigm is absent or disintegrating, policymakers may be much more vulnerable to outside pressure" (Hall 1993, 290).

In contrast, Nordlinger has identified four structural determinants of state autonomy. The first is the state's boundedness vis-à-vis society, such as the ease with which individuals can move back and forth between positions of authority. Another is the internal differentiation of the state, which results in greater expertise and competence. A third is the cohesiveness of the state, which is a function of both centralization and ideology. The last is the state's policy capacities, or the effectiveness of its policy instruments (Nordlinger 1987, 377–84). This analysis, however, treats the latter feature as a separate dimension of state strength, to which we now turn.

Domestic Capacity

So far, we have discussed the autonomy of the state to define public policy based on its own preferences. But what good is such autonomy if the state has little ability to implement its policy preferences? Although this project takes a broader view of state strength, the concept has often been equated with the capacity of governments to enforce or carry out policy decisions or, more generally, to exert control over political and economic outcomes (Ikenberry 1988, 203; Hollifield 1990, 58–59; Jessop 2006, 126). Here, however, we describe this characteristic of the state as its "capacity."

Theda Skocpol has defined state capacity as the ability of states "to implement official goals, especially over the actual or potential opposition of powerful social groups or in the face of recalcitrant socioeconomic circumstances" (1985, 9). In a similar vein, Glenn Fong has written that "state strength or state capacity refers to the ability of government to extract resources from society, implement policies even in the face of societal opposition, and influence social groups. 'Strong' states can resist societal pressures, change the behavior of private actors, and transform the structure of its society and economy" (Fong 1990, 276). The basic sources of state capacity are manifold (Skocpol 1985, 16–18). They include

- the legal authority and formal powers of the state
- the administrative capacity of the state, including the loyalty and expertise of public officials
- other material and organizational resources of the state, including information
- the specific policy instruments available to the state
- perhaps most subjectively, the legitimacy of the state and its various activities

These basic features of the state broadly determine the opportunities and constraints confronting government officials as they seek to implement policy (Ikenberry 1986). Indeed, Ikenberry has argued, "The policy instruments and institutional resources available to government elites form the most important determinants of adjustment policy when crisis presents new challenges to government" (Ikenberry 1986, 106).

Ikenberry has gone on to categorize the generic types of policy instruments available to states. The first is what he terms the organizational instrument, or government possibilities for direct control over investment and production. Another is the credit instrument, or the state's ability to direct finance to private firms. A third is the fiscal instrument, including both taxation and spending. Finally, there is the market or regulatory instrument, which influences "the rules and conditions under which societal and economic groups interact." The latter includes antimonopoly laws, tariffs, price controls, and production quotas (Ikenberry 1986, 122–33).

In 1996, the International Energy Agency published a similar menu of energy policy instruments (IEA 1996, 21–30). It included

- economic and fiscal instruments, including taxes (and tax exemptions), subsidies, grants, and credit applied to fuels, services, or equipment
- trade instruments, including tariffs, quotas, licenses, bans/embargoes, and selective government procurement

- government ownership and administration, including ownership of companies, equity participation, provision of government services (market information provision, technical assistance, etc.)
- regulation, including prices, production volumes, markets (access, licensing, monopolies, cartels, among others), and environmental and technical matters
- research and development, whether involving the public sector directly, support for the private sector, or international collaboration

As we will see, there is likely to be considerable variation across states in terms of the availability of these different types of policy instruments (Ikenberry 1986, 123 and 137).

One item missing from both of these lists is the coercive instruments of the state (Skocpol 1985, 7; Weir and Skocpol 1985, 118). But given the nature of the cases considered in this study, these are likely to be invoked only infrequently on the domestic front, except to enforce other legal and regulatory instruments. Rather, coercive capacity is much more likely to be relevant in the international sphere, a subject to which we now turn.

International Capacity

As discussed in the previous chapter, policies pursued in response to concerns about energy security may have both internal and external dimensions. Typically, a range of policy options lies in the international environment. Thus to understand the choices states make both within and across these two arenas, one must also consider a third component of state strength: international capacity, or the ability of the state to pursue and achieve its goals with respect to outside actors and structures.

International capacity may be implicit in some discussions of state strength, but it deserves to be distinguished from domestic capacity and considered in its own right.[2] As we will see in the case studies, there is not necessarily a strong correlation between international and domestic capacity. A state may have substantial domestic capacity but little international capacity, and vice versa.

Like its internal counterpart, this international dimension of state capacity may have numerous sources, such as international prestige and moral authority, diplomatic skill, military power, economic, financial, and technical resources, and the legal authority to grant or withhold access to national markets. Some of these components of state capacity may be intrinsic to the state itself. For example, the state may be free to enter into certain types of agreements with international actors unconstrained by the broader society. Likewise, its ability to conduct effective diplomacy may depend primarily on its administrative capacity.

Other sources of international capacity, however, may be bound up with certain aspects of domestic capacity, especially the ability to extract and mobilize domestic resources that can then be deployed in the international sphere. In this regard, it is useful to distinguish, as has Fareed Zakaria, between state power and national power. National power is the sum total of material resources—economic, financial, technical, human, and other—potentially available to the state within its geographical boundaries or under the control of its subjects/citizens. State power is that portion of national power that the government can employ for its own purposes (Zakaria 1998, 9 and 38).

Thus state power, and international capacity more precisely, depends in no small part on the ability of the state to convert national wealth and power into tools and resources that can be deployed on the international stage (see also Lamborn 1983, 125). In the words of Mastanduno, Lake, and Ikenberry, "Wealth provides a basis for international power, but is not synonymous with power. The state must convert wealth into power by taxing, requisitioning, or expropriating social resources" (Mastanduno et al. 1989, 462). To be successful in democracies, moreover, this process must rest on a substantial basis of consent. Thus an important determinant of success is "the deftness of state officials in cultivating public opinion, educating the citizenry, and bolstering the authority of government institutions" (Mastanduno et al. 1989, 460).

The relationship between international and domestic capacity has been concisely summarized by Klaus Knorr:

> The volume and quality of material resources mobilized for use in foreign affairs depends on two factors: first, the productive capacity and wealth of the country, and second, the share of these resources or outputs that is allocated to foreign policy. This allocation results from the ability of the government to extract appropriate inputs, diverting them from alternative uses, by means of requisitioning (e.g., drafting military manpower) and purchase; the rate of extraction being, in turn, a function of the government's authority to requisition and to secure finance by taxation or borrowing. (Knorr 1975, 38–39)

Clearly, then, states will vary in both the amount of underlying national wealth and resources potentially at their disposal and their ability to draw on this power in the pursuit of external goals. No two states are likely to have the same international capacity.

Illustrations of State Strength

Based on such considerations, some scholars have drawn broad conclusions about the relative strength of the five states examined in this study, albeit without necessarily considering the threefold distinction developed above. In his pathbreaking study of state strength, Krasner argued that there are modal differences in the power of the state among the advanced market economies (1978a, 58–60). Scholars have typically regarded France and Japan as the strongest states. As Hollifield has observed, the French state "is generally viewed as strong and autonomous, having the independence to formulate policies in the 'national interest' and the administrative capacity for implementing those policies, even in the face of adverse social and economic conditions" (1990, 59). Indeed, in the words of Ambler, "France is often perceived to be the most perfect embodiment of the strong and centralized state" (1988, 469). Similarly, Krasner described Japan as coming "closest to the pole of strength, at least for the period before 1976" (1978a, 60). Although other scholars have found a more "deliberative, consensual style at the stage of policy formulation," most have nevertheless agreed that the Japanese state possessed a substantial capacity to implement policy (Weatherford and Fukui 1989, 588; Fong 1990, 276).

In contrast, the United States has been seen as the quintessential weak state. As Krasner has put the matter, "In the US, private groups can penetrate the decision-making process more easily. There are many decision-making nodes where state initiatives can be vetoed. US leaders have relatively few policy instruments for intervening in the economy" (1978b, 66). These blunt characterizations of the weakness of the U.S. state have been echoed by many other scholars (Skocpol 1985, 12; Nordlinger 1988, 877; Ikenberry 1988, 43)

As we shall see in the empirical chapters below, however, these five states are not so easily pigeonholed. When it comes to their responses to energy security, there has been much more variation across the three dimensions of state strength than the foregoing characterizations admit.

Caveats and Qualifications

We conclude this discussion of state strength with several caveats. For analytical purposes, we have distinguished between three components, dimensions, or "faces" of state strength. But it is important to recognize, first, that there is often a high degree of interdependence among them. We have already noted the degree to which international capacity may be dependent on the ability of the state to mobilize and extract domestic resources, which might more properly be said to lie within the realm of domestic capacity. As Ikenberry has explained, "The ability of the state to protect or enhance the nation's international position hinges in important respects on the internal political and material resources of the nation and the state's access to them" (Ikenberry 1988, 37). There is not necessarily a one-to-one correspondence between international and domestic capacity, however. As also noted above, some elements of international capacity do not depend on the resources residing in the broader society that the state represents. Also, it might be more or less easy to mobilize and extract resources for external or internal purposes depending on the relative degree of legitimacy associated with the relevant activities.

Likewise, strong interaction effects may exist between what policies states choose to pursue and state capacity, both internally and externally. As Skocpol has argued, "The explanation of state capacities is closely connected to the explanation of autonomous goal formation by states, because state officials are most likely to try to do things that seem feasible with the means at hand" (Skocpol 1985, 16). Or as Hall has put the matter, "A state's choice of policies will be heavily influenced by its existing capacities to carry out a range of policies. Those that require costly development of new capacities are less likely to be pursued" (Hall 1986, 16). Thus even officials in a highly autonomous state will be disinclined to adopt policies reflecting their preferences if they know they will lack the ability to implement them (Knorr 1975; Weir and Skocpol 1985, 118; Nordlinger 1987, 383).

Nevertheless, the above quote from Hall raises a second important issue: the malleability of state capacity. State capacity is more or less fixed in the short term. Thus a state's initial response to concerns about energy insecurity is likely to be strongly shaped by the institutional resources and policy instruments already at hand.

But state capacity is not immutable. It can change or be altered over time. Indeed, the transformation of state capacity may be a principal focus of government policy. As Ikenberry has written, "At moments of national crisis, politicians and administrative officials have sought with varying degrees of success to expand their capacities to respond to economic crisis and change" (Ikenberry 1988, 41; see also 1986, 121). Thus it may be useful to distinguish between short-term policy responses that take state capacity as a given and longer-term responses that involve efforts to modify state capacity and open up a wider range of options.

Nevertheless, as Ikenberry also cautions, the state's resources and policy instruments tend to be stable over time. "Responses to the energy crises depended on existing institutions even as they sought to effect changes. . . . Enduring institutional structures and established policy repertoires, despite efforts to move beyond them, became the central mechanisms for state policy" (Ikenberry 1986, 118). Indeed, it is the stability of state structures that is the basis of their explanatory power (Ikenberry 1986, 121).

A third qualification concerns the potential for variation in state strength within a given state across policy areas. Thus far, the discussion has implied a monolithic assessment of state strength in each of the three dimensions. In fact, however, even within a single state, the dimensions of state strength may vary by sector. We should not necessarily expect a state to be characterized by a certain degree of autonomy or capacity in all policy areas (Suleiman 1987, 275; Krasner 1978a, 58; Atkinson and Coleman 1989, 47; Hollifield 1990, 59; Jessop 2006, 119). As Krasner has noted, "The ability of public leaders to accomplish their goals also depends on the decision-making arena in which an issue is decided" (Krasner 1978a, 89).

In the United States, for example, the executive branch is generally accorded greater autonomy on foreign policy and national security issues than on domestic policy issues (Skocpol 1985, 17–18). And within the executive branch, the White House and Department of State, where much of external policy is determined, have enjoyed a relatively high degree of insulation from societal pressures (Krasner 1978a, 11). Conversely, Atkinson and Coleman have observed, "The supposedly centralized, autonomous French state is . . . not only responsive to, but sometimes captured by, societal interests. And when it is not captured, the French state often coordinates its policy closely with the business community" (1989, 48). With regard to state capacity, Skocpol and Finegold have found that the American state has had a greater ability to intervene in the economic affairs of agriculture than in those of industry (Skocpol and Finegold 1982, 261).

A final issue concerns the centralization of the state. Some scholars have equated a higher degree of state centralization with greater degrees of autonomy and capacity, especially since centralization implies cohesion and coherence (Doner 1992, 399; Zakaria 1998, 39). In particular, decentralized states have been seen as vulnerable to capture by private groups. But this is not necessarily the case. As Suleiman has observed, "Centralized structures that allow for the concentration of jurisdiction in an arm of the state often do not prevent, but on the contrary facilitate, the take-over of the state by private groups. . . . [Thus] a state's organizational structure does not define the degree of power, or strength, or autonomy that the state possesses" (1984, 260–61). Likewise, Ikenberry has noted that "whether centralized bureaucracies are stronger or weaker depends on the nature of the socioeconomic crisis at hand and on the possibilities of finding an effective fit between the available instruments and particular problems" (1988, 204). Thus the relationship between centralization and state strength is ultimately an empirical question.

Policy Legacies and Path Dependence

A final theoretical consideration concerns the impact of earlier policy choices on later energy security concerns and responses. As noted above, state capacities are not forever fixed but may change over time, especially when policy is designed to alter them. By the same token, other potential determinants of energy policy, including societal interests and material factors, may be reshaped, at least over the long term, by policy decisions, whether intentionally or not. Even more profoundly, the choices that are made at one point may determine the potential sources of vulnerability in subsequent periods. Thus, over time, many of the opportunities and constraints that states face may become endogenous to the analysis. In order to explore these ideas, we draw on the literature on critical junctures, policy legacies, and path dependence. These concepts may be especially useful for shedding light on the even more divergent energy security concerns and responses that characterized the major developed democracies in the 2000s.

Theory

It may be useful to think of moments of heightened energy insecurity, when potentially consequential and long-lasting policy decisions are made, as critical junctures. Capoccia and Keleman have defined a critical juncture as "a situation in which the structural influences on political action are significantly relaxed for a relatively short period, with two main consequences: the range of plausible choices open to powerful political actors expands substantially and the consequences of their decisions for the outcome of interest are potentially much more momentous" (Capoccia and Keleman 2007, 343). Thus three characteristics of critical junctures stand out. One is the boundedness of the period during which decision making occurs. Another is the possibility of significant departures in the direction of policy. And a third is the potentially lasting impact of those decisions, which close off, at least temporarily, alternative policy pathways (Capoccia and Keleman 2007, 341 and 348).

Of course, whether a critical juncture turns out to be truly "critical" depends on the longer-term effects of the choices made, which leads to the question of path dependence. And here, given the focus of the project on state policy responses, we are particularly concerned with what have been termed "policy legacies."

Path dependence means that "once a particular option is selected, it becomes progressively more difficult to return to the initial point when multiple alternatives were still available" (Mahoney 2000, 513). Institutions and policies may continue to evolve, "but in ways that are constrained by past trajectories" (Thelen 1999, 387). As a result, "the relative benefits of the current activity compared with other possible options increase over time, while the costs of exit—switching to some plausible alternative—rise" (Pierson 2000, 252).

Scholars have identified a number of different mechanisms of path dependence. In an early study of policy feedback, Paul Pierson described these as fixed costs, learning effects, coordination effects, and adaptive expectations as well as increasing returns (Pierson 1993, 608; see also Pierson 2000, 255). Later, Kathleen Thelen differentiated between two broad types of feedback mechanisms (Thelen 1999, 392–94):

1. incentive structure or coordination effects: once a set of institutions is in place, actors adapt their strategies in ways that reflect but also reinforce the logic of the system
2. distributional effects: political arrangements and policy feedbacks actively facilitate the organization and empowerment of certain groups while actively disarticulating and marginalizing others

And in a more recent effort to model formally the causes of path dependence, Scott Page distinguished among four principal ones (2006, 88):

1. increasing returns: the more a choice is made or an action is taken, the greater its benefits
2. self-reinforcement: making a choice or taking an action puts in place a set of forces or complementary institutions that encourage that choice to be sustained
3. positive feedback: an action or choice creates positive externalities when that same choice is made by other people
4. lock-in: one choice or action becomes better than any other because a sufficient number of people have already made that choice

In more concrete terms, policies can have the following effects that may cause them to be self-perpetuating. They may establish laws, rules, and procedures that modify the costs and benefits of alternative behaviors and strategies. They may involve the augmentation of existing—or the creation of new—government resources and policy instruments. They may entail significant investments and commitments that become sunk costs. They may, through the allocation and redistribution of material and political resources, result in the formation or strengthening of particular interests groups (who become vested interests), sometimes at the expense of others. They may establish precedents that affect the legitimacy of various courses of action. And they may contribute to the development of shared values, beliefs, and expectations that may further influence behavior (see also Pierson 1993; Pierson 2004). In short, the choices made at one point establish the actors, rules, tools, and ideas that condition choices at later times.

Application to Energy Policy

Energy policy in general and state responses to energy insecurity in particular should provide fruitful terrain for the application of these concepts. First, moments of acute energy security involve periods when new options become possible and perhaps necessary, and energy policy often, but not necessarily, heads off in new directions. In particular, it may be useful to view the oil shocks of the 1970s and the resulting policy decisions as critical junctures.

Second, energy policies often promote and sometimes require substantial investments in particular modes of energy production, consumption, and transportation. Indeed, when one considers individual consumers, large-scale energy users, energy producers, importers, transporters, and distributors, and the state itself, the range of potentially affected investment decisions is mind boggling. These investments in turn serve as sunk costs that usually require years and sometimes decades to amortize. Power stations, transmission lines, and pipelines, for example, are typically expected to last thirty years or more.

Third, the sale of energy constitutes a substantial percentage of the economy in the developed democracies. Within the United States, for example, spending on energy has ranged between 5.9 and 13.7 percent of GDP since 1970 (EIA 2012, 13). As a result, any shifts in patterns of energy production and consumption as the result of new policies can occasion a significant redistribution of resources within societies and between society and the state. New interest groups may spring up while the balance of power among existing ones may shift in decisive ways.

Dieter Helm has nicely summed up the relevance of critical junctures and path dependence to the study of energy policy: "Energy policy is typically the prisoner of its past. Policies are put in place in particular contexts, usually as the result of crises sufficiently great to render what has gone before as no longer workable. So, at any point in time, the energy policy framework is one that has been designed for a different context. As time goes on the mismatch becomes greater" (Helm 2008, 13). In the remainder of this book, we will be watchful in particular for the ways in which the policy choices of the 1970s left distinct policy legacies, sending patterns of energy consumption, production, and imports off in notably different directions.

In the three preceding chapters, I have developed a conceptual and theoretical framework for analyzing state responses to energy insecurity. In the next part of the book, we turn to the task of using this framework to characterize and explain the policy responses of the five major developed democracies to their energy security concerns of the 1970s and in the first decade of the twenty-first century.

PART TWO: CASE STUDIES

CHAPTER FIVE

Britain

From Fossil Fuel Importer to Exporter—and Back

> We have entered a decade or more of dramatic transition, heralding a century
> of serious energy uncertainty. We are moving from a position of relative en-
> ergy independence to one of significant dependence on imports.
>
> —Malcolm Wicks, *Energy Security*

Britain's energy security concerns in the 1970s and in the 2000s bear superficial similarities to one another. But beneath the surface, they were strikingly different. In the earlier period, Britain faced what was then a common problem: a substantial dependence on oil imports and their attendant costs. But apart from the immediate financial consequences of a quadrupling of the price of oil, British concerns about the security of its energy supplies were not nearly as acute as those in many other industrialized countries. The recent discovery of large quantities of natural gas and then oil in the North Sea meant that Britain could look forward to attaining self-sufficiency in energy, and possibly to becoming a net energy exporter. Thus the principal issues faced by British policymakers concerned not whether Britain could reduce its dependence on foreign oil, but how much oil Britain should produce and what role the government should play in its exploitation. Just as important as energy security considerations were financial and fiscal ones, since oil production promised to generate increased government revenues and result in a substantial improvement in the country's problematic balance of payments position.

What saved Britain in the 1970s, however, proved to be the country's undoing three decades later. In the 2000s, Britain's primary energy security concerns actually stemmed from its reliance on North Sea oil and gas. As a result of declining gas production in particular, Britain faced a potentially acute energy shortage by the middle of the decade and growing import dependence in the following years. The solutions to the problem were fairly straightforward: increased gas import capacity in the form of terminals for liquefied natural gas and undersea pipelines and, in the longer term, more renewable electricity and nuclear power plants to replace gas-burning generating stations. But by then, the state lacked the capacity and even the inclination to address the problem directly.

Instead, it had come to rely almost entirely on the private sector to address the country's energy needs. In the end, energy companies provided sufficient gas import capacity to avert a serious supply disruption and, at the beginning of the next decade, they were poised to make substantial investments in renewable energy and nuclear power. But the long-term outlook remained uncertain, as the markets alone did not necessarily provide sufficient incentives to induce private actors to take the steps required to allay Britain's new energy security concerns.

The 1970s: British Responses to the Oil Shocks

Like most other industrialized democracies, Britain had rapidly grown dependent on imported oil between the late 1950s and early 1970s. And as a result, it was initially hit hard by the first oil shock. Although Britain did not suffer any severe shortages of petroleum products, the quadrupling of oil prices put a tremendous strain on the economy, which was already struggling to balance its international payments.

But a solution was already in the works. During the previous years, oil companies had discovered substantial amounts of oil and natural gas on Britain's continental shelf in the North Sea. It was only a matter of time before the oil would be flowing in large quantities. The question was not whether domestically produced oil would displace imports, but how quickly, and how much domestic production might eventually exceed consumption, making Britain a net oil exporter. By 1979, Britain was able to absorb the second oil shock without much difficulty, since its economy benefitted as much as it suffered from the higher oil prices. Thus the government could be as much concerned with ensuring that the public secured a fair share of the expected economic rents as it was with promoting the exploration and development of North Sea oil resources in the first place.

At the same time, the government recognized that the bounty of the North Sea would not last forever. Thus it took some steps to limit oil and gas consumption and to ensure that other forms of energy, especially coal and nuclear power, would be available to pick up the slack when oil and gas production started to decline. Nevertheless, British policy overall was characterized by a relatively high degree of complacency, especially when it came to energy efficiency and the execution of the nuclear power program.

Background

Historically, Britain had been a major producer and user of coal. Until the late 1940s, coal provided more than 90 percent of British energy consumption, and well after that, it remained the primary input for the electricity and gas industries. Because of its use in the transportation sector as well as its advantages in some industrial applications, imported oil was gradually making inroads, and beginning in the late 1950s, the availability of cheap oil in seemingly unlimited quantities ushered in an era of rapid substitution for coal, both in industry and electric power generation. Coal's share of primary energy consumption plummeted from about 85 percent in 1956 to 60 percent in the mid-1960s and then to just 35 percent in 1972. Likewise, domestic coal production dropped dramatically, from a peak of 224 million tons in 1957 to just over half that amount in 1972. Meanwhile, oil consumption grew rapidly, reaching more than 110 million tons and 50 percent of primary energy consumption (PEC) by 1972 (Chesshire et al. 1977, 37 and 40; DOE 1977, 193; Robinson and Morgan 1978, 190–91; Lucas 1982, 96–97; DECC 2012a, table 2.1.1; BP 2013).

The other significant development in Britain's energy mix prior to the first oil shock was a rise in natural gas consumption. Before the 1970s, most gas consumed in Britain was derived from coal, so-called town gas. In 1965, however, natural gas was discovered on the British continental shelf in the North Sea, and by the end of the decade, significant amounts were being brought ashore. As a result, British gas consumption grew from a nominal amount in the late 1960s to more than 10 percent of PEC in 1973 (Bending and Eden 1984, 37; BP 2013).

Through the early 1970s, the primary objective of British energy policy was to produce as much energy as possible in order to keep up with rising demand (Helm 2004, 2). Of course, there are different ways to achieve this goal, and prior to the first oil shock, the energy sector was largely run by the state through integrated, public-owned monopolies. After World War II, the government had nationalized the coal, gas, and electricity industries, which were headed by the National Coal Board (NCB), the Gas Council, and the Central Electricity Generating Board (CEGB), respectively. Only the oil industry remained largely in private hands, with the state exercising control primarily through its powers of regulation (Chesshire et al. 1977, 36–37; McGowan 1996b, 134; Helm 2004, 14). Although exploration and development of the North Sea resources was initially conducted by oil companies, the 1965 Gas Act gave the Gas Council the exclusive right to purchase all the gas produced there, at prices negotiated with the producers (DOE 1977, 191 and 196; Lucas 1982, 99).[1]

Until the late 1950s, British policy proceeded on the assumption that supplies of fossil fuels, especially oil and gas, would be limited. One consequence of this belief was that the government made an early commitment to the development of nuclear power. A 1955 white paper described nuclear energy as "the energy of the future" and announced a 10-year program based on the British-developed

Magnox reactor technology to build 2,000 megawatts (MW) of commercial generating capacity, or enough to satisfy 25 percent of Britain's electricity needs. Following the Suez crisis the following year, which closed the canal and raised concerns about the reliability of Middle Eastern oil supplies, the size of the program was tripled (Helm 2004, 28–29; WNA 2012a).

Then in the mid-1960s, the government announced a second nuclear power program based on the new advanced gas-cooled reactor (AGR) technology. The aim was to install up to 8,000 MW of additional generating capacity by 1975, although the first orders were not placed until 1970. With an eye to the longer term, the government also ordered in 1966 a 250-MW prototype fast breeder reactor, which would be able to use the plutonium produced as a byproduct of both military and civilian nuclear programs and extract up to 60 times more energy from uranium than could conventional reactors (Chesshire et al. 1977, 45; Bending and Eden 1984, 173; Helm 2004, 91).

As early postwar concerns about limitations on the availability of foreign oil quickly turned to expectations of a virtually unlimited world supply at a price below the long-run marginal cost of domestically produced coal, the government turned its attention to slowing and managing the seemingly inevitable decline of the coal industry. It imposed a substantial duty on imported oil and a virtual ban on coal imports. It imposed a tax on fuel and heating oils, which was initially equivalent to 30 percent of the price of industrial fuel oil. It established a substantial preference for coal in electricity generation. And it gave substantial direct aid to the NCB. As one analyst concluded, "British energy policy has been consistently aimed at supporting coal in whatever way it could" (Chesshire et al. 1977, 43; Evans 1979, 116–17).

Despite these efforts, the future of coal looked bleak in the face of so much cheap oil. A 1967 white paper on fuel policy anticipated that domestic coal production would fall to only 120 million tons in 1975 and then just 80 million tons in 1980 (Chesshire et al. 1977, 45–47; Lucas 1982, 100; Helm 2004, 35). And the situation for coal became only more dire with the discovery of natural gas and oil in the North Sea.

Initially, British policy emphasized developing the North Sea gas and oil as quickly as possible (Chesshire et al. 1977, 45; Robinson and Morgan 1978, 19; Lucas 1982, 99; McGowan 1996b, 135). In the case of natural gas, rapid exploitation would help to obtain the overall lowest cost of supply for consumers. Gas, however, did not represent a substantial threat to coal, since it was intended for so-called "premium" markets, like space heating, and as a raw material for industry, which competed mainly with oil, although it did spell the demise of the coal-based town gas industry. But oil was another story, and within four years of the first discovery in 1969, starts had been made on some 15 oil fields, with government incentives expediting the process. Companies were allowed to write off 175 percent of their investment costs before paying any tax on revenue, which meant that during the early years of production in a given field, the government might receive only the 12.5 percent royalty (Schneider 1983, 372).

Prior to the 1970s, a significant justification of postwar British foreign and defense policy had been the need to ensure access to Persian Gulf oil supplies. Even after the loss of its base at Suez, Britain reaffirmed its commitment to defend its interests in the Persian Gulf and Aden, near the entrance to the Red Sea. It maintained close political ties with Kuwait, Bahrain, and the Trucial states, which later became the United Arab Emirates, and it stationed a naval presence in the gulf, with facilities at Bahrain, as well as a garrison at Aden, where its Middle East Command was based. In 1961, Britain even dispatched a military task force to Kuwait when the latter was threatened by Iraq (Northedge 1974, 294–95; Schneider 1983, 121–22; Dockrill 1988, 68, 78–79, and 87–89).

Because of financial pressures and growing local opposition, however, Britain was forced to liquidate these commitments in the late 1960s. In 1967, it hastily evacuated its forces from Aden, and following the financial crisis that required Britain to devalue the pound late that year, the government announced that it would terminate its protective treaties and withdraw all remaining forces from the Persian Gulf area by 1971 (Schneider 1983, 121–22; Dockrill 1988, 94–95). Henceforth, it would have to rely on diplomacy and U.S. power to protect its foreign oil interests.

British Energy Security Concerns in the 1970s

The OPEC production cuts in 1973 "brought to the fore long dormant anxieties about security of supply" (Chesshire et al. 1977, 47). But Britain suffered less than did its European neighbors. The oil supply during the first quarter of 1974 was down just 6 percent from its forecast level, compared with 15 percent reductions in France and West Germany (Schneider 1983, 246). As a result, no significant shortages materialized. In addition, the government froze product prices, not lifting the controls until late 1974 (Krapels 1982, 137).

Nevertheless, the rise in oil prices eventually had a negative effect on the British economy. The growth of Britain's gross national product (GNP), which had averaged 3.2 percent from 1960 to 1973, slowed to an anemic 1.1 percent over the next six years. Likewise, the rates of both unemployment and inflation roughly doubled over the same time periods (Deese and Miller 1981, 185). Perhaps most acute of all was the impact on the already troubled current account. Because oil imports made up half of Britain's total energy supplies, the fourfold increase in oil prices resulted in a serious balance of payments problem. In 1974, oil imports accounted for two-thirds of Britain's trade deficit of £5.26 billion (Chesshire et al. 1977, 47; Bending and Eden 1984, 1).

Still, the energy security concerns raised by the first oil shock were largely overshadowed by problems with the domestic coal industry. There, British energy policy expert Dieter Helm has argued, "*the combination of state ownership and monopoly had provided the very conditions to endanger security of supply,* by providing a basis for the growth and sustaining of union power, notably in the form of the National Union of Mineworkers (NUM). . . . Only the miners dimmed the lights in postwar Britain" (Helm 2004, 16; emphasis in the original). Thus a strike by the miners over wages in 1972 had raised doubts about the security of the coal supply (Ashworth 1984, 326). On that occasion, a state of emergency had restricted electricity consumption by large industrial consumers, resulting in the layoffs of some 1.2 million industrial workers (Helm 2004, 69). Then in early February 1974, at the height of the oil crisis, the miners struck again. Coal production was reduced by about 60 percent, leading to a three-day work week and the fall of the Conservative government in elections held at the end of the month. In the view of another analyst of British energy policy, the coal disputes of the early 1970s "were quite as damaging as the Arab oil restrictions on British energy supplies" (Evans 1979, 119; see also Prodi and Clo 1975, 102; Helm 2004, 37).[2]

Overview of British Policy Responses

The outgoing Conservative government of Edward Heath had no time to fashion a comprehensive response to the starker new realities of Britain's energy situation. In early 1974, it did establish a Department of Energy; the previous Ministry of Fuel and Power had been subsumed in 1969 by the Ministry of Technology, which in turn was incorporated into a Department of Industry in 1970 (Helm 2004, 36). But it was left to the incoming Labour government of Harold Wilson to reconsider British energy policy in the face of the OPEC price hike (Helm 2004, 40).

The overall approach adopted by the government was twofold. In the short term, it sought to reduce Britain's dependence on imported energy by increasing domestic production, with the ultimate goal of attaining energy self-sufficiency. This objective, however, did not appear difficult to achieve. By 1974, it was widely anticipated that oil production in the North Sea would increase rapidly during the second half of the decade, equaling and then exceeding import levels by the early 1980s. More problematic would be what happened after that. The government already expected the supply of North Sea oil and gas to begin to decline in the late 1980s or 1990s. Thus it also started to take steps to achieve "an optimum balance of energy supplies" by the turn of the century, when the country could no longer rely so heavily on indigenous oil and gas (IEA 1980, 203).

In part because the achievement of energy self-sufficiency, at least temporarily, seemed assured, an altogether different consideration played an important role in the government's thinking. The existing laws provided no means for capturing much of the substantial economic rent that was now anticipated, thanks to the combination of upward revisions in the magnitude of the North Sea oil reserves and the quadrupling of world oil prices. Under the existing tax system, major oil companies would be able to shelter corporate income tax for some years with accumulated losses from their Middle East operations and with capital allowances on investments outside the region. As a result, the oil companies would "reap enormous and uncovenanted profits on their investment." A further concern was that half or more of the post-tax profits were likely to be remitted overseas, placing a heavy strain on Britain's balance of payments (Dam 1976, 103–5).

Thus one of the first steps taken by the Labour government was to review the country's offshore oil and gas policy, issuing a white paper on the subject in July 1974. The white paper set forth three primary objectives: to redress the balance between oil company profits and government revenues, to maximize the gain to the British balance of payments, and to safeguard the national interest in an important resource that belonged to the nation. To this end, it contained three main sets of proposals. It called for direct government participation in the future development of North Sea oil. It proposed to reform the corporation tax structure in order to eliminate any sheltering of future North Sea profits by losses or capital allowances on investments elsewhere as well as to introduce a new supplementary tax on North Sea operations. And it called for additional regulatory powers, including the power to control the rate of production (Dam 1976, 103–11; see also Robinson and Morgan 1978, 24–26; Evans 1979, 89–90).

Subsequent policy statements emphasized the goal of achieving a balance of energy supplies over the longer term, once self-sufficiency was achieved. A 1976 Department of Energy Report on research and development concluded that the main priorities of the future should be nuclear power, coal, and conservation and recommended a large nuclear energy program, including a fast reactor program to avoid dependence on imported uranium (Chessire et al., 1976, 61; see also Mc-Gowan 1996b, 137). Likewise, a 1978 Green Paper on energy policy called for the development of a range of indigenous energy sources backed by a substantial research commitment to technologies that would be expected to bear fruit only in the medium to long term, though renewable sources of energy were not expected to make a major contribution before the end of the century (Department of Energy [UK] 1978, 86; McGowan 1996b, 137).

The Conservative government of Margaret Thatcher that took office in May 1979 largely maintained the objectives of its predecessor. As an IEA report put it, "The overall energy policy orientation of the United Kingdom government remains unchanged: the economic development and use of the four main domestic energy sources (coal, oil, natural gas and nuclear) with a view to attaining and prolonging energy self-sufficiency" (IEA 1982, 339). Rather, the principal difference between the Conservative and Labour governments would concern how to go about achieving this goal. As will be discussed later, the former came to place an unprecedented degree of emphasis on privatization and market liberalization.

Domestic Policy Responses

What concrete steps did the British government take to promote energy security following the first oil shock? As noted above, the primary emphasis was on increasing domestic energy production, beginning with oil and gas. Coal and nuclear power were seen as important long-term options that had to be preserved and developed during the medium term while indigenous supplies of oil and gas were still plentiful (Lucas 1982, 101). Although not entirely neglected, the reduction of oil and energy consumption through conservation received less attention than other initiatives.

DOMESTIC PRODUCTION OF OIL AND GAS

The Labour government supported a rapid buildup of North Sea oil production for several reasons. One, of course, was to increase the country's security of supply by reducing its heavy dependence on oil imports. Just as important, however, were the potential fiscal and economic benefits in the form of tax revenues and a substantial improvement in the balance of payments. Nevertheless, there was also growing interest in ensuring that the oil companies did not deplete the oil and gas resources too quickly (Chesshire et al. 1977, 48; Eckbo 1979, 73–74; Lucas 1982, 103; Bending and Eden 1984, 2004; Bromley 1991, 172).

Under the circumstances, the desired increase in oil production largely took care of itself. The oil companies had substantial incentives to find and develop North Sea oil fields as quickly as possible. Thus Labour government policies focused primarily on exerting greater control over offshore development and production and obtaining as much of the economic benefits as possible. To this end, it passed two major pieces of legislation in 1975: the Petroleum and Submarine Pipelines Act (PSPA) and the Oil Taxation Act (Lucas, 1982, 102).

The PSPA established the British National Oil Company (BNOC) as the principal vehicle of government participation in offshore operations. The BNOC was granted broad powers to engage in the oil business, including the power to operate pipelines, tankers, and refineries, and many of the PSPA's provisions applied to existing North Sea licenses. From the perspective of energy security, one of the most important powers was the right to purchase 51 percent of each company's production at market prices. This arrangement ensured that in the event of a future disruption of foreign supplies, oil could be landed in Britain for the home market. The BNOC also acquired some of its own North Sea assets and was authorized to negotiate participation agreements with existing licensees. Beginning with the next round of offshore licenses, moreover, the BNOC would receive an equity share of 51 percent in each new development and a voice in all decisions affecting operations. Thus a majority of the profits would accrue to the BNOC, although it would also have to put up 51 percent of the development and operating funds (Dam 1976, 112–13, 118; DOE 1977, 198–200; Evans 1979, 90–92; Lucas 1982, 102–3; Bending and Eden 1984, 201; Helm 2004, 40).

The 1975 PSPA also gave the government extensive powers to control depletion rates. In particular, in combination with existing legislation, the minister of energy could regulate the rate at which new territory was licensed for exploration, control development and production programs, delay the use of production capacity, and require that production from existing wells be reduced (Lucas 1982, 102; see also Robinson and Morgan 1978, 32). Nevertheless, the government recognized that the existence of such powers might cause the oil companies to limit their investments, putting at risk the goal of achieving self-sufficiency in oil. Thus at the end of 1974, before the law went into effect, the Department of Energy issued a statement clarifying the government's intentions with respect to their use. Most important, it would distinguish between discoveries made by the end of 1975 and those occurring later, and between delays imposed on the development of new fields and controls on the rate of production once a field entered into service. For fields discovered before 1976, no delays would be imposed on development and no controls would be imposed on production until 1982 or four years after the start of production, whichever was later. In addition, reductions in production would be limited to 20 percent (Dam 1976, 114–15; IEA 1979, 135; Lucas 1983, 248; Bending and Eden 1984, 201).

The 1975 Oil Taxation Act included additional measures "to secure a fair share of the benefits from offshore oil for the British people and to maximize the gain to the balance of payments" (DOE 1977, 200). First, it modified the rules for corporate taxation to establish a "ring fence" around the profits from North Sea oil and gas. No longer would the oil companies be able to charge losses and capital allowances stemming from investments elsewhere against the 52 percent corporation tax payable on North Sea income. In addition, the act introduced a new Petroleum Revenue Tax (PRT) that was limited to North Sea activities. The PRT was initially set at 45 percent and then raised to 60 percent in 1979 and 70 percent in 1980, though it also contained safeguards so as not to discourage the development of less-productive fields. Between royalties, the corporation tax, and the PRT, the government expected to capture 70 to 85 percent of the revenues from North Sea production, and it estimated that North Sea oil could improve Britain's balance of payments by more than 3 percent of GNP by 1980 and 5.0–5.5 percent by 1985 (Dam 1976, 108–9, 124–27; DOE 1977, 198–200; IEA 1979, 136; Evans 1979, 89; Lucas 1982, 103; Bending and Eden 1984, 200).

Initially, the Thatcher government largely continued these policies. It quickly expressed its intention to increase the tempo of exploration activity and held a further round of licensing in 1980 (IEA 1980, 207; IEA 1981, 288). At the same time, however, it also announced plans to enforce some control over the rate of oil depletion by deferring some production to later years in order to "maximize indigenous hydrocarbon production on a long-term basis" (IEA 1982, 342; see also IEA 1981, 289; Turner 1983, 185). Also in 1980, the government introduced a fourth tier of tax—the Supplementary Petroleum Duty—that would go into effect the following year and bring the marginal tax rate to more than 90 percent (IEA 1982, 344). In the face of a drop in offshore oil field development in the early 1980s, however, it reversed course in 1983 and reduced the tax burden in order to incentivize new efforts by the oil companies (Commission 1984, 157).

DEVELOPMENT OF ALTERNATIVES TO OIL

Even as oil production took off in the second half of the 1970s, the Labour government sought to lay the foundation for long-term energy security. First, it made a commitment to coal as key part of Britain's solution to the oil crisis. Following the resolution of the 1974 strike, the new government set up a group of representatives from the government, unions, and the NCB to examine the future of the industry. In 1973, the NCB had already begun to develop a longer-term strategy for coal, and this became the basis for the so-called Tripartite Discussions, which endorsed it as a broad strategy for the industry. The 1974 Plan for Coal estimated the probable market for coal at between 120 and 150 million tons in 1985, with the midpoint of 135 million tons to be used as a general guide. To be able to meet this demand, the government endorsed the goal of creating 42 million tons of new capacity at an estimated capital cost of £600 million in 1974 prices, and nearly half of the capital projects were approved by September 1976 (Lucas 1982, 102; Ashworth 1984, 353–60; Helm 2004, 17 and 72).

For a variety of reasons, implementing the Plan for Coal proved much more difficult than had been hoped. By 1976, the estimated capital costs had risen by 74 percent because of inflation. Nevertheless, the government pressed on with the policy, and the plan was reaffirmed by the Thatcher government, even though the Conservative Party did not view coal as a secure source of supply after the events of the early 1970s. The new government maintained high levels of capital investment, although the emphasis shifted from long-term expansion to attaining short-term economic viability and phasing out operating subsidies by increasing productivity (IEA 1981, 290; IEA 1982, 346; Ashworth 1984, 362–63; Helm 2004, 17).

The Labour government also moved quickly to renew the country's commitment to nuclear energy. In July 1974, it announced a third nuclear power program based on yet another British design, the steam-generating heavy water reactor (SGHWR). Although none of the AGRs of the second nuclear program had yet been completed, authorization was given for six new reactors with a capacity of 660 MW, for a total of 4 gigawatts (GW). Development of the SGHWR technology, however, proved to be prohibitively expensive. The program was postponed in 1976, as part of the cost-cutting measures resulting from the financial crisis that year, and then cancelled in 1978. Instead, the government announced that it would instead build two more AGRs and would consider introducing the now proven U.S.-developed pressurized water reactor (PWR) in the 1980s (IEA 1979, 136; Williams 1980, 233–34 and 258; Lucas 1982, 105; Bending and Eden 1984, 173–74; Helm 2004, 92–95).

The subsequent Thatcher government also quickly affirmed a belief in the importance of nuclear energy. As the new secretary of state for energy told the House of Commons, "Even with the full exploitation of coal and conservation, and with great efforts on renewable energy sources, it would be difficult to meet the country's long-term energy needs without a sizeable contribution from nuclear power," and he recognized the need to build one PWR a year for a decade (Helm 2004, 51; see also IEA 1981, 290; IEA 1982, 348; McGowan 1996b, 140). For the Conservatives, moreover, the nuclear program held an additional attraction: as a potential weapon against the coal miners in the event of a future strike (Helm 2004, 100). Nevertheless, although the new government initially suggested that it supported an ambitious program to build 10 new power stations with a combined capacity of 15 GW beginning as early as 1982, it refrained from making any concrete commitments, pending the completion of a lengthy study that dragged on until the middle of the decade (Helm 2004, 99–103).

Energy conservation was the stepchild of British domestic policy responses to the oil shocks. Prior to 1973, the government had done almost nothing to promote energy conservation or efficiency (Bending and Eden 1984, 239; Anderson 1993, 45). Indeed, beginning in 1970, the nationalized fuel industries had been prevented from passing along their cost increases as part of the government's anti-inflation policies (Chesshire et al. 1977, 50–51).

In response to the first oil shock, the government quickly took a number of steps to reduce the consumption of energy and oil in particular. It increased taxes on gasoline and imposed a 50 mile per hour speed limit. It belatedly agreed to allow domestic energy prices to rise in line with their costs, although not always to world market levels. It passed a building regulation that was the first to set significant thermal insulation requirements. It declared that new oil-fired electricity generating capacity would be approved only in exceptional circumstances, although it allowed 11 GW of capacity ordered before 1973 to proceed. And at the end of 1974, it adopted a 12-point program of additional energy saving measures (Chesshire et al. 1977, 50–51; IEA 1979, 137; Schneider 1983, 325; Bending and Eden 1984, 240; Anderson 1993, 46).

All in all, however, the government's initial energy conservation efforts were modest. It undertook no significant financial outlays, and it avoided heavy regulation. Likewise, a 1976 white paper on energy conservation put primary emphasis on voluntary, rather than mandatory, measures. Thus the principal effort to promote fuel efficiency in the automobile sector, where petroleum use was increasingly concentrated, was a voluntary agreement by the car manufacturers to achieve a 10 percent improvement in gasoline consumption of new cars by 1985 (Chesshire et al. 1977, 52; IEA 1980, 205; Lucas 1982, 106; Bending and Eden 1984, 244).

At the end of 1977, the government finally took a major step forward when it announced a 10-year program intended to save 11 million tonnes of oil equivalent (mtoe) per year, or about 5 percent of British energy consumption. The government allocated some £450 million for the first four years of the program, including £270 million for the insulation of public sector housing and other buildings and £100 million to subsidize insulation in private homes. In addition, about £75 million were made available to help industry and business to reduce energy use. Although largely focused on insulation, this program was described as "the first real evidence of a major commitment to energy conservation" (Bending and Eden 1984, 243; see also IEA 1979, 135; IEA 1980, 205–6; Anderson 1993, 46). As the IEA noted, British policy "is now beginning to include some mandatory provisions and a higher level of financial incentives." Nevertheless, the IEA also found that motor fuel prices remained 20–40 percent below most other European countries, and the cost of natural gas was still artificially low (IEA 1979, 135).

Starting in 1979, the new Conservative government took a very different approach to conservation. It placed much greater emphasis on market pricing and taxation, as opposed to regulation and government spending, to promote reductions in energy consumption and substitution. In its view, all fuels should be priced on an economic basis, taking into account costs and market conditions. As a general rule, the government opposed the use of mandatory regulations, except for energy conservation in buildings (IEA 1981, 291; IEA 1982, 340–41; Commission 1984, 155–56; Bending and Eden 1984, 245). And in 1982, it noted, perhaps overoptimistically, that "the explicit role of market prices in determining energy demand removes the need for a separate allowance for energy conservation" (Anderson 1993, 46).

Thus in early 1980, the government announced that the real price of natural gas would rise by 10 percent per year over the next three years. That year, the government also raised the tax on gasoline by more than 20 percent, and it imposed another significant increase on gasoline and diesel fuel the following year. As a result, the taxes on motor fuels amounted to about half of the pump price (IEA 1980, 204; IEA 1981, 291; IEA 1982, 340–41).

Still, there was no significant decline in government spending on conservation during the first few years of the Thatcher government. It budgeted approximately £150 million per year, continuing to provide substantial assistance for home insulation, public buildings, and the conversion of industrial boilers from oil to coal (IEA 1981, 291; IEA 1982, 341–42). In 1983, moreover, it even created an Energy Efficiency Office within the Department of Energy, reflecting "a recognition of the need to do more to help market forces operate more effectively" (Commission 1984, 156). Still, per capita financial support for energy conservation remained below half the average in the European Community (Commission 1984, 156).

EMERGENCY PREPARATIONS

Thanks to the fact that Britain would soon be self-sufficient in oil, the government felt little need to make any special preparations for a future supply

disruption. It did remain subject to European Community stockpiling requirements, but as domestic oil production rose, its obligation was reduced to 76.5 days
of consumption. Even then, the government left it entirely up to the oil companies to hold and manage the stocks, and it was reluctant to create any spare or
surge production capacity in the North Sea (Deese and Miller 1981, 200; Turner
1983, 164; Lucas 1983, 237; Commission 1988, 130). The government took
only a slightly more precautionary approach to the security of Britain's gas supplies, developing one gas field as a seasonal supply facility and converting another
into seasonal gas storage (Commission 1984, 160).

External Policy Responses

During the 1970s and early 1980s, the primary focus of British energy security
policy was on developing the country's indigenous energy resources, both in the
short term and for the long run. In contrast, Britain made only limited efforts in
the international sphere to promote its energy security. And more often than not,
it found itself resisting cooperative arrangements that might have restricted in
any way its use of North Sea oil and gas.

Like other states, one of Britain's initial reactions to the first oil shock was
to try to gain secure access to Middle East oil supplies. It sought to establish
special relationships with its erstwhile protectorates in the Persian Gulf as well
as Saudi Arabia and Iran, the two largest oil producers in the region (Lieber
1976, 30). It concluded one bilateral deal with Iran for 5 million tons of oil, or
about 5 percent of one year's consumption, but overall, these efforts were not
particularly successful (Lieber 1976, 29–30; Schneider 1983, 255–56).

Britain joined the European Community at the beginning of 1973, just months
before the first oil shock. But in the area of energy, it found itself almost immediately playing an obstructionist role. Central to British policy was the desire to retain complete control over the exploitation of its North Sea energy resources. Consequently, British leaders blocked almost every attempt by the EU Commission to
develop a Community energy policy. They believed that Britain had little to gain
from a common approach, given that it would soon achieve energy self-sufficiency.
Thus the EC was unable to adopt an emergency sharing scheme until the end of
1977, and even then, Britain was reluctant to divulge the details of its emergency
preparations for fear of having to make North Sea oil supplies available to other
member states (Prodi and Clo 1975, 107; Lieber 1976, 34; Deese and Miller 1981,
199; Schneider 1983, 340; McGowan 1996b, 158; McGowan 2011, 197–98).

Britain displayed a somewhat more cooperative attitude at the transatlantic
level. British leaders were not enthusiastic about the U.S. proposal for coopera-

tion among the consumer countries, but they supported it just the same, preferring the broader IEA to the EC as a forum for discussing energy policy matters. In addition, the IEA imposed few demands on Britain because of its position as an oil producer and, eventually, a net oil exporter. It had no IEA obligation to maintain oil reserves nor to draw down stocks in the event of a crisis, and only light obligations under the emergency allocation scheme (Prodi and Clo 1975, 107; Turner 1983, 164–68; McGowan 2011, 199). Later, Britain was active in helping to draft emergency plans for stock drawdowns, sharing imports, and possibly reallocating North Sea oil in the event of a shortage, but it was reluctant to agree in advance to increase production during a crisis (Deese and Miller 1981, 200).

Evaluation of British Policy Responses to the Oil Shocks

A decade after the first oil shock, Britain's energy security was much improved. Certainly, Britain was more secure than any of the other major developed democracies. Whereas Britain had depended on oil imports to meet half its energy needs in 1973, it was now self-sufficient in energy, and even a net exporter of oil. Oil production had begun in the North Sea in 1975 and grew steadily thereafter, exceeding the level of domestic consumption in early 1981 and then reaching 2.7 MBD in 1985 when Britain briefly held the honor of being the world's fifth largest oil producer (figure 5.1). As a result, by 1979, Britain was already largely sheltered from the direct effects of disruptions in the world oil market. In particular, large price increases no longer caused a large transfer of wealth from Britain, and much of the resulting revenue windfalls would go to the government. Only two caveats marred this otherwise bright picture of oil independence. One was the fact that Britain was able to use only a fraction of the very light North Sea oil in its own refineries. It continued to need to import heavier crudes from the Middle East in order to produce the correct mix of refined petroleum products (DOE 1977, 197). The other was the fact that Britain had little capacity to increase oil production in the short run, and the government had no plans to create a strategic reserve (IEA 1982, 343).

Britain also remained self-sufficient in coal. Because of efforts by the Conservative government to make the industry more efficient, production was slowly declining in the early 1980s, but it still exceeded domestic consumption, resulting in a steady buildup of stocks and net exports. Coal reserves were equivalent to 300 years of supply at the current rate of consumption. Meanwhile, electricity generated from nuclear power plants roughly doubled as 10 more reactors came online between the late 1970s and mid-1980s, although the construction of the first PWR was greatly delayed. Only in the natural gas market did Britain rely on

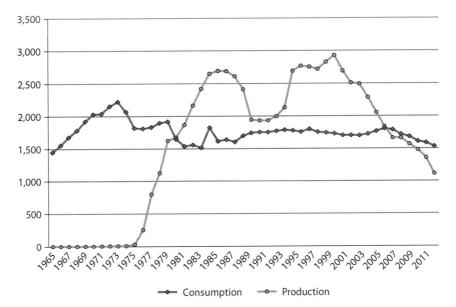

Figure 5.1 Consumption and production of oil in Britain, 1965–2012 (thousand barrels per day). *Source*: BP 2013.

imports to meet demand. Gas production had risen by one-third since 1973, but consumption had grown even faster, leaving a gap of about 20 percent to be filled from abroad. Nevertheless, the construction of gas storage facilities together with increased production flexibility provided by the Morecambe field meant that the industry was in a reasonably strong position to cope with major supply disruptions (Commission 1984, 152–53; Commission 1988, 131; DECC 2012a, table 2.1.1 and table 2.1.2).

Paralleling the rise in oil production had been a significant decline in British oil consumption, from nearly 2.3 MBD (113 million tonnes) in 1973 to around 1.6 MBD (75 million tonnes) in the mid-1980s. Over the same period, oil's share of British PEC also dropped, from around half to less than 40 percent. Most of the savings were achieved in the industrial sector, which saw petroleum consumption fall from 28.7 million tonnes to just 12.0 million tonnes between 1973 and 1983, and electric power generation, where the use of oil fell from 18.1 million tonnes to 5.1 million tonnes over the same 10-year period. Only in the transportation sector did oil consumption increase, and even there, the fuel economy of new automobiles had improved by some 15 percent by 1983 (IEA 1984, 179; DECC 2012a, table 1.1.5 and table 5.1.1).

More generally, Britain experienced an improvement in its energy efficiency. Energy intensity fell by around 18 percent overall between 1973 and 1982, and by even more in the industrial sector, where total energy consumption dropped by more than one-third. Nevertheless, the rate of improvement had been one of the slowest in the European Community, where Britain still had one of the highest levels of energy intensity in every sector (Commission 1984, 156; Commission 1988, 129; DECC 2012a, table 1.1.5). A 1983 report concluded that take-up of energy conservation measures had been poor and that progress on conservation had been unsatisfactory (Bending and Eden 1984, 248), while a Department of Energy survey of 80 companies found that energy efficiency had risen only 10 percent between 1973 and 1981 and thus that the potential for further energy savings was considerable (Chesshire 1986, 406).

How much could these improvements in Britain's energy security be attributed to government policies? One authoritative analysis concluded that "for most of the period prior to 1979, therefore, the government conducted an official Energy Policy which was in many respects, highly effective, notably in the development of North Sea resources over the 1960s and 70s. . . . The mix of government ownership and clear objectives worked well in developing oil and gas reserves and in building a national network for natural gas" (McGowan 1996b, 137).

It could be argued, however, that the government did not have to do much to promote the increase in oil and gas production. The oil companies had substantial incentives of their own to do so; the government's main task was to keep out of the way. A clearer contribution can be identified in the development of coal and nuclear power, although all of the new nuclear capacity that became available by the mid-1980s had been authorized before the first oil crisis. Nevertheless, without government involvement, the levels of investment might have been lower.

The contribution of government policy to reducing energy consumption and energy intensity was even more questionable. In the view of one expert, "the UK, some 13 years after the first oil shock in 1973 . . . has failed to develop a coherent, comprehensive strategy for enhancing the nation's energy efficiency" (Chesshire 1986, 403). The IEA concluded that the "economic pricing" of oil had been the single most effective measure for bringing about reduced oil use through fuel substitution, conservation, and increased energy efficiency (IEA 1982, 340). And the growth of oil consumption in the transportation sector, especially for road transport, suggested that government programs had been inadequate (IEA 1982, 341; DECC 2012a, table 1.1.5). Even the rapid improvement in automotive fuel economy raised the question of whether the voluntary targets established in 1979 had been sufficiently stringent to make any difference by themselves (IEA 1984, 110). As for electricity and gas, where prices continued to be subsidized for much of the period, the level of consumption remained roughly constant or grew (Commission 1984, 155; DECC 2012a, table 5.1.3 and table 4.1.1).

Finally, the medium- to long-term prospects for British energy security appeared dim. Beginning in the late 1970s, the government and other experts consistently predicted that British oil production would peak in the mid-1980s and then begin to decline, absent substantial new discoveries in the North Sea. In 1985, the IEA projected that Britain would once again become a net oil importer sometime between 1995 and 2000 (Lucas 1983, 248; Commission 1984, 152; IEA 1985, 497). The situation for gas looked potentially even more bleak. Because of an anticipated decline in production, the IEA also projected a potential gap between supply and demand of as much as 30 billion cubic meters (bcm), or approximately two-thirds of consumption, by the mid-1990s (IEA 1985, 483; Chesshire 1986, 398–99). Thus, as one study concluded, the crucial question for British energy revolved around the balance between coal, nuclear power, and alternative energy sources, which collectively accounted for only about 40 percent of PEC in the mid-1980s (Evans 1979, 111).

British Responses to Energy Insecurity in the 2000s

In fact, energy security did not become a major issue again in Britain until the mid-2000s. During the 1980s, the Thatcher government had embarked upon a far-reaching program of privatization and deregulation, one consequence of which was a substantial rise in natural gas's share of the energy mix. Then in the 1990s and early 2000s, British energy policy became preoccupied with the problem of climate change. At the turn of the century, however, production of both oil and gas in the North Sea peaked and then began to decline. By the middle of the decade, Britain had once again become a net importer of natural gas, even as the country was becoming increasingly dependent on gas for heating and electricity generation, and it would soon become a net importer of oil (figure 5.2)

This fairly sudden shift in Britain's external energy dependence, in combination with deepening concerns about climate change, prompted a fundamental review and revision of British energy policy beginning in 2006. The review, which culminated in several major pieces of legislation, resulted in a redoubling of existing efforts to promote energy efficiency and the production of renewable sources of energy. But it also saw a reversal of the government's previously dismissive at-

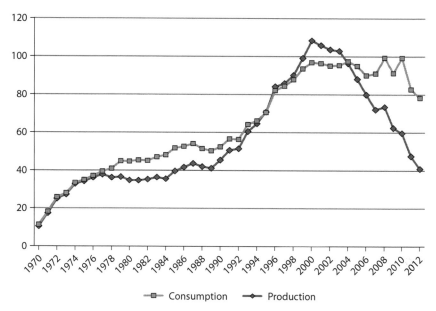

Figure 5.2 Consumption and production of natural gas in Britain, 1970–2012 (billion cubic meters). *Source*: BP 2013.

titude toward nuclear power, and the government sought to simplify the planning and licensing process governing major energy projects. Externally, the government continued its efforts to advance the liberalization of the European energy markets, especially for gas, and became a leading proponent of a common European external energy policy, which was expected to give the EU greater leverage and influence in its dealings with external energy partners such as Russia.

Despite the high degree of government activity to promote energy security in the 2000s, the government's response to the renewed concerns differed fundamentally from the types of measures taken in the 1970s. In contrast to the earlier period, the government was no longer directly involved in the production and supply of energy or even the construction of energy infrastructure. Rather, it was left to the private sector to make the necessary investments. The government's role was largely limited to structuring market incentives and facilitating the desired private behavior. To an important extent, this approach nevertheless proved successful, as energy companies often stepped forward to deliver the investments regarded by the government as necessary to enhance British energy security. But Britain's energy security remained dependent on market forces that the government could not control.

Background

Between the early 1980s and the early 2000s, the British energy scene changed in profound ways. The first was a fundamental shift from direct government involvement in the energy sector to a liberalized energy market, which was completed in the 1990s. The other was a belated but growing emphasis on the need to address climate change.

ENERGY MARKET LIBERALIZATION

In the 1970s, as discussed above, the government was deeply involved, either directly or through state-run industries, in the energy sector. It set levels of production. It built coal-fired and nuclear electric generating plants. It purchased, sold, and delivered all the natural gas consumed in Britain. Through its ownership of BNOC and British Petroleum, it even participated in the exploration, development, and production of North Sea oil and gas. By the end of the decade, almost the entire energy supply sector had been brought into public ownership or under close public control (Bending and Eden 1984, 34).

Beginning in the early 1980s, however, the conservative government of Margaret Thatcher engineered a fundamental "shift of emphasis away from government planning toward the market" (McGowan 1996b, 140). This shift was most famously heralded in a 1982 speech by Energy Minister Nigel Lawson, who stated that the government's principal task was not to plan the future shape of energy production and consumption or even to try to balance demand and supply for energy, but to "set a framework which will ensure that the market operates in the energy sector with a minimum of distortion and that energy is produced and consumed efficiently" (McGowan 1996b, 141). During the following years, the government more or less steadily introduced competition through privatization and deregulation. Although Britain was not the first major European state to employ a market approach to energy policy, it embraced the market far more thoroughly than did any other European state and, arguably, even more than did the United States under President Ronald Reagan.

The liberalization process began in earnest in 1982, when the government sold off its majority stake in BNOC. That same year, a new law opened up the national pipeline system and allowed private suppliers to compete with British Gas for large and medium-sized customers, while the 1986 Gas Act privatized the national gas company. In the 1990s, the gas supply and transportation functions were legally separated, and the gas market became fully competitive, with all customers free to choose their suppliers (Bending and Eden 1984, 201; McGowan 1996b, 133, 142, 148).

Meanwhile, the government also moved to privatize and deregulate the electricity industry. The 1983 Energy Act allowed private companies to generate electricity, while the 1989 Electricity Act broke up the CEGB into separate production and transmission companies. Initially, the government had intended at least to keep nuclear power in the public sector, but in the mid-1990s, all but the older Magnox plants were transferred to a new company, British Energy, and privatized. Even the coal industry was sold off in 1995 (McGowan 1996b, 148; WNA 2012a).

As a result of these moves, by the late 1990s, the energy sector had been almost completely liberalized. In sharp contrast to the 1970s, the government now played little or no role in supplying energy. Rather,

> energy policy is now characterized by private firms competing in relatively open markets and by the absence of a well articulated government role. Government continues to intervene but its activities are much less pervasive than in the past and to the extent that public authorities are active in the sector most of the time it is the regulatory agencies which are to the fore, operating on an agenda far narrower than what used to be considered energy policy's realm. (McGowan 1996b, 160; see also Helm 2007a, 4)

Importantly, even the security of energy supplies would no longer be the direct responsibility of the government, "but would instead be the outcome of market forces" (Helm 2004, 2). Energy had become just another commodity that was not subject to special treatment (McGowan 1996b, 151).

THE ENERGY MIX AND ENERGY SELF-SUFFICIENCY

Between 1985 and 2000, British PEC grew slowly, from around 200 mtoe to around 225 mtoe per year. Thanks to a substantial reduction in the energy intensity of the British economy, however, total PEC in 2000 stood at almost exactly the same level as it had in 1973, despite substantial economic growth in the interim. Similarly, total oil consumption remained roughly constant at 80 mtoe throughout this period, and well below its 1973 peak of 113 mtoe (BP 2013).

What had changed were the relative importance of coal and natural gas in the energy mix. After stabilizing at around 70 mtoe following the first oil shock, coal consumption began a steady decline in the late 1980s and fell by nearly half by 2000. Meanwhile, consumption of natural gas, which had grown steadily in the 1970s, experienced a renewed surge in the 1990s, nearly doubling between 1989 and 2000 from 45 mtoe to 87 mtoe. Indeed, gas overtook oil as the single most important source of energy, reaching almost 40 percent of PEC in 2000 versus only 35 percent for oil (BP 2013).

The principal cause of this shift was the so-called "dash to gas" in the electricity sector, where deregulation led to heavy investment in relatively inexpensive gas-fired power plants. During 1990s, gas-based production mushroomed from just 1 percent to some 40 percent of total electricity generation. Over the same period, the share of electricity generated by coal plummeted from nearly two-thirds to just one-third (IEA 2002b, 115–16).

Because the use of oil to generate electricity had dropped to almost nothing, the remaining demand for electricity was met by nuclear power. As the AGR reactors begun in the 1970s and early 1980s came online, the share of electricity provided by nuclear energy climbed to as high as 30 percent in the mid-1990s before leveling out at about one-quarter, or about 10 percent of PEC, in 2000 (IEA 2002b, 115–16).

The year 2000 also represented the high water mark in British energy self-sufficiency. The fears of the mid-1980s that oil and gas production would soon peak were allayed as both showed major gains in the 1990s. As the decade ended, overall oil production still exceeded consumption by nearly half, and Britain became a net exporter of natural gas with the opening of the UK-Belgium interconnector pipeline in the late 1990s. Paradoxically, the only exception to this picture of energy independence was coal, which had once been the foundation of British energy production. Because of a steep decline in domestic coal production in the 1990s, imports accounted for more than 40 percent of consumption by 2000 (BP 2013).

CONCERNS ABOUT CLIMATE CHANGE

A final development that would constrain future British energy policy making was growing concern about the environmental consequences of energy production and use, especially climate change (McGowan 1996b, 149). Indeed, by the early 2000s, climate change had arguably become the principal focus of British energy policy, as suggested by the subtitle of the energy white paper published in 2003: "Creating a Low Carbon Economy."

In the late 1990s and early 2000s, Britain undertook commitments to cut greenhouse gas emissions substantially. Under the 1997 Kyoto Protocol and the legally binding EU burden-sharing agreement of the following year, Britain agreed to lower its total greenhouse gas emissions by 12.5 percent below 1990 levels by 2008–12. At the same time, the government set an even more ambitious national target of reducing CO2 emissions below 1990s levels by 20 percent in 2010. Then, in 2000, the Royal Commission on Environmental Pollution recommended that Britain cut its CO2 emissions by 60 percent by 2050, a goal the government endorsed in the 2003 white paper (IEA 2002b, 43; DTI 2003; Helm 2005, 16).

To achieve these ambitious goals, the government adopted a comprehensive climate change program in 2000. Among the most important measures were the Climate Change Levy (CCL); climate change agreements between energy-intensive sectors of industry and the government; a voluntary UK-wide Emissions Trading Scheme (ETS); and a Carbon Trust. Introduced in 2001, the CCL was a tax on the use of gas, electricity, liquefied petroleum gas (LPG), and coal in industry, commerce, agriculture, and the public sector. Businesses could reduce their payments, however, by up to 80 percent by participating in voluntary climate change agreements that established stringent targets to reduce energy consumption or emissions. The UK ETS started in 2002, three years ahead of the planned EU emissions trading system and required participating organizations to make absolute reductions in emissions against a 1998–2000 baseline. Finally, the Carbon Trust was established in 2001 as a nonprofit organization with the aim of accelerating the take-up of cost-effective, low-carbon technologies and other measures by business and the public sector (IEA 2002b, 46–55).

On the supply side, the fight again climate change prompted efforts to promote renewable energy sources and other power generation technologies that produced little or no carbon. In 2000, the government announced the goal of generating 10 percent of all electricity from renewable sources by 2010, up from less than 3 percent that year (IEA 2002b, 116). To achieve this goal, it introduced in 2002 a Renewables Obligation (RO) that would incentivize power generators to provide steadily increasing amounts of renewable electricity over time. Under this program, licensed electricity suppliers were required to ensure that a specified proportion of their supplies came from renewable sources (IEA 2002b, 63–67). Britain also sought to stimulate the production of renewable fuels directly. It introduced incentives for biodiesel and bioethenol in 2002 and 2005, respectively, and the 2004 Energy Act paved the way for the introduction of a Renewable Transport Fuels Obligation (RTFO) modeled after the RO (IEA 2007b, 100).

INTERNATIONAL DIMENSIONS OF BRITISH POLICY

Finally, on the international plane, Britain had begun to take a more proactive stance toward the European Union, in contrast to the obstructionism that characterized British policy in the 1970s. Consonant with the liberalization of the British energy market, Britain quickly became the leading supporter of European

Commission proposals for liberalizing the EU's electricity and gas markets in the 1990s and, later, of the EU's emissions trading system. Nevertheless, and despite its own growing concern about climate change, Britain opposed an EU-wide carbon tax and was skeptical of the need to make energy policy a formal part of the union's mandate (McGowan 1996b, 159; McGowan 2011, 200, 203–4).

The Reemergence of British Concerns about Energy Security

Energy security did not once again become a concern in Britain until the early 2000s, but by the middle of that decade, it had joined climate change as one of the two main foci of British energy policy. The principal cause was the rapid and seemingly irreversible decline in North Sea oil and gas production that began at the beginning of the decade. In the mid to late 2000s, Britain was expected to go from being a net exporter to a net importer of oil and gas and thereafter to become increasingly dependent on foreign sources for both.

Of particular concern was the situation with respect to gas. Before the discoveries in the North Sea, Britain had already long been a substantial importer of oil. Not so with gas, and during the 1970s, 1980s, and 1990s, domestic production had provided for most of Britain's gas needs. Thus in a relatively short period of time, Britain would have to acquire the means to meet a rapidly growing share of its gas consumption through imports.

To complicate matters, Britain was expected to become increasingly dependent on gas, especially for the generation of electricity. Most of the aging nuclear power plants were scheduled to be shut down by the middle of the 2010s, and the use of coal-fired generating capacity would be increasingly constrained by the need to limit CO_2 emissions. Although Britain had set an ambitious target for renewable electricity, most of the growing gap in power generation would most likely have to be made up by gas.

DECLINING DOMESTIC PRODUCTION AND GROWING IMPORT DEPENDENCE OF OIL AND GAS

Throughout the 1980s and 1990s, Britain had produced substantial volumes of oil in the North Sea. In 1999, however, British oil production peaked at about 137 million tons and then began what was expected to be an irreversible decline. Because Britain then produced significantly more oil than it consumed, it was not forecast to become a net importer until about 2010. But after that, production was expected to fall rapidly, resulting in an ever higher degree of import dependence (PIU 2002, 22; JESS 2006b, 13; DTI 2006b, 3). British natural gas production did not take off until the 1990s, but it too peaked in 2000 and then began to fall. Because gas production exceeded consumption by only a small margin, moreover, it was estimated that Britain could become a net importer of gas as soon as the middle of the 2000s (PIU 2002, 22–23; DTI 2003, 78; POST 2004, 1).

Becoming once again a net oil importer was not regarded as a major problem. Britain had always imported substantial amounts of crude oil and oil products, even during the years of high domestic oil production (JESS 2006b, 61). Thus an adequate import infrastructure was already in place. Because of the global nature of the oil market, moreover, oil prices in the UK had always been sensitive to developments in other parts of the world. Although British officials expressed concerns about growing competition for energy supplies, insufficient investments by producer countries, increased resource nationalism, and instability in oil exporting states, such trends would have impacted the British oil market anyway (for a list of concerns, see DTI 2006a, 11 and 19).

The situation with gas, in contrast, appeared to be more dire for several reasons. First, there was simply less time to prepare, since the shift from exporter to importer was expected to take place very quickly. Indeed, Britain became a net importer sooner than expected, in 2004 (DTI 2005, 17). Second, Britain was less prepared. The country had long imported some gas by pipeline from Norway and could potentially import an additional amount via the recently completed UK-Belgium interconnector, but its total import capacity in the early 2000s of less than 20 bcm per year represented only a fraction of the annual domestic demand of nearly 100 bcm. Yet early estimates suggested that Britain would need to import up to 50 percent of its gas requirements by 2010, and as much as 90 percent by 2020 (HL 2004, 7; POST 2004, 1 and 4; DTI 2005, 17; DTI 2006a, 18; DTI 2006b, 35). Thus the 2007 energy white paper concluded, it was "in the gas market where the significant rise in expected import levels presents the most significant challenge" (DTI 2007, 116).

SHORT-TERM CONCERNS

The short-term risks appeared to be particularly acute, owing to the fact that gas consumption was highly seasonal. Because a large percentage of gas was used for space heating, demand in the winter exceeded average consumption by a substantial amount, and on an extremely cold day, it could be as much as twice as high as on average (JESS 2002, 32; DECC 2011b, 36). In the past, this seasonal variation in demand was addressed primarily by varying the rate of domestic production, and Britain had required very little gas storage. As one study put the matter, "The UK gas fields are the strategic storage for the UK" (POST 2004, 3). But as production peaked and then began to decline, so did this swing production capacity. Since the completion of the pipeline with the continent in the late 1990s, Britain had imported gas to meet peak winter demand, and by 2004, it was reaching the limits of its import capacity. Moreover, the total gas storage capacity of 3.3 bcm was the equivalent of just two weeks of supply, in contrast to the supplies of up to 80 to 90 days typically maintained on the continent (JESS 2002, 34; DTI 2006b, 37). As a result, one 2004 study concluded, "We are uneasy about the position in the UK over the next two to three winters where the supply and demand balance is already tight . . . it is not clear that the market-based balancing of supply from all available sources against the highest daily demand peak in 20 years could be achieved" (HL 2004, 7). Indeed, the available supply could fall well short of the "one-in-twenty-years" peak day demand benchmark that the supply network was expected to be able to meet (POST 2004, 1–4; HL 2004, 33–40).

As long as gas supplies remained tight, there would be a significant risk of interruption, and any interruption would not be just a matter of people doing without until sufficient gas once again became available. In the event of a supply failure, there would be a risk of air entering the pipeline system, "thereby creating a highly explosive and dangerous situation" (S/STI 2006a, 7). Every supply point would have to be shut off at the meter, and restoring service once adequate gas was again available would be a manpower- and time-intensive process. One exercise confirmed that full recovery from a large-scale loss of gas supply would take upward of two months. Thus, even more than petroleum products or electricity, gas supply continuity was extremely important to maintain, even under the most trying circumstances (HL 2004, 34; S/STI 2006a, 7).

These fears were nearly realized during the winter of 2005–6, which was the coldest in parts of Britain in a decade. Because of a faster decline than expected in British gas production and maintenance work in several gas fields, domestic output and Norwegian imports reached only 94 percent of the forecasted amounts. To make matters worse, LNG supplies were limited by increased U.S. imports in the wake of hurricanes Katrina and Rita, which had disrupted gas production in the Gulf of Mexico, and gas flows through the UK-Belgium interconnector averaged only 60 percent of total capacity, despite higher prices in Britain. To top it all off, a fire disabled the main gas storage facility in February. As a result, wholesale gas prices jumped by as much as 300 percent and Britain "came very close to running out of gas" (Helm 2008, 22). Disaster was only averted because electricity generators and big industrial users were able to reduce their demand (BBC News 2006; S/STI 2006b, 9–11; DTI 2006a, 22; JESS 2006a, 14; DECC 2010a, 30–31).

LONG-TERM CONCERNS

Nevertheless, the medium- to long-term outlook was more positive. By the middle of the decade, a substantial amount of new import capacity was either under construction or planned. In the fall of 2005, the first LNG terminal for receiving imports opened, although it did not achieve full capacity until the following March, after the winter crisis had passed. That facility, on the Isle of Grain, would eventually be able to handle 15 bcm, while a second LNG terminal with a capacity of 10 bcm would open the following year. At the same time, the import capacity of the interconnector with the continent was being doubled, to 16.5 bcm per year, and a second pipeline that could deliver up to 20 bcm of gas from Norwegian fields was being built. Altogether, those and several other planned projects were likely to bring Britain's total gas import capacity to approximately 100 bcm by the end of the decade. In addition, a number of new storage projects in development or under consideration were expected to increase total storage capacity by some 50 percent over the same time frame (HL 2004, 27; S/STI 2005, 14–15; S/STI 2006a; S/STI 2006b, 17).

Despite these reasons for optimism, several sources of concern remained. First, even the increased gas storage capacity could meet only about a third of maximum peak day gas demand, and much of it might be needed to compensate for the intermittency of wind power, which was expected to provide a growing share of electricity production. Thus even more import capacity would eventually be needed to meet periods of peak demand (DTI 2007, 118; Wicks 2009, 67; DECC/ Ofgem 2011, 38).

Second, as Britain became increasingly reliant on gas imports, its energy security would inevitably depend more and more on conditions and events beyond its direct control. Norway could be counted on as a reliable supplier, although even its exports to Britain were disrupted in January 2010 by bad weather (DECC 2010a, 32). But the reliability of LNG imports would depend on the development of a deeper global market, and growing interconnections with the continent would expose Britain to the same types of supply disruptions that roiled Europe in early 2006 and 2009. Thus the 2007 energy white paper concluded, "We will benefit from greater diversity of supply, but be more exposed to the risk and impact of any overseas disruptions to energy supplies as supply routes become longer and cross more countries" (DTI 2007, 116; see also Wicks 2009, 67 and 83).

GROWING DEPENDENCE ON GAS

To complicate matters, Britain's natural gas consumption was poised to increase over the following two decades as the country became more dependent on gas for electricity generation, necessitating even more import capacity. Gas was already integral to the electric power industry. Of the 75 GW of generating capacity in Britain in the middle of the 2000s, approximately one-third was provided by modern combined-cycle gas turbines, and gas accounted for some 36 percent of all electricity generated (DECC 2011a, ch. 5). And these figures were only likely to grow, because over the next two decades a substantial share of the existing coal and nuclear generating capacity was expected to be retired.

In the early 2000s, coal was an equally important source of power, with about 30 GW of dedicated or dual-fired (with oil) generating capacity. In 2001, however, the EU adopted the Large Combustion Plant Directive (LCPD), which imposed sharp restrictions on emissions of sulfur dioxide (SO_2) and nitrogen oxide (NO). Power plants that were unable to comply with the new limits could opt out, but they would have to close after 20,000 hours of operation or at the end of 2015, whichever came first. As a result, Britain would lose as much as 11 GW of coal and oil-fired generating capacity by the middle of the next decade, and coal's share of electricity generation could shrink from one-third to as low as 15 percent over the next 10 to 14 years (JESS 2006a, 18–19; DTI 2006b, 39; DTI 2007, 128–29; Helm 2008, 6 and 16).

An even more drastic curtailment of Britain's nuclear generating capacity was expected over the same period. In 2005, Britain had 23 nuclear power plants with about 12 GW of capacity in operation, meeting about 20 percent of electricity demand. Almost all of these reactors had been started in the 1960s and 1970s, however. Consequently, the majority were scheduled to shut down by the mid-2010s, and only one, the single PWR approved in the 1980s, might be in operation after 2023. Nuclear power's contribution to electricity production was expected to be less than 10 percent of the total by 2015 and to continue declining thereafter (IEA 2002b, 133; DTI 2003, 10 and 86; JESS 2006b, 34; DTI 2007, 181).

Because of these developments and expected increases in electricity demand, the government estimated that Britain would need around 20–25 GW in new generating capacity by 2020, or the equivalent of nearly one-third of existing capacity, and up to an additional 10 GW over the following decade. Some of this need would be met by renewable sources of electricity, but the majority would have to be provided by gas. Indeed, a majority of the proposals for building new generating capacity at the time involved gas-fired facilities. As a result, the share of electricity provided by gas was forecast to grow to around 50 percent by 2010 and as high as 60 percent by 2020 (POST 2004, 1; HL 2004, 23; S/STI 2006b, 3; DTI 2007, 128–29 and 184; see also DECC/Ofgem 2011, 3).

PLANNING OBSTACLES

Finally, acquiring any needed gas infrastructure and new power generating facilities of any type would not necessarily be easy. Given the previous liberalization of the energy sector, it would be up to the private sector to make the necessary investments, but private investors might well be discouraged by the British planning system. As the 2007 energy white paper noted, "Planning is consistently one of the top concerns for investors. . . . it can take too long . . . it can create too much uncertainty. In extreme cases, the cost and uncertainty can deter the private sector from proposing projects that would improve the reliability of our supplies" (DTI 2007, 255).

According to one report, potential investors had to allow for three to five years to obtain planning consent for most major gas projects, and even applications for gas storage and onshore wind farm projects had had to wait on the order of two years for a final decision. In 2006, moreover, three of the four major decisions on gas supply infrastructure projects resulted in refusals. Thus the government concluded, "There is a risk that planning delays or unpredictable decisions will prevent new infrastructure of national significance from coming on line in a timely fashion" (DTI 2007, 141–42, 146, and 255–56; see also JESS 2002, 34).

Overview of British Policy Responses

How did the government respond to these new concerns about energy security? Although such concerns were expressed as early as 2002, efforts to address them did not become a major component of British energy policy until after the middle of the decade. In February 2003, the government published an energy white paper, which represented the first comprehensive review of energy policy since at least the early 1990s. The white paper listed four goals, including maintaining the "reliability" of energy supplies, but the bulk of the report was devoted to the goal stated in its subtitle, "creating a low carbon economy." Less than 20 pages of the 142-page document were devoted to the issue of energy reliability, and most of the proposed measures consisted of monitoring the situation and working more closely with other interested parties at home and abroad. No major shifts or innovations in British policy were regarded as necessary to address the issue at the time (DTI 2003).

Energy security received somewhat more prominence in the brief international energy strategy published in October 2004, but the real turning point was the comprehensive energy review conducted in 2006, just three years after the publication of the white paper. With regard to energy security, the initial consultation document on which the review was based noted that "the UK has become a net importer of gas sooner than expected, and is also becoming a net oil importer. . . . With heightened concerns about energy security, we need to ask ourselves if we are doing enough to identify and manage potential risks in this new situation" (DTI 2006b, 1).

The resulting energy review report elevated energy security to the same status as climate change, noting that "we face two major long-term energy challenges: tackling climate change . . . and delivering secure, clean energy at affordable prices, as we become increasingly dependent on imports for our energy needs" (DTI 2006a, 10). The "energy security challenge" consisted in turn of two particular challenges: "managing increased dependence on oil and gas imports; and ensuring that the market delivers substantial and timely investment in electricity generating capacity and networks" (DTI 2006a, 18).

The energy review culminated in three separate white papers and several sets of related legislation over the following two years. In May 2007, the government published simultaneously a new energy white paper and a white paper on reforming the national planning system. The following January, it issued a separate white paper on nuclear power and introduced three sets of legislation concerning energy, climate change, and planning, all of which were adopted in November 2008. Finally, in July 2009, the Parliament adopted a detailed national strategy for energy and climate change, the Low-Carbon Transition Plan (LCTP), that promised to reduce natural gas demand by 29 percent in 2020, thereby limiting gas imports to just 45 percent of supply (HMG 2009a, 28 and 35).

The following sections detail the concrete steps taken by the government through these policy statements and pieces of legislation to increase Britain's energy security. Nevertheless, two principal themes ran through them. One was that many of the measures intended to reduce carbon emissions would also enhance Britain's energy security.

> Reducing greenhouse gas emissions and safeguarding energy security are, in general, complementary aims. A low carbon energy system is likely to use a more diverse balance of energy sources. Using several different forms of energy, such as renewables, nuclear and fossil fuels with [carbon capture and storage], will help to make the system more resilient by offering more options for

electricity generation and reducing dependence on any one energy source. . . .
[I]n the longer term, the low carbon transition is likely to decrease reliance on
imported oil and gas and will thereby help to reduce the risks associated with
high levels of energy dependency. (DECC 2010a, 16)

Thus there would be little or no conflict between the two main goals of British
energy policy.

The other central theme was a continued reliance on markets to deliver the
new investments required to ensure Britain's energy security. The government
was no longer in the business of building power plants, pipelines, storage facilities, and other energy infrastructure. It would not even specify particular targets
for the amount of investment that was needed. Rather, its role would continue
to be limited to shaping the legal, fiscal, regulatory, and informational environment in which private actors would make the decisions that would determine the
level and reliability of energy supplies (BERR 2008, 11).

Domestic Policy Responses

At home, the government attacked the problem on multiple fronts. It took steps
to maximize domestic production of oil and gas, but it could at most slow, rather
than, reverse the general trend of declining output and rising import dependence.
Instead, the most promising routes to greater energy security lay in reducing consumption and promoting substitutes for oil and gas, especially renewable sources
of energy and nuclear power. In addition, the government made changes in the
planning and approval processes to facilitate the construction of new infrastructure for the import, transportation, and storage of gas.

DOMESTIC PRODUCTION

Efforts to maximize the production of oil and gas had begun soon after the
decline in production had begun. The 2002 Finance Act, for example, altered
the tax regime for offshore exploration, development, and production to make it
one of the most favorable for investment in the world (DTI 2003, 84). The government also introduced new types of licenses to attract small investors and encourage exploration of new areas. These efforts continued during the following years
as concerns about energy security increased. The government further diversified the types and costs of licenses to attract the widest range of investors, and
the 2009 budget introduced a new incentive for bringing smaller and more
technically challenging oil and gas fields into production (DECC 2010a, 2;
DECC 2010b, 25). Nevertheless, the potential for slowing the decline was very

limited. According to one estimate, a continued high level of investment could deliver up to an extra 30 mtoe of oil and gas after 2020, but this would have amounted to less than 15 percent of total production in 2000 (DTI 2007, 123). Instead, the greatest promise for enhancing energy security lay elsewhere.

REDUCING CONSUMPTION OF GAS AND OIL

One more promising area was in reducing the consumption of gas and oil. Increasing energy efficiency and reducing carbon emissions had already been high priorities of British energy policy. The 2007 energy white paper, a 2007 energy efficiency action plan, and the 2009 LCTP all reinforced and added to these existing measures with a range of new actions. For example, the government introduced a mandatory cap and trade scheme, the Carbon Reduction Commitment (subsequently renamed the CRC Energy Efficiency Scheme), that applied to large nonenergy intensive private and public sector organizations with electricity consumption of greater than 6 gigawatt-hours per year. It progressively tightened building regulations and required commercial premises and rental properties to post energy performance certificates that describe a building's energy ratings. The government raised energy performance standards for appliances and worked to phase out the sale of inefficient light bulbs (DTI 2007, 9–11). A new Carbon Emissions Reduction Target (CERT) required all domestic energy suppliers with more than 50,000 (later 250,000) customers to make savings in the amount of CO_2 emitted by households (Ofgem 2013). And the government raised the fuel duty and the Vehicle Excise Duty for the most polluting cars (DTI 2007, 241). In 2009, the government estimated that these measures would reduce net natural gas demand by 29 percent in 2020, or about 27 bcm, to around just 66 bcm (HMG 2009a, 103).

RENEWABLE ENERGY

Similar savings in oil and especially gas consumption were expected to come through the rapid and extensive introduction of substitutes, namely renewable sources of energy, nuclear power, and possibly coal with carbon capture and storage (CCS). In 2009, in the context of the EU, Britain adopted a legally binding goal of obtaining 15 percent of its energy from renewable sources by 2020, which would represent a sevenfold increase over 2008. It also set more specific targets of obtaining more than 30 percent of its electricity (which accounted for 49 percent of PEC), 12 percent of its heat (30 percent of PEC), and 10 percent of its transportation energy (21 percent of PEC) from renewables. If successful, Britain would reduce its overall fossil fuel demand by around 10 percent and gas imports by

20–30 percent compared with what they would otherwise have been in 2020 (HMG 2009b, 8 and 10; DECC 2011b, 26).

Introducing renewable energy in the transportation sector would mainly help to reduce Britain's need for oil imports, since transportation accounted for some two-thirds of oil consumption. The primary mechanism for doing so was the RTFO, which the government had announced in 2005 and was introduced in 2008–9. The RTFO required suppliers of transport fuel to ensure that at least 5 percent of sales were from renewable sources by 2010–11. In the 2006 energy review and 2007 energy white paper, the government expressed its intention to increase the obligation to a higher level, perhaps as much as 10 percent, assuming that robust sustainability and carbon standards for biofuels could be developed. By 2010, however, concerns about the environmental impact of biofuels had led to a shift in emphasis to ultra-low emission vehicles. The government now planned to spend several hundred million pounds to incentivize the purchase of plug-in hybrid and electric vehicles (EV) and another £30 million to support the deployment of an EV charging infrastructure in key cities (DECC 2010b, 18; DECC 2011c, 101–2).

The biggest contribution to meeting the overall goal for renewable energy, however, was to come from renewable sources of electricity. The original goal of the RO had been 10 percent of electricity production by 2010. This objective had been raised to 15 percent by 2015, and the 2006 energy review and 2007 energy white paper had expressed the intention of achieving 20 percent by 2020 (DTI 2006a, 16; DTI 2007, 14). Thus the final target of 30 percent by 2020 was extremely ambitious.

To help achieve the higher target, the government took several steps. In 2010, it introduced a feed-in tariff scheme to encourage the deployment of small-scale (less than 5 MW capacity), low-carbon electricity generation. It provided hundreds of millions of pounds in direct support for key emerging technologies, especially offshore wind and wave and tidal power generation (HMG 2009b, 17; DECC 2011c, 6). Most important, the government introduced "banding" to the RO to provide differentiated levels of support to different renewable technologies, depending on their relative maturity, development cost, and associated risks. In particular, banding would increase the level of support for technologies in the early stages of development, such as offshore wind, wave, and tidal power, while reducing that for well-established technologies in order to avoid oversubsidization of the latter. Overall, the RO was expected to provide £1 to £2 billion annually in support for the deployment of renewable electricity (DTI 2007, 14).

It was clear, however, that renewable energy would not be a panacea. In particular, the intermittent nature of many renewable sources of electricity in combination with the inability to store large amounts of electricity meant that Britain would still require a substantial amount of other forms of generating capacity in order to provide backup when the availability of renewable sources was low. Indeed, the government concluded, increasing reliance on renewable electricity meant that Britain would need to increase its total generating capacity, by perhaps as much as 100 percent (DECC 2011b, 19–20).

CARBON CAPTURE AND STORAGE

If Britain were to limit the amount of CO_2 emissions from power generation, there were just two main options. One was the widespread use of carbon capture and storage (CCS) technology at fossil-fuel-fired power plants. According to one government estimate, CCS had the potential to reduce carbon emissions by up to 90 percent. To prepare for the deployment of CCS technology, the government required that all new commercial scale (over 300 MW) combustion power stations would have to be designed and built "carbon capture ready" and that any new coal power station demonstrate the effective use of CCS on at least 300 MW of its generating capacity. Government planning proceeded on the assumption that CCS would be proven by 2020, and to promote the development of the technology, the government offered financial support for up to four commercial-scale demonstration projects (HMG 2009a, 65–66; DECC 2011b, 31–32). In the mid-2000s, however, the affordability of CCS remained far from certain, and as of 2011, not a single commercial demonstration project had begun. Perhaps as a result, the government projected that less than 2 percent of electricity would be generated by coal with CCS between 2020 and 2030. Thus the greatest hope for meeting much of Britain's future electricity needs, at least in the short to medium term, lay with nuclear power.

NUCLEAR POWER

As recently as the 2003 energy white paper, the government had shown little interest in nuclear power. At that time, it concluded that "current economics make [nuclear power] an unattractive option for new, carbon-free generating capacity" and that it should concentrate its efforts on energy efficiency and renewables. At best, the government would keep the nuclear option open, but it would not provide any support for new nuclear construction (DTI 2003, 12 and 44).

Within just three years, however, the government had radically altered its position. In the 2006 energy review report, it found that "under likely scenarios for gas and carbon prices, new nuclear power stations would yield economic bene-fits in terms of carbon reduction and security of supply." Thus it concluded that "nuclear has a role to play in the future UK generating mix alongside other low carbon generating options" (DTI 2006a, 113). Indeed, if Britain were simply to maintain the existing level of nuclear capacity, its gas consumption would be some 13 percent lower in 2030 (DTI 2006a, 17).

This preliminary view was repeated and then finalized in the 2007 energy white paper and the 2008 white paper on nuclear power, respectively. The latter concluded that "energy efficiency and renewable technologies alone will not be enough to meet the twin challenges of climate change and energy security" (BERR 2008, 16). Henceforth, it would be in the public interest for new nuclear power stations to have a role to play in Britain's future energy mix alongside other low-carbon sources and thus to allow energy companies the option of investing in them. Conversely, preventing them from doing so "would increase the risk of not achieving our long-term climate change and energy security goals, or achieving them at higher cost." The government judged that the risks associated with nu-clear power were small and that they could be effectively managed by the existing regulatory regime (BERR 2008, 10 and 31–32; see also DTI 2007, 17 and 204–5).

Despite the cautious language contained in the white papers, "it [was] abso-lutely clear that the government wants nuclear power stations built" (Helm 2007b, 1). And as time passed, the government's interest in seeing a rapid buildup of nuclear generating capacity only grew. As a 2011 government statement put the matter, "It is important that new nuclear power stations are constructed and start generating as soon as possible and significantly earlier than 2025" (DECC 2011b, 30).

Nevertheless, the government was quick to note that it was not itself propos-ing to build new nuclear power stations. Rather, it would be for the private sec-tor to initiate, fund, construct, and operate them. In addition, the owners and op-erators would have to set aside funds to cover the full costs of decommissioning the new reactors when the time came and their full share of long-term waste manage-ment and disposal costs (DTI 2007, 204–5; BERR 2008, 10 and 147). Although the government found, on the basis of cost-benefit analysis, that nuclear power was likely to be an attractive economic proposition, ultimately, markets would decide how many, if any, new nuclear plants to build (BERR 2008, 20; Helm 2008, 10).

But the government would still have a role to play. Potential developers had made clear that before they would consider investing in new nuclear power plants, the government would have to address a number of regulatory barriers (DTI 2006a, 121; DTI 2007, 144). Thus, in view of the potential public policy benefits of new nuclear build, the government decided to take a number of facilitative actions designed to reduce the regulatory and planning uncertainty and risks associated with investing in new nuclear power stations, especially during the preconstruction period. These included

- strengthening the EU emissions trading system so that investors would have greater confidence in carbon price signals when making decisions
- establishing a strategic siting assessment process to develop criteria for determining the suitability of sites for new nuclear power stations; following consultation, the government would assess appropriately nominated sites against these criteria
- conducting a process of justification as required by the EU to test whether the economic, social, and other benefits of specific nuclear power technologies outweighed the health detriments
- assisting nuclear regulators with a process of Generic Design Assessment (GDA) of industry-preferred nuclear power plant designs; the GDA would limit the need to discuss these issues in depth during the site specific licensing process
- providing a legislative framework for funding decommissioning and waste management liabilities
- simplifying the planning system for major electric power projects by ensuring that it gave full weight to the decisions on strategic, policy, and regulatory issues that had already been taken at the national level and did not allow such issues to be reopened in relation to individual applications (DTI 2007, 207; BERR 2008, 34–35 and 134–35)

Assuming that these measures could be adopted quickly, the government hoped that the first new nuclear plants could be operating as early as 2018 (BERR 2008, 36 and 139; see also DECC 2011b, 30).

GAS INFRASTRUCTURE

A further major component of British policy at home was to facilitate the construction of new LNG terminals, gas pipelines, and storage facilities. A good deal of additional import capacity had come online in the mid- to late-2000s, helping to avert a winter supply disruption. And gains in energy efficiency and renewable sources of electricity might slow the predicted rise in annual gas imports. At certain times of peak demand, however, import requirements on a short-term basis could become much greater. Thus even more import and storage infrastructure was likely to be needed by 2020 if Britain were to continue to have reliable and affordable gas supplies (S/STI 2006a, 1 and 3–4; DTI 2006a, 21 and 86; DTI 2007, 253; Wicks 2009, 57).

Once again, however, the government's role in addressing these needs would be highly circumscribed. For example, the government considered the idea of providing or commissioning strategic gas storage but rejected it on a number of grounds. In particular, there was a risk of undermining other actions taken to promote energy security, such as by discouraging commercial investment in gas storage. Instead, as with the energy sector in general, the government concluded that the private sector was best placed to deliver the needed additional gas supply infrastructure (S/STI 2006a, 6; DTI 2006a, 89–90; DECC 2010a, 55–58).

And once again, the government's primary role would be to establish the right regulatory framework. The government took action to enable and incentivize the timely development of appropriately sited gas supply infrastructure projects through reforms to the relevant planning and approval processes (DTI 2007, 120). Part of this effort consisted of revising the legal regime covering innovative offshore gas storage and import facilities. For example, the government anticipated that companies would soon be able to use new technology to create salt caverns offshore for storing gas and to unload LNG tankers at mooring buoys connected by pipelines to the shore. The groundwork for such projects was laid by the 2008 Energy Act, which established a new licensing system for offshore facilities (S/STI 2006a, 14; DTI 2007, 21; DECC 2010a, 5).

But the problem was not limited to offshore projects. As one analysis noted,

> the planning regimes concerning onshore gas supply infrastructure have developed over the years in a piecemeal fashion and do not properly reflect in terms of delivery of gas infrastructure the major changes in the structure of the British gas industry in recent years nor the advances in gas technology, particularly vis-à-vis the growing importance of LNG and innovative gas storage projects. (S/STI 2006a, 10)

As a result, potential developers of supply infrastructure were faced with increasing risk, through uncertainties over planning time scales and outcomes, long delays, and procedural costs (S/STI 2006a, 10). Thus the effort to promote security of gas supplies also converged with the government's more general efforts to reform the planning and approval process for energy infrastructure.

REFORMING THE PLANNING PROCESS

In sum, many of the projects that the government hoped the private sector would develop—renewable energy, nuclear power plants, and natural gas infrastructure—faced significant obstacles in the planning process. Consequently, a further major prong of government policy on energy security came to be simplifying and streamlining the planning and approval processes for large-scale energy projects. The overall goals were straightforward: to make the system more predictable, to limit delays, to strike a better balance between local concerns and national needs by limiting planning inquiries as much as possible to local issues, and, more generally, to minimize the costs and risks to developers (S/STI 2006a, 3; DTI 2006a, 16 and 20 and 164; DTI 2007, 21 and 130; HMG 2009a, 14). The proposed reforms were first presented in a separate 2007 white paper, "Planning for a Sustainable Future," and then formally proposed as legislation in a Planning Act, which was approved in November 2008.

The Planning Act created a new system of development consent for "nationally significant" infrastructure projects, including many types of energy projects. In particular, it covered all electricity generating stations, including renewable and nuclear, of more than 50 MW onshore and 100 MW offshore and virtually all onshore gas storage and import facilities. For each type of infrastructure, the government would issue a National Policy Statement (NPS) that would establish the national need. A new independent body, the Infrastructure Planning Commission (IPC), would then be responsible for examining and making decisions on all applications for development consent of qualifying projects. The new procedures set a deadline of six months for carrying out the examination procedure and then a further three months for taking a decision, and the IPC would give substantial weight to national considerations of need (BERR 2008, 137–38; DECC 2010a, 4 and 23; DECC 2011b, 2–3 and 17). The IPC was established in late 2009 and started work the following March.

External Policy Responses

Efforts to increase British energy security in the 2000s also had an external dimension. The most immediate objective was to secure oil and gas supplies at reasonable prices as British production declined. More generally, however, British policy was concerned with ensuring the stability, transparency, openness, and liquidity of international energy markets. Concrete goals included promoting political and economic reforms, such as market liberalization and private investment, in key supplier and transit countries as well as encouraging sustainable energy consumption in major energy consuming countries (FCO/DTI/Defra 2004; DTI 2006b, 34).

Some of this work was necessarily conducted on a bilateral basis. Britain signed treaties with Norway and the Netherlands to lay the legal groundwork for new gas import pipelines. It also sought to deepen its engagement and promote good relations with other important energy-producing and transit countries, such as Russia, Saudi Arabia, Iraq, Qatar, and Nigeria. These bilateral dealings had multiple objectives, such as ensuring that British importers had equal access to foreign energy supplies, encouraging continued investment in exploration and production, promoting political and economic stability and good governance, and improving the climate for foreign investment (DTI 2003, 80–81; DTI 2006a, 19 and 81–82; DECC 2010b, 9–10). One noteworthy success of these efforts was the decision of Qatar's state-controlled gas company to invest in an LNG terminal in Wales underpinned by long-term supply agreements (Wicks 2009, 98).

The external aspects of British efforts to increase energy security were largely focused on the EU, however. Indeed, during this period, Britain became increasingly supportive of policy initiatives that moved the EU in the direction of a common energy policy. The EU could help Britain achieve its goals on both the supply and demand sides.

On the one hand, Britain continued to push forcefully for liberalization of the EU's gas and electricity markets. As Britain became more dependent on imports, especially for gas, the continental energy market would become an increasingly important source of energy. It was vital to ensure that gas and electricity could flow freely across the English Channel in response to differences in prices and demand (S/STI 2005, 2; S/STI 2006b, 2; JESS 2006b, 6; DTI 2007, 120). Consequently, Britain was perhaps the most fervent supporter of the liberalization packages proposed by the EU Commission. And once the packages had been adopted by the member states, Britain worked tirelessly for their complete and rapid implementation. It also encouraged the commission to make full use of its enforcement powers, including those provided by EU competition law, to address market abuses (DTI 2006a, 19 and 22; DTI 2007, 108; DECC 2010b, 6–7).

Britain also became a strong supporter of developing a well-defined common external energy policy and integrating energy into other EU policies with an external dimension. It recognized that the members of the EU would carry more weight when speaking with one voice. Hence the EU needed to adopt a more collective approach to dialogue with major energy suppliers, current and potential transit countries, and even major energy consumer nations (DTI 2006c). Of particular interest to Britain in this context was the development of a "southern corridor" that would bring gas to Europe by pipeline from the Caspian and Middle East regions (DECC 2010a, 5; DECC 2010b, 7).

On the demand side, Britain was a strong proponent of extending and tightening the EU emissions trading system. For example, it wanted the third phase to last more than five years and to include transport and aviation fuel. Although strengthening the ETS would further constrain the use of coal, it would also help to drive advances in energy conservation, and by establishing a firm carbon price, encourage investment in renewable energy and nuclear power (DTI 2006a, 12–14; DTI 2007, 11). Britain also called for an ambitious EU energy efficiency action plan, including higher standards for vehicle fuel efficiency and the energy efficiency of appliances and other energy-consuming products (DTI 2006d, 2; DTI 2007, 9).

Taken together, these steps suggested "a more fundamental shift in the UK's view of the value of and need for a common energy policy" (McGowan 2011, 204). Indeed, in a speech to the European Parliament in late 2005, Prime Minister Tony Blair said, "I believe it is time that we developed within Europe a common European energy policy. For far too long we have been in the situation where, in a haphazard and random way energy needs and energy priorities are simply determined in each country according to its needs, but without any sense of the collective power we could have in Europe if we were prepared to pool our energy and our resources" (Blair 2005). Subsequently, Britain endorsed the inclusion of an energy chapter in the 2009 Lisbon Treaty, which for the first time made energy policy a formal competence of the EU.

Evaluation of British Policy Responses in the 2000s

British efforts to promote energy security in the first decade of the 2000s seemed to be in a period of transition. On the one hand, the government still relied heavily on market forces. Whether the issue was natural gas production, imports, storage, nuclear power plants, or renewable energy, it would be up to the private sector to deliver the necessary investment. The government was simply no longer in the business of producing, transporting, or supplying energy.

On the other hand, the government was doing more and more to incentivize businesses to deliver the outcomes that it considered necessary for British energy security. At a minimum, the government sought to reduce or eliminate regulatory obstacles that might discourage private investment, as in the case of gas infrastructure and nuclear power. In other areas, however, the government was increasingly intervening to shape the market so that it would generate the results it desired. In the case of renewables, argued British energy policy expert Dieter Helm, there was "not much 'market' left. The [2007 energy] white paper is littered with initiatives, strategies, subsidies and interventions for almost all aspects of renewables" (Helm 2007b, 2). And this intervention sometimes came with a high price tag. In Helm's estimation, "The RO is one of the developed world's most expensive interventions—some wind is costing up to £500 per tonne of carbon abated" (Helm 2007b, 2).

It remained to be seen, moreover, just how successful this approach would be at enhancing British energy security. As the next decade unfolded, there were some early indications of success, but much uncertainty remained, and the government felt compelled to take further steps to ensure the security of energy supplies.

GAS SUPPLIES

One bright spot was gas import infrastructure. As discussed above, Britain had narrowly avoided a winter gas supply crisis in the mid-2000s, when new import capacity came online just in time. During the remainder of the decade, gas imports continued to rise, reaching 37.5 bcm or about 40 percent of consumption in 2010. But import infrastructure grew even faster. By 2011, it totaled more than 150 bcm per year, roughly evenly divided between LNG facilities, pipelines from Norway, and pipelines connecting Britain to the continent (DECC/Ofgem 2011, 30–31; see also DECC 2010a, 4). As a result, there already appeared to be ample capacity to meet Britain's gas needs up to 2020 and beyond, notwithstanding an expected further decline in domestic production (DECC 2010a, 36; DECC/Ofgem 2013, 43).

In contrast, total gas storage capacity had grown only modestly, but here too there was reason for optimism. The first license for an offshore gas storage project was issued in 2010, and, in 2011, three more facilities were under construction and another 16 had been proposed, of which half had received the necessary planning consents. By late 2013, total capacity had increased by 20 percent and, perhaps more important, daily deliverability rates had almost doubled compared to 2010. (DECC 2010a, 4–5 and 22–23; DECC/Ofgem 2011, 39; DECC/Ofgem 2013, 45–46). Nevertheless, doubts remained as to how many of these facilities would actually be built because the major energy companies were not convinced of their commercial viability (Blair 2011).

In 2013, there was potentially good news with regard to indigenous gas production. Initially, the use of hydraulic fracturing was seen as having very limited potential in Britain. The British Geological Survey (BGS) had originally estimated onshore shale gas reserves at just 150 bcm, or less than twice Britain's annual consumption, and the first commercial exploratory wells triggered small earthquakes, prompting the government to impose a temporary halt in May 2011. In late 2012, however, the government lifted the ban and established a new office to promote the development of unconventional gas and oil by streamlining regulation. Then in 2013, the BGS issued a new estimate for central Britain that put the reserves there at between 23 and 65 trillion cubic meters. If even only 10 percent of that amount could be brought to market, it would be enough to meet Britain's gas needs for some 45 years (Reed 2012; Reed 2013b). To realize this potential, however, the government and industry would still have to overcome the strong opposition of environmental groups and many local interests.

ALTERNATIVE GENERATING CAPACITY

The outlook for alternative sources of electric power was also positive. At the end of 2013, Britain had just over 20 GW of renewable generating capacity, or more than 20 percent of the total. Another 3.6 GW of renewable projects were under construction, 14.5 GW of projects had received planning permission, and more than 20 GW of projects had submitted planning applications. As a result, the government projected that total renewable generating capacity would reach nearly 38 GW by 2020, or about 40 percent of all generating capacity, and that renewables would be providing more than one-third of all electricity.[3]

Meanwhile, the government had laid the regulatory groundwork for a rapid buildup of nuclear capacity. In mid-2007, nuclear regulators began a GDA on four nuclear reactor designs proposed by industry, although two were later withdrawn. The process was expected to be completed by 2011, but the process was delayed pending an analysis of the lessons of the accident at Fukushima Daiichi in March of that year (BERR 2008, 143; WNA 2012b). The government's initial strategic siting assessment was completed in 2010, and in 2011, the Parliament approved the NPS for nuclear power generation, which listed eight sites as suitable for deployment of new power stations (DECC/Ofgem 2011, 14; WNA 2012b).

Initially, the nuclear industry responded favorably to these developments. EDF Energy announced plans for four new reactors at two sites and, in late 2011, applied for consent to build the first two. It hoped to have the first of these connected to the grid in 2018. Two other energy companies expressed their intentions to build as many as seven to nine more reactors between 2020 and 2025, for a total of at least 16 GW in new nuclear capacity (DECC 2011b, 30; WNA 2012b). In 2011, the government's own projections were more cautious, but still included 4.8 GW in new nuclear capacity by 2025 and 12 GW by 2030 in the most likely case.[4]

Despite these positive initial developments, it appeared that Britain could face two potential threats to the security of its electricity supplies later in the decade. The first was insufficient low-carbon generating capacity to make up for the expected loss of some 20 percent of Britain's existing power sources by the end of the decade while meeting the country's ambitious carbon reduction goals. Eight GW or one-third of Britain's coal-fired capacity would have to close at the end of 2015 as a result of the EU LCPD, and all but 3.7 GW of Britain's nuclear capacity would reach the end of its design life by the end of the decade, with 2.5 GW more following in first half of 2020s (IEA 2007b, 155–56). In addition, Britain would need more backup generating capacity, mostly fired by gas, to compensate for the growing amount of intermittent renewable power on the system and the inflexibility of nuclear base load. The government estimated that more than £100 billion in private sector investment in new generating capacity and grid infrastructure would be needed by 2020 alone. And as the decade wore on, the problems were exacerbated by the U.S. shale gas revolution, which drove the price of coal in Britain down below that of gas and caused a number of gas-fired power stations to be mothballed.

In response to these developments, the government devised a comprehensive Electricity Market Reform (EMR), which was introduced as legislation in 2012. One key feature was a new type of feed-in tariff scheme for low-carbon production called Contracts for Difference, which was intended to incentivize investment in renewables, nuclear power, and fossil fuels with CCS. Under this system, the government would set a strike price for each technology that would be guaranteed for 15 to 35 years. If the market price for electricity fell below the agreed strike price, electricity suppliers would make up the difference, and if the market price was higher, the generator would pay back the difference. The second feature was a capacity market, in which generators and other potential providers of electricity, such as storage, would be paid to maintain reliable capacity to delivery electricity at times of increased demand. According to one estimate, this mechanism would help bring forth up to 26 GW of new gas-fired capacity needed by 2030 (Hosker 2013). The EMR also included a carbon floor price and an emissions performance standard that would effectively block the construction of any new coal-fired plants that lacked CCS. In combination, these measures would constitute a major change in how investment decisions were made. Indeed, one analysis described the EMR as granting the government "powers to intervene in the market on a scale not seen since the industry was privatized" (EurActiv 2012b).

Nevertheless, the EMR was much criticized during the following months. Some expressed concerns about the likely impact on consumers' electricity bills. Others viewed the Contracts for Difference as a hidden subsidy for nuclear power. And yet others claimed that its provisions would violate EU rules on state aid.

Explaining British Responses to Energy Insecurity
Energy Resource Endowments

During both of the periods examined in this chapter, energy resource endowments importantly conditioned British energy security concerns and policy responses. In the 1970s, the recent discovery of abundant reserves of oil and natural gas in the North Sea gave Britain options that most other developed democracies could only envy. As a result, Britain did not experience the pressure that others did to secure and protect foreign oil supplies, by whatever means necessary.

This rise in fossil fuel self-sufficiency also had negative consequences, however. In particular, it reduced the urgency to pursue other domestic policies that might have helped to increase British energy security in the longer term. Although Britain possessed one of the most advanced nuclear programs at the time, a significant expansion in the program could not be justified, given expectations that the combination of coal and North Sea oil and gas would meet most of Britain's energy needs until the 1990s. Partly as a result, only one reactor of the PWR design was every built, leaving Britain almost entirely reliant on the older Magnox and AGR technologies. Likewise, Britain's relative energy plenty and self-sufficiency contributed to a greater degree of complacency about improving energy efficiency than was found in some other countries (Chesshire et al. 1977, 48 and 51; Evans 1979, 93; Lucas 1982, 105; Commission 1984, 161; Chesshire 1986, 403; Anderson 1993, 52).

It is also worth speculating about whether Britain's abundance of energy resources also facilitated the sharp shift to a free market orientation in the 1980s. Energy expert Francis McGowan has written that "As the UK achieved self-sufficiency, the Thatcher government was able to afford the luxury of a radical reorientation of energy policy" (McGowan 1996b, 151). In addition, North Sea gas and oil presumably made it easier for the government to confront the coal miners' union in the middle of the decade, since by then gas had largely displaced the use of coal for space heating and oil could be substituted for the main remaining use of coal, electricity production.

Whereas the exploitation of domestic energy resources had provided a solution to the oil crises, the eventual decline in oil and especially gas production set the stage for the renewed concerns about energy security in the 2000s. Although the drop in domestic output could be compensated to a significant extent by increased imports, the additional costs and risks inevitably associated with the latter meant that Britain had to take more seriously measures to reduce consumption as well as to develop substitutes like renewable energy and nuclear power.

Economic Conditions and Policy Constraints

The overall state of the British economy also played a role in shaping British responses to energy security, especially in the 1970s. At that time, Britain was still struggling to limit its balance of payments deficits in order to maintain the value of the pound on foreign exchanges (Hall 1986, 76–80). Indeed, the government was eventually forced to turn to the International Monetary Fund for a $4 billion loan in 1976. Balance of payments concerns impacted British policy in at least two ways. First, they provided another reason for developing North Sea oil reserves as quickly as possible, since doing so would reduce and eventually eliminate net oil imports. Second, they constrained the use of military forces in the pursuit of external policy objectives. In fact, Britain had withdrawn its last forces from the Persian Gulf just before the first oil shock, leaving it with far more limited options.

In the 2000s, British efforts to promote energy security were constrained less by budgetary limitations than by the country's efforts to fight climate change. The 2008 Climate Change Act committed Britain to reduce its greenhouse gas emissions by 80 percent below the 1990 level by 2050. This goal was widely viewed as requiring Britain to decarbonize electricity production by the 2030s. Subsequently, the government adopted interim emission reduction goals of 34 percent by 2020 and 50 percent by 2027 (IEA 2012a, 31). Continued reliance on coal to generate power would have increased the security of Britain's electricity supplies. But in the absence of large-scale CCS, these aggressive emission reduction targets required Britain to phase out coal-fired plants and to invest instead in large amounts of low-carbon generating capacity, even though doing so would introduce new sources of insecurity, such as the intermittency of many renewables, into the power supply.

Ideology

A very important determinant of British responses to concerns about energy security has been the dominant beliefs, or ideology, held by British leaders about the appropriate role of the state. More than in any other of the countries examined in this study, these beliefs underwent a major shift between the two periods under consideration.

In the 1970s, British leaders in both parties generally believed that the state should play a major role in the energy sector. This attitude has been well summarized by Helm: "For most politicians in the postwar period, the importance of energy has naturally translated into the assumption that governments need to control its production and distribution. Until the 1980s, it was a conventional wisdom that markets are hopelessly inadequate in providing appropriate energy supplies. State-owned companies were deemed to be so natural they were made *statutory* monopolies" (Helm 2004, 1; see also 14). Likewise, others have noted "the British economic establishment's view that government intervention is almost invariably both benevolent and advantageous to society as a whole" and that the energy crisis only encouraged the belief that Britain's energy problems required deep government involvement (Robinson and Morgan 1978, 18 and 192). Interestingly, however, policymakers tended to focus on the supply side of the energy equation and thus to overlook how government might address demand-side issues, such as energy conservation and efficiency.

By the beginning of the next century, a sea change had occurred in the dominant beliefs of British leaders. The Conservative governments of the 1980s and 1990s had championed a free market approach to energy policy that treated energy as just another tradable commodity, and this intellectual framework was eventually adopted by the Labour Party under the leadership Tony Blair, which returned to power in 1997. Indeed, in the words of McGowan, the subsequent New Labour governments "not only left the previous policy in place but enthusiastically embraced and advanced it" (McGowan 2011, 193; see also Helm 2004, 24).

This market oriented "policy paradigm" (Hall 1993, 279; see also Kuzemko 2009) placed significant constraints on British policy responses to energy insecurity in the 2000s. The default position of the government was never to intervene directly to ensure that energy supplies were adequate and reliable. Rather, as government reports and white papers repeatedly emphasized, the private sector was best placed to channel investment in the most effective directions. In particular, "competitive energy markets [were] the most cost-effective and efficient way of generating, distributing, and supplying energy" (DTI 2007, 26). The government's role should be limited to establishing very broad objectives and creating the right incentives and conditions through an appropriate regulatory framework, but preferably one of a very limited nature (DTI 2003, 87; S/STI 2006a, 2; JESS 2006b, 7; DTI 2006b, 38; DTI 2007, 8 and 26).

Only at the very end of the decade, as the limited ability of markets to provide for Britain's energy security became clearer, did government officials begin to question this approach. In a personal review of British energy security in 2009, a former minister of energy argued that "the era of heavy reliance on companies, competition and liberalisation must be reassessed. The time for market innocence is over. We must still rely on companies for exploration, delivery and supply, but the state must become more active—interventionist where necessary" (Wicks

2009, 1). And in the broader LCTP issued that same year, the government concluded that "market forces on their own will not achieve the necessary change towards a low-carbon energy mix sufficiently quickly and radically" (HMG 2009b, 13). How quickly the government could in fact change course, however, remained to be seen.

State Strength

These shifting views about the appropriate role of the state contributed to equally momentous changes in the domestic capacity of the state to shape energy security outcomes. During the postwar era, when the dominant ideology favored state involvement, Britain built up a substantial state capacity, as exemplified by the publicly owned monopolies for coal, electricity, and gas. Thus in the 1970s, the government did not hesitate to build additional capacity, such as the BNOC, when doing so seemed useful for achieving its policy goals.

By the 2000s, this situation had been almost entirely reversed. Much of the state capacity that had been built prior to the 1980s had been dismantled through the process of privatization and deregulation. The capacity of the government was now largely limited to developing national policies, mainly by the energy group within the Department of Trade and Industry—the original Department of Energy had been abolished in 1992 and a new Department of Energy and Climate Change was not created until late 2008—and regulating the energy markets. Hence the government had little choice but to rely heavily on the private sector to address the new energy challenges of the decade.

In contrast to the wide variation in state capacity, the central government institutions concerned with energy policy maintained a relatively high degree of policymaking autonomy. By the 1970s, the nationalization of the various energy industries had resulted in the dominance of the national government over local interests. Within the central government, the key actors engaged in policy making were limited in number—a few ministers and a somewhat larger body of senior permanent officials—and formed a relatively close group centered on the Department of Energy (Chesshire et al. 1977, 52–53; Evans 1979, 106; Lucas 1982, 93; McGowan 1996b, 138).

The principal exception to the autonomy of the central organs of government during this earlier period was the influence wielded by the powerful state-owned energy industries themselves. This may help to explain why energy policy in the 1970s was primarily concerned with the problem of supply, and Helm has argued that the 1979 decision to build a family of PWR's "reflected the degree of capture by [electricity] industry over the Department [of Energy] and its ministers" (Helm

2004, 52). Nevertheless, the interests of these entities tended to coincide with the immediate needs of the central government officials (Bending and Eden 1984, 31; Anderson 1993, 53; McGowan 1996b, 136 and 160).

The breakup of the state-owned monopolies removed this constraint, but it was accompanied by several other encroachments on the autonomy of the central government. One of these was the devolution in the late 1990s of some powers to the authorities in Scotland, Wales, and Northern Ireland. Thus, for example, the Scottish authorities gained responsibility for energy efficiency and renewable energy policy as well as the right to approve the construction of all power stations with a capacity of greater than 50 MW (IEA 2002b, 13 and 26; DTI 2006a, 16; DTI 2007, 207).

A second was the result of an increasingly transparent and participatory policymaking process that was designed to maximize consensus. Rather than simply issue a policy statement or white paper, in the 2000s, the government would typically provide multiple opportunities for public comment before finalizing its official positions. For example, the year and a half long review of policy that culminated in the 2007 energy white paper began with the issuance of a "consultation document" that invited comments on the full range of issues. This was followed by a preliminary "energy review report" that provided a further opportunity for consultation by interested individuals and groups on the government's proposals. Rather than simply constraining policy making, however, it could be equally argued that this process also enabled government officials to shape public opinion and build support for the positions they hoped to adopt on potentially controversial issues, such as nuclear power.

Finally, over time, changes in the planning process had ceded ever greater powers to local authorities. As a result, it often became difficult or took longer for large energy projects to gain approval. Nevertheless, as discussed above, the government was able to take important steps toward recentralizing the planning and consent process in the 2000s so that local interests could not so easily block projects that were deemed to be in the national interest.

This last development resulted in a somewhat paradoxical situation. On the one hand, the government itself now lacked the capacity to build projects, like nuclear power plants or gas infrastructure, that it might find useful for addressing its overall goals. For that, it had to rely on the private sector. On the other hand, the government was able to limit the ability of other societal actors to obstruct projects that market actors found profitable. In that sense, then, it maintained a high degree of autonomy. Thus Britain exhibited elements of both a strong and a weak state on the domestic front.

External state capacity was not central to improving Britain's energy security, though it would not have been substantial if called on. In the 1970s, Britain did not need to be particularly active on the international front, thanks to the reality and promise of increasing flows of North Sea gas and oil. As discussed above, however, Britain had just relinquished much of the military capacity that had enabled it to exert much influence in the Persian Gulf after Word War II. By the 2000s, the government possessed only diplomatic and limited financial means to assist energy companies in their efforts to secure access to foreign gas supplies. Instead, it sought primarily to promote Britain's energy security in the context of the EU. Membership in the EU enabled Britain to leverage its limited external capacity but also made the achievement of its policy goals hostage to the interests of the other member states.

Policy Legacies and Path Dependence

The British case contains several clear examples of how earlier policy choices shaped later energy security concerns and responses. The most striking example involves Britain's fairly aggressive exploitation of the oil and gas reserves discovered in the North Sea. This choice did much to enhance Britain's energy security—as well as its economic well-being—over the following three decades. But the degree of dependence that it engendered also set Britain up for a renewed bout of energy security concerns when gas production went into a steep and seemingly irreversible decline.

A related choice was Britain's relative neglect of nuclear power in the 1970s. Although Britain had been a leader in the field, the sudden abundance of gas and oil led it to make only modest investments in the nuclear program during that and subsequent decades. This policy meant, however, that just when Britain faced the need to find substitutes for domestic natural gas, much of which was used to produce electricity, its nuclear generating capacity and the domestic nuclear industry more generally were also in decline.

Finally, the long-term impact of the profound shift to a market-based approach to energy policy that occurred in the 1980s should not be underestimated. The resulting processes of privatization and deregulation left the government with a very limited set of policy instruments for coping with the energy security concerns that emerged in the 2000s. Thus many of its efforts focused on developing new tools for addressing the failure of energy markets to deliver new energy supplies and infrastructure.

Conclusion

During the two periods under consideration, Britain faced two very different sets of energy security concerns, although there was an important link between them. In the 1970s, they revolved to an important extent—but not exclusively—around Britain's growing dependence on imported oil. But thanks to the recent discovery of North Sea gas and oil, those initial concerns were soon allayed, and Britain enjoyed a relatively high degree of energy security for the next several decades.

Those same resource endowments, however, turned out to be been an important source of Britain's more recent energy security concerns. Rapidly declining production in the North Sea, especially of gas, meant that Britain would have to find alternative sources abroad or substitutes at home, and fairly quickly. This task was complicated, moreover, by the fact that Britain's fossil fuel bounty had inhibited the development of potentially competing energy sources, especially renewables and nuclear power, during the intervening decades.

Equally striking are the differences in how Britain responded to its energy security concerns in the two periods. During the 1970s, the government and state-owned enterprises played a major role in energy production and distribution. In the 2000s, in contrast, the government relied heavily on the private sector to take the actions needed to enhance the country's energy security. The role of the state had become largely confined to shaping the markets, and even here government officials emphasized the limited use of regulation. The capacity of the British state had swung from one extreme to the other.

CHAPTER SIX

France

Nuclear Power and Its Discontents

Energy security remains the key priority area of French energy policy.

—International Energy Agency, *Energy Policies of IEA Countries: France 2009 Review*

In contrast to Britain, France has had very few indigenous energy resources. As a result, it entered the 1970s with one of the highest degrees of energy insecurity among the developed democracies. Since then, however, it has become one of the most secure. The secret to this transformation was France's heavy investment in nuclear power following the first oil shock. At that time, France depended on imports for more than three-quarters of its energy needs, nearly 70 percent of which were met by foreign oil. By the early 2000s, France had 58 nuclear power plants in operation, providing for nearly 40 percent of its primary energy consumption (PEC). In contrast, oil's share of PEC had fallen to just over 35 percent.

Although France has found itself in a relatively secure position in recent years, its principal energy security concern has stemmed, paradoxically, from its previous success. By the mid-2000s, French leaders had to confront the approaching need to replace the country's now aging nuclear plants. The oldest reactors would not reach the end of their useful lifetimes before late in the following decade, but there was little time to lose in planning for their replacements, given the long lead times associated with the construction of new plants. This time, however, the French government found itself much more constrained than it had been in the 1970s. Consequently, the renewal of French nuclear policy was forced to proceed more cautiously and on a much more modest scale than before.

The 1970s: French Responses to the Oil Shocks

Of the three major West European states examined in this study, France had become by far the most dependent on imported energy and, especially, foreign oil by 1973. Oil accounted for more than two-thirds of French PEC, and only 1 percent of that was produced at home. Thus France was most vulnerable to the consequences of oil supply disruptions.

In response to the first oil shock, France acted aggressively both at home and abroad to promote its energy security. Perhaps more than any other state, it sought to negotiate bilateral arrangements with oil producers that would ensure access to foreign supplies in the future. On the domestic front, it embarked upon the largest nuclear power program the world has ever seen outside the United States, and it took a number of steps to limit oil use. Overall, concluded Michael Hatch, "French energy policy in the 1970s was characterized by active state intervention in almost all energy-related activities with the express purpose of controlling energy production and consumption patterns" (Hatch 1986, 190).

Largely as a result of these efforts, by 1985, France's energy security was much improved. Oil's share of PEC had declined to just 43 percent and was still dropping. Oil had been largely replaced by nuclear power, whose share of PEC had risen from less than 2 percent in 1973 to more than one-quarter, with many more nuclear plants scheduled to come online over the following decade. Indeed, it now appeared that the nuclear sector had been overbuilt, and France would become a net exporter of nuclear electricity. Much less successful had been France's efforts in the international arena, but this failure did not substantially detract from the great progress that had been made at home.

Background

Prior to the first oil shock, the French state played a dominant role in the energy sector. It exercised direct control over the coal, natural gas, and electricity industries through state-owned enterprises established immediately after World War II. Charbonnage de France (CDF) had a monopoly on the production and sale of coal. The production, transportation, and distribution of gas were the purview of Gaz de France (GDF). Électricité de France (EDF) was responsible for the transmission of electricity and acquired most of the generating plants and almost all of the distribution facilities, even though it did not receive a formal monopoly on production. In 1945, the government also established the Commissariat à l'énergie atomique (CEA), which was given responsibility for the promotion and coordination of every aspect of nuclear energy, both military and civilian. Among the CEA's duties were basic research and the development of nuclear reactors up to the prototype stage (de Carmoy 1977, 56–57; DOE 1977, 115–118; Lucas 1985, 1, 10, and 13).

The state's role in the petroleum industry was less direct but still substantial. The overall aim of French oil policy was to gain a greater share for French companies in the world oil market and to strengthen French influence over all stages of the process of bringing petroleum products to the domestic market

(Menderhausen 1976, 18; Katzenstein 1976, 35–38). To this end, the government employed two complementary approaches (see also Feigenbaum 1982, 115). First, it used legislation and regulation to exercise tight control over the importation, refining, and sale of oil in France. A 1928 law established a government monopoly on the import of crude oil and petroleum products, which it exercised by allocating import rights to oil companies that were reviewed on a periodic basis. The law also instituted a system of refining quotas that were intended to promote the domestic refining industry, and it stipulated that French companies must control at least half of the domestic market. To improve the security of French oil supplies, a March 1958 decree required all importers to maintain a stockpile equivalent to three months of domestic sales. Indeed, France was the first country to establish regulations for the purpose of maintaining a civilian emergency reserve (DOE 1977, 111; Saumon and Puiseux 1977, 141 and 168; Krapels 1980, 59–60 and 68–69; Giraud 1983, 166).

Second, the government participated directly in the oil market through the promotion of national champions that could compete with the major international oil companies. The first of these was Compagnie française des pétroles (CFP), which was established in the 1920s and in which the government held a controlling 35 percent share. After World War II, the French government created several additional firms, such as the Bureau de recherches de pétrole (BRP), to stimulate petroleum exploration in French territories and to expand the oil-refining industry. In 1966, the government formed the fully state-owned Entreprise de recherches et d'activités pétrolières (ERAP) out of the BRP and other public agencies to serve as an agent in negotiations with producer countries. It assisted ERAP directly with long-term, interest-free loans and by designating it as the sole supplier to various state agencies (Prodi and Clo 1975, 96; Katzenstein 1976, 35–38; de Carmoy 1977, 56–57; DOE 1977, 111–14; Lucas 1985, 25).

Two more specific goals of postwar French oil policy were that the production capacity controlled by French companies be equal to domestic consumption and that the geographical sources of French oil be as diverse as possible. A major step toward the achievement of the first goal occurred when a French company discovered oil in Algeria in the mid-1950s. By the early 1960s, a third of crude imports came from Algeria, with another 20 percent originating in Iraq, and the government issued a decree requiring that all refineries accept crude oil from French-controlled territories, even if it was more expensive (Menderhausen 1976, 20; Saumon and Puiseux 1977, 127; DOE 1977, 114; Krapels 1982, 60; Lucas 1985, 16–17). In 1971, however, Algeria nationalized the bulk of its oil resources, affecting some 80 percent of ERAP's crude oil production. As a result, France had to accept more oil from the major international oil companies and from the Middle East, jeopardizing both goals of French international oil policy (Menderhausen 1976, 29; Katzenstein 1976, 38; Lucas 1985, 39; Hatch 1986, 30).

In the meantime, the government had been promoting the use of oil at home. The overriding concern of French economic policy in the 1960s was to ensure the competitiveness of French industry as the implementation of the Common Market and international negotiations reduced barriers to trade. And one way to promote competitiveness was to ensure that industry had access to abundant supplies of energy at the lowest possible price. By the late 1950s, moreover, it had become clear that large amounts of oil could be produced in the Middle East and elsewhere and transported to Europe at a cost much lower than that of mining indigenous coal (Saumon and Puiseux 1977, 139 and 168–69; Cohen 1982, 36; Lucas 1985, 13–15). The belief, widely accepted among those responsible for the energy sector, that oil prices would continue to be low lasted until at least the end of the decade (Saumon and Puiseux 1977, 144).

Thus the government withdrew its support from the coal industry and reduced barriers to the free inflow of oil, allowing market forces for the most part to dictate the patterns of energy consumption. Indeed, France offered less protection to the coal industry than any other country in Western Europe. Although gasoline was taxed heavily, the government did not tax heavy fuel oil, which competed directly with coal, and in 1968, it made the value-added tax on heavy fuel oil deductible, so that the effective price became the lowest in the Common Market. When this policy of cheap oil triggered protests in coal mining regions and violent strikes by coal miners, the government refused to make concessions and closed the mines (Saumon and Puiseux 1977, 141–144 and 168; Cohen 1982, 36; Lucas 1985, 14; Hatch 1986, 17–19).

As a result of these policies, French oil consumption skyrocketed. Between 1960 and 1973, it grew at an annual rate of 12 percent, or nearly fivefold. Whereas oil had represented less than 15 percent of PEC in 1949 and still just 30 percent in 1960, by 1973 it had reached more than two-thirds. At that time, some 60 percent of energy demand in industry and power plants as well as 100 percent in the transportation sector was met by oil (Saumon and Puiseux 1977, 125; de Carmoy 1977, 56; Krapels 1980, 97; Lieber 1983, 70; Commission 1984, 97; Taylor et al. 1998, 42; BP 2013).

Coal's share of the energy supply fell in tandem. In 1950, coal had accounted for 77 percent of total energy use, and it still made up more than half of the energy mix in 1960. But production peaked that year at 60 million tons and then began a steady decline. By 1973, coal consumption was down to 46 million tons, representing just one-sixth of PEC, and a growing share of that was imported (de Carmoy 1977, 56; Saumon and Puiseux 1977, 128; Cohen 1982, 36; Giraud 1983, 175; Lucas 1985, 17; Hatch 1986, 15; BP 2013).

A further noteworthy development in the French energy picture was the emergence of natural gas as a significant energy source. Large-scale consumption began in 1960, following the discovery of significant domestic reserves in the mid-1950s. Between 1960 and 1973, gas consumption increased tenfold, to 8.5 percent of PEC. But demand had already outstripped domestic supply, and by 1973 more than half of the gas used in France was imported (Saumon and Puiseux 1977, 129; Taylor et al. 1998, 46–48).

As a result of all these trends, France became increasingly dependent on energy imports. In 1950, domestic energy production had provided for some 70 percent of national requirements. In 1960, however, when oil began to displace coal rapidly, the level of energy self-sufficiency was down to 62 percent, and by 1973, it had fallen to less than one-quarter. To make matters worse, France was almost entirely dependent on imports to meet its need for oil, and a growing share of those imports was coming from the Persian Gulf: from just over 20 percent in 1965 to nearly two-thirds in 1973 (de Carmoy 1982, 113; Giraud 1983, 165; Lucas 1985, 39; Hatch 1986, 196, T5; Saumon and Puiseux 1977, 119). Thus emphasis in French policy on minimizing the cost of energy had led France to become highly dependent on oil imported from a small number of oil-exporting countries (Saumon and Puiseux 1977, 168–69; Cohen 1982, 36).

The one bright spot for French energy security was the country's nascent civilian nuclear energy program. Around the time of the 1956 Suez crisis, the government had approved the construction of three small natural uranium gas-cooled reactors (GCR) of French design, which were completed by 1966. In 1963, EDF initiated a second round of three larger GCRs. During the late 1960s, however, the nuclear program languished while French officials debated the merits of continuing with the indigenous GCR or adopting the light-water reactor (LWR) that had been developed in the United States. At the end of the decade, the government finally opted for the latter and decided to build as many as 10 LWRs over the next five years. When the first oil shock occurred, six of the new reactors had been ordered, but nuclear power still accounted for just 2 percent of French PEC (Saumon and Puiseux 1977, 130–132 and 146–148; Lucas 1985, 19 and 47–48; Hatch 1986, 142; Price 1990, 49–51).

French Energy Security Concerns in the 1970s

In the Middle East, French policies had been pro-Arab since 1967, but this stance did not provide much protection against the first oil shock. Although France was not specifically targeted by the Arab oil exporters, it experienced supply reductions comparable to those of other West European countries because the major international oil companies allocated the available petroleum in proportion to each country's level of consumption. During the height of the Arab production cuts, from December 1973 through March 1974, French supplies were 7 percent lower than the level of the previous year (Lieber 1980, 143–44; Lieber 1983, 80).[1]

According to Robert Lieber, the impact of the first oil shock led to

> a dramatic realization by both government and public that France was seriously vulnerable. Not only did the crisis evoke memories of wartime privation, but it brought awareness that as a result of oil import dependence, France ran the risk of seeing its industry, transportation, and entire life brought to a halt through some future upheaval in the international energy supply system. In short, energy and oil had become security issues par excellence. (Lieber 1983, 80)

Even after the initial fears subsided, it was widely assumed that oil scarcity would eventually return and that, in the meantime, a political event could at any moment disrupt the oil supply (Giraud 1983, 167; Kapstein 1990, 184).

By mid- to late 1974, after production had returned to its previous levels, the economic impact of the new, much higher price of oil became the dominant concern. The growth of France's gross domestic product, which had been galloping at an annual clip of 5–6 percent, slumped to half that level, while the rates of inflation and unemployment more than doubled (Menderhausen 1976, 74–75, 86–87, and 92–93; Lieber 1980, 144; Deese and Miller 1981, 185; Hatch 1986, 197, table 6). Because France imported so much oil, its balance of payments was hit harder than that of any West European country but Italy by the quadrupling of oil prices. The cost of oil imports jumped from 14.6 billion French francs (FF) in 1973 to 43 billion FF in 1974, while the total bill for imported energy tripled to 50 billion FF. France went from running a slight surplus to a $6 billion deficit in its current account (Saumon and Puiseux 1977, 119 and 150; Lieber 1983, 79–80; Giraud 1983, 167; Hatch 1986, 40 and 197). Because France had not substantially reduced its oil consumption by 1979, the second oil shock had a similar impact. The cost of energy imports more than doubled, and what was a hard-earned surplus in the current account once again became a substantial deficit. As before, GDP growth was cut in half while inflation returned to double-digit levels (de Carmoy 1982, 132; Lieber 1983, 79; Hatch 1986, 197).

Overview of French Policy Responses

Successive French governments responded quickly, decisively, and consistently to the oil shocks. The overriding goal of French policy in the 1970s and early 1980s was to reduce the country's dependence on foreign sources of energy, especially oil. France would reduce its energy consumption, increase domestic energy production, and diversify its energy imports, both by type of energy and by geographical origin (de Carmoy 1982, 118; Giraud 1983, 167; Commission 1988, 78; Price 1990, 51).

Following the first oil shock, the center-right French government, then headed by Prime Minister Pierre Messmer, quickly conducted a sweeping review of energy policy, which was announced in March 1974. The revised energy program established several ambitious goals for 1985 (Menderhausen 1976, 91; Carmoy 1982, 131; Cohen 1982, 34; Lucas 1985, 57; Hatch 1986, 53–55; Finon 1996, 33):

- reducing France's dependence on all imported energy sources from the current level of 76 percent to 55–60 percent of PEC, and the share of oil from nearly 70 percent to just 40 percent
- reducing energy consumption by up to 45 million tonnes of oil equivalent (mtoe) from the previously projected level of 285 mtoe, or 16 percent (although that amount would still represent an increase of more than 25 percent above the 1973 level)
- raising the share of PEC provided by nuclear power to 25 percent and its contribution to electricity generation to 70 percent
- limiting the amount of oil imported from any single country to 15 percent of the total

In 1980, the government established new goals for 1990 that went even further. Oil's share of PEC would fall to less than one-third, while that of nuclear power would rise to 30 percent, and more emphasis would be placed on energy savings (de Carmoy 1982, 132–33; Lieber 1983, 80–81; Commission 1984, 98; Hatch 1986, 142–43).

In 1981, with the election of President François Mitterrand, the Socialists took power for the first time in the history of the Fifth Republic. Despite their differences on many issues, however, they largely maintained their predecessor's energy policies. The Socialist energy program placed even more emphasis on conservation and the development of renewable sources of energy, setting a target of 30–40 mtoe more in energy savings by 1990. But it also reaffirmed the objective of reducing oil's share of energy consumption, and the largest single element in reducing France's dependence on imported oil remained the nuclear program (de Carmoy 1982, 134; Commission 1982, 19; Commission 1984, 98–100; Lucas 1985, 58).

Domestic Policy Responses

At home, French policy emphasized reducing energy consumption in general and oil use in particular and rapidly increasing the contribution of nuclear energy (Commission 1988, 77; Finon 1996, 34). Indeed, in the view of Robert Lieber, "During and after the first oil shock, France carried out the most coherent and vigorous domestic energy program of any of the principal oil consuming states. Of all the OECD countries, it undertook the most serious long-term effort to develop nuclear power, conserve energy, and reduce oil import dependence" (Lieber 1983, 76).

MANAGING DEMAND: REDUCING OIL IMPORTS AND CONSUMPTION

The first line of attack in French policy was to reduce energy consumption, and especially that of oil. The government used several strategies to this end. In 1974, it decided to limit the amount that could be spent on oil imports the following year to 51 billion FF, which at the prevailing price would hold imports at 10 percent below their 1973 level. To help achieve that goal, the government quickly imposed restrictions on the use of fuel oil, raised the price of gasoline and other petroleum products, ended low rates for large consumers of electricity, established lower speed limits, set quotas for sellers of heating oil, and mandated various other conservation measures (Lieber 1976, 32; de Carmoy 1977, 57; Schneider 1983, 324; Hatch 1986, 54–55; Ikenberry 1988, 102).

Although price controls were retained on gasoline, diesel fuel, and heating oil through the 1970s, the ceilings were adjusted upward to reflect the rise in crude oil prices, and government taxes made gasoline prices among the highest in Europe. In addition, energy prices to domestic and small industrial consumers tended to be above average for the European Community (de Carmoy 1977, 57; Krapels 1982, 61–63; Lieber 1983, 81; Commission 1984, 100).

These efforts to discourage oil consumption were complemented by an extensive, more general energy conservation program. In 1974, the government raised insulation standards for new buildings, prohibited heating above 20 degrees centigrade, offered tax deductions to individuals for energy saving investments, and restricted public and commercial lighting at night. It also created the Agence pour les économies d'énergie (AEE) to conduct educational campaigns and oversee other conservation programs. Between 1976 and 1980, the government subsidized 3,100 energy savings projects in industry at a cost of more than 8.5 billion FF.

There were, of course, limits to how far the government was willing or able to go. In 1977, for example, it refused to adopt several proposed measures, including binding contracts with auto manufacturer requiring them to raise fuel efficiency, a financial penalty for electricity and gas customers who consumed more than specified amounts based on previous consumption, and a 2 percent energy tax on the country's 5,000 largest consumers (Saumon and Puiseux 1977, 150; Giraud 1983, 171; Lieber 1983, 81; Lucas 1985, 37 and 57; Finon 1996, 35). Nevertheless, concluded one analysis, "The most ambitious effort to reduce oil consumption was made by France" (Schneider 1983, 324), and further measures were adopted in the wake of the second oil crisis (Lucas 1985, 58).

As noted above, the Socialist government that took office in 1981 reinforced these energy conservation measures. It planned to invest 40 billion FF over the following decade in energy savings, and in 1982 it created a new agency, l'Agence française pour la maîtrise de l'énergie (AFME), to implement the program. Spending on such measures as district heating, the insulation of public buildings and public housing, and energy-saving industrial equipment reached 4.4 billion FF in 1984 (Commission 1984, 93; Lucas 1985, 58; Finon 1996, 36 and 39).

PROMOTING SUBSTITUTES FOR OIL

The other major prong of France's domestic response to the oil shocks was to promote substitutes for oil. As Andre Giraud noted, "Energy policy has provided strong action to replace oil with nuclear, coal, and renewable energies" (Giraud 1983, 173). The most promising way to achieve this goal in the short run was to substitute coal for oil in industry and electric power generation, where coal had until recently been the dominant fuel. EDF immediately began to convert oil-burning power plants back to coal as well as to build some new coal-fired stations, and coal consumption for the purpose of generating electricity grew steadily through the 1970s. By 1980, all the original coal-fired plants had been reconverted, and the use of coal in the sector had roughly doubled. In addition, the government offered financial incentives to encourage the use of coal in industry. Nevertheless, domestic coal production continued to fall, with the growing difference between consumption and production being made up by imports. Although the Socialist government initially attempted to arrest the decline and even to increase coal production by as much as 50 percent, subject to a ceiling on government subsidies, it soon abandoned this goal because of the high cost. Thus substituting coal for oil would mean trading one form of import dependence for another (de Carmoy 1982, 120, 123, and 134; Commission 1982, 134; Giraud 1983, 175; Lucas 1985, 47; Hatch 1986, 58; Price 1990, 52).

Instead, then, France's principal response was to increase greatly the scope of its existing nuclear program. As Lieber and others have noted, "France pursued the most ambitious nuclear power program of any Western country during the 1970s" (de Carmoy 1982, 126; Lieber 1983, 81; see also Hatch 1986, 142; Ikenberry 1986a, 111). Previously, the government had planned to order a total of 10 reactors between 1971 and 1975, or approximately 2 per year, for a total of less than 10 GW in new generating capacity. In March 1974, however, the Messmer government ordered a drastic acceleration and expansion of the program. It called for the construction of no less than 6 900-MW reactors that year and 7 in 1975, to be followed by 6 to 7 more units per year until 1980, for a total of more than 40 GW in new capacity. Limits on the capacity of the nuclear industry to build so many reactors and difficulties with securing sites in the face of local opposition prompted the government to reduce the rate of orders slightly, to 5 or 6 per year, after 1975. But between 1974 and 1981, more than 40 reactors were ordered, with the average size increasing from 900 MW to more than 1.3 GW (figure 6.1) (Menderhausen 1976, 90; Saumon and Puiseux 1977, 150; de Carmoy 1977, 58; de Carmoy 1982, 126; Giraud 1983, 173; Hatch 1986, 142; Price 1990, 51–53).

In 1981, the Socialists took office promising to reexamine the nuclear program. Prior to the election, they had proposed freezing it, completing only those plants already under construction. Doing so would have meant a total capacity of just 39 GW in 1990, well short of the outgoing government's target of 65 GW. Once in power, the Socialists immediately cancelled one controversial power station and suspended work on 18 other units (Lucas 1985, 55–56).

Ultimately, however, the Socialist's program review resulted in only marginal changes, and these might have been taken by any government in response to lower projections of future electricity consumption and thus concerns about the creation of excess capacity. The revised program set a goal of 56 GW by 1990, with nuclear power still providing 27 percent of France's PEC. The new government decided to order six new units in 1982 and 1983, only three less than previously planned. An October 1981 parliamentary vote reaffirmed the national commitment to nuclear power. Only after 1983 did the rate of orders fall sharply, reflecting the new economic realities rather than any fundamental change of doctrine (de Carmoy 1982, 134; Lieber 1983, 81; Fagnani and Moatti 1984, 264 and 273; Lucas 1985, 55–56; Hatch 1986, 170; Price 1990, 53–54).

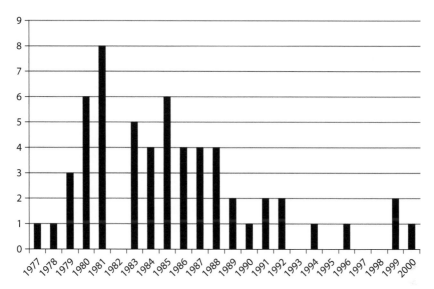

Figure 6.1 French nuclear power reactors (year of entry into commercial service).
Source: World Nuclear Association, "Nuclear Power in France" (updated February 2014), www.world-nuclear.org/info/Country-Profiles/Countries-A-F/France/.

Also of note is France's commitment to developing all aspects of the nuclear fuel cycle. France had constructed a prototype fast breeder reactor before the first oil crisis, and in the 1970s, it built a uranium enrichment plant as the leading member of a consortium of European countries and a reprocessing plant to handle irradiated fuel from light water reactors. The Socialist government maintained even the more controversial parts of the nuclear program, expanding the reprocessing plant and deciding to complete the commercial breeder reactor begun by its predecessor. In the early 1980s, France had the most advanced breeder program in the world, and it was well ahead of other countries in reprocessing technology (Cohen 1982, 35; Fagnani and Moatti 1984, 264 and 268; Lucas 1985, 30–33).

External Policy Responses

France also actively used external policy tools to promote its energy security after the first oil shock. Indeed, "at the international level, successive French governments undertook an ambitious energy diplomacy aimed at dealing with the political and economic consequences of oil import dependence" (Lieber 1983, 76). Most notable were France's efforts to negotiate bilateral arrangements with oil producers that would ensure access to oil and its complementary strategy of promoting closer European political relations with the Arab world. The flip side of these activities was its strong opposition to U.S.-led efforts to forge cooperation among the consumer countries, especially where it might involve confronting the oil producers (see also Lieber 1980, 147).

Following the outbreak of the first oil crisis, France wasted little time in trying to lock up oil supplies through bilateral agreements with producers. By December 1973, it had reached a deal with Saudi Arabia for 27 million tons of oil over three years at 93 percent of the posted price, and by the end of the following January, it had concluded provisional negotiations with the Saudis for 800 million tons of oil over a 20-year period, or enough to cover nearly a third of its consumption at the time, although it eventually had to settle for only 12 million tons per year. Later that year, France signed an agreement with Iraq for 20 tons of oil per year, though at the cost of promising to provide the latter with a nuclear research reactor (Lieber 1976, 30; Menderhausen 1976, 73–74; Deese and Miller 1981, 205; Schneider 1983, 255; Ikenberry 1986a, 113; Finon 1996, 33–34).

These efforts continued through the decade. In 1978, Iraq agreed to increase its annual oil shipments to 30 million tons. In early 1980, following the second oil shock, President Valéry Giscard d'Estaing made a trip to the Middle East where he pledged support for Palestinian self-determination in order to buttress French relations with the Arab states. And after the Iran-Iraq War once gain disrupted world oil supplies, he traveled to Mexico, where he gained a commitment of 5 million tons of oil per year, and to other countries in search of new government oil deals (Lieber 1980, 150; Krapels 1982, 66; Schneider 1983, 465; Kemezis and Wilson 1984, 92). As two scholars concluded at the time, "France exhibits the most consistent devotion to bilateral deals" (Deese and Miller 1981, 205).

Along with its bilateral efforts, France strongly advocated the establishment of a special relationship between the European Community and the Arab states. The signature element of this strategy was its proposal for a Euro-Arab dialogue, which was endorsed by European leaders at a late 1973 summit meeting (Lieber 1976, 18; de Carmoy 1982, 122; Schneider 1983, 259).

Simultaneously, France worked to block or at least to dilute the U.S. proposal for cooperation among the consumer countries. Prior to the February 1974 Washington conference, it led the other EC countries to adopt a joint position that largely endorsed the French position: that the gathering was not to be used to confront the oil-exporting countries, that no new organization was to be created as a result of the conference, that Europe must retain its freedom to establish direct relationships with the exporting countries, and that a dialogue with the exporting countries and non-OPEC less-developed countries be entered into by April.

Although the French foreign minister attended the conference, he did so mainly to prevent any unfavorable commitments on the part of the European Community, and France alone refused to subscribe to the most significant parts of the resulting communiqué. Subsequently, France also declined to join the International Energy Agency, which was established later that year (Prodi and Clo 1975, 108; Lieber 1976, 2–23; de Carmoy 1982, 122; Schneider 1983, 260; Venn 1986, 150). In the words of J. L. Plummer and John Weyant, "The French disliked what they saw as confrontational aspects of the program and American leadership in pushing it (calling it an 'energy NATO')" (1982, 261).

Evaluation of French Policy Responses to the Oil Shocks

By the mid-1980s, France's energy situation was much improved. Even though primary energy consumption had increased by about 5 percent since 1973, oil use had dropped by one-third, from 127 million tons to just 84 in 1985. Likewise, oil's share of French PEC had declined from more than two-thirds to 43 percent and was still falling. Oil consumption decreased dramatically in almost every sector. The only exception was the transportation sector, where it grew from 31 to more than 35 million tons per year (Taylor et al. 1998, 45; BP 2013).

Over the same period, France registered a roughly 50 percent increase in natural gas consumption and hydroelectric power. But oil had been replaced mainly by nuclear power, which now met more than one-quarter of France's energy needs. In 1985, France produced 15 times as much nuclear electricity as it had in 1973, and nearly two-thirds of all electricity was generated in nuclear power plants. Not least important, the contribution of nuclear power was expected to rise substantially as more nuclear plants came online in the late 1980s and early 1990s (figure 6.2) (Commission 1988, 84; Finon 1996, 34; Taylor et al. 1998, 52; BP 2013).

Because of the significant drop in oil consumption, France was also much less dependent on energy imports by 1985. Although a growing percentage of coal and natural gas came from abroad, less than 60 percent of PEC was now imported. At the same time, France had diversified the geographical sources of its energy imports. Significant quantities of oil now came from the North Sea and Africa as well as the Middle East, while natural gas was arriving from Norway, the Soviet Union, Algeria, and the Netherlands in roughly equal amounts (Commission 1988, 80; Finon 1996, 23; IEA 2004, 40).

Finally, France had made major strides in the area of energy efficiency. Between 1973 and 1985, overall energy intensity (PEC divided by GDP) had fall by approximately one-fifth. This decline was a principal reason why total energy consumption in 1985 was down almost 20 percent from the level of 240 mtoe predicted

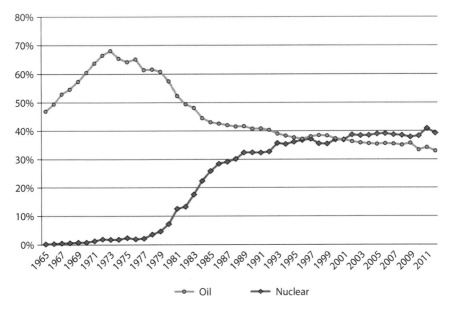

Figure 6.2 Oil and nuclear power as shares of primary energy consumption in France, 1965–2012. *Source*: BP 2013.

10 years before. Some of the biggest gains were the result of changes in the construction standards for new housing, retrofitting old housing and public buildings, investments in energy intensive industries, and better automotive fuel economy (Commission 1988, 79; Finon 1996, 22–23 and 40–41).[2]

Overall, as Hanns Maull was able to note as early as 1981, France had a "relatively impressive energy adjustment record" (Maull 1981, 295), and much of this success could be attributed to government action. Certainly, the rapid buildup of nuclear-generating capacity seems hardly possible without the massive intervention of the government. Likewise, the country's energy conservation efforts yielded substantial fruit. According to an estimate by the IEA, between 1973 and 1986, French policy effected a savings of 30 mtoe annually (IEA 2004, 81; see also Finon 1996, 40–41).

This is not to say, however, that there was no room for improvement. France was still far from being self-sufficient in energy and thus vulnerable to potential supply interruptions abroad. France was still almost entirely dependent on foreign sources of oil, and its dependence on natural gas and coal from abroad was growing. In 1985, imports accounted for some four-fifths of natural gas consumption and more than half of the coal used in France (Lieber 1983, 82; Commission 1988, 78 and 81; BP 2013).

In some respects, moreover, the aggressive nuclear program had been too successful. The pace of orders had assumed a rate of growth in electricity demand that turned out to be greatly exaggerated. In the mid-1980s, however, it appeared that France could have as many as 7 to 10 more nuclear power plants than it needed to meet domestic demand by the end of the decade. The problem was not recognized until 1983, at which point the building program was abruptly and substantially scaled back (Commission 1988, 84 and 102; Price 1990, 55; Finon 1996, 36). Another response was to promote greater electricity consumption by industry and in the home, but this move contradicted those aspects of French energy policy that emphasized conservation and may have contributed to a prolonged stagnation in improvements in energy efficiency that began in the early 1980s (Fagnani and Moatti 1984, 274; Finon 1996, 38–39).

Finally, the rapid buildup of nuclear energy was facilitated by a high degree of standardization in the design of the nuclear power plants, which reduced costs and delays. But standardization also had a downside, since it could multiply the negative consequences of any defects. If generic faults were to be found, they could necessitate repairs on potentially dozens of reactors (Cohen 1982, 38; Finon 1996, 34).

France's external policy initiatives were much less fruitful. Although France struck bilateral oil deals with several countries, and CFP obtained over 200,000 barrels per day from Iran through its participation in the Iranian oil consortium, these arrangements did little to enhance France's energy security in the end, and its approaches to other countries did not pan out. France received no significant break on the prices that it paid—and it sometimes paid more than prevailing world prices—for the privilege of guaranteed access, and the oil supplies in question turned out to be no less vulnerable to disruption. France was not spared from the loss of Iranian oil during the revolution that seized that country in 1978–79, and Iraqi oil deliveries plunged by more than 90 percent during the subsequent Iran-Iraq War. France was able to pay for the oil through the export of industrial goods, technology, and advanced weapons, but this too sometimes put France in an awkward position, as when it took the controversial step of providing Iraq with a nuclear research reactor (Lieber 1980, 148; Deese and Miller 1981, 205–206; de Carmoy 1982, 120–21; Krapels 1982, 61; Lieber 1983, 84–91 and 147–148; Schneider 1983, 462).

France's initial efforts in multilateral fora were no more successful. In particular, its attempt to lead the European Community in a direction divergent from that favored by the United States failed. It was unable to block the U.S. initiative for consumer country cooperation, which resulted in the establishment of the

IEA. And the Euro-Arab dialogue that it promoted was troubled from the out-set by issues such as whether to grant representation to the Palestinian Libera-tion Organization and made little headway (Lieber 1980, 147–148; Deese and Miller 1981, 206; de Carmoy 1982, 122; Ikenberry 1988, 91).

As it became clear that its efforts to court the oil producers would not yield significant benefits, France belatedly tacked back toward a more cooperative pol-icy with the consumer countries. Although it remained outside the IEA, it coop-erated informally through its membership in the EC and the Organization of Economic Cooperation and Development (OECD). And beginning in 1979, it ac-tively promoted consumer solidarity, calling for limits on oil imports and better coordination of stockpile programs (Lieber 1980, 152; Plummer and Weyant 1982, 261; Schneider 1983, 267; Cowhey 1985, 274).

French Responses to Energy Insecurity in the 2000s

In the 2000s, France was not immune to concerns about energy security, but they were arguably not as acute there as in the other states examined in this study. Thanks largely to its heavy investment in nuclear power following the oil shocks of the 1970s and a dramatic decline in oil's share of PEC, France had achieved a remarkable degree of energy self-sufficiency for a country that was almost entirely lacking in fossil fuel resources. Nevertheless, by the middle of the 2000s, French leaders were voicing concern about the rising price of oil, and they also had to address the aging of their nuclear power plants, the first of which would be ap-proaching the end of its original 40-year lifetime in a decade.

In part to address these energy security concerns while continuing its efforts to reduce greenhouse gas emissions, France adopted a comprehensive energy law in 2005 that was followed by a series of more concrete policy initiatives intended to achieve the law's broad goals. Central to French policy was a renewal of France's commitment to nuclear power. French authorities hoped to extend the lifetimes of the existing plants while embarking on the construction of the first of a new generation of reactors. In addition, they redoubled their emphasis on reducing energy consumption and, for the first time, began to promote heavily the devel-opment of renewable forms of energy as substitutes for nuclear power and fossil fuel imports.

Given the progress France had made since the 1970s, it arguably needed to do the least to maintain a high level of energy security. Nevertheless, French policy was dogged by obstacles and uncertainties. Although the role of the French state in the energy field remained substantial, it lacked the degree of autonomy and capacity that had enabled it to achieve its ambitious goals of the 1970s. Through its control of EDF, it was able to initiate the construction of the first EPR, but the future of the existing plants now depended on the rulings of the recently created and highly autonomous Nuclear Safety Authority (ASN) and would thus be hostage to unanticipated events, such as the 2011 disaster at Fukushima Dai-ichi in Japan. Likewise, the development of alternatives was now hamstrung by the types of local concerns that had long plagued policy initiatives in other developed democracies.

Background

By the 2000s, France's energy security was much improved over the 1970s and relatively high in comparison with the other developed democracies. Overall energy consumption had grown by about one-third, but energy intensity had continued to decline, dropping roughly one-third between 1973 and 2001 (IEA 2004, 74). More impressively, whereas imports had provided for three-quarters of France's energy needs in 1973, roughly half of France's PEC was now domestically produced; 58 nuclear power plants generated nearly four-fifths of France's electricity supply with much of the rest provided by hydroelectric power. Indeed, France had a substantial overcapacity in electricity and was exporting more than 10 percent of its electricity production.

Although France now imported almost all of the fossil fuels it consumed, it also boasted the lowest level of oil dependence (just over 35 percent of PEC), the second lowest share of PEC from natural gas (approximately 15 percent), and the lowest level of coal consumption (roughly 5 percent) of the five major developed democracies (IEA 2004, 9–10, 40–41; BP 2013). In addition, France's foreign sources of natural gas were among the most diverse, making it less vulnerable to a major supply disruption (IEA 2004, 114). And France maintained substantial reserves of both oil and gas. French law, updated in 1992, required suppliers to hold stocks equivalent to 27 percent of the previous year's consumption, which exceeded the IEA requirement of 90 days of imports, and gas reserves also totaled about three months of supply (IEA 2004, 40 and 44).

Although environmental concerns had begun to color French energy policy, they had had little impact as of 2000. In 1992, France had created an interministerial group on the effects of greenhouse gases, but thanks to the abundance of nuclear power, its greenhouse gas emissions were already relatively low. Thus under the Kyoto protocol, France agreed only to stabilize its greenhouse gas emissions at their 1990 level by 2008–2012 (Méritet 2011, 162). Likewise, the abundance of nuclear energy removed any incentive to limit electricity consumption. Nevertheless, in the middle of the 1990s, France introduced a modest program to promote wind power, and in 2000, the government imposed a feed-in tariff system requiring EDF to purchase renewable electricity from plants with a capacity of less than 12 MW. That year, France also adopted a National Program for Tackling Climate Change (PNLCC), although it sought to rely primarily on voluntary agreements with energy-intensive industries in order to reduce greenhouse gas emissions (Finon 1996, 47–49; IEA 2004, 62 and 88; FEI 2010, 15–16).

Perhaps the biggest constraint on French energy policy was France's increasing political and economic integration with its European neighbors. As early as 1996, French energy expert Dominique Finon observed that

> the appearance on the scene of a new power center (the European institutions) advocating new rules is progressively moving things in a liberal direction, less oligopolistic and more decentralised. . . . European integration necessarily entails a weakening of the French State's instruments of intervention, given the emphasis on free markets and the transfer of responsibilities to the community level. . . . The construction of a greater Europe is in conflict with the French interventionist tradition, public service culture, and the interests of the public monopolies. (Finon 1996, 33 and 49)

In the energy sector, this process was accelerated by the EU's adoption in the late 1990s of the first directives to liberalize the electricity and gas markets. In response, France created the Commission of Energy Regulation (Commission de régulation de l'énergie, CRE), an independent authority with responsibility for opening first the electricity and then the gas markets. Among its duties were to ensure open access to all transmission and distribution networks and the independence of those networks from any historical or ownership influences (IEA 2004, 34). In addition, the traditionally state-owned monopolies, EDF and GDF, became partially privatized with boards of directors. As French energy expert Sophie Méritet has written, the European requirements were "a shock for the French culture of *dirigisme*" (Méritet 2011, 158). Nevertheless, the government retained a controlling ownership stake in both companies and resisted further EU measures that would have required legally separating their production and transmission functions.

In addition, in the early 2000s, the government began to develop multiyear indicative investment programs (PPI for electricity and PIP for gas) in order to ensure that the investment choices of the energy companies were in line with government goals with respect to desired future capacities. The PPI for the electricity sector, for example, established objectives for new generation capacity by technology, energy source, and geographic zone. If the objectives of PPIs were not attained, the government could issue invitations to tender offers for new production facilities that will be guaranteed a certain price (MEEDDAT 2009a and 2009b; IEA 2010, 23, 28, and 106; Méritet 2011, 156).

French Energy Security Concerns in the 2000s

Nevertheless, concerns about energy security had never gone away completely in France. In 1998, for example, when France's reliance on energy imports had dropped to less than half of PEC and world oil prices were low, the French Senate established a commission of inquiry on French energy policy, which "concluded that energy independence should remain a priority and that France needed a policy that would simultaneously guarantee security of supply, respect for the environment in the framework of international engagements, and the competitiveness of French business" (Revol 1998; Revol and Valade 2001, 3).

Then, during the first half of the next decade, French officials began to voice concern about rapidly rising energy prices, which became a political issue because of their impact on the economy. Much of the problem was due to the increasing cost of energy imports, which roughly doubled between 2003 and 2006. As recently as early 2004, French forecasts had assumed that the price of oil would remain approximately $30 per barrel (DGEMP/OE 2004, 4). Just two years later, when oil reached $70 per barrel, Prime Minister Dominique de Villepin spoke of a "petroleum crisis" and warned that oil would be expensive for decades to come. That year, the net cost of energy imports reached 46 billion euros, just short of the all-time high of just over 50 billion euros in 1981, and the bill would have been higher but for France's export of electricity (DGEMP 2006a; MINEFI 2007).[3]

Of even greater concern was the aging of France's nuclear power plants. Of the 58 commercial reactors in operation in the early 2000s, all but four had commenced commercial operation between the late 1970s and the early 1990s. In 2002, the French nuclear safety authority approved a 10-year operating extension for all 34 of the older 900 MW reactors. But even in the event that these reactors were able to achieve the 40-year lifetimes that had been originally envisioned, a large number of replacements would have to begin to come online by 2020. And even if the lifetimes could potentially be extended beyond 40 years, there was little time to lose in determining how France's future electricity needs would be met, given the long lead times for nuclear power plant development and construction (Bataille and Birraux 2003; Fontaine 2003; WNA 2011).

Overview of French Policy Responses

A major review of French energy policy began in 2002, even before the Iraq war and the subsequent run up in world oil prices. The timing of the review reflected the longer view of French concerns about energy security. The process involved a so-called "national energy debate" consisting of more than 250 government-organized symposia around the country and culminated with the publication of a white paper (*Livre blanc*) in late 2003 and then the adoption of a major energy policy law (Loi de programme fixant les orientations de la politique énergétique, LPOPE) in July 2005 (Fontaine 2003; DGEMP 2005; Méritet 2011, 154–56).

The new French energy policy laid out four general aims, the first of which was "to contribute to national energy independence and to guarantee the security of energy supplies." This goal meant limiting the exposure of the French economy to fluctuations in energy prices and ensuring the availability of sufficient capacity to cope with potential shortages of electricity, gas, and oil. The other goals included assuring a competitive energy price, protecting health and the environment, in particular by fighting against the effects of greenhouse gases, and assuring energy access to all (LPOPE 2005; DGEMP 2006b).

To achieve these broad aims, the policy defined four general approaches, or "axes": managing energy demand, diversifying energy sources, promoting research, and ensuring adequate means of transmission and energy stocks. It then went on to establish a number of more specific targets, many of which would help to enhance France's energy security. By 2010, France would reduce its energy imports by 10 mtoe, or the equivalent of more than 10 percent of France's oil imports, it would meet 10 percent of all of its energy needs and generate 21 percent of its electricity from renewable sources, and it would increase the share of biofuels in the fuel supply from almost nothing to 7 percent. Over the longer term, France would seek to reduce its energy intensity by 2 percent per year until 2015 and then by 2.5 percent per year thereafter. And it would maintain the nuclear option by building a demonstration reactor of the latest design by 2015 (LPOPE 2005).

Over the next several years, the government defined even more ambitious targets. That for biofuels was raised to 10 percent by 2015. France would obtain 23 percent of its final energy consumption from renewables by 2020. And it would stabilize electricity consumption at the current level of less than 500 terawatt hours (TWh) per year (DGEMP 2006a; MEEDDAT 2009c; IEA 2010, 93).

Domestic Policy Responses

At home, France took action on several fronts to achieve these energy-security-related targets. The most important of these measures were the introduction of a broad energy savings scheme, a renewal of France's commitment to maintaining a large base of nuclear power, and the promotion of renewable sources of electricity and heat, although additional efforts were also made to reduce France's need for oil imports.

REDUCING ENERGY CONSUMPTION

As noted above, the first axis of the new French energy policy was to reduce consumption. As one government document noted, "Any policy aimed at improving the security of supply goes through, in the first instance, the implementation of measures to manage demand" (DGEMP/OE 2006). The most important step in this regard was the establishment by the LPOPE of a new scheme of energy savings ("white") certificates, which aimed to stimulate improvements in energy efficiency through the use of market-based instruments. Beginning in 2006, the scheme imposed an obligation on energy suppliers to generate energy savings by their customers, though the suppliers would be free to choose the precise means for meeting their obligations. A certificate would be issued for each gigawatt-hour of savings, and failure to accumulate the required number of certificates would result in a fine of 20 euros per megawatt-hour, though suppliers could purchase certificates from others who had accumulated a surplus. During the first phase, which ran through mid-2009, the scheme focused on the residential and service sectors, which were responsible for 42 percent of France's energy consumption, and set a target of 54 TWh in cumulated energy savings over the lifetime of the measures taken. Most of the burden fell on EDF, GDF, and heating oil suppliers. In the second three-year phase, which began in 2011, the target was raised to a total of 345 TWh, and the scheme was extended to the transportation sector, which was responsible for 32 percent of French energy use. Motor fuel suppliers were obliged to obtain the equivalent of 90 TWh of cumulated savings by the end of 2013 (Togeby et al. 2007, 21–22; IEA 2010, 46–47; Leinekugel 2011). If successful, the second phase would generate savings equal to roughly 60 percent of one year of electricity generation.

The LPOPE set the stage for new thermal regulations that would reduce energy consumption in new construction by 15 to 20 percent in comparison with previous legislation. A subsequent law established an even more ambitious program for new buildings and an unprecedented retrofitting program for existing ones. It would limit energy consumption in the former to less than 50 kilowatt-hours per year per square meter in the former by further tightening the thermal regulations, and it would reduce energy use in the latter by 38 percent by 2020 by rehabilitating 400,000 houses annually and renovating 800,000 public housing units (Secretariat-General 2006, 6; IEA 2010, 44 and 48).

RENEWING THE COMMITMENT TO NUCLEAR POWER

On the supply side, France renewed its commitment to relying heavily on nuclear power to meet its energy needs. Indeed, given the potential consequences of doing nothing, this could be regarded as the most important component of recent French energy security policy. Before taking any action, however, the government sought to relegitimize nuclear power in the public mind, which was an important purpose of the open process leading up to the issuance of the 2003 white paper and the adoption of the new energy policy law in 2005.[4]

The government took several additional measures to ensure public support. A June 2006 law defined a national policy for the management and disposal of radioactive waste, asserting that the ultimate responsibility rested on the operators of the nuclear plants. A second law passed the following month defined new guidelines on nuclear transparency and security and mandated safety reviews every 10 years. The July law also created an independent Nuclear Safety Authority (Autorité de sûreté nucléaire, ASN) that would have to approve all lifetime extensions (IEA 2010, 10 and 19; Méritet 2011, 156).

The first step in reaffirming the critical role of nuclear power was to ensure that France could obtain the maximum use from the 58 existing reactors. In 2006, France's 20 second-generation 1300 MW units, all commissioned between 1986 and 1994, were cleared for another 10 years of operation, and in 2009, the ASN approved in principle, based on a generic safety assessment, the operation of the older 900 MW units for a full 40 years, although each reactor would still be subject to a careful inspection at the 30-year mark (WNA 2011). The government also initiated discussions about extending the lifetimes of the existing power plants beyond 40 years. Indeed, the central scenario of the 2009 PPI involved doing just that. EDF conducted an assessment of the prospects for running all reactors as long as 60 years, concluding that this would be possible but that it would have to replace the steam generators and make other upgrades at a cost of 400 to 600 million euros per unit. If the government and EDF did decide to pursue such a course, however, they could not proceed without the approval of the new nuclear safety authority (MEEDDAT 2009b, 13; MEEDDAT 2009c; IEA 2010, 124–27; WNA 2011).

Consequently, the government could not rely exclusively on lifetime extensions to maintain a robust nuclear generating capacity. It would also have to start laying the groundwork for the deployment of another generation of reactors that would be based on a new design, the so-called European Pressurized Water Reactor (EPR), to be ready as early as 2020. Indeed, there was no time to waste. As the new energy policy law noted, the construction in the very near future of a demonstration EPR was indispensable to optimize technically and financially the subsequent deployment of new power stations (LPOPE 2005).

Thus it came as no surprise when, in 2006, EDF submitted an application to build the first 1650 MW EPR at Flamanville, Normandy. Construction began the following year, with completion expected in 2012. Then just two years later, the government announced that EDF would build a second EPR at Penly, with construction starting in 2012. As the 2009 PPI noted, French plans "must include a margin of security in terms of electricity generation capacity corresponding to the uncertainties associated with the safety of existing nuclear reactors. This concern, combined with the need to promote investment in the nuclear park, justifies the construction of two new generation reactors and could justify the creation of additional EPRs following the completion of Penly" (MEEDDAT 2009b, 54). If all went well with the first two reactors, EDF would be in a position to begin serial construction of EPRs in the middle of the next decade, just as the first generation of reactors approached the 40 year mark. In the event that no further lifetime extensions were granted, France would have to build 40 EPRs over 20 years in order to maintain total nuclear generating capacity at roughly the same level (MEEDDAT 2009, 54; WNA 2011; ASN 2011a, 276).

OTHER SOURCES OF ENERGY

Although the government hoped that nuclear power would remain by far the largest single source of energy, it did not want to put all of its eggs in that one basket. For the first time, the government began to place considerable emphasis on renewable energy, especially for electricity production and, as a means of reducing electricity consumption, heat generation. It set a goal of raising the share of renewables in final energy consumption to 23 percent by 2020, up from just 7 percent in 2007. The percentage of electricity generated by renewables would rise from 14 to 27 percent over the same time period, while the contribution of renewables to heating and cooling would climb from 15 to 33 percent (IEA 2010, 35; MEEDDM 2010, 12). In late 2008, the government released a comprehensive renewable energy action plan that outlined 50 specific measures for achieving these goals (IEA 2010, 95).

In the area of electricity generation, the greatest opportunities appeared to lie with wind power. At the beginning of 2005, France had only 0.4 GW of wind generating capacity. The 2006 PPI, however, set a goal of adding 17 GW more by 2015, and the 2009 PPI raised this target to a total of 25 GW by 2020. Much lower targets were set for other renewable sources of electricity, such as biomass and biogas, hydro power, and solar cells, though they were not neglected. The government estimated that, by 2020, wind would be providing some 58 TWh of electricity, or nearly as much as hydroelectric power. To achieve these goals, the government relied primarily on attractive feed-in tariffs. In 2006, it introduced 15-year contracts starting at a rate of 8.2 euro cents per kilowatt-hour for onshore wind facilities and 20-year contracts starting at 13 euro cents per kilowatt-hour for offshore wind. Generous tariffs were also available for small hydroelectric and photovoltaic solar installations. And when those incentives failed to generate the desired amount of private investment, the government announced tenders for a 3 GW offshore wind project in 2011 (Gipe 2006 and 2008; MEEDDAT 2008, 17 and 28; MEEDDAT 2009b, 70; MEEDDM 2010, 99–100; IEA 2010, 90 and 97; EurActiv 2011). To promote renewable heat, the government created a special fund in 2009. The plan was to invest 1 billion euros per year for several years followed by an annual contribution of about 800 million euros thereafter, with the goal of increasing renewable heat production by 5.5 mtoe by 2020 (MEEDDAT 2008, 8).

As noted above, France's consumption of natural gas was relatively low in comparison with other advanced industrialized countries, but it was growing. In particular, the government expected that gas would provide a rising share of electric power generation, to more than 10 percent by 2020. In 2009, nine gas-fired power plants were under construction, and 10 additional projects were under consideration (IEA 2010, 57, 84, and 102).

The government took several steps to ensure that this growing reliance on gas would not result in a new set security of supply concerns. It sought to diversify the sources and routes of its gas supply; with the exception of Norway, which accounted for approximately one-third of France's gas supply, no single country provided more than 20 percent of the total. It steadily increased its import capacity; a third LNG terminal opened in 2010 with three more under consideration. It relied heavily on long-term contracts with supplier countries. It developed a comprehensive emergency plan for potential gas supply disruptions. And it made plans to expand its gas storage capacity by 50 percent (IEA 2010, 12, 58, 60, and 64–67).

Finally, France took steps to reduce the dependence of its transportation sector on foreign oil supplies. It modified the purchase and registration taxes for vehicles to encourage consumers to buy cars that produced fewer CO_2 emissions and thus used less fuel (IEA 2010, 50). At the same time, the government sought to increase the share of biofuels in the transportation fuel supply. It had offered a tax deduction to blends of gasoline and diesel containing ethanol and vegetable oil, respectively, since 2002, and in 2004 and 2005, it rolled out a Plan Biocarburants (Biofuels Plan) for achieving its ambitious goals—7 percent of the fuel supply by 2010 and 10 percent by 2015—in that domain. In addition to maintaining the existing tax deductions, the government exempted biofuels from the General Tax on Polluting Activities, and it considered adding an obligation to including a certain percentage of biofuels in the fuel supply (IEA 2010, 97–98).[5]

External Policy Responses

In the 1970s, France's external responses to the oil shocks consisted largely of efforts to secure access to foreign oil supplies. In the 2000s, in contrast, the international dimensions of French energy security policy were focused primarily on the EU. France's overall strategy was to introduce as many of the ideas contained in the 2005 energy law as possible into the EU agenda. Hence it promoted its system of energy savings certificates, encouraged investment in new gas storage capacity as well as gas pipeline interconnections and LNG terminals, and advocated the adoption of a new EU directive on renewable heat to supplement the existing EU directives on renewable electricity and biofuels (Secretariat-General 2006).[6]

France also strongly supported the development of a common external energy policy so that Europe could speak with a single voice in international fora on energy matters. As a concrete step to that end, it proposed the creation of a special energy representative attached to the office of the EU High Representative. More generally, the government argued that the EU should give the energy climate issue greater prominence in all of its external dealings. At the same time, it continued to resist measures to liberalize further the internal electricity and gas markets, especially the breakup of vertically integrated energy companies and the suppression of regulated tariffs (Secretariat-General 2006).[7]

Overall, however, France's external policy responses were quite limited in comparison with what the government attempted on the domestic front. Given the particular problems that it faced, France's most promising options for maintaining and increasing its energy security, such as conservation, nuclear power, and renewables, were to be found at home.

Evaluation of French Policy Responses in the 2000s

France's efforts to improve its energy security had a mixed record of success. On the positive side, the country had halted, at least temporarily, the historic trend of rising energy consumption. In 2004, the government projected that the primary energy supply would rise by 11.6 percent between 2000 and 2010. In fact, at the end of the decade and for the next several years, PEC was almost exactly what it had been 10 years earlier. Although only a small fraction of that difference could be attributed to French energy savings measures, the further extension of the white certificate scheme promised to help reign in future growth in energy use (DGEMP/OE 2004, 10; Leinekugel 2012; BP 2013).

At the same time, French efforts to maintain and even increase the level of domestic energy production had encountered a number of obstacles and setbacks, starting with the nuclear program. The construction of the first EPR at Flamanville suffered a series of delays and cost overruns, which resulted in a more than doubling of the expected final tab, from 3.3 billion euros to more than 8 billion euros. This rapid cost inflation cast doubt on the affordability of new nuclear power plants (Buchan 2014). Then the disaster at Fukushima Daiichi in early 2011 raised questions about how long the existing nuclear reactors could be kept running as well as when the first new reactors would come online.

One of the first casualties of the heightened scrutiny was the new reactor program. The ASN asked EDF to fix a series of gaps and weaknesses in the Flamanville project, which was expected to delay its completion until 2016, four years behind schedule. In addition, the planned public hearings for the second EPR at Penly were postponed for at least a year because of new safety tests that EDF was ordered to carry out, and in 2013, the project was suspended indefinitely (Boxell 2011; Boxell 2012; ASN 2012b; Buchan 2014).

The consequences of the Japanese disaster for the continued use of the existing reactors were potentially even more serious. In January 2012, the ASN imposed what were described as "radical safety standards" (Butler 2012). None of the facilities would have to be shut down immediately, but the ASN concluded that "for the continuation of their operation, an increase in the robustness of the facilities to extreme situations, beyond their existing safety margins, is necessary, as rapidly as possible." In particular, they would have to be prepared to deal with a combination of natural phenomena, such as earthquakes and flooding, on an exceptional scale and exceeding the levels used in the design or the previous safety reviews of the facilities, and with severe accident situations following a prolonged loss of electrical power or cooling that could affect all the installations on a given site. Thus EDF would be required to develop quickly a "hard core" of material and organizational measures for each facility that was likely to include additional generators, pumps, supplies of coolant, and hardened emergency management centers. In addition, ASN required that EDF gradually deploy a national "nuclear rapid response force" comprising specialist crews and equipment able to take over from the personnel on a given site. EDF estimated that these measures would cost at least 13 billion euros to adopt (ASN 2011b; Boxell 2012; Butler 2012; ASN 2012a; ASN 2012b).

The intrusion of domestic politics also cast a shadow over the future of nuclear power. During the 2012 presidential election, the ultimate victor, François Hollande, called for reducing the share of electricity generated by nuclear power plants to 50 percent by 2025, which by any measure would require closing a number of the existing reactors. Hollande also pledged to shutter the oldest nuclear power station, at Fessenheim, before the next presidential election in 2017, about the time the new EPR at Flamanville was now expected to be completed.

Although less dramatic, the development of renewable sources of energy encountered its share of difficulties. Between 2005 and 2012, wind power capacity increased by roughly 1000 MW per year, to 7.7 GW. But it would need to grow even faster during the remainder of decade to achieve the government's 2020 goal of 25 GW. Yet, as the IEA noted in 2010, "wind farm developers face significant challenges related to the complexity of the permitting process and to public opposition" (IEA 2010, 121). Wind turbines could be installed only in specified zones that were a minimum distance from areas designated for housing. And in 2011, the government created additional obstacles by establishing more cumbersome review procedures for wind mills over 50 meters tall and requiring that wind farms have a minimum of at least five turbines. Thus there were good grounds to expect that because of environmental, aesthetic, or other concerns, the development of wind power would proceed more slowly than the government had hoped (IEA 2010, 98 and 121; Ochs and Serre 2010).

Likewise, production of biofuels rose substantially in the mid- to late 2000s but then began to level out well short of the government's goal of 10 percent of transport fuel consumption. Between 2005 and 2008, ethanol output increased from 75 to 510 kilotons of oil equivalent while that for biodiesel jumped from 328 to 1887 ktoe. As a result, France was able to meet its renewables target of 5.75 percent of the transport fuel supply that year. But this figure still represented only about 3 percent of France's total oil consumption, and biofuel production showed little further growth during the following years (MEEDDM 2010, 120; IEA 2010, 93; BP 2013).

Finally, increased domestic gas production through the use of hydraulic fracturing was not a near-term eventuality. The U.S. Energy Information

Administration estimated that France might possess on the order of 4–5 trillion cubic meters of technically recoverable shale gas, which would put it near the top of European gas reserves. But strong public concerns about the potential environmental impact of fracking led the Parliament to prohibit the practice in 2011, and Hollande vowed to maintain the ban after taking office the following year.[8]

Explaining French Responses to Energy Insecurity

How are we to understand the pattern of French responses to energy insecurity? Clearly, material factors, especially France's lack of indigenous energy resources, have played an important role. With the exception of coal, France has been almost entirely dependent on imports of fossil fuels, and even the share of coal consumption met by domestic production has steadily declined to nothing, with the last coal mine closing in 2004 (Méritet 2011, 48). This lack of conventional energy resources has heightened concerns about the security of energy supplies and provided a rationale for an active policy focused on the reduction of import, and especially oil, dependence (Katzenstein 1976, 42; Finon 1996, 21).

French Political Culture

This quest for greater self-reliance in energy has arguably been reinforced by broad French national predispositions or political culture. Dominique Finon has described the "dominant culture [as] somewhat supply oriented, interventionist and nationalist" (Finon 1996, 54). In particular, as Robert Lieber noted some three decades ago, "driven by a nationalist legacy most explicitly—although by no means exclusively—expressed in Gaullism, successive French governments have sought a maximum degree of national autonomy in their domestic and foreign policies" (Lieber 1983, 76; see also Finon 1996, 33). And this search for national independence in turn, observed Michael Hatch in the mid-1980s, "has been the underlying theme and the unifying rationale throughout the definition and execution of French energy policy" (Hatch 1986, 161). After all, a deep striving for political leadership and economic self-sufficiency was not compatible with a heavy dependence on energy imports (Fagnani and Moatti 1984, 267). Indeed, France sought to exploit the first oil crisis to raise its international profile and "establish itself as the key intermediary between the commodity producing countries and the developed world" (Schneider 1983, 259). Hatch has also argued that the decisiveness that characterized France's response to its domestic energy problems was "underpinned and reinforced by a commonly held set of values or world view among those in positions of political power" (Hatch 1986, 159).

These general national predispositions were prominently on display in France's reaction to the U.S. proposals for cooperation among the oil-consuming countries following the first oil shock. But they also help to explain the French nuclear program, which was "considered the sine qua non of national independence" (Fagnani and Moatti 1984, 265). Within the government, a large nuclear program was universally viewed as indispensable for French security (Hatch 1986, 152–53). There was also a general consensus among almost all the political parties in support of an ambitious nuclear program. Within the opposition, both the Communist Party and the left wing of the Socialist Party were staunch supporters, and although the official position of the Socialist Party was initially critical, the party quickly swung behind nuclear energy when it came to power in 1981 (Fagnani and Moatti 1984, 270–71; Hatch 1986, 154). Likewise, despite some protests, "the attitude of the general public toward the implementation of the nuclear program [was] less critical than in a number of European countries" (de Carmoy 1982, 129; see also Giraud 1983, 175). Even after the concerns raised by the Three Mile Island accident in the United States, a majority of the population favored continuation of the program in the early 1980s (de Carmoy 1982, 129).

These material and dispositional imperatives alone, however, did not guarantee that France would be able to make significant progress toward enhancing its energy security. Rather, the nature of the French state has been critical in that regard. Traditionally, scholars have viewed France as having a strong state, in terms of all the dimensions emphasized in this study. Indeed, among the advanced industrialized democracies, France has epitomized the strong state. Below, I will consider in turn the autonomy and the capacity of the French state and how they have shaped French responses to energy insecurity.

State Autonomy

The autonomy of the French state has been a common theme in studies of French public policy. One of the most extensive analyses of this phenomenon was provided by John Zysman during the middle of the energy crises of the 1970s. Zysman noted that "from the beginning the state was an instrument of centralizing power, created apart from the society, almost in opposition to it, and thus at least partially autonomous . . . the French state often seems to reach out to capture private allies for its own purposes, and certainly in many economic affairs the initiative lies with the state" (1977, 194).

In its modern form, this autonomy had its roots in the Grand Corps system, which tended "to insulate the state bureaucracy from the society because the mechanism of recruitment severely restrict[ed] access to high positions within the bureaucracy" (Zysman 1977, 196). But it was reinforced by the structure of the Fifth Republic, which further isolated the executive and the bureaucracy from interest groups, French society as a whole, and even the National Assembly (Zysman 1977, 7, 194, 197). Thus, Zysman concluded, "the state is open to influence only through narrowly defined channels that are controlled by one political group. . . . The channels of influence are sufficiently narrow so that many groups now feel themselves powerless to exert any pressure within the state bureaucracy" (1977, 197). Indeed, in his view, "the discretion open to the French bureaucracy and to the government of the Fifth Republic has been most remarkable on some issues" (Zysman 1977, 198).

These views have been echoed in other analyses of French policy making (Sulieman 1974, 335; Fagnani and Moatti 1984, 265; Hatch 1986, 151–52). But the autonomy of the state has not been viewed as detrimental to the development of effective public policy. As Peter Hall has noted, "The French have traditionally believed that the state should remain independent from the pressure of social groups in order to guard the public interest" (Hall 1986, 176).

Nor should one exaggerate the degree of insulation of the state from societal pressures. As Ezra Sulieman noted as early as 1974, there could be a close relationship between the administration and certain interest groups, especially professional organizations. Likewise, Hall detected an "increasing interpenetration between the higher civil service and the management of large enterprises" that had resulted, paradoxically, from the highly statist postwar planning process, which brought managers and government officials closer together" (Hall 1986, 170–71). Indeed, in Harvey Feigenbaum's words, "the French administration is plagued by a considerable degree of clientelism whereby public agencies tend to adopt the point of view of the industries they regulate" (Feigenbaum 1982, 119).

In what ways has the autonomy of the French state shaped French responses to energy insecurity? Notwithstanding the caveats registered above, analysts have generally found that the French state has enjoyed considerable decision-making autonomy with regard to energy policy, at least in the 1970s and 1980s, especially if one includes the state-controlled energy companies as part of the state.[9] As Hanns Maull wrote in 1981,

> The powerful position of the state and the relatively closed character of the political system have confined energy policy to the administrative and industrial level. . . . The government has been able to avoid the intrusion of politics and the widening of the range of actors and participants in policy-formulation quite effectively. . . . The subordination of energy policy in France has thus been not

to social forces and demands, but to key government objectives. The centrepiece of French energy policy, the nuclear programme, is strongly linked to the government objective of turning France into one of the industrially most advanced economies. (Maull 1981, 295–96)

Likewise, Dominic Finon noted in 1996 that "many major decisions are taken within the framework of the close relations existing between the state energy enterprises and the ministries, which restrict the scope of the planning process. . . . Most of the decisions have been made behind close doors, away from the relatively open procedures of the Plan and away from the political arena. Politicians therefore play a low-key role in the matter of energy policy" (Finon 1996, 30). Even the legislative branch was largely excluded from the formulation of energy policy. Debates were rare, and "the Parliament was hardly consulted except to approve the plans" worked out by the technocrats (Saumon and Puiseux 1977, 168; see also Hatch 1986, 152–53; Finon 1996, 31).

This phenomenon was particularly evident with respect to the nuclear energy program of the 1970s and early 1980s. As Fagnani and Moatti observed, "Decision-making in France is centralized and concentrated among a relatively small circle of politicians and entities, located mainly in Paris. . . . All nuclear related decisions are made by officials of the executive branch and by the relevant publicly owned utilities. . . . Decisions, for example, regarding the choice of sites for new reactors were all made by the central administration" (Fagnani and Moatti 1984, 265). By the same token, public opinion had little impact because of the decision-making structure of the government and the absence of referenda. Indeed, the French authorities made few attempts at public consultation on the nuclear program (Marsh 1981, 147; Fagnani and Moatti 1984, 271).

By the 2000s, in contrast, the government felt it must be more inclusive and appear more responsive to public opinion in order to maintain support for its preferred policies. Hence the organization of the "national energy debate," even if the purpose was more to prepare the public for a renewal of the nuclear energy program than a sincere effort to solicit input, and the government's quick resort to parliamentary approval of a major energy law, which nevertheless gave the government much leeway with regard to the means of implementation.

Nevertheless, the government remained in the driver seat when it came to the formulation of energy policy. Perhaps the principal exception was in the area of biofuels, where the agricultural sector exerted considerable influence over the decision to increase their share of the transportation fuel supply from almost nothing to as much as 10 percent.[10]

State Capacity

Paralleling this high degree of decision-making autonomy has been a substantial state capacity for action, which has facilitated an interventionist policy, especially on the domestic front. The government had long enjoyed a powerful policy instrument in the financial system, and the relatively high degree of centralization facilitated strategic coordination by the chief executive (Zysman 1977, 195–96, 199). In the energy field, these general strengths have been supplemented by a powerful regulatory capacity, price and tax controls, public subsidies, and, especially, the presence and, where necessary, the creation of new powerful public and semi-public enterprises (Finon 1996, 24 and 30; see also Ikenberry 1986a, 125; Méritet 2011, 147). As Guy de Carmoy noted in 1982, "the government has the means to implement its goals through a highly centralized state-control system over the agencies and companies operating in the various sectors of energy," referencing its ownership of CDF, GDF, and EDF and their respective monopolies or quasi-monopolies on production, transportation, and distribution as well as its substantial positions in the CEA, Framatome, the sole supplier of nuclear reactors, and CFP and Elf-Aquitaine, the major French oil companies (de Carmoy 1982, 118).

These tools of state power proved especially useful for promoting the government's ambitious goals with respect to nuclear energy in the 1970s and 1980s. They ensured that the program had the funding and other resources it needed to advance rapidly and helped to clear away potential obstacles. Opponents had extremely limited avenues for blocking or even slowing the program, even when public opinion soured in the late 1970s. Indeed, EDF was able to offer financial incentives to win over reluctant local authorities and communities, and its educational efforts helped to rebuild popular support. As a result, implementation of the nuclear program proceeded with unmatched speed (Lieber 1983, 81; Fagnani and Moatti 1984, 267; Lucas 1985, 55; Ikenberry 1986a, 113 and 125–26; Hatch 1986, 141 and 158–59; Price 1990, 56–60).

In the 2000s, the government retained some of these tools, although they were being increasingly diluted by privatization and market liberalization. By 2010, its stake in EDF was just 84.4 percent, and its ownership share in the recently merged natural gas conglomerate GDF Suez was just 35.7 percent (IEA 2010, 22). Thus the government was able to proceed with its new program to build EPRs, albeit on a much more modest scale. But in order to maintain public support for nuclear power, it further tied its hands through the creation of the independent nuclear safety authority, the ASN, in 2006. Only the ASN had the authority to extend the lifetimes of existing reactors, and it could slow the construction of new plants by increasing safety requirements, as it did after the disaster at Fukushima.

In the 1970s, the capacity of the state also afforded France advantages as it sought to secure access to foreign oil supplies. It had a strong tradition of state intervention in commercial arrangements, and because it already had large state-owned companies, it could move quickly to negotiate bilateral contracts with oil producers (Kemezis and Wilson 1984, 97; Ikenberry 1986a, 113; Ikenberry 1988, 102). In the end, however, the government was able to secure only a small fraction of France's energy needs through such deals, reflecting the shift in power to the oil producers and the relative decline in France's material resources in the postwar years.

Policy Legacies and Path Dependence

The policy choices of the 1970s led directly to the situation France faced three decades later, especially its high degree of reliance on nuclear power. In large measure, this was a positive outcome, as France enjoyed a relatively high degree of energy security. But it also meant that France would soon have to address the aging of its nuclear plants, a task that was greatly complicated by the renewed concerns about the safety of nuclear power raised by the disaster at Fukushima Daiichi in 2011.

Conclusion

France has been able to achieve a relatively high degree of energy security, notwithstanding its paucity of fossil fuel resources. Much of France's success in improving its energy security can be attributed to the strength of the French state, especially in terms of its decision-making autonomy and domestic capacity. This strength was particularly evident in the 1970s in the areas of energy conservation and, especially, nuclear power. Following the first oil shock, the government greatly accelerated the existing nuclear program, and over the next seven years alone, it authorized contracts for some 50 nuclear reactors. French leaders were able to act quickly and decisively, and they were able to overcome or neutralize what opposition to the program there was in French society. The program continued largely unabated, even as popular support for nuclear power evaporated in other developed democracies. In the end, it was only the saturation of the domestic market for electricity that caused the construction of new reactors to stop.

In the 2000s, however, the state found itself somewhat more constrained than it had been in the 1970s. Public backing for nuclear power had softened over the years, and the state had less ability to forge ahead with expensive and potentially controversial programs. Thus the government took pains to cultivate popular and parliamentary support, and it ceded significant powers to an independent safety authority. Partly as a result, the renewal of French nuclear policy proceeded more cautiously and on a much more modest scale than it had in the 1970s.

CHAPTER SEVEN

Germany

From Dependence on Persian Gulf Oil to Russian Gas

Of the countries examined in this study, the Federal Republic of Germany represents an intermediate case in terms of the magnitude of the threats that it has faced to its energy security and the natural resources at its disposal.[1] In the 1970s, it was much less dependent on foreign oil than was either France or Japan, but with the exception of coal, it lacked the indigenous fossil fuel resources of either Britain or the United States. Nevertheless, West Germany's response to the oil shocks emphasized what it could do at home, where it pursued a strategy that first emphasized the substitution of coal, nuclear power, and natural gas for oil and, later, energy conservation. Beyond backing the development of new natural gas import routes, the government's external efforts to enhance the country's energy security were minimal.

The resulting increased reliance on coal, nuclear power, and natural gas, however, was not without its drawbacks. By the early to mid-1980s, the future limits on their use had already become clear. Coal and nuclear power raised deep environmental and, in the case of the latter, safety concerns that would constrain how Germany could respond to future threats to its energy security. But it was the growth in dependence on imported gas, especially from the USSR and later Russia, that set the stage for united Germany's principal energy security challenges in the 2000s.

Until the mid-2000s, German energy policy was dominated by growing concern about climate change and the decision to phase out the use of nuclear power by the early 2020s. More traditional worries about the security of energy supplies reemerged only as a result of the first Russia-Ukraine gas crisis of 2006, which resulted in natural gas shortages in Western Europe. Germany responded by conducting over the next two years a thorough review of its energy policy, which placed primary emphasis on increasing energy efficiency and the use of renewable energy sources. By the time the review was completed in late 2007, however, concerns about climate change had returned to the fore, and the new German policy contained no measures specifically intended to promote energy security. A further energy policy review conducted at the end of the decade by a new governing coalition made no significant changes in emphasis, although it briefly flirted with a delay of the planned nuclear phaseout.

Although the impact of path dependence is perhaps least prominent in the German case, the case does provide much evidence of the importance of state strength for understanding policy responses to energy insecurity. German policies often reflected the limited autonomy of the state, which was pressured on one side by strong public sentiments and on the other by powerful interest groups. At the same time, policy has been importantly shaped by the state's limited capacity. These limits have been most pronounced in the international realm, helping to account for the heavy emphasis on domestic policy responses. But even at home, the federal government has possessed relatively few instruments for pursuing its policy goals, relying instead primarily on the private sector, and it has had limited ability to overcome determined societal resistance to its objectives. Despite these limitations, however, the German state has played a not insignificant role in helping to ensure relatively favorable policy outcomes.

The 1970s: West German Responses to the Oil Shocks

Because of the important role that coal had played in the German economy and society, the Federal Republic of Germany had not (yet) become nearly as dependent on foreign oil as was either Japan or France, and it was only slightly more so than Britain, at the time of the first oil shock. In addition, although the government generally took a free market approach to energy policy, it had already begun to anticipate the risks of foreign oil dependence and had outlined an ambitious nuclear power program. Thus, while West Germany may not have been hit quite as hard as other states, the government still took the situation seriously and was able to prepare quickly an energy plan that projected a significant reduction in oil's share of primary energy consumption (PEC) by 1985.

The initial emphasis of West Germany's response to the oil shocks was to seek to substitute coal and natural gas for oil while reinforcing the nuclear plans that had already been outlined. During the following years, however, the energy program was revised several times, especially as political opposition to nuclear power mounted. Over time, the projections for future domestic energy production and consumption steadily declined as the emphasis in German policy shifted from the supply side to conservation.

Partly as a result of these efforts, West Germany was able to improve its energy security significantly during the decade after the first oil shock. By 1985, it had reduced its oil consumption both in absolute terms and as a share of PEC by one-quarter, largely through the substitution of nuclear energy and natural gas and by arresting the previous slide in coal production. In addition, West Germany's oil supplies were much more diversified, with a plurality now coming from the North Sea, and it had accumulated substantial emergency stocks.

At the same time, however, the seeds of future energy security problems had been sown. Environmental and safety concerns had already begun to constrain the degree to which West Germany could rely on coal and, especially, nuclear power, the development of which had fallen far short of initial expectations. At the same time, West German was becoming increasingly dependent on imports of natural gas, a large share of which was now coming from the Soviet Union.

Background to the 1970s
WEST GERMANY'S ENERGY MIX

Like most of the other developed democracies, West Germany experienced a significant shift in its energy mix in the decades prior to the oil crisis, although not to the extent of some other countries. Germany had traditionally been a major coal producer, and during the first decade after World War II, domestic coal dominated the energy supply. As late 1957, coal still accounted for as much as 85 percent of West German PEC, with oil a distant second at only 11 percent (Hatch 1986, 194, T1; Bundesregierung 1973, 3).

A central principle of postwar German energy policy, however, was to provide basic materials industries, such as iron and steel, chemicals, cement, nonferrous metals, and paper products, with low-cost energy, and beginning in the late 1950s, domestically produced coal became increasingly uncompetitive with oil. Although the price of German coal stayed roughly the same between 1957 and 1967, that for fuel oil dropped by more than half over the same period. Largely as a result of this growing price differential, coal production and consumption peaked in 1956 at about 150 million tons and then declined steadily, falling to just 31 percent of PEC in 1973, while oil's share grew commensurately, reaching more than 56 percent of PEC in 1973 (de Carmoy 1977, 53; Schmitt 1982, 138; Meyer-Abich and Dickler 1982, 223–25; Lucas 1985, 213 Hatch 1986, 11–12 and 94). The other noteworthy change in West Germany's energy mix was a rapid rise in natural gas consumption. From almost nothing in 1960, gas use grew to more than 10 percent of PEC in 1973 (BP 2013).

As a result of these developments, West Germany went from being a net energy exporter in the mid-1950s to a substantial energy importer by the early 1970s. The country produced a small amount of oil, but most of the growing demand for oil had to be met by production from abroad, which accounted for more than 98 percent of oil consumption by 1973. Thus oil—and total energy—imports grew from 6 percent of PEC in 1957 to more than half of PEC in 1973. Thanks to the recent discoveries in the North Sea, West Germany also produced a significant amount of natural gas, but consumption grew even faster, exceeding domestic production around 1970 (Bundesregierung 1973, 4; BP 2013; DOE 1977, 129; Hatch 1986, 27).

With just a few exceptions, discussed below, West Germany energy policy prior to the first oil shock was largely characterized by a free market orientation. Consistent with its focus on minimizing energy costs to industry, the government showed a strong preference for a market economy operating under a private enterprise system, and it generally allowed commercial considerations to determine levels of consumption and imports. This approach was especially true of the increasingly important oil market, where there were no restriction on the entry of firms, no controls on prices, and no attempts to influence investment. The government also made little or no real effort to prevent the takeover of German firms by foreign companies. Hence most of the domestic market for petroleum products was sourced by subsidiaries of the international oil companies (Menderhausen 1976, 18; DOE 1977, 125; Krapels 1980, 65; Lucas 1985, 189).

Despite this overall laissez-faire approach, the government did take a few steps to safeguard the country's oil supplies. In 1965, it began to require refiners of crude oil and importers of refined petroleum products to maintain stocks of 65 and 45 days, respectively. In 1970, it decided to create a reserve of 8 million tons of oil, about 60 million barrels, or the equivalent of 25 days of imports at the time, although construction of the reserve did not actually begin until two years later. And it sought to ensure that German-owned firms controlled at least 25 percent of the market (Menderhausen 1976, 25; DOE 1977, 125; Krapels 1980, 65).

In the late 1960s, growing concern about the security of oil supplies also prompted the government to spearhead the formation of a joint enterprise for oil exploration and development abroad. It used the promise of substantial subsidies to secure the participation of the eight largest German-owned oil companies. The new concern, Deutsche Erdölversorgungsgesellschaft, or DEMINEX, was intended to increase the direct access of the parent companies to foreign sources of oil through a variety of means, including its own exploration efforts, the acquisition of production rights in existing oil fields, participation in exploration ventures with other groups, and long-term purchasing arrangements. For the period 1969 to 1974, DEMINEX received a government subsidy of DM 575 million in the form of project loans that needed to be repaid only if they resulted in successful discoveries. In addition, if the company bought into a proven oil field, the government would provide 30 percent of the purchase costs (Menderhausen 1976, 25; DOE 1977, 125; Kemezis and Wilson 1984, 111; Lucas 1985, 191–93).

The government's biggest departure from free market principles prior to the first oil shock, however, occurred in the coal industry. The industry employed more than half a million people throughout the 1950s, and hard coal production was concentrated in the Ruhr region, which often played a decisive role in West German general elections. Thus for both social and political reasons, the government took a large number of measures to protect domestic coal production in the face of less expensive imports of both oil and coal. These measure included quotas and later a tax on coal imports; voluntary limits by the oil industry on oil imports; taxes on light and heavy duty fuel oil; direct grants, subsidies, and tax credits to the coal mining industry; restrictions on new power stations using fuel oil and natural gas; and subsidies for the use of coal in electric power plants (Menderhausen 1976, 23–24; de Carmoy 1977, 51; Schmitt 1982, 137 and 140–43; Lucas 1985, 213; Hatch 1986, 11–14).

Notwithstanding these efforts, employment in the coal industry had fallen by half by 1968. Thus the government finally passed a law intended to reduce coal production to a competitive level and to concentrate the industry into economical units. Even then, the industry continued to sustain heavy losses despite continued government aid in the form of subsidies and import quotas (DOE 1977, 126; Schmitt 1982, 141; Lucas 1985, 213; Hatch 1986 1986, 11–14).

The government also took some steps to promote nuclear power, although not nearly to the same extent as it supported coal. It initiated a civilian nuclear energy program in 1955, the same year that West Germany regained most of its political sovereignty, and the first two nuclear research centers were established the following year. Between 1956 and 1976, the federal and state (*Land*) governments provided approximately $7.5 billion in funds for research and development. The federal government also agreed to cover most of the costs of a fast breeder reactor that was begun in 1972, but it expected industry to pay for the development and production of conventional nuclear reactors. Thus at the time of the first oil crisis, West Germany had only two nuclear power plants of more than 500 MW in operation, with a handful of others under construction (DOE 1977, 126; Lucas 1985, 209–10 and 244).

Impact of the Oil Shocks

Even before the first oil shock, West German government officials had become concerned about rising oil prices and potential supply bottlenecks because of growing international demand and the concentration of production in a relatively small number of countries. These concerns were reflected in a comprehensive energy program that was developed during the first nine months of 1973 and published on September 26, just weeks before the crisis began (Bundesregierung 1973). The program called for reducing risks related to oil by increasing the security of oil supplies; the speedy buildup of economical energy sources, especially natural gas, nuclear power, and brown coal, that would contribute to a reduction of the risks associated with oil; and the use of hard coal where it was financially justifiable and economically necessary.

Most of the 17-page text concerned matters of energy supply. It devoted just one short section (4 paragraphs) to the rational use of energy. The program projected that West German energy consumption would grow to about 430 million tonnes of oil equivalent (mtoe) in 1985, an increase of 72 percent over the 1972 level. Petroleum would remain by far the single most important source of energy, although its growth as a share of PEC would be arrested and then reduced slightly to 54 percent. Coal would continue its decline, from 32.3 percent of PEC in 1972 to just 14 percent in 1985. The brunt of the reduction, however, would be borne by hard coal; consumption of brown coal would increase by nearly one quarter. Coal would be replaced by natural gas and nuclear energy, whose shares of PEC would both increase to 15 percent.

Perhaps most notably, the energy program called in particular for building up Germany's nuclear generating capacity as quickly as possible, to 18 GW by 1980 and then at least 40 GW—and ideally 50 GW—by 1985 (Bundesregierung 1973, 10; Evans 1979, 79). This goal was extremely ambitious, given that only 7.2 GW of capacity had been built or was under construction at the end of 1972. At about the same time, the government also released its fourth atomic energy program, for the period 1973–76, which affirmed the long-term goal of achieving approximately 45 GW of generating capacity by 1985 and called for spending DM 6.1 billion, mostly on basic research and the development of nuclear technology. The program assumed that the limits of natural gas and brown coal would be reached by the end of the decade, after which growth in electricity production would depend on the availability of sufficient nuclear power (Schaff 1999/2000).

As farsighted as the 1973 energy program may have been, the first oil shock quickly invalidated many of its assumptions and estimates (Hatch 1986, 42). West German concerns went through two phases. For the first several months, attention focused on potential shortages of petroleum products, especially of heating oil, which consumers started to hoard. Because of the largely free market in petroleum products, however, supply and demand adjusted more quickly than in countries that did not immediately allow internal prices to rise (Prodi and Clo 1975, 99; Menderhausen 1976, 78; Hatch 1986, 69–70).

Thus by March 1974, concerns about shortages had dissipated and attention shifted to the broader macroeconomic consequences of the jump in oil prices. The German government was particularly concerned about economic growth, which slowed to a crawl and then reversed in 1975, and unemployment, which doubled in 1974 and then again the following year. In contrast, inflation remained the lowest among the major advanced industrialized countries, and West Germany continued to run a substantial balance of payments surplus (Menderhausen 1976, 86–87 and 92–93; Hatch 1986, 39–40 and 197, table 6).

Overview of German Policy Responses

The West German response to the oil shocks went through several phases, which were represented by revisions of the 1973 energy program. The consistent overriding goal of German policy was to reduce the country's dependence on oil, most of which was necessarily imported, as summarized by the slogan "Weg vom Öl" (Away from Oil). But how the government proposed to achieve this goal evolved over time. Initially, it emphasized replacing oil with coal, natural gas, and nuclear energy. As obstacles to this supply-side approach emerged, policy shifted to place more emphasis on conservation and reducing energy consumption. Throughout, German policy continued to rely as much as possible on market forces, except where some further impetus or correction of market failures was deemed necessary (IEA 1979, 67; Meyer-Abich and Dickler 1982, 221 and 238; Schneider 1983, 325; IEA 1986, 253–54).

THE FIRST REVISION OF THE ENERGY PROGRAM

The first revision of the government's 1973 energy program *(Erste Fortschreibung des Energieprogramms der Bundesregierung)* was published in October 1974, one year after the beginning of the first oil shock. In contrast to the original program, it called for reducing oil's share of PEC to just 44 percent by 1985 and, to help achieve this goal, for reversing the previously projected decline in coal. In particular, hard coal consumption, which stood at 83.7 million tons in 1972 and was projected to fall to just 50 million tons in 1985, would now be maintained at around 80 million tons, and coal's overall share of PEC was to drop only to 21 percent, not 15 percent as previously projected. In addition, the share of PEC met by natural gas would now rise to 18–19 percent, versus only 15 percent in the original plan. The revision also raised the targets for nuclear power, to 20 GW of generating capacity by 1980 and 45–50 GW by 1985, although its projected share of

PEC remained at 15 percent (DOE 1977, 131 and 134; de Carmoy 1977, 52–53; Evans 1979, 70 and 79; Meyer-Abich and Dickler 1982, 231; Lucas 1985, 243; Hatch 1986, 42–43, 70, and 198).

The first revision also contained several elements directly concerned with the security of oil supplies. It called for limiting West Germany's imports from any single country to a maximum of 15 percent. It also advocated measures for coping with future oil supply disruptions, such as an increase in obligatory private sector stocks of crude oil and petroleum products and an accelerated program of government crude oil stockpiling (Menderhausen 1976, 88; DOE 1977, 129)

Like the original program, however, the first revision placed little emphasis on energy conservation. Its projection of demand in 1985—about 388 mtoe—was 9 percent lower than in the original program, but this still represented a 57 percent increase over the level in 1972. And much of the reduction could be accounted for by lower expectations for future economic growth. The revised program still assumed that energy consumption would rise nearly as fast as GDP (de Carmoy 1977, 52; Meyer-Abich and Dickler 1982, 231).

THE SECOND REVISION OF THE ENERGY PROGRAM

As political opposition to the rapid growth of the nuclear power industry rose over the next few years, however, the government, which had been led by the Social Democratic Party (Sozialdemokratische Partei Deutschland, or SPD) since 1969, felt it necessary to review the energy program yet again. The outlines of a second revision emerged in March 1977, with the publication of a set of "interim guidelines" (*Grundlinien und Eckwerte für die Fortschreibung des Energieprogramms*). The interim statement forecast a further decline in 1985 energy consumption of 9 percent. More significantly, it expressed a need for just 30 GW of nuclear capacity, a full one-third or more less than the amount projected just two and a half years before (DOE 1977, 133; Fells 1977, 341; Hatch 1986, 95–97; Price 1990 86).

The second revision of the energy program, which was published in December 1977, went even further in this direction, reflecting the uncertainties generated by the public debate over the future of nuclear energy and the resulting delays in the construction of several nuclear power plants. It further lowered the projection for PEC in 1985 to about 340 mtoe, or 13 percent below the figure contained in the first revision, and it adopted a much more reserved approach toward nuclear power, which would be developed only to the extent "absolutely necessary to secure electricity supply." Thus the emphasis shifted from as much nuclear energy as possible to only as much as was needed to meet the country's overall energy requirements. Henceforth, the main purpose of nuclear power would be to fill the gaps left by coal, not to become a leading energy source in its own right. Although the second revision reaffirmed the need to expand nuclear power production beyond then existing levels, the revised nuclear energy targets for 1985 were just 24 GW of generating capacity and 11 percent of PEC (IEA 1979, 67–68 and 70; IEA 1980, 118; Meyer-Abich and Dickler 1982, 232 and 235; Hatch 1986, 97; Schaaf 1999/2000). The achievement of this goal would require only a small increase in capacity over the amount already in operation (6.5 GW) or under construction (14.5 GW) (Fells 1977, 341).

Nuclear energy was no longer regarded as an easy substitute for oil. One consequence of the deemphasis of nuclear power was that there was no further reduction in the projection for oil's share of PEC, although achievement of the lower target for total energy consumption would allow oil imports to be substantially reduced from their previously projected levels. The second revision also envisioned an even greater reliance on coal in the long term (IEA 1979, 70; IEA 1980, 115; Hatch 1986, 44 and 101; Price 1990, 86).

Instead of the supply side, however, the second revision gave top priority for the first time to energy conservation. Previously, the rational use of energy had received relatively little attention in energy policy because the view of the government was that ensuring the economic use of energy was the responsibility of industry and the consumer. Now, the government reversed course, and henceforth, it would strengthen national efforts in energy conservation as well as basic research and development and coal utilization as means of reducing West Germany's dependence on imported oil (IEA 1979, 67–68; Meyer-Abich and Dickler 1982, 232 and 235; Lucas 1985, 231; Hatch 1986, 97 and 101; Schaff 1999/2000).

Nevertheless, German energy policy would continue to be constrained by the philosophy that

> an optimal solution of our energy-supply problems can only be expected within the framework of decentralized decisions. . . . Government interventions are often considered less flexible and reversible than decisions resulting from market forces. . . . Adaptability cannot be administered; it can only be realized through a market system based on competition, . . . Therefore, it is the objective of the German energy program to strengthen market forces and to intervene only when market imperfections lead to politically unacceptable results or where market forces need support or correction because of high risks, long lead times, or external effects. (Schmitt 1982, 148)

THE THIRD REVISION OF THE ENERGY PROGRAM

In November 1981, less than a year before losing power, the SPD-led government adopted a third revision of the energy program. This time there was no major change of emphasis. The revised program once again gave top priority to energy conservation, followed by the substitution of coal, nuclear power, and natural gas for oil. It restated the government's intention to rely primarily on the market and the price mechanism to bring about the necessary changes in supply and demand, although it also recognized a role for continuing regulatory, fiscal, and financial incentives to facilitate the process of adjustment in certain sectors (Meyer-Abich and Dickler 1982, 237; IEA 1983, 165; Commission 1984, 13).

Consistent with the previous revisions, it projected a further decline in PEC in 1985 of about 9 percent, to 280 mtoe, which represented an overall decrease of more than one-third in the projection since the original energy program was announced in 1973. The expected share of PEC from oil was reduced slightly to 43 percent, but that for nuclear power fell even more, to just 11 percent. Now, the government estimated that just 18 GW of generating capacity would be available. The slack would be made up by coal, whose projected share of PEC was now 29 percent, more than double the figure anticipated in 1973 (Meyer-Abich and Dickler 1982, 238; IEA 1982, 170).

The Christian Democrat-led government that took office in 1982 made no further changes in German energy policy. As a report by the European Commission noted in 1988, "One of the cornerstones of Germany energy policy in the past has been the consensus between Federal Government, the major opposition party, and all the Länder on the general direction of national energy policy, especially the combined development of nuclear and indigenous coal" (Commission 1988, 59bis).

Domestic Policy Responses

Within the framework of the energy program and its successive revisions, the West Germany government took a number of specific measures intended in whole or in part to increase German energy security following the first oil shock. These fell into roughly four categories:

1. directly reducing or discouraging the use of oil through taxes and regulations
2. promoting alternatives to oil, especially coal, but also natural gas and nuclear energy

3. promoting energy conservation more generally, especially after 1977
4. improving West Germany's ability to withstand a future oil supply disruption

DIRECTLY REDUCING OIL CONSUMPTION

As noted above, the overriding goal of German policy was to reduce the country's dependence on oil. And the most direct way to do so was to prevent or to discourage oil consumption through taxes and regulations as well as by allowing prices to rise in response to world market conditions. West Germany had imposed high taxes on most petroleum products, such as gasoline, diesel fuel, and heavy fuel oil, prior to the first oil shock. After 1973, these taxes were kept in place and in some cases increased. In 1978, the government doubled the tax on heating oil, and over the next three years, it raised the taxes on gasoline and diesel. By the time of the second oil shock, the tax per liter on gasoline stood at DM 0.44, that on diesel at DM 0.42, and that on heavy fuel oil at DM 0.14. The government also sought to limit the use of heating oil to produce electric power and banned the construction of new oil-fired power plants (Fells 1977, 342; IEA 1979, 65 and 67; IEA 1980, 116; IEA 1982, 172; Schmitt 1982, 151; Meyer-Abich and Dickler 1982, 231 and 235; and Jochem et al. 1996, 64).

SUBSTITUTION

Simultaneously, the government promoted the substitution of other energy sources for oil. It devoted its biggest efforts to boosting coal, because the fate of the coal industry had much larger political, economic, and social implications. In the case of natural gas, the government relied much more heavily on market actors to make the necessary investments, and it expected the electrical utilities to pay for new commercial nuclear power plants.

After the first oil shock, the downward adjustment process for the hard coal industry that the government had developed in the late 1960s was immediately halted (Schmitt 1982, 144). Instead, the government erected a series of policies to support the use of hard coal, especially for electricity production, and to prevent a further decline in domestic hard coal production. First, it maintained an import quota of about 5 million tons per year on coal from non-European Community countries. The quota was only raised in 1981, and then only to 6.6 million tons, in order to promote the substitution of coal for oil in industry (IEA 1980, 118; Schmitt 1982, 155; Lucas 1985, 214).

Within the electricity sector, the government provided subsidies to cover the extra capital cost of building coal-fired plants or converting existing oil-fired plants to coal (Lucas 1985, 246). It also strongly encouraged long-term contracts between the electric utilities and the coal mines to ensure demand for domestic hard coal. Under the initial agreement, signed in 1977, the utilities committed to take 33 million tons of coal per year for 10 years. In 1981, the agreement was extended through 1995, with the quantity gradually increasing to 40 million tons in 1985, 45 in 1990, and 47.5 in 1995 (Fells 1977, 342; Lucas 1985, 214, 222, 241, and 246).

The electric utilities did not like the agreements, but they went along, fearing that the alternative was government legislation. In addition, they received a substantial subsidy that was financed by a tax of 4 to 5 percent on electricity consumption. In 1980 alone, the tax raised more than DM 1.8 billion. Overall, federal and state support for the coal industry reached at least DM 6 billion per year in the early 1980s (IEA 1982, 177; Lucas 1985, 246 and 256; Hatch 1986, 45; see also IEA 1979, 70; IEA 1980, 118).

In 1980, the government announced a major program to create synthetic fuels from coal. It sought to demonstrate the feasibility of both coal gasification and liquefaction on a large scale and offered to subsidize investments at a level of up to 50 percent. The government had already spent DM 1 billion on research on coal conversion technology and budgeted an additional DM 2 billion for the program through 1985 (Schmitt 1982, 151; IEA 1982, 178; IEA 1983, 170; Lucas 1985, 247).

Beyond their high financial costs, the government's efforts to promote domestic coal consumption and production encountered several obstacles. In the mid-1970s, a recession in the steel industry and stagnating demand for electricity caused declining sales, growing stockpiles, and even greater financial losses in the coal industry. In addition, local opposition hindered the construction of a handful of large coal-fired power plants with the capacity to burn a total of 14 million tons per year. And increases in the output of brown coal, which was much cheaper than hard coal but was produced in open pit mines in heavily populated areas, were limited by environmental concerns (Schmitt 1982, 146–47; Hatch 1986, 43–44 and 86).

In contrast to coal, the government did little to promote the substitution of natural gas for oil. Here it relied primarily on the market to increase supplies and stimulate demand, but it was not entirely passive. Within West Germany, the government provided subsidies for deep drilling, and it worked to extend the regional gas transmission network (DOE 1977, 131; Evans 1979, 67 and 76; IEA 1980, 118). At the same time, it offered to help German companies secure gas supplies from abroad with general political support and financial guarantees. The contract with the Netherlands, from which the country had received most of its gas imports, was set to expire at the end of the 1970s. But West Germany had begun to import gas from the Soviet Union in 1973, and with the government's blessing, German companies negotiated a string of additional long-term contracts over the following decade. These included a second deal with the Soviet Union in 1974, an arrangement to import gas from Norway following the completion of an undersea pipeline in 1977, a complicated five-country agreement with Iran that would ship Iranian gas to the USSR in return for increased Soviet deliveries to Western Europe, a contract with Algeria for liquefied natural gas (LNG), and, most controversially, a third Soviet contract in 1981. Under the terms of the 1981 Soviet agreement, West Germany would import an additional 10.5 billion cubic meters (bcm) (9.45 mtoe) per year starting in the mid-1980s, potentially bringing the Soviet contribution to West German gas consumption up to 30 percent (Bundesregierung 1973, 9–10; DOE 1977, 131; Meyer-Abich and Dickler 1982, 237; IEA 1983, 166; Stern 1983, 67; Lucas 1985, 197; Hatch 1986, 51 and 99).[2]

In response to criticism of the final Soviet deal, the government took steps to allay concerns that it was abetting undue dependence on a potentially unreliable supplier. It stated that it would not allow the Soviet share of German gas to exceed 30 percent. And in the third revision of the energy program, it called for a tripling of Germany's gas storage capacity to 7.5 bcm, or approximately two months of consumption at the time (Meyer-Abich and Dickler 1982, 240; IEA 1986, 264; Jochem et al. 1996, 71).

In the late 1960s and early 1970s, all the major political parties considered nuclear power to be the most promising primary energy source of the future (Jochem et al. 1996, 67). Thus it is not surprising that, immediately after the first oil shock, the government had projected that nuclear energy would grow the most as a share of PEC, from 1 to 15 percent by 1985, and thus be the principal substitute for oil. Nevertheless, it was not prepared to play a major role in helping to realize this ambitious projection. In the first revision of the energy program, the government promised to provide more support for research on such matters as reactor safety, reprocessing, and waste disposal. Indeed, nuclear research continued to receive about 70 percent of all government research appropriations through the 1970s. The government also promised to increase spending on the fast breeder reactor and high-temperature reactor demonstration projects. The government's contribution to the prototype breeder alone totaled more than DM 3 billion. And it called for standardization of commercial reactors types in order to speed up the process of planning, licensing, and construction. But it relied on the electrical utilities to finance all new commercial nuclear generating capacity (Schmitt 1982, 151; Meyer-Abich and Dickler 1982, 231 and 236; Lucas 1985, 209 and 256; Schaaf 1999/2000).

This arrangement of a limited government role and primary reliance on the private sector might have been sufficient to realize the original projections had the nuclear program not encountered significant popular opposition. The first protests seemed to appear out of the blue in 1975 when the government approved the construction of a 1.3 GW reactor at Whyl on the Rhine River in southwestern Germany. The next year, more than 1,000 organizations participated in demonstrations at nuclear sites. And in 1977, the antinuclear movement reached a peak, with riots at two different locations. Simultaneously, opponents used the legal system to block the construction of several reactors. As a result of this opposition, the issuance of initial construction permits slowed to a crawl—only four were granted from 1975 to 1977—and in 1977, a de facto moratorium took effect when a court ruled that no new licenses for nuclear plants could be given out until at least a permit had been issued for the construction of a spent fuel processing and storage facility (Fells 1977, 341; IEA 1980, 118; IEA 1982, 178; Meyer-Abich and Dickler 1982, 249–50; Schneider 1983, 342; Lucas 1985, 199 and 238; Hatch 1986, 73–73 and 79–82; Price 1990, 86).

The vehemence of the popular resistance to nuclear power caused the governing parties to rethink their positions on the issue. As its 1979 party conference, for example, the governing SPD agreed that plants under construction should be completed, but only put into operation when a satisfactory means of waste management was assured or when sufficient intermediate storage capacity existed, and new power stations should be approved only when the first, more demanding, condition was met (Lucas 1985, 242). These shifts were reflected in the second and third revisions of the energy program, which increasingly deemphasized the role of nuclear power, as discussed above.

Nevertheless, the government did not abandon the nuclear program altogether. It continued to work on the problem of the storage of nuclear waste, making enough progress that the prior injunction against new licenses was lifted. And in 1981, it succeeded in streamlining the licensing procedure, paving the way for approval of three more plants the following year. Those, however, would be the last to be built in West Germany (Meyer-Abich and Dickler 1982, 240; IEA 1982, 166; Lucas 1985, 237–38).

Perhaps surprisingly, given developments in more recent years, the government paid little attention to alternative sources of energy, such as wind and solar power. At the time, they were thought to have only marginal potential. Even in the third revision of the energy program, renewables were not expected to begin to make a significant contribution before the next century. In addition, the government believed that the costs of developing renewable forms of energy could and should be borne by the private sector (Fells 1977, 343; Meyer-Abich and Dickler 1982, 241; Lucas 1985, 234).

REDUCING ENERGY CONSUMPTION: CONSERVATION AND EFFICIENCY PROGRAMS

An increasingly important domestic component of the West German response to the oil shocks was to reduce energy consumption, including oil consumption, through conservation measures and gains in energy efficiency. Initially, the government's principal approach was simply not to shield the consumer from energy price increases, allowing the market alone to determine energy demand. The main conservation measures adopted by the government were intended to deal with emergency situations, such as when it imposed speed limits and temporarily banned Sunday driving in late 1973. Its initial support for research and development of energy saving technologies and products amounted to just DM 120 million per year. Not until several years after the first oil shock did the government begin to implement substantial long-term programs to promote conservation, which was finally given formal priority in the second revision of the energy program in December 1977, and by the mid-1980s, it had taken scores of actions to reduce energy use. By the late 1980s, total subsidies for energy savings since 1973 amounted to some DM 13 billion. Nevertheless, West German policy shied away from mandatory measures for reducing oil consumption, especially in the auto sector, preferring instead to alter behavior through a variety of financial incentives and voluntary agreements with industry (IEA 1979, 69; IEA 1980, 116–17; Meyer-Abich and Dickler 1982, 226 and 238; Lucas 1985, 232; Hatch 1986, 39 and 51; Jochem et al. 1996, 62).

Perhaps the biggest efforts to reduce consumption were made in the building sector, which accounted for some 40 percent of primary energy use and where heating oil was widely used. In 1976, the government passed an energy savings law that empowered it to establish thermal insulation standards for, and to require efficient heating and cooling systems in, new buildings (IEA 1979, 68; IEA 1980, 116; Schmitt 1982, 149–50; Meyer-Abich and Dickler 1982, 231–33; Jochem et al. 1996, 63). In December 1977, the second revision proposed a complementary retrofitting program aimed at home owners. The resulting Housing Modernization Act of 1978 provided DM 4.35 billion in grants and tax credits over five years to encourage energy savings investments in existing homes, such as better insulation and upgraded heating systems (IEA 1979, 67–68; IEA 1980, 116; IEA 1982, 173; Schmitt 1982, 149; Lucas 1985, 232; Hatch 1986, 51; Jochem et al. 1996, 62). The third revision strengthened these measures, raising insulation and efficiency standards for new buildings, setting requirements for existing buildings for the first time, and adding a new DM 1 billion program to improve the thermal performance of public buildings (IEA 1982, 174; IEA 1983, 165 and 168).

A second set of programs, which complemented the government's efforts to promote the use of coal, concerned district heating and combined heat and power (CHP) systems. Prior to the second revision, the government had authorized DM 680 million in grants to encourage waste heat recovery from power stations. The second revision established a new DM 730 million scheme to provide subsidies of up to 35 percent for the costs of new coal-fired district heating plants. An amendment to the Investment Allowance Act allowed companies to take a 7.5 percent tax deduction for investments in CHP plants and heat recovery systems. And in the early 1980s, the government extended the district heating program for five years at a cost of DM 1.2 billion and created a new DM 6.3 billion program of interest subsidies on loans for energy conservation and fuel-switching investments in small and medium-sized industries (IEA 1979, 70; IEA 1980, 116–17; IEA 1982, 171 and 175; IEA 1983, 171; Lucas 1985, 220).

The government's approach to energy conservation in the transportation sector was less direct. Rather than use regulations or financial incentives other than taxes on vehicle sales, it sought voluntary agreements with the auto industry to improve the fuel economy of new vehicles, with the implied threat of legislation should a satisfactory agreement not be reached. In 1978, the car makers pledged to reduce fuel consumption by at least 10 percent by 1985, and in 1981, they set the more ambitious goal of 15 percent. Similar agreements were reached with the makers of electrical appliances and other energy using consumer goods (IEA 1980, 117; Schmitt 1982, 149–50; Meyer-Abich and Dickler 1982, 231 and 235; IEA 1983, 168; Lucas 1985, 232; IEA 1986, 261; Jochem et al. 1996, 63).

EMERGENCY PREPARATIONS

Finally, the government took several steps to increase West Germany's preparedness for a possible future oil shock. Construction of the planned government reserve of 8 million tons of oil had begun in 1972, and the 1973 energy program had called for increasing the storage requirements for refiners (from 65 to 90 days) and importers (from 45 to 70 days) beginning in 1975 (Bundesregierung 1973, 8; Krapels 1980, 65; Hatch 1986, 48). Following the second revision, the government passed a stockpiling law that established a public corporation, the Erdöl-beforratungsverband (EBV), to manage stockpiles for private companies. The EBV was authorized to hold reserves of up to 65 days on behalf of the participants, thereby limiting the amounts that refiners and importers would have to maintain by themselves. In return for paying an annual fee, the companies were able to keep most of the required stocks off of their balance sheets. In addition, the EBV reserves would be segregated administratively and to some extent physically from commercial inventories, further ensuring their availability in a crisis (Krapels 1980, 66–68; Deese and Miller 1981, 193–95; Hatch 1986, 48–49). In addition, the government established a system for allocating and, if necessary, rationing petroleum products as well as setting maximum prices if necessary (Menderhausen 1976, 79; Deese and Miller 1981, 195–97).

External Policy Responses

The external dimensions of West Germany's response to the oil shocks were much more limited, but still noteworthy. As discussed above, the government provided diplomatic and financial support for German companies seeking to secure natural gas supplies from abroad. It also increased its financial support for DEMINEX, the oil exploration and development company that had been set up in the late 1960s. Between 1975 and 1985, it invested an addition DM 2 billion in the concern in three roughly equal installments, and by 1976, DEMINEX was involved in as many as 22 projects in 14 different countries (DOE 1977, 128; IEA 1982, 171 and 176; Lucas 1985, 192).

In addition, the government sought to create a state-controlled oil company that could secure oil directly from producers. The 1973 energy program designated the energy company VEBA, in which the government held a 40 percent stake, as the principal vehicle for promoting national oil interests, and in 1974 VEBA negotiated a three-year contract with Saudi Arabia guaranteeing the delivery of 12 million tons of oil (80 thousand barrels per day). In 1974, the government orchestrated VEBA's takeover of another company, Gelsenberg, over the objections of the Federal Cartel Office and provided the resulting venture with roughly $100 million in annual subsidies over the following six years (Menderhausen 1976, 77 and 86; DOE 1977, 123, 125, and 128; de Carmoy 1977, 51–52; Lucas 1985, 193).

In the multilateral realm, West Germany was generally supportive of U.S. initiatives, in stark contrast to France. At the Washington energy conference in early 1974, it assumed a leading role in persuading other EEC countries to adopt a comprehensive action program along the lines of that advocated by the United States.

It also agreed with the United States on the need for a code of conduct limiting bilateral deals with oil producers and on the desirability of a broad a measure of consumer country cooperation. In the view of the West Germans, the energy crisis was too big to be managed on an exclusively European basis. Subsequently, within both the IEA and the European Community, Germany sought to promote oil market transparency and careful preparations for crisis management (Lieber 1976, 22; Schneider 1983, 260; Lucas 1985, 251). In 1980, West Germany also expressed some support for the U.S. actions taken in response to the Iranian revolution and the Soviet invasion of Afghanistan to ensure access to Persian Gulf oil supplies, although it was able to make only a very modest military contribution of its own, deploying a task force of four ships to the Indian Ocean (Bax 1981, 39).

Evaluation of German Policy Responses to the Oil Shocks
IMPROVEMENTS IN GERMAN ENERGY SECURITY

Overall, West Germany experienced a significant improvement in its energy security during the decade following the first oil shock, although perhaps not to the same extent as did Britain, France, or even Japan. By 1985, the country had reduced its oil consumption by some 25 percent over 1973, from 150 mtoe to 113 mtoe. While oil remained West Germany's single most important energy source, its share of PEC had fallen by a comparable amount, from 56.5 to 42.2 percent, over the same period, and outside observers expected it to drop below 40 percent in the next few years (Commission 1988, 52).

Oil consumption had been largely replaced by nuclear energy and natural gas. The former saw its share of PEC rise dramatically, from just 1 to more than 10 percent, and by 1985, some 30 percent of West Germany's electricity was being generated in nuclear power plants (IEA 1987, 207). Meanwhile, the use of natural gas increased by more than 50 percent. Also important in facilitating the reduction in Germany's oil dependence, however, was the arrest of the previous inexorable decline in coal consumption. Whereas the government had forecast in 1973 that coal's share of PEC would fall by more than half by 1985, from more than 30 to just 14 percent, coal consumption remained roughly constant in both relative and absolute terms over the next 12 years (figure 7.1) (Bundesregierung 1973; BP 2013).

At the same time that West Germany had diversified its energy mix to place much less reliance on oil, it had also diversified the foreign sources of its oil and natural gas. By the mid-1980s, the North Sea was the single leading source of German oil imports, accounting for approximately one-third (IEA 1986, 254). Domestic production and imports from the Netherlands and the Soviet Union

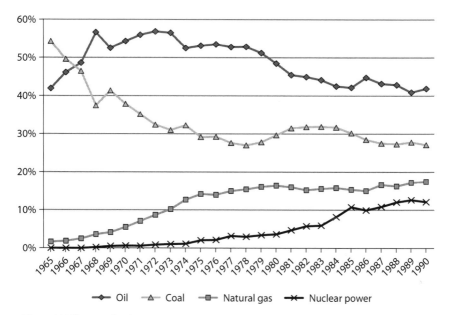

Figure 7.1 Shares of primary energy consumption in West Germany, 1965–90.
Source: BP, Statistical Review of World Energy (various years).

each met 25 to 30 percent of the demand for gas, with the remainder provided by Norway (IEA 1986, 256; Commission 1988, 54).

More generally, West Germany experienced a significant improvement in its overall energy efficiency. In 1985, PEC was only slightly higher than it had been at the time of the first oil shock. Yet despite the resulting economic setbacks, the economy had grown by approximately one-quarter, resulting in a decline in energy intensity of about 20 percent. Contributing to this improvement was a decrease in the fuel consumption of new automobiles of some 23 percent between 1978 and 1985 (Commission 1988, 53).

Not least important, West Germany had accumulated substantial stockpiles of oil and coal. In 1977, it exceeded the IEA oil stockpiling requirement of 90 days of supply and by 1980, the system contained the equivalent or more than 100 days of consumption. The government had also established hard coal reserves of 10 million tonnes, or about an eighth of annual production (DOE 1977, 130; Deese and Miller 1981, 193–94; Schmitt 1982, 152).

LIMITATIONS

Despite these important measures of progress, there were also important limitations to how much West Germany's energy security had improved. Although oil consumption and imports had fallen, oil use was increasingly concentrated in the transportation sector, where ready substitutes were not available. Because more and more natural gas was coming from abroad, moreover, the country's overall dependence on energy imports had not declined, remaining at around 55 percent. As noted above, moreover, gas imports from the Soviet Union were already expected to increase to about 30 percent of total demand when the third contract went fully into effect (Commission 1988, 54; Jochem et al. 1996, 71).

Meanwhile, other domestic sources of energy production were increasingly constrained. The heady days of the nuclear energy program appeared to be over. No new plants were ordered after 1982, and delays continued to hamper the completion of some that were under construction. As a result, there was little reason to hope for any significant future increase in generating capacity (Schmitt 1982, 151 and 155; Price 1990, 95). At the same time, the use of coal to produce electricity was increasingly constrained by environmental concerns. In 1983, the government adopted stringent emissions standards for coal- and oil-fired plants with capacities of more than 50 MW, and additional regulations governing installations down to 1 MW capacity were adopted in 1986 (IEA 1986, 257–58 and 263; Commission 1988, 55).

There was also reason to be concerned on the demand side. Since 1982, the rate of increase in energy efficiency had slowed significantly, while the consumption of transportation fuels had increased regularly, despite the success in improving the fuel economy of new cars. Following the change of government in 1982, the new Christian Democrat-led coalition reduced the budget for energy conservation research and development by more than 70 percent (Commission 1988, 53, 56, and 59bis).

Finally, West Germany made little progress in securing access to foreign oil supplies. Although the government had pursued direct negotiations with producer countries through VEBA, these efforts proved less successful than had originally been hoped. Likewise, DEMINEX made only a small contribution to German-controlled oil production. In 1981, for example, it produced just 2.4 million tons of oil, the equivalent of just 2 percent of West German imports of crude oil and petroleum products that year (Kemezis and Wilson 1984, 99; Hatch 1986, 39 and 46).

CONTRIBUTIONS OF GOVERNMENT POLICY

Both these improvements and their limitations can be attributed in no small part to West Germany's response to the oil shocks, or perhaps more precisely the lack thereof, given the government's generally laissez-faire approach to energy policy.

As one observer noted, "West Germany has relied almost exclusively on higher prices, allowing all its energy prices to rise to world market levels" (Schneider 1983, 325; see also IEA 1986, 253).

On the supply side, the government took some steps to incentivize and subsidize private firms, but with the principal exception of coal, it left investment decisions largely up to the private sector. There was no direct government involvement in the domestic production of nuclear power and natural gas, and its participation in international oil ventures remained quite limited. Even the government's strong support for and protection of the coal industry did little more than arrest the sector's previous steep decline in output. The government did, however, play a major role in ensuring the accumulation of substantial oil reserves.

On the demand side, market prices and taxes did much to discourage oil consumption. Beyond that, however, it took the government several years to appreciate the potential for promoting conservation and energy efficiency more generally, and its investments in that area remained relatively modest (Maull 1981, 297; Meyer-Abich and Dickler 1982, 242). According to one estimate, the government spent between six and nine times as much on increasing the energy supply as on improving efficiency during the 1980s (Jochem et al. 1996, 92). Thus as much as 60 percent of the sharp decline in German energy consumption between 1979 and 1982 was the unintended result of reduced economic activity rather than policy (Hatch 1986, 53). Perhaps the biggest success of government policy was in the residential space heating market, where the response of homeowners to the incentives offered to undertake conservation measures was strong (IEA 1983, 167).

German Responses to Energy Insecurity in the 2000s

In Germany, concerns about energy security also came abruptly to the fore in the mid-2000s.[3] As in Britain, moreover, they revolved primarily around the country's dependence on imports of natural gas, although the specific sources of those concerns were different. Following the oil shocks, Germany had successfully limited oil consumption, but its use of natural gas had grown since the early 1970s and had continued to increase after unification, reaching nearly one-quarter of PEC in 2005. At the same time, Germany now relied on imports to meet more than 80 percent of demand, and a growing percentage of them came from a single country, Russia.

For years, however, German leaders evinced little concern. Indeed, the Red-Green coalition (1998–2005) negotiated a phaseout of nuclear power by the early

2020s, which could increase the country's dependence on gas to generate electricity, and in 2005, the government backed an agreement by German and Russian companies to build a new gas pipeline that would directly link the two countries via the Baltic Sea. Thus it required the January 2006 gas conflict between Russia and Ukraine to propel energy security to the top of the political agenda. The decision by the Russian natural gas concern Gazprom to cut off supplies to Ukraine over an unresolved commercial dispute called into question Russia's reliability as an energy supplier. Although the recently elected Black-Red coalition (2005–9) had already decided to conduct a comprehensive review of energy policy, the gas crisis gave considerable impetus to the process.

The energy policy review culminated in the adoption of a comprehensive integrated energy and climate program in the second half of 2007. The program included 29 separate measures primarily aimed at increasing energy efficiency and the use of renewable forms of energy that could reduce Germany's dependence on natural gas imports. When fully implemented in 2020, these measures were expected to increase the contributions of renewable energy to electricity production to 25–30 percent while raising energy productivity by 3 percent per year.

As ambitious as the new program may have been, however, it placed much more emphasis on fighting climate change than on enhancing Germany's energy security. Although greater energy efficiency and the use of renewables could reduce energy imports, the program contained few if any measures primarily intended to address Germany's dependence on imported natural gas in particular. The same was true of the comprehensive energy concept adopted in 2010 by the subsequent Black-Yellow coalition, elected in 2009, which established an even more ambitious goal for renewable electricity—35 percent by 2020—and called for reducing PEC by 20 percent over the same period.

At the beginning of the following decade, it appeared that Germany might just achieve these ambitious goals. In 2011, the share of electricity generated by renewables passed the 20 percent mark, and although the economy was strong, PEC was down 8 percent from its 2005 level. Partly as a result of these positive trends, natural gas consumption had dropped nearly 10 percent over the same time period, rather than rising. In the longer term, however, the success of German energy policy—and Germany's energy security—would require overcoming several major challenges, including the rising cost of renewable electricity, the substantial indirect costs of adapting the power system to accommodate an ever larger share of renewables, and the limited options for achieving Germany's ambitious energy efficiency goals.

Background

As the twenty-first century dawned, Germany's energy situation looked much like it had in the mid-1980s. PEC was up by just 23 percent, notwithstanding Germany's unification, which increased the population by one-quarter, and substantial growth in GDP per capita. Oil's share of PEC had continued to fall, albeit more slowly, to under 40 percent. Coal's share of PEC had resumed its earlier decline and also dropped, to 26 percent, reflecting efforts to rationalize the industry and reduce government subsidies, although coal still accounted for more than half of electricity production. Meanwhile, natural gas had continued rise as a share of PEC, to about 22 percent, although its use was largely confined to the industrial and residential sectors. According to the IEA, the government had not wanted Germany to become highly dependent on gas for electricity generation. Instead, the second largest source of electricity after coal was nuclear energy, with 19 operating plants generating some 30 percent of Germany's power supply (IEA 2002a, 10, 27, 66–67, and 111).

Dependence on foreign energy sources remained Germany's Achilles heel. In fact, the overall share of energy from imports had been gradually rising since the 1980s, reaching about 60 percent in 2020, not including uranium. Not only was most oil still imported, but imports now provided for nearly 80 percent of Germany's gas consumption, and most of those came from just three counties: Russia, Norway, and the Netherlands (IEA 2002a, 25 and 76; BMWi/BMU 2006).

Mitigating this import dependence, however, were several factors. One was the much greater liquidity of the world oil market, which had largely eliminated fears of potential shortages. Another was the limited reliance on oil and gas for electricity production. A third was the substantial stockpiles of both oil and gas that had been accumulated. Although the oil stockpiling law had been amended to end the stockholding obligations for producers and the government had sold its crude oil reserves, the stocks maintained by the EBV contained the equivalent of more than 100 days of net imports. Likewise, the gas industry maintained the equivalent of about 90 days of consumption in storage capacity. Finally, interruptible contracts covered some 10 to 20 percent of all gas consumption, potentially facilitating a substantial cutback in use in an emergency (IEA 2002a, 27 and 59–60).

Nevertheless, two long-term developments were placing increasingly tight constraints on German energy policy, with potential implications for energy security. One was growing concern in Germany about climate change. In 1995, the government had adopted a national target of lowering CO_2 emissions by 25 percent from their 1990 levels by 2005. And under the Kyoto protocol, Germany agreed to reduce its total greenhouse gas emissions by 21 percent by the end of the first commitment period (2008–12), although this goal was not formally ratified by the parliament until 2002 (IEA 2002a, 38). To this end, Germany put forward a comprehensive National Climate Protection Program in 2000, although the government had begun to take concrete steps as much as a decade before.

One set of actions sought to promote greater energy savings and efficiency. In 1996, German industry entered into a voluntary agreement with the government to reduce its CO_2 emissions by 20 percent by 2005 below 1990s levels, and this target was raised to 28 percent in 2000 in a new agreement that also aimed to lower overall greenhouse gas emissions by 35 percent by 2012. During this same period, the auto industry committed itself to producing new cars that reduced fuel consumption by 25 percent by 2005 (IEA 2002a, 38–39).

In 1999, the government introduced a new "ecological tax" on motor and heating fuels and electricity that was gradually raised over the next several years. The tax was partially intended to promote energy conservation, although its revenues were used to reduce the social security contributions of companies and their employees. Thus the structure and level of the tax did not clearly reflect the environmental externalities of energy use, and it contained a number of exemptions (IEA 2002a, 29 and 44; IEA 2007a, 34). Finally, in the early 2000s, the government adopted new regulations governing the energy efficiency and emissions of buildings, with the goal of reducing consumption in new buildings by 30 percent, and it established a program to provide financial support for efficiency improvements in existing buildings (IEA 2002a, 39 and 49–50).

Even more noteworthy were Germany's efforts to promote renewable forms of energy, which helped the country to become a world leader in the field (see Runci 2005). As early as 1991, the government adopted the Electricity Feed Law (Stromeinspeisungsgesetz), which obliged power companies to buy all the electricity generated from renewables in their distribution areas at up to 90 percent of the average retail price (IEA 2002a, 93; IEA 2007a, 68). This initial effort was replaced in 2000 by the Renewable Energy Law (Erneuerbare-Energien-Gezetz, or EEG), which expanded and improved on the original provisions. The EEG provided more certainty by guaranteeing rates for a prolonged period (typically 20 years) and using fixed feed-in tariffs based on the cost of each technology, so that those that had previously been prohibitively expensive, such as solar photovoltaic (PV), would now be competitive. It also ensured that renewable installations would have access to the grid as well as transmission and distribution networks (BMWi 2001, 17; IEA 2002a, 94–95; IEA 2007a, 68–69).

The goal of the EEG was to increase the share of renewables in electricity generation to 12.5 percent by 2010. To this end, Germany also adopted several other complementary programs. A 1999 program provided low interest loans for the installation of PV equipment on private homes. A 2000 law guaranteed a minimum feed-in price for electricity produced by CHP plants operated by public utilities (IEA 2002a, 9–10, 92–96).

The other constraining long-term development was heightened public opposition to nuclear power. The environmentally focused German Green Party was in part an outgrowth of the nuclear protests of the 1970s, and it was joined in opposition to nuclear power by the SPD following the Chernobyl disaster of 1986, which gave a tremendous boost to the antinuclear movement. The SPD quickly proposed to phase out nuclear power over 10 years, and by the early 1990s, some of the major utilities had declared their unwillingness to invest in the development of new nuclear power plants as long as a national consensus on the future role of nuclear energy did not exist (Price 1990, 90–94; McGowan 1996a, 8–9; Jochem et al. 1996, 68).

Thus it came as no surprise when one of the first decisions of the Red-Green coalition that took power in 1998 was to move forward with a nuclear phaseout. Negotiations led to an agreement between the government and the energy utilities (signed in 2001) that was enshrined in amendments to the Atomic Energy Act in 2002. Under the terms of the agreement, the 19 operating power plants would be shut down when they reached an average age of 32 years, with the last going off line in the early 2020s (IEA 2002a, 10, 35, and 113).

Both of these developments had potentially significant implications for Germany's energy security. The phaseout meant that Germany would have to turn to substitutes to generate the 30 percent of electricity provided by nuclear power, while the need to reduce CO_2 emissions greatly circumscribed how much Germany could rely on coal, which already accounted for some half of power production. Thus, given the embryonic state of renewables, it seemed likely the demand for natural gas—and gas imports—would grow substantially. A 2001 *Energy Report* estimated that if Germany were to reduce CO_2 emissions by 40 percent in the energy sector by 2020 while phasing out nuclear power, the share of electricity generated by gas would rise to 54 percent, and gas would constitute more than 40 percent of the total energy supply, even assuming robust growth in renewables (BMWi 2001, 42 and 47; IEA 2002a, 23–24). And much of this additional gas would almost certainly have to come from Gazprom (IEA 2007a, 8, 36–37, and 154).

German Concerns about Energy Security

Despite Germany's already high level of dependence on energy imports and the prospect of even greater dependence on imports of natural gas in the future, especially from Russia, neither German leaders nor the public showed much concern about or paid much attention to energy security in the early 2000s (Umbach 2006). For example, none of the key actions areas defined by the "energy dialogue" conducted by the government in 2000 explicitly concerned security (IEA 2002a, 19 and 22). Likewise, the 2001 *Energy Report*, which was based on the outcome of the energy dialogue, made only general references to the goal of security of supply (BMWi 2001).

Yet the warning signs continued to mount. By the mid-2000s, Germany produced only 18 percent of the gas it consumed, and of the remainder, as much as 37 percent came from Russia, which also accounted for some 44 percent of gas imports (BMWi/BMU 2006; EIA 2006b; IEA 2007a, 96–97). Over time, moreover, the amount of gas produced at home was expected to decline, while, according to one authoritative estimate, the share of imports from Russia could rise to more than 70 percent by 2020 (Kemfert and Müller 2007). Because almost all of Germany's natural gas imports arrived via fixed pipelines, moreover, they could not be easily replaced in the event of a supply disruption (Müller 2007).

Still, as late as 2005, German political leaders evinced little concern about energy security in general and Germany's growing import dependence in particular. Indeed, just 10 days before the September federal election that year, Chancellor Gerhard Schröder presided over the signing of an agreement by German and Russian companies to construct a new gas pipeline underneath the North Sea that would connect Germany directly to Russian gas supplies. Scheduled for completion in 2010, the pipeline would have an initial capacity of 27.5 bcm per year, half of which would be dedicated to Germany, with plans to later double its size (Götz 2005). As the International Energy Agency subsequently warned, "Germany should be wary that its security of gas supply depends to a large degree on the activities of one company, Gazprom. While the planned Nord Stream pipeline will help increase diversity of supply routes, it will inevitably further increase German dependence on Russian gas and, therefore, on Gazprom" (IEA 2007a, 114).

Shortly after the election, the new Black-Red coalition government of the center-right Christlich Demokratische Union Deutschlands / Christlich-Soziale Union (CDU/CSU) and the center-left SPD demonstrated a somewhat greater interest in energy policy. The coalition agreement called for the development of a new comprehensive energy policy concept (*Gesamtkonzept*) and devoted nearly four pages (out of some 125 pages in the section on "Areas of Action") to energy (Bundesregierung 2005b). Likewise, energy policy was one of 20 or so topics addressed by the new chancellor, Angela Merkel, in her first general policy address (*Regierungserklärung*) on November 30, 2005 (Bundesregierung 2005a). Perhaps most significantly, Merkel announced that she would be convening a national energy summit early the following the year.

Even then, however, energy security remained a low priority. The energy sections of the coalition agreement and the chancellor's remarks seemed motivated much more by concerns about climate change and high energy prices (and their implications for economic competitiveness) as well as deep differences within the coalition over the future of nuclear power. Whereas the agreement contained detailed and sometimes ambitious goals for renewable energy (increasing the share of renewables in electricity production to at least 20 percent and in total energy consumption to at least 10 percent by 2020), energy efficiency (doubling energy productivity by 2020 compared with 1990), and energy research, it contained no mention of Germany's import dependence, and it explicitly ruled out any revision of the phaseout agreement and resulting amendments to the Atomic Energy Act (Bundesregierung 2005b; IEA 2007a, 27).

Rather, it was not until early 2006 that energy security finally, and rather suddenly, became the focus of a broader political debate. The trigger was the gas dispute between Russia and Ukraine that broke out at the very beginning of the year. Much of the natural gas that Germany and other EU countries bought from Russia passed by pipeline through Ukraine. Unable to reach a new agreement with Ukraine on natural gas prices and transit fees, the dominant Russian natural gas concern Gazprom cut exports to Ukraine on January 1. Although Gazprom continued to feed gas intended for its other European customers into the pipeline, many European countries immediately experienced a sharp drop in the supply of gas.

Given that the disruption occurred during the middle of winter, when gas demand for space heating is high, European leaders responded with alarm and sought to broker a quick resolution of the dispute. Although Russia was widely portrayed in the media as the culprit, German leaders were careful not take sides. Nevertheless, the episode had the effect of focusing German minds on the question of energy import dependence and supply security (*Versorgungssicherheit*) (Umbach 2006; Umbach 2007).

Although pressure in the trans-Ukraine pipeline was quickly restored to normal levels, a series of similar events continued to raise questions in Germany about the reliability of Russian energy supplies over the following year. On

January 22, 2006, for example, mysterious explosions ruptured the pipelines supplying Russian gas to Georgia. And the next January, following a dispute very similar to the one involving Ukraine, Russia cut off oil exports to Belarus, affecting 20 percent of Germany's oil supply.[4]

Overview of German Policy Responses

By chance, the principal vehicle used to address the energy security concerns raised by the 2006 gas crisis was the energy summit that Merkel had announced the previous November, which evolved into an extended process. What turned out to be only the first of three summits was held in April. In attendance were the chancellor; the federal ministers for economics and technology, the environment, education and research, and foreign affairs; and 21 high-level representatives from the energy sector, industrial and private consumers, unions, research institutes, and environmental and other NGOs. Security of energy supply, along with energy prices, climate protection, modernization of the electricity supply, innovation and technology, and international cooperation, was among the half dozen central themes discussed at the summit, and perhaps the most prominent of them (IEAa 2007, 28).[5]

The participants agreed to hold a second summit in the fall, and in preparation for that meeting, they established three working groups that would present reports in September on (1) international aspects of energy policy, (2) national aspects, and (3) research and energy efficiency. The three working groups duly submitted their initial reports as planned, and as might have been expected, the reports devoted considerable attention to the issue of security of supply.[6] The second energy summit was held in October. The discussion at the summit was largely limited, however, to the results of the first and third working groups, reflecting deep divisions within the working group concerned with national aspects of energy policy. The chancellor announced that there would be a third summit the following spring, and the working groups were asked to prepare a further set of reports.[7]

The three working groups issued their final reports at the very end of the spring, and the third and final energy summit was held in July 2007, somewhat later than originally intended.[8] Perhaps most striking about the results of the summit was the shift in emphasis that had occurred since the previous gathering. Although the summary of the proceedings reiterated the usual three general goals of energy policy—security of supply (*Versorgungssicherheit*), economic efficiency (*Wirtschaftlichkeit*), and environmental sustainability (*Umweltverträglichkeit*)—now the focus was on the creation of an "integrated energy and climate program."[9]

As Chancellor Merkel stated, "With this program, we are taking on the central challenge of the 21ˢᵗ century, climate change."[10] In contrast, the importance of addressing concerns about security of supply appeared to have diminished. Instead, the conclusions reached at the summit suggested that Germany would be able to enhance its energy security through its efforts to combat climate change. Certainly, few if any potential conflicts between these two goals were acknowledged.

This renewed emphasis on climate change—and the corresponding deemphasis of energy security—persisted through the end of the year. In August 2007, the cabinet approved a 29-point Integrated Energy and Climate Program (Integriertes Energie- und Klimaprogramm, or IEKP).[11] And in December, the cabinet adopted a detailed report on the plans for implementing each element of the program and proposed a comprehensive package of 14 laws and regulations to that end, with the promise of a second, smaller package of additional measures to follow in the spring (Bundesregierung 2007; BMU 2007a; BMU 2007b).

As foreshadowed by the July summit, the IEKP placed much more emphasis on reducing greenhouse gas emissions than on enhancing Germany's energy security. Although many of the proposed measures could reduce Germany's energy imports, the purportedly comprehensive program contained few if any measures specifically intended to address Germany's dependence on imported oil and natural gas per se. Thus, by the end of 2007, the concerns about energy security that had initially animated the policy review process had largely dissipated.

Domestic Policy Responses

Apart from references to promoting the export of German energy technology and active participating in the formation of the European energy policy framework, the essential fields of action (*Wesentliche Handlungsfelder*) identified at the July 2007 summit lay primarily in the domestic policy arena. Indeed, these elements had already been largely spelled out by the environment minister in an April 2007 statement to the Bundestag on the government's climate policy.[12] Likewise, the IEKP emphasized what Germany could do at home.

One important area of action would be increasing energy efficiency. Doing so would allegedly allow Germany to reduce the consumption of all forms of energy, and electricity in particular. The July 2007 summit had reaffirmed the goal expressed in the November 2005 coalition agreement of doubling energy productivity by 2020, and Working Group 3 presented a comprehensive action program containing dozens of concrete recommendations for doing so. Subsequently, the IEKP identified 30 different ways to reduce energy consumption, and the December package contained five detailed proposals for new legislation, regulations, and guidelines in this area. Among these were an amendment to double the share of electricity produced from high-efficiency CHP plants from 12 to 25 percent by 2020, an amendment to the Energy Savings Ordinance to increase the efficiency of new buildings by an average of 30 percent, and a 1.4 billion euro per year program to rehabilitate old buildings (BMU 2007b; IEA 2007a, 56).

A second important area would be the promotion of renewable forms of energy, to which most of the rest of the package was devoted. Among the specific actions were amendments to existing laws that would incentivize and facilitate the development of offshore wind farms and the use of biogas as well as the adoption of a new Renewable Energies Heat Act. When fully implemented in 2020, these measures were expected to increase the contributions of renewable energy to electricity production from 13 percent to 25–30 percent and to space heating to 14 percent. The IEKP would also amend the Biofuels Quota Act to increase the share of biofuels in the transportation sector from 6.6 percent to 20 percent by volume (and 17 percent by energy content) by 2020, and the Bundestag quickly moved to raised the interim biofuels obligations for 2010 and 2015 (Bundesregierung 2007; IEA 2007a, 35, 66, and 72; BMU 2007b).

Progress in each of these areas would allow Germany to reduce significantly its greenhouse gas emissions, thereby contributing directly to the goal of preventing or minimizing climate change. At the same time, it would presumably reduce Germany's dependence on imports of oil and natural gas as well, thereby enhancing the country's energy security. But these additional potential benefits were not explicitly spelled out. Indeed, the IEKP was silent on several issues of particular relevance to the security of energy supplies. For example, it contained no measures intended to diversify the sources of Germany's natural gas imports, such as promoting the construction of LNG terminals. Nor was there any discussion of the possible contribution of nuclear power to energy security (as well as to reducing greenhouse gas emissions). There would be no revisiting of previous nuclear phaseout decision.

External Policy Responses

Foreign policy considerations were largely absent from the final energy policy documents agreed to in late 2007. Only 3 of the 29 key points in the IEKP had any bearing on the external aspects of energy policy, and these emphasized the goals of climate protection and energy efficiency rather than energy security. Nevertheless, since early 2006, the Foreign Office had made substantial efforts to establish the importance of having an energy foreign policy (*Energieaußenpolitik*), especially as a means for promoting energy security. Thus the biggest question raised by the final summit and the resulting IEKP was how well Germany's energy foreign policy would be integrated into the overall Gesamtkonzept, or whether the internal and external (environmental and security, respectively) dimensions of energy policy would proceed largely on separate tracks.

The new energy foreign policy had several more specific aims of relevance to energy security. One was to help diversify the foreign sources of energy and transit routes so as to reduce Germany's vulnerability to supply disruptions, whether politically motivated or not. Another was to promote a stable and open investment climate in supplier countries so as to increase the production and export of natural gas and oil in particular. And a third was to promote greater energy efficiency and the use of renewable energy sources in other countries so as to reduce the global demand for fossil fuels (Sander 2007).

How were these aims to be achieved? The overall approach propounded by the Foreign Office was to promote greater dialogue among producer, consumer, and transit countries. As Foreign Minister Frank-Walter Steinmeier argued in early 2007, "Energy security must be organized in a cooperative way—globally and in Europe" (Steinmeier 2007a). He lamented that in this sensitive area, there was what he saw as a lack of adequate dialogue. To remedy this deficiency, he repeatedly called for the creation of a system of cooperative energy security modeled after the Organization for Security and Co-operation in Europe, which would help to build mutual understanding and trust (Steinmeier 2007a; Steinmeier 2007b). In addition, Germany was a strong backer of the creation of the global International Renewable Energy Agency (IRENA) and the Desertec Industrial Initiative, which sought to develop the tremendous renewable energy potential of North Africa.

Germany's foreign energy policy also had a strong EU component. One purpose would be to reinforce and promote the domestic goals with regard to climate protection, energy efficiency, renewables, and market liberalization through action at the regional level. But the EU was also seen as a crucial vehicle for pursuing the desired dialogues with other consumer, producer, and transit countries. The Foreign Office very much supported the development of a European external energy policy that would enable the EU to speak with a single voice.[13]

Perhaps needless to say, of particular concern in German energy diplomacy were relations with Russia. Echoing the theme of German efforts to overcome the division of Europe during the cold war, "change through rapprochement" (*Wandel durch Annäherung*), Germany policy toward Russia was described as "change through increased interdependence" *(Wandel durch Verflechtung)* (Wagner 2006; Kempe 2007). Steinmeier placed considerable emphasis on inducing Russia to ratify the Energy Charter Treaty, which would provide a solid, market-based framework for reciprocal trade and investment. That failing, because of Russian resistance, he also strongly supported the negotiation of a new EU partnership and cooperation agreement with Russia that would contain a substantial chapter on energy grounded in the principles contained in the unratified charter (Steinmeier 2006a, 2006b, 2007b). Another German goal was to help Russia to make improvements in energy efficiency, thereby potentially greatly reducing its domestic demand for natural gas and freeing up more gas for export.

Overall, however, it seemed unlikely that all these international activities could make as large a contribution to German energy security as those actions taken at home. In addition, Germany's external actions were not entirely consistent with one another. The government continued to support German energy companies in their efforts to gain direct access to Russia's substantial natural gas reserves through asset swaps, even though such unilateral moves were viewed by many as undermining the goal of establishing a unified EU position toward Russia (e.g., Kramer 2006; Bhadrakumar 2006). Likewise, the German government resisted certain aspects of the EU's efforts to liberalize and integrate the gas and electricity markets, such as ownership unbundling and the so-called "reciprocity clause," which would have prevented non-EU companies from controlling gas and electricity networks in the absence of an agreement allowing foreign access to assets in their home countries. Such moves were seen as reducing the political leverage and energy security of the EU as a whole (IEA 2007a, 114–15; Westphal 2008; Duffield and Westphal 2011, 178–80).

Evaluation of German Policy Responses in the 2000s
SUBSEQUENT DEVELOPMENTS IN GERMAN ENERGY POLICY

German energy policy experienced several more dramatic twists at the end of the decade and the beginning of the next, but its basic thrust, emphasizing energy efficiency and renewables, remained largely unchanged. Concerns about energy security were abruptly raised once more by an even more serious supply disruption as a result of a second Russia-Ukraine gas crisis in January 2009. This time, Russian exports to the EU member states were cut off completely for two weeks, and southern Germany, the region most dependent on imports of Russian gas, experienced a 60 percent reduction in deliveries (Westphal 2009, 22–24; Pirani et al. 2009, 4).

Then, the election of a new center-right coalition government in September 2009 consisting of the more nuclear friendly Christian Democrats (CDU-CSU) and Liberals (FDP) provided an opportunity to conduct a further review of

German energy policy. The coalition partners promptly declared that they were prepared to modify the nuclear phaseout, although they would maintain the ban on the construction of new power plants, and in November, they announced their decision to develop a new energy concept, to be completed by the following October (Merkel et al. 2009; Ackland 2010, 1).

The overall purpose of the resulting energy concept was to design and implement a long-term overall strategy for the period up to 2050, but it also included interim goals for the next 10 years. It established an even more ambitious 2020 target for renewable electricity of at least 35 percent—up from the 25–30 percent contained in the IEKP—and called for reducing PEC by 20 percent and electricity use by 10 percent over the same period. To achieve these goals, the energy concept identified some 120 individual measures, including doubling the rate of building renovation and a massive expansion of both solar and wind power generating capacity.[14]

Most of these proposed measures, however, simply built on efforts that had been included in the IEKP or had been started in earlier years, such as the EEG (BMU 2010; IEA 2013a, 9). Rather, the energy concept's most significant departure from existing policy was its proposal to slow the long-planned nuclear phaseout, extending the operating lives of Germany's nuclear power plants by an average of 12 years. It described nuclear energy as a bridging technology that would be needed until it was certain that renewable sources could meet the country's electric power needs (BMWi/BMU 2010). Nevertheless, the new concept, like the IEKP before it, played down Germany's dependence on imported gas and the energy security risks that dependence posed. There was no mention of gas imports or the Russia-Ukraine gas conflict of the previous year, nor was there any separate discussion of energy security. Instead, the concept emphasized the potential contributions to reducing greenhouse gas emissions and fighting climate change.

Less than six months after the publication of the energy concept, moreover, the March 2011 disaster at the Fukushima Daiichi nuclear power station in Japan prompted yet another reversal in Germany's nuclear policy. The government abruptly shut down eight of the oldest reactors and restored the goal of phasing out the remaining nine by 2022. In June 2011, the cabinet adopted a comprehensive energy package consisting of six laws and one ordinance intended to implement the provisions contained in the energy concept on an accelerated basis. As one subsequent report noted, "The faster withdrawal from nuclear power requires swifter implementation of the far-reaching measures defined in the Energy Concept to restructure the energy system" (BMWi 2012, 6 and 7). Thus Germany's future energy security would depend heavily on the success of its efforts to reduce energy consumption and promote renewable sources of energy, especially in the electric power sector, which collectively became known as the *Energiewende*, or "energy transition."

PROGRESS TOWARD GREATER ENERGY SECURITY?

As the next decade moved on, there were reasons to be optimistic. In 2011 and 2012, PEC was down nearly 10 percent from the middle of the previous decade and electricity production had remained stable, notwithstanding Germany's relatively strong economy. Natural gas consumption had declined by nearly 10 percent from its 2006 peak, and the share of gas imports from Russia dipped below 40 percent. Perhaps most remarkably of all, the amount of electricity generated from renewable sources grew rapidly, reaching 25 percent in 2013 (figure 7.2) (BP 2013; BMWi 2014, tables 4, 8, 17, and 22). The largest fraction of this came from wind power, but the contribution of solar energy was catching up. Indeed, from 2010 to 2012, installed solar photovoltaic generating capacity alone increased by more than 7 GW per year, bringing the total up to well over 30 GW (Buchan 2012, 16; IEA 2013a). Thus Germany seemed on track to meet its ambitious renewable power goal for 2020.

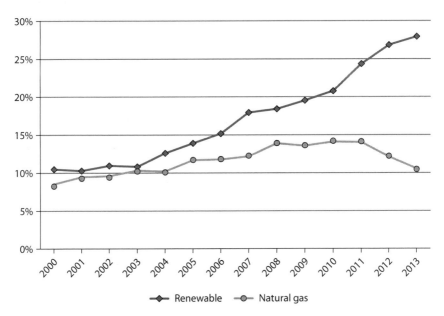

Figure 7.2 Shares of gross electricity production in Germany, 2000–2013.
Source: BMWi 2014, table 20.

A set of scenarios prepared by three independent organizations in 2010 just prior to the adoption of the energy concept, moreover, suggested that these positive trends were likely to continue. Even assuming no further change in policies, PEC was projected to decline by 14.4 percent and electricity production by 9.2 percent from their 2008 levels by 2020 while renewables would rise to 16.4 percent of PEC and to 33.7 percent of electricity over the same period. Meanwhile, and partly as a result, both gas consumption and imports were projected to drop by around 20 percent, and the contribution of gas to electricity production would fall to just 7 percent (EWI/GWS/Prognos 2010, A1-5, A1-9, and A1-12). Thus the measures contained in the energy concept and the energy package would presumably result in even bigger improvements in each of these indicators, and private companies were expected to increase Germany's gas storage capacity by 40 percent, from 20 to 28 bcm, between 2015 and 2025 (IEA 2007a, 109–110; Rümler et al. 2010). To an important extent, however, the short-term decline in gas consumption was a fluke due to the relatively high cost of burning gas to generate electricity in comparison with coal. The price of most gas imports was indexed to oil product prices and thus reflected the high world price of crude oil. Meanwhile, the explosion of shale gas production in the United States had driven down the price of U.S. coal exports to Germany, and the price of European carbon permits remained low. As a result, not only was less gas being used, but virtually no investments were being made in new gas-fired capacity, and Deutsche Bank predicted that as much as one quarter of the existing capacity would close by 2015. Nevertheless, forecasts made after the 2011 decision to restore the 2022 nuclear phaseout indicated that the share of power generated from natural gas would have to rise (EWI/GWS/Prognos 2011, 39; Katakey 2012; Mikulcak 2012; Buchan 2012, 23–24).

Nor was Germany likely find help at home with meeting its gas needs anytime soon. The CDU-FDP coalition had drafted legislation to enable the use of hydraulic fracturing, but had decided to postpone introducing the legislation until after the federal elections scheduled for 2013 because of environmental concerns. The election returned a new CDU-SPD grand coalition, however, which agreed to maintain the existing moratorium on fracking for the time being (Wacket and Busemann 2013).

REASONS FOR CONCERN

In the longer term, moreover, the success of German energy policy depended on overcoming several major challenges. One was the rising cost of the feed-in tariff scheme, which was driving up electricity prices as the volume of subsidized renewables increased. The total subsidy under the EEG reached 13.5 billion euros in 2011, 4 billion euros more than predicted as recently as 2007, and then more than 20 billion euros in 2013. At the same, large users of electricity were largely exempt from paying for the subsidy, placing most of the burden on individual consumers. As a result, the EEG surcharge per kilowatt-hour had grown from just 0.2 euro cents in 2000 to 3.6 euro cents in 2012, and then jumped to 5.3 euro cents in 2013. According to one estimate, the surcharge would account for nearly 23 percent of the average power bill that year (IEA 2007a, 70; BMWi 2012, 8–9; Buchan 2012, 8 and 16; Neubacher and Schroeder 2012; Mikulcak 2012; Euractiv 2012a; IEA 2013a, 116).

In a belated effort to stem the hemorrhage of funds, the government started to reduce the tariffs for PV annually and then abruptly cut them by 20 to 30 percent in 2012, to be followed by small additional reductions every month. It also placed a cap on total PV capacity of 52 MW. But the tariffs already paid to existing installations would not be touched (IEA 2013a, 124–25).

Also to be factored in were the indirect costs of adapting the rest of the electric power system to accommodate a substantial volume of intermittent and geographically dispersed renewable energy. To move renewable power from where it was produced to where it was most needed, Germany needed to build several thousands of kilometers of new high voltage power lines, equivalent to 10 percent of the existing grid, by 2020 at a cost of around 20 to 25 billion euros (Buchan 2012, 19; Mikulcak 2012; Hockenos 2012; Eddy 2012). An even larger investment would be required to upgrade many of the country's 870 distribution systems. And Germany would need a much greater amount of storage capacity and/or back-up gas or coal generating capacity—in addition to as much as 17 GW more of base load capacity by 2022 to replace nuclear reactors. But fossil-fuel generating capacity was becoming less and less profitable as ever more renewable power was fed into the grid, discouraging investment, while the potential for quickly expanding storage capacity, such as pumped storage using water, was very limited absent a major advance in a new technology such as batteries or hydrogen. Indeed, in 2013, power companies began to close thermal plants that had become unprofitable (Hoshi 2013). Even if everything went well, the total estimated cost of the necessary infrastructure expansion ran as high as $195 billion over the next 10 years, which would mean even higher electricity prices (BMWi 2012, 8; Hockenos 2012; Dohmen et al. 2012; IEA 2013a, 13–15).

Finally, grave doubts remained about the feasibility of achieving Germany's ambitious energy efficiency goals. The 2005 coalition agreement had called for a doubling of energy productivity by 2020 over the level of 1990, which would have required average annual increases of 3 percent. The 2010 Energy Concept had effectively reduced this target to just 2.1 percent per year, but even that seemed difficult to achieve. Between 2000 and 2008, the average improvement had been only 1.1 percent, and industry had already gone to great lengths to use energy more efficiency. Instead, the greatest potential for energy savings lay in the renovation of existing buildings, some three-quarters of which dated from before the first thermal insulation ordinance took effect in 1979. As of 2012, however, the rate of renovation was already lagging as the existing government incentives were not deemed sufficient to offset the high costs. Thus a 2012 study concluded that Germany would probably fail to meet its 2020 target of a 20 percent reduction in energy use and that it was even less likely to achieve a 10 percent cut in electricity consumption (IEA 2007a, 53–54; Buchan 2012, 28–30 and 33; Hockenos 2012).

Explaining German Responses to Energy Insecurity

As in most cases, material factors have set the stage for determining both the nature of Germany's energy security concerns and how Germany has responded to them. In contrast to the United States and Britain, but like France and Japan, Germany has not possessed large reserves of oil and gas, making it dependent on imports of those valuable energy sources. But in contrast to Japan, it has enjoyed relatively ready access to substantial amounts of piped gas from neighboring or nearby countries, though as we have seen, these too can be a source of insecurity depending on the reliability of the supplier. In addition, and in contrast to France and Japan, Germany has been favored with large stocks of domestic coal, which is a substitute for oil and gas in electricity generation and many industrial applications. Nevertheless, the use of coal has been increasingly constrained because of the relatively large amounts of pollution its combustion produces. A further limiting factor has been a paucity of locations for siting nuclear reactors because of Germany's high population density and the limited amount of cooling capacity in the form of either extensive coastline or large rivers without substantial concentrations of people nearby, which hampered the growth of the nuclear power industry (Lucas 1985, 237). Thus Germany represents an intermediate case in terms of resource endowments (see also Maull 1981, 297).

Societal Factors

In addition, several features of German society have been of potential relevance to energy policy and Germany's responses to concerns about energy insecurity in particular. These include several broad political dispositions, the most longstanding of which has been a strong market orientation. As one analysis observed in the 1970s, "One aspect of West Germany's energy policy that is frequently emphasized by all branches of political opinion is the determination to keep the fuel and power industry largely in the private sector, the only exception being subsidies to the coal industry as a matter of social policy. The operation of a 'free market' is constantly emphasized" (Fells 1977, 343). In the early 1980s, another study noted a "rigid market orientation" when energy efficiency is at issue, and in the 1990s, a group of German experts wrote that German energy policy was "based on the assumption that the free market is the best way to attain [its] goals" (Meyer-Abich and Dickler 1982, 241; Jochem et al. 1996, 57).

Beginning in the 1970s, this free market orientation was joined by a strong antinuclear sentiment, which was based on a combination of "fears over the potential damage that would be caused by a major accident in highly populated areas, the necessity for the safe storage of nuclear wastes over many centuries, and the potential military misuse in politically unstable countries" (Jochem et al. 1996, 67; see also Ackland 2009, 42). And in the 1980s, these worries broadened to include a range of other environmental issues relevant to energy policy, such as acid rain and climate change. As one study noted in the mid-1990s, "German concerns over the environment are arguably much stronger than in much of the rest of the EU" (Jochem et al. 1996, 81).

At the same time, German society has been marked by a number of powerful interest groups with a strong interest in aspects of energy policy. Most prominent among these have been the major energy companies, especially the gas and electric utilities. These companies have tended to be vertically integrated, with interests in production, transmission, distribution, and retail sales. They have also grown larger through mergers over time. Thus the number of gas companies that owned the major pipeline systems and accounted for most of Germany's natural gas imports declined from six to as few as four during the 2000s, while electricity generation and transmission have been increasingly dominated by just four supraregional companies that, by the mid-2000s, controlled about three-quarters of Germany's generation capacity and accounted for an even higher percentage of the electricity actually produced (IEA 2007a, 10, 30 and 127).

State Strength

These societal characteristics might not have mattered but for certain features of the German political system, which helped to give them expression in German energy policy. The overall effect has been to limit the autonomy and the capacity of the German state, which has found itself constrained by both types of social forces when it comes to both the formulation and implementation of energy policy.

Turning first to the question of autonomy, the state has often found itself pressured on both sides by strong public sentiments and the demands of powerful interest groups. On the one hand, institutions such as proportional representation and the party system have made elected officials highly attentive to public opinion. The electoral system, which results in relatively small swings in party representation in the Bundestag from election to election, has also militated against dramatic shifts in policy and usually results in coalition governments that depend on compromise. Likewise, parliamentary government ensures that the executive remains highly constrained by the majority in the Bundestag (Hatch 1986, 99 and 191–92).

On the other hand, the political system has also provided multiple access points for special interests to shape energy policy. The most influential of these have been the major energy companies, which have enjoyed a close relationship in particular with the Federal Ministry of Economics (BMWi). Indeed, as one analysis averred in the mid-1980s, "It is not possible for the federal government to make policy in the electrical or nuclear sectors without the consent of RWE [the largest energy company in West Germany]" (Lucas 1985, 260). And more recently, in the view of senior German energy policy analyst, Friedemann Müller, the BMWi has reflexively defended the interests of the energy industry under almost any circumstances (Müller 2005, 177–78; see also Müller 2007, 33; Westphal 2008, 105).

But the beneficiaries of interest group politics have not been limited to the major energy companies. Following the first oil shock, "even the symbolically important step of speed limits could not be taken" because of opposition by the drivers' association and the automobile industry (Maull 1981, 292). And even antinuclear protestors were "not at all locked out of the consultative opportunities to influence decision-making" in the 1970s (Marsh 1981, 148). Nor have the major energy companies always prevailed when their interests clashed with public opinion. In the 2000s, for example, the nuclear power producers enjoyed a brief victory when the Black-Yellow coalition decided to extend the nuclear phaseout, but it was unable to prevent the government's subsequent reversal in the face of heightened antinuclear sentiment following the disaster in Fukushima Daiichi (Mikulcak 2012). And as the renewable energy industries have grown in the last decade, they have become increasingly influential in policymaking circles (Bosman 2012).

Nevertheless, the state has still enjoyed some room for maneuver in the definition of energy policy and not simply been a mouthpiece for public sentiment or special interests. Thus, for example, it has been able to produce comprehensive energy programs and detailed policy proposals that shaped the energy sector, even if it could not override strong societal interests on a regular basis, for instance, the phaseout of the nuclear power program in 2000s. Along the lines of Ikenberry's "irony of state strength," the West German state was able to let higher international prices flow through the economy, incentivizing users to cut their consumption to the maximum extent.

These limits on state strength have also extended to the area of domestic capacity. One limitation has concerned the range of policy tools available to the state. Because of Germany's free market orientation, the government has generally not been inclined to play a direct role in the provision of energy. It has relied on the private sector to make the necessary investments. Instead, the government's role has been restricted to using taxes, regulation, market-based instruments (such as emissions trading), and subsidies for immature technologies that were not yet ready to compete in the market (IEA 2007a, 26–27). Nevertheless, as exemplified by the initial success of the nuclear program in the 1970s and the EEG in the 2000s, even such indirect methods have sometimes been able to generate substantial results.

A second important limitation is that individuals and environmental groups have been able to exploit the decentralized nature of the political system and the courts to slow or block the implementation of policies that they opposed. Under Germany's federal system, much power and authority resides at the Land (regional government) level. In particular, the Länder have been the primary planning authorities. Indeed, the federal government has not even had the power to impose military facilities on the Länder (IEA 1979, 71; Lucas 1985, 207). Meanwhile, the postwar German judicial system has emphasized the protection of individual rights against the power of the state (Fells 1977, 342; Hatch 1986, 139–40).

A prime example of these constraints in action was the throttling of Germany's nuclear power ambitions in the late 1970s, when "the government's view that rapid expansion was imperative did not guarantee swift implementation of the nuclear program" (Hatch 1986, 68). Under the Atomic Energy Act of 1959, the licensing of nuclear plants was done at the state level. Under West German law, moreover, any citizen had the right to object to the issuing of a license if he/she believed his/her personal rights or interests were affected, and a court decision could take years. Thus antinuclear forces skillfully exploited these opportunities to bring the nuclear program almost to a complete halt (Fells 1977, 341; Lucas 1985, 235–36; Price 1990, 85). In the words of Hanns Maull, this was "a sign that Germany can no longer rely on the traditionally powerful role of the state" (Maull 1981, 297).

A more recent if less dramatic example of this phenomenon has been the frustratingly slow expansion of the the electric power grid in order to accommodate the rapid growth of renewables. In a classic case of NIMBYism, few localities have been willing hosts to massive new power lines. In an effort to speed the process, the federal government was forced to pass two laws, in 2009 and 2011, that it was hoped, would centralize planning and shorten judicial review (Buchan 2012, 19–22).

Germany has possessed even less international capacity that could be used to promote its energy security. In the 1970s, West Germany sought to create a national oil company, VEBA, but had difficulty competing with the better established state-controlled enterprises and the multinationals (Kemezis and Wilson 1984, 99). Instead, perhaps its biggest assets have been its large energy market and its advanced technology, but the government's ability to control and manipulate access to these resources has been quite limited because of its broader commitment to an open market economy. In addition, Germany has been constrained by its history of militarism and aggression and by its postwar dependence on other Western states for its security and political legitimacy. Thus, following the first oil shock, West Germany did not aggressively pursue bilateral deals with Middle East oil producers, as did France, and instead exhibited substantial deference to the approach preferred by the United States, which emphasized greater cooperation among the consumer countries. And in the early 1980s, when West Germany sought firmer ties with Saudi Arabia as a means of ensuring access to oil supplies, it ultimately backed down from selling weapons to the Saudis in the face of arguments that they might be used against Israel (Kemezis and Wilson 1984, 66).

Paradoxically, some of these constraints came into conflict following the Soviet invasion of Afghanistan, when the desire to support the new U.S. focus on the Persian Gulf collided with Germany's limited military capabilities and domestic opposition to participation in any out-of-area operations (Bax 1981, 39). The West German pursuit of energy security by expanding and diversifying its foreign natural gas supplies also led to tensions with the United States over the sale of advanced pipeline technologies to the Soviet Union.

In the 2000s, a united Germany relied mainly on diplomacy to promote its energy security. As a result, progress depended heavily on the cooperation of its dialogue partners, especially Russia, which was often not forthcoming. Perhaps the most significant achievements took place in the area of EU energy policy, but here too Germany sometimes found itself at odds with its European partners (Duffield and Westphal 2011).

Nonfactors

In closing, it is worth noting factors that have not significantly shaped German responses to energy insecurity. One might expect, for example, party politics to have had a major impact. In fact, however, the record reveals a high degree of policy continuity during the periods despite changes in the governing coalitions. Thus, the Christian Democrats made no major revisions when they took office in 1981, and the 2000s were marked by steady emphasis on renewables and energy efficiency as the principal elements of policy through three distinct coalitions. Prior to the reemergence of energy security concerns in the mid-2000s, the Red-Green coalition did orchestrate a fundamental change in nuclear energy policy, but the later Black-Yellow coalition never sought to repudiate it, just to extend the period of time over which the phaseout would be implemented.

Likewise, intragovernmental bureaucratic politics have at most influenced policy at the margins. During the 1970s and early 1980s, energy policy was under the exclusive purview of the BMWi. In the 2000s, however, responsibilities were more divided, with the Federal Ministry of the Environment (BMU) now in charge of renewables policy and nuclear safety issues, while the Foreign Office made a bid to be fully involved in the international aspects of energy policy. Each department, moreover, sought to develop or maintain competencies in the areas that fell outside its formal mandate, and this natural organizational competition for influence was sometimes reinforced by ministers with strong personalities and higher political ambitions. A possible effect of the outcome of these struggles was the short life of energy security at the top of the policy agenda, reflecting the failure of the Foreign Office to gain a greater voice in the shaping of energy policy. But that result is also readily explained by developments in the external environment, including the quick restoration of gas supplies following the 2006 conflict and heightened societal concerns about climate change following the release of the Intergovernmental Panel on Climate Change's *Fourth Assessment Report* in early 2007.

Policy Legacies and Path Dependence

In the case of Germany, it is more difficult to argue that the policy choices of the 1970s greatly shaped the energy security concerns of later years and how Germany responded to them. The best example of this would be the government's support for increased imports of natural gas, including from the then Soviet Union. This policy set the stage for the concerns raised by the shortages resulting from the

Russia-Ukraine gas conflicts. At the time this course of action was embarked upon, however, the immediate benefits seemed to outweigh the possible future risks. Not only did importing gas from the Soviet Union provide an alternative to foreign oil, but it served the broader political purpose of helping to knit more closely together the two halves of Europe and thereby to overcome the division of Germany.

Moreover, it would be easy to exaggerate the resulting degree of energy insecurity. Gas still accounted for less than one-quarter of Germany's energy consumption, and Germany had accumulated substantial stocks. In addition, as the European gas market became more integrated, Germany could increasingly count on being able to access supplies from other sources, although integration also made Germany more vulnerable to a wider set of possible disruptions. Thus, outside a small circle of experts, concerns about gas supplies evaporated almost as quickly as they had arisen.

How Germany responded to the renewed energy security concerns of the 2000s was conditioned more by recent choices rather than the earlier responses to the oil shocks. One was the decision to phase out nuclear power, which took an important potential option off the table. But that decision merely reflected the country's deep and long-standing antinuclear sentiment, as revealed when the Black-Yellow coalition quickly reversed its decision to extend the phaseout following the disaster Fukushima Daiichi. Another was Germany's previous efforts to promote renewable sources of energy, especially in the form of the EEG, as well as its substantial experience with energy conservation measures. These experiences, rather than serving as constraints, provided a broad foundation on which to build a response that could reduce Germany's dependence on imported gas while helping the country to achieve its climate change goals.

Conclusion

Overall, Germany has addressed fairly effectively its principal sources of energy insecurity. Following the first oil shock, it was able to reduce substantially its oil consumption and thus its dependence on oil imports, primarily through the substitution of nuclear power and natural gas while arresting the previous decline in coal consumption. In the 2000s, it was able to prevent its dependence on gas imports from growing to dangerous levels. Indeed, the central elements of recent German energy policy—the aggressive promotion of renewable sources of energy and ever higher levels of energy efficiency—could, if fully implemented, bring about a marked improvement in Germany's energy security situation. And as the

2010s began, there were promising signs of progress, especially in the deployment of renewables, although the longer-term success of the policy would require overcoming several major challenges.

Arguably, Germany's energy security concerns have been less acute than those of some of the other major developed democracies, and it has possessed significant energy resources, located both on its own territory and nearby, on which it could draw. Nevertheless, the German state has played a not insignificant role in helping to produce these generally favorable outcomes. In terms of both policymaking autonomy and domestic capacity, Germany has occupied an intermediate position. The state has been constrained by broad public sentiments and powerful special interests, but it has still enjoyed some latitude to define energy policy. Likewise, government officials have generally had access to only a limited set of policy instruments. In particular, the state has played almost no role as an energy provider and has instead generally emphasized a market-based approach. It has contented itself with the use of taxes, subsidies, and regulations intended to influence the behavior of private actors. Yet these, applied consistently over prolonged periods of time, have often turned out to be effective tools, making considerable contributions to the achievement of energy conservation in the late 1970s and early 1980s and the rapid deployment of renewable energy in the 2000s. Only in the international realm has Germany lacked any significant state capacity to help promote its energy security goals.

CHAPTER EIGHT

Japan

Across-the-board Energy Insecurity

Japan . . . has been obsessed with the question of energy security for much of
the past century.

—Robert Manning, *The Asian Energy Factor*

Of all the states examined in this study, Japan has arguably experienced the most
acute concerns about energy security during the periods under consideration. As
in the case of France, these concerns have reflected Japan's profound lack of indigenous energy supplies, which has made Japan extremely dependent on imports. Since the 1970s, Japan has imported more than 80 percent of its primary
energy consumption (PEC), and the figure is closer to 95 percent if imports of
uranium are taken into account. Unlike France, however, Japan is geographically
separated from friendly and reliable sources of energy. All of Japan's energy imports arrive by sea, and usually from quite distant sources. Thus the International
Energy Agency concluded in a 2003 review, "Energy security issues are more critical in Japan than in most IEA countries owing to its isolated location and limited domestic resources" (IEA 2003, 7).

In view of the magnitude and breadth of Japan's energy security concerns, the
government of Japan has arguably made the most extensive efforts to improve the
country's energy security. These efforts have spanned almost the entire spectrum
of possibilities, from ensuring access to foreign sources of energy, to diversifying Japan's energy mix, to reducing energy consumption, to establishing stockpiles. And these efforts have yielded large dividends in terms of a significant improvement in Japan's energy security. In 1973, Japan relied on oil to meet nearly
80 percent of its PEC. By 2000, oil's share of PEC had dropped to well under half,
and it has continued to decline. Oil has been replaced by natural gas, nuclear
power, and to a lesser extent, coal. In addition, Japan has established one of the
world's largest stockpiles of oil and petroleum products in terms of days of supply. And the Japanese economy has boasted the highest levels of energy efficiency
in the industrialized world.

Although Japan's energy security has improved significantly, however, it remains perhaps the most precarious of the major industrialized countries. Japan

remains the most heavily dependent on energy imports, and along with the oil-producing United States, the most dependent on oil. In addition, many Japanese have voiced concern that so much of the oil comes from a single region, the Middle East, although given the relative ease with which oil and petroleum products can be traded, there are grounds for questioning just how much more vulnerable this makes Japan. At the same time, renewable sources of energy have still contributed only a small share of PEC. And Japan's 2010 plan to increase energy security placed considerable emphasis on the expansion of nuclear power, an emphasis that was called into serious question by the 2011 disaster at the Fukushima Daiichi nuclear power plant.

The 1970s: Japanese Responses to the Oil Shocks

The oil shocks of the 1970s hit Japan especially hard. In 1973, Japan was more dependent on oil, which accounted for nearly 80 percent of PEC, than any of the other countries reviewed in this study, and it relied almost entirely on imports to meet its oil needs. Nevertheless, it took Japan a number of years to formulate a response, but the policies that it did eventually adopt were very comprehensive. The government worked to establish substantial petroleum stockpiles. It took a number of measures to promote energy conservation and improvements in energy efficiency. It sought to reduce the country's dependence on oil by promoting the use of substitutes such as coal, natural gas, and especially, nuclear power. And it made strenuous efforts to secure Japanese access to oil and other energy resources from abroad.

To a significant extent, Japan's response to the oil shocks was successful. By 1985, Japan had reduced its oil consumption by nearly one-quarter while accumulating stocks equivalent to four months of supplies. Meanwhile, the Japanese economy, and especially Japanese industry, had become much more energy efficient. And Japan had struck direct deals with foreign governments for nearly half of the oil it imported. In other respects, however, Japan's energy security had not greatly improved. Although its energy supply was more diversified, it still depended on imports to meet most of its needs, and more than two-thirds of its oil still came from the Middle East. In addition, the buildup of nuclear power that Japan had counted on to reduce its oil and import dependence fell well short of the original goals.

Background

After World War II, Japan, like much of Europe, relied heavily on coal to meet its energy needs, and Japan produced much of the coal it consumed. As late as

1950, solid fuels, chiefly domestically produced coal, and hydroelectric power accounted for nearly 95 percent of the country's primary energy supply, and until the late 1950s, foreign exchange pressures limited Japan's ability to import oil. In 1958, however, Japan ended controls on crude oil imports just as the world price of crude oil began to decline. As a result, Japanese industry quickly switched over from coal to oil, because of the latter's growing abundance, versatility, ease of use, and relative cheapness. Thus oil surpassed coal as the chief energy source as early as 1961, and its share of Japanese primary energy consumption (PEC) grew steadily, from 38 percent in 1960, to 72 percent in 1970, to some 78 percent in 1973. Coal's share of PEC declined in parallel, reaching less than 16 percent in 1973. The bulk of the remainder was generated by hydroelectric power (Schneider 1983, 54–55; Fujime 1997, 179; EDMC 2010, 234–36).

As oil's share of Japan's PEC grew, so did Japan's dependence on energy imports. As late as 1958, some 70 percent of Japan's energy supply came from domestic sources, mainly coal and hydroelectric power. By 1973, however, some 90 percent of its energy was imported. Most of this was crude oil, although by then Japan was also importing three-quarters of its coal because of a rapid decline in domestic coal production after 1961 (Oshima et al. 1982, 87; Shibata 1983, 129–32; Schneider 1983, 55). Not only that, but virtually all of Japan's crude oil came from the Middle East, and some 80 percent of that was controlled by the major independent oil companies. The one Japanese company with significant overseas production, the Arabian Oil Company, supplied less than 10 percent of Japan's needs (Tsurumi 1975, 118; Bromley 1991, 184). Of the major economic powers, then, Japan was the most vulnerable to the shock that was to come.

One final fact about Japan's energy profile is worth noting. In 1973, industry alone accounted for nearly two-thirds of all energy consumption (ECCJ 2009, 3). Thus the biggest potential energy savings were likely to be found in that sector. This situation is not surprising, given that Japan's highest economic priority after the war had been to rebuild its industrial economy. Thus the overwhelming priority of Japanese energy policy before 1973 was to make sure that industry obtained all the energy it needed, which was increasingly oil and petroleum products, at the lowest possible price (Tsurumi 1975, 116; Vernon 1983, 82).

This single-minded focus had several consequences that would later have implications for Japanese energy security. It meant that the government preferred to keep the structure of the Japanese oil industry fragmented in order to promote price competition (Tsurumi 1975, 116). In addition, the government had no incentive to arrest the decline of the domestic coal industry, which because of its relatively small size and political weakness lacked the clout to obtain government support. And the absence of any strong domestic interests to protect meant that the government placed no restrictions on energy imports. Thus Japanese industries and other importers were free to obtain energy from the least expensive sources, even if this heightened the country's dependence on a single source of energy imported from a single distant region (Shibata 1983, 130 and 133).

This is not to say that the government did not intervene at all in the energy market. In the late 1940s and early 1950s, it had established rules to encourage the efficient and careful use of coal, which was then in short supply, but these had become increasingly irrelevant with the rise of oil (Dore 1983, 96). The 1962 Petroleum Industry Law authorized the Ministry of International Trade and Industry (MITI) to regulate the domestic petroleum industry, including licensing refineries and approving the acquisition of imported crude oil. In 1967, the Japan Petroleum Development Corporation (JPDC) was created to promote overseas exploration and development by Japanese firms through subsidies and other forms of financing. At least partly as a result, between 1968 and 1973, the number of Japanese firms engaged in overseas exploration rose from 8 to 49 and expenditures on exploration and development increased tenfold, from $44 million to $488 million (Krapels 1980, 63; Morse 1982, 264; Vernon 1983, 94–96). In general, however, the approach of the government to energy policy emphasized market competition.

Impact of the Oil Shocks

In these circumstances, it is not surprising that the first oil shock had a significant political impact in Japan (see Morse 1982, 259–60). Indeed, as Ronald Dore wrote, "It was the Japanese who invented the term 'oil shock'" (Dore 1983, 94). According to one estimate, the actual decline in Japan's oil supply was quite modest. Total petroleum stocks dropped from 58 to 46 days, but never ran out (Morse 1982, 259–60). Rather than shortages, the principal material impact was the result of the quadrupling of oil prices. As a result, "the damage incurred in Japan was deeper and wider than in most other countries because of her industries' heavy dependence on imported oil" (Shibata 1983, 135). Japan's gross national product, which had been growing at roughly 10 percent per year, stagnated for two years before returning to a more modest 5 percent average rate of increase. The higher oil prices also caused wholesale and consumer prices to jump by 25 percent in 1974, and they added some $15 billion per year to Japan's international payments (Shibata 1983, 129 and 135–36; see also Hatch 1986, 197, table 6; EDMC 2010, 216–19).

Nevertheless, perhaps the biggest impact of the first oil shock was psychological in nature. Indeed, one observer described the reactions as a "national nervous breakdown" (Dore 1983, 94). Not since the early postwar years had Japan seemed to face the prospect of serious supply shortages (Chrisstoffels 2007, 9). The Japanese were also shocked when the Arab oil producers initially classified Japan as an "unfriendly" country (Tsurumi 1975, 123). However unjustified this designation may have been, the result of the Arab oil embargo and production cuts was "panic over the possibility that a prolonged shortage of crude oil would destroy Japanese industry" (Tsurumi 1975, 113–14). Thus, one analyst later concluded, "the immediate impact of the crisis does seem to have been greater in Japan than in most other countries" (Dore 1983, 94). Henceforth, the security of the nation's energy supply, especially with regard to oil, would be a major policy consideration (Vernon 1983, 82).

This conclusion was reinforced by the second oil shock, which in some ways hit Japan even harder. In 1978, Japan had reduced oil's share of PEC by only a few percentage points, and total oil consumption was actually higher than it had been in 1973 (BP 2013). In addition, the major international oil companies still supplied some two-thirds of Japan's crude oil, and when the crisis struck, they diverted as much as 1 MBD of the oil destined for Japan. Japanese importers were forced to make up for their losses by buying oil on the spot market, which did much to drive up the world price. As in 1973, no major shortages materialized, but the experience heightened existing fears that Japan could not count on its oil suppliers, and the sharp jump in prices threw Japan's balance of payments back into deficit (Eguchi 1980, 264; Yorke 1981, 433–44; Krapels 1982, 56; Schneider 1983, 446; Kemezis and Wilson 1984, 87; Hatch 1986, 197, table 6). Thus the events of 1979 gave further impetus to Japanese policy development, and according to one source, energy security was the most important item in the 1980 *Report on Japan's Comprehensive National Strategy* (Jain 2007, 32; see also IEA 1981, 175).

Overview of Japanese Policy Responses

Japan's policy response to the first oil shock unfolded unevenly and somewhat slowly, given the magnitude of the shock, during the following years. In part, this may have been due to a lack of administrative capacity as well as the consensus-based approach to policy making that Japan has often followed since the war. The Agency for Natural Resources and Energy (ANRE) within MITI, which has played the lead role in the formulation of energy policy, had been created only months before the oil crisis began, in July 1973 (Samuels 1981, 144; Morse 1982, 258). Only following the initial shock, in 1974, did MITI create an Advisory Committee on Energy charged with developing national goals and the policies by which they might be achieved (Vernon 1983, 96). And the Advisory Committee for Energy issued its final report only in October 1978 (IEA 1979, 91). Finally, only in late 1980 did the cabinet approve comprehensive targets for Japan's 1990 energy mix (Suttmeier 1981, 114).

Nevertheless, all the major elements of Japan's policy response were in place by the time the second oil shock once again roiled energy markets in 1979. The Japanese response was rather comprehensive but can be summarized in terms of three main goals. The first was to reduce the country's high level of dependence on oil, both by promoting energy conservation and by developing alternative energy sources. Since Japan would still be heavily dependent on oil imports for some time, the second goal was to ensure access to foreign oil supplies by strengthening political and economic ties with existing producer countries, diversifying the sources of Japan's oil, and increasing the amount of oil produced by Japanese companies. And just in case another oil supply disruption were to occur, the third goal was to create substantial petroleum stockpiles in Japan (see, for example, Evans 1979, 43; IEA 1979, 91; Oshima et al. 1982, 88).

Domestic Policy Responses
EMERGENCY PREPARATIONS

Perhaps not surprisingly, some of the first actions taken by the government sought to address how Japan might cope with a future oil supply disruption. In 1973, during the first oil crisis, the Japanese Diet hastily passed the Petroleum Supply and Demand Adjustment Act, which gave the government authority to establish petroleum supply targets, to issue restrictions on the use of petroleum, and to impose allocation and rationing schemes, among other things (Morse 1981a, 43). During the initial phase of a crisis, the government would seek to rely on administrative guidance and voluntary restraint. But if those measures proved insufficient, the cabinet could resort to compulsory demand restraint measures for both large and small energy users (Morse 1981a, 43; Morse 1982, 263; IEA 2003, 70–71).

Equally important were the steps that the government took to stockpile oil for a possible future crisis. Even before the oil shock, in 1972 the private sector began a stockpiling program (JOGMEC 2009, 18). But this initial effort was reinforced in 1975, when the Diet adopted the Petroleum Stockpiling Act that went into effect the following year. This law required refiners, marketers, and other importers to maintain emergency stocks equivalent to 70 days of the previous year's domestic consumption, although the government offered loans on generous terms to private companies to buy or build storage facilities and to buy the oil needed to fill them. Meanwhile, the Petroleum Supply and Demand Adjustment Act empowered the government to order the companies to draw down stocks in a declared emergency (Evans 1979, 44; Krapels 1980, 63–64; Niquet 2007, 13).

Beginning in 1978, moreover, these burgeoning private stockpiles were complemented by government-owned stocks. The government created the state-owned Japan National Oil Company (JNOC) to establish a stockpile that would hold 30 million kiloliters (180 million barrels) of oil, or the equivalent of about 36 days of consumption. The target was later increased to 50 million kiloliters (300 million barrels), or more than half the size ever achieved by the U.S. Strategic Petroleum Reserve until the 2000s (Krapels 1980, 64; Krapels 1982, 52).

ENERGY CONSERVATION AND EFFICIENCY

The government's most extensive set of policy responses was in the area of energy conservation and efficiency (IEA 1981, 176; Dore 1983, 102–18; Ikenberry 1986a, 114). It raised taxes on oil and petroleum products. It provided information, advice, and financial assistance for taking steps to reduce energy consumption. It invested in basic research and development. It established regulations to promote energy efficiency in the energy-intensive industries. And through its industrial policy, it issued administrative guidance and provided support to promote a shift to less energy-intensive industries.

Equally important was what the government did *not* do. With just a few exceptions, such as kerosene for household use, it did little to shield business and consumers from the sudden rise in the cost of oil and petroleum products. Instead, it allowed the increased prices to be passed through with only modest delays. Thus the government relied heavily on the free market price mechanism to promote conservation (IEA 1979, 92; IEA 1981, 176; Krapels 1982, 52; Oshima et al. 1982, 88 and 99).

The government reinforced the impact of market forces by steadily increasing taxes on petroleum products. The gasoline tax, which stood at 28.7 yen per liter (y/l) before the oil crisis, was raised to 34.5 y/l in 1974, then 43.1 y/l in 1976, and finally to 53.8 y/l in 1979. The tax on fuel oil went from 15 y/l to 24.3 y/l over the same period. And the aviation fuel tax was doubled, from 13 y/l to 26 y/l. Only the tax on liquefied petroleum gas (LPG), which was widely used in homes, was never increased. And to top it all off, the government slapped a general 3.5 percent tax on petroleum in 1978 (Krapels 1982, 167, table 14; PAJ 2009, 62).

The government also took a number of steps that were directly aimed at increasing conservation. In a symbolic move, it declared February to be Energy Conservation Month as a way of raising public awareness of the issue. In 1978, it established an Energy Conservation Center to educate the public and provide technical advice for business. And that same year, it started the Moonlight Project for research and development of energy-saving technology, whose budget quickly grew, from roughly $10 million in first year to approximately $100 million in FY 1980 (IEA 1981, 177; Dore 1983, 97).

Most of the direct steps taken by the government to promote conservation, however, were focused on the industrial sector (IEA 1979, 92). This focus made a good deal of sense, since industry was responsible for as much as two-thirds of Japanese energy consumption in 1973 (ECCJ 2009), and the government had prior experience with managing coal consumption in factories.[1] Those industries that had grown the most rapidly and achieved the greatest degree of competitiveness in the postwar period were all energy intensive, because they had been able to take advantage of Japan's relatively low energy prices (Shibata 1983, 134). What had been a virtue in previous years, however, was now a threat to national security.

First, the government offered a number of financial incentives to industry. These included low interest loans for the purchase of more energy efficient equipment and accelerated depreciation allowances and property tax reductions for investments in the same (IEA 1979, 82; IEA 1981, 177–78; Dore 1983, 102–18; Shibata 1983, 140). Nevertheless, the International Energy Agency questioned whether the terms offered by the government were sufficient to induce the desired level of investment (IEA 1979, 92). Another scholar reported that "few of the managers I met were inclined to attribute any more than the most marginal importance to the tax and credit incentives offered by the government. . . . Prices were generally acknowledged to be the most effective determinant of the energy-saving effort" (Dore 1983, 139).

Instead, the potentially most important direct step taken to promote energy conservation in industry was the adoption in 1979 of the Law Concerning the Rational Use of Energy, also known as the Energy Conservation Act. Although the act did not set any specific targets for improvement in energy efficiency, it required all factories that consumed more than 3,000 kiloliters of oil equivalent per year to participate in an energy management program. They would have to appoint trained energy managers, who would seek to rationalize and improve the use of fuels and provide regular reports of energy use (Dore 1983, 97–100). The act also allowed the government to impose fines in the event of noncompliance, although it contained no direct sanctions for industries that failed to meet established standards (IEA 1980, 144). The potential for energy conservation was substantial, as the act covered 4,500 factories accounting for 80 percent of total industrial energy consumption (IEA 1981, 177–78).

Finally, the government sought to facilitate a shift from more- to less-energy intensive industry in Japan. For the most part, according to one contemporary analysis, the process was left to market forces, but government policy nevertheless played an important subsidiary role (Dore 1983, 117–18). It used a combination of administrative guidance and government-controlled investment funds to help steer the economy toward more knowledge-intensive, high-tech, high-valued-added industries. (Dore 1983, 117–18; Shibata 1983, 152; Ikenberry 1986a, 113–14; Bromley 1991, 185). Thus between 1970 and 1985, the share of Japanese exports accounted for by machinery and equipment rose from 46.3 to 71.8 percent, while the share accounted for by chemicals, metals, and metal products fell from 26.1 to 14.9 percent (Bromley 1991, 18).

In response to the oil shocks, the government did much less to promote energy conservation in the transportation, commercial, and residential sectors. The 1979 Energy Conservation Act authorized the government to set standards for building insulation and automotive fuel efficiency, among other things. For example, it established a fuel efficiency target of 30.1 miles per gallon (mpg) in fiscal year 1985. The law also provided some financing for home improvements intended to conserve energy (IEA 1980, 144–45; IEA 1981, 180; Dore 1983, 100–101). But the government did not impose binding regulations and relied instead primarily on voluntary measures in these other sectors as well as the testing and labeling of cars and appliances (Eguchi 1980, 274; Dore 1983, 100–101).

PROMOTING SUBSTITUTES FOR OIL

Conservation could only improve Japan's energy security so much. Thus the government also placed substantial emphasis on substituting other energy sources for oil, especially in industry and electric power generation. In 1980, for example, the cabinet adopted targets for reducing oil dependence by 1990 (from 75 to 50 percent) while increasing the share of the nation's energy that came from coal (from 12.9 to 17.7 percent), natural gas (from 4.0 to 10.2 percent), and nuclear power (from 3.6 to 10.9 percent) over the same time period (Suttmeier 1981, 114).

Here, too, the government relied heavily on market forces. For example, according to the IEA, substituting imports of liquefied natural gas (LNG), which had first arrived in the early 1970s, was a critical element in Japanese policy (IEA 1979, 93). But apart from providing some financial inducements, such as low interest loans, for the construction of LNG transports and receiving terminals, the government generally considered the private sector to be responsible for encouraging increased use of LNG (IEA 1981, 183; see also Morse 1982, 266; Shibata 1983, 142).

Nevertheless, the government did take a number of measures on the margins to speed the transition away from oil. Most directly, it banned the construction of new oil-fired power plants, except for those that had already been planned, and no new plants could be started after the mid-1980s (IEA 1979, 94; Eguchi 1980, 268; Shibata 1983, 139). At the same time, the government took several steps to encourage the use of coal in the industrial and electric power sectors. For example, it offered subsidies to offset partially the cost differential between coal and oil. It provided preferential loans for the construction of new coal-fired power plants, and it offered compensation to municipalities that agreed to accept them. It provided financing to cover the capital cost of large-scale centers for handling coal shipments. And it used subsidies and loans (approximately $300 million in 1980) to encourage the development of local coal supplies. Concluded an IEA study in 1981, "There is little doubt that the government is making considerable effort to meet its targets for increased coal use" (IEA 1980, 146; Eguchi 1980, 268; IEA 1981, 183–84).

The government's biggest push, however, occurred in the area of nuclear power. As the IEA noted, "Nuclear power is the first priority in reducing oil-based electricity generation" (IEA 1981, 185). It was the one area in which Japan could hope to become independent. The government set its sights on establishing a complete nuclear fuel cycle, including uranium enrichment, fuel fabrication, and reprocessing (Samuels 1981, 162), and it established ambitious targets for nuclear power production. One long-term energy plan produced by MITI in the mid- to late 1970s foresaw an increase to 65.8 million tonnes of oil equivalent (mtoe) by 1985 and 99.5 mtoe by 1995, or approximately 19 percent and 28 percent, respectively, of Japan's total PEC at the time (Eguchi 1980, 267).

Consistent with its overall free market approach, the government left it up to the private utilities to build the nuclear power plants. But the government helped to move the process along in three ways. In the short term, it sought to generate general public acceptance and to overcome local opposition to the construction of nuclear power plants. To this end, it used public relations campaigns and offered various forms of financial assistance and inducements to the residents of areas in which power plants would be located. Using this "cooperation money," it paid for public works, made grants to individuals and businesses, and subsidized electricity consumption, among other things. According to the IEA, the government provided about $300 million in compensation for each gigawatt (GW) of capacity to affected local municipalities (IEA 1979, 94; Suttmeier 1981, 121–23; IEA 1981, 185; Oshima et al. 1982, 97; Shibata 1983, 141; Samuels 1987, 246; Kohalyk 2008, 72).

The government also subsidized the nuclear power program directly. It constructed a pilot uranium enrichment plant and a fuel reprocessing facility at Tokai (IEA 1979, 94). And it devoted ever more substantial sums to research and development on nuclear technologies, including the construction of the Joyo experimental fast breeder reactor (FBR) as well as nuclear fusion. By the end of the decade, expenditures on nuclear research and development represented approximately 18 percent of all government spending on science and technology (IEA 1980, 147; Samuels 1981, 162; Suttmeier 1981, 112).

During the 1970s, much less attention was placed on renewable sources of energy, which were seen as only a much longer-term solution to Japan's energy security concerns. Nevertheless, the government did establish the Sunshine Project in 1974 to support research on alternative sources of energy, such as coal liquefaction and solar power. And in 1980, following the second oil shock, the Diet passed the Alternative Energy Act, which established the New Energy Development Organization (NEDO) to coordinate and finance research, development, and exploration of energy sources other than oil and increased the level of funding for those purposes (IEA 1980, 147; Morse 1981b, 11–12; Samuels 1981, 150 and 157; Dore 1983, 101).

External Policy Responses

The final important component of the government's response to the oil shocks was its strenuous efforts secure Japan's access to oil and other energy resources from abroad. These efforts began rather awkwardly when, in a state of panic, the government endorsed the position of the Arab oil producers in the Middle East conflict in the hopes that doing so would induce them to lift the oil supply restrictions placed on Japan, an action that has been described as "the first open break with American foreign policy in post-war diplomatic history that Japan had dared to make" (Tsurumi 1975, 124; see also Yorke 1981, 434; Morse 1982, 260). The acts of supplication continued over the next several months as first the deputy prime minister and then the head of MITI made hastily arranged visits to the Persian Gulf, offering billions of dollars in credits and investments (Yorke 1981, 436). For example, in January 1974, Japan agreed to lend Iraq $1 billion in return for 160 million tons of crude oil and products over 10 years (Schneider 1983, 255). Thus the oil crisis had "jolted Japan into assuming an independent diplomatic posture" (Tsurumi 1975, 126) and, in the words of one analyst, abandoning "the principal on which its postwar external relations had been based: the separation of economic and political matters" (Yorke 1981, 434).

Once the initial fears of shortages had subsided, however, the government developed a longer-term strategy that was set out in a July 1974 report by the Oil Group of the Overall Energy Investigation Council. The report recommended that the government both seek to conclude direct deals with the governments of oil-producing countries for the purchase of oil and provide support for Japanese companies seeking to obtain concessions exploration and development (Tsurumi 1975, 126). In addition, Japanese leaders also sought to repair the breach with the United States, readily attending the Washington Energy Conference, although they did not want to be too seen as too closely associated with the United States for fear of being associated with U.S. policy toward Israel, nor did they want to sacrifice their freedom to deal independently with oil-exporting countries (Schneider 1983, 261). Through this combination approaches, Japan would diversity and secure its supplies of crude oil from abroad on a long-term basis (IEA 1979, 93).

The first approach, subsequently termed "resource diplomacy," came to the fore in Japan's foreign policy (Yergin 1991, 654). It involved using a variety of means, such as financial assistance, investments, and technology sharing, to cultivate close political and economic relations with oil producers. By the end 1976, the government had signed economic and technical cooperation agreements with Iraq, Saudi Arabia, Iran, and Qatar, including an offer by MITI to finance one-half of a Mitusbishi investment in a petrochemical complex in Saudi Arabia. As a result of such efforts, Japanese investment in the Middle East soared (Vernon 1983, 96–97; see also Evans 1979, 44; Eguchi 1980, 273; Morse 1981a, 41).

Japan's resource diplomacy was not limited to the Persian Gulf. In 1978, the government signed a long-term trade agreement with China that would eventually result in imports of 300,000 barrels of oil per day, and the Japanese Export-Import Bank began to authorize a series of loans for the development of China's oil and coal resources. Likewise, it entered into an agreement with Mexico whereby the latter would export 100,000 barrels a day to Japan in return for a $500 million loan (Eguchi 1980, 272–73; Bromley 1991, 187; Kohalyk 2008, 56).

At the same time, the government stepped up its efforts, begun in 1967 with the creation of the JPDC, to support Japanese energy companies engaged in overseas exploration and development, setting a goal of having 30 percent of crude oil imports come from Japanese owned oilfields (Schneider 1983, 462). To this end, it aided searches for new sources of oil by providing low-interest loans, assuming certain risks, supplying information, helping companies negotiate with foreign governments through diplomatic channels, and equity participating with private interests in a number of oil development projects (Shibata 1983, 142; see also Tsurumi 1975, 120; Chrisstoffels 2007, 10–12). By the spring 1975, about 50 Japanese projects for oil and gas were operating abroad (Tsurumi 1975, 126). And in 1978, the government further increased the level of financing available for overseas exploration activities from 50 percent to 70 percent of the costs (IEA 1979, 93). That same year, the JNOC was created to assume the responsibilities of JPDC as well as oversee the national stockpile effort (Morse 1982, 264).

Government assistance was not limited to the search for oil but also extended to coal and natural gas, as part of the more general strategy of diversifying Japan's fuel mix and reducing its dependence on oil in particular. The government promoted direct Japanese investment in overseas coal development that would result in long-term supply contracts, for example, by providing guarantees for private loans (IEA 1979, 93; IEA 1980, 147; Eguchi 1989, 267–68;). Likewise, it supported the LNG industry through loans and investments for exploration and the construction of liquefaction plants in producer countries (Morse 1982, 266).

Evaluation of Japanese Policy Responses to the Oil Shocks
ACHIEVEMENTS

By the middle of the 1980s, Japan's energy security was much improved. In each of the areas targeted by government policy, noteworthy progress had been made. One area in which the progress could be easily measured was that of oil stockpiles. First the private and then the government stocks grew rapidly. By 1981, they covered slightly over 100 days of use, and by the middle of the 1980s, when the government stockpile was two-thirds full, they equaled more than four months of consumption. Although the majority of the stocks were still in private hands, the government could be expected to have unquestioned control over the supplies in an emergency (Vernon 1983, 114; IEA 1986, 321).

The increase in the stockpiles in terms of days of supply was abetted by an overall decline in oil consumption. Although the progress was not linear, by 1982, oil use had dropped by some 23 percent (to less than 210 mtoe) and remained at that level until late in the decade (figure 8.1). And although total energy consumption increased slightly over the same period, it was accompanied by a nearly 30 percent decline in energy intensity. Thus, while annual economic growth averaged around 4 percent from 1973 to 1985, primary energy consumption grew just 0.8 percent per year or less (IEA 1986, 335; Fujime 1997, 182). Overall, Japan's performance in energy conservation "was better than that of other IEA countries" (McKean 1985, 335).

The decline in oil consumption was accompanied by a major shift in Japan's energy mix. Oil's share of PEC dropped from 77.5 percent in 1973 to 56 percent

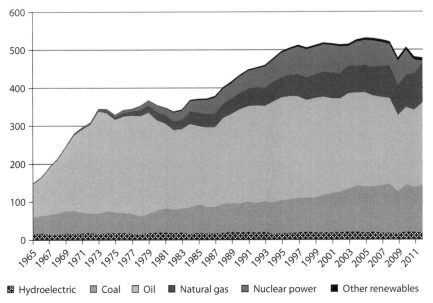

Hydroelectric   Coal   Oil   Natural gas   Nuclear power   Other renewables

Figure 8.1 Primary energy consumption in Japan (million tonnes of oil equivalent). *Source*: BP 2013.

in 1985 (BP 2013). Over the same period, the share attributable to coal increased from 15.5 to 19.9 percent, to natural gas from 1.5 to 9.6 percent, and to nuclear from 0.6 to 9.3 percent (figure 8.2) (Fujime 1997, 176; BP 2013). This rapid transformation was especially impressive, given the amount of new infrastructure that needed to be built. In 1973, the Japanese domestic energy system was almost entirely oriented toward oil (Shibata 1983, 141). Japanese companies had limited experience with nuclear power plants, which in any case were expensive to construct. And the growing use of LNG required large capital outlays for both the importation (liquefaction plants, transportation vessels, receiving terminals) and domestic distribution systems.

This shift in the energy mix could be seen in both the industrial sector, which also experienced a significant improvement in energy efficiency, and the electric power sectors. Industry's dependence on oil as a whole dropped from 61 percent of energy consumption to less than 48 percent, and the decline in some manufacturing areas was even more dramatic (EDMC 2010, 60). In the cement industry, for example, oil's share of energy dropped from 80 to 32 percent, while in the steel industry, it declined from 61 to 40 percent (Dore 1983, 120, table 3). Meanwhile, the use of oil to generate electricity plummeted, from nearly three-quarters in 1973 to just 25 percent in 1985. That year, it was surpassed by nuclear (27.2 per-

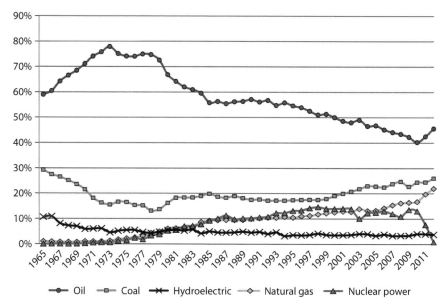

Figure 8.2 Shares of primary energy consumption in Japan, 1965–2012.
Source: BP 2013.

cent) as the principal source of electricity, with natural gas not far behind (21.7 percent) (Herberg 2004, 354; JAEC 2007, 10; Nishiyama 2008, 28). Only the transportation sector remained almost entirely dependent on oil.

There was also some improvement in diversifying and securing access to foreign oil supplies. By 1980, direct deals with foreign governments were generating 45 percent of Japan's crude imports (Vernon 1983, 97; see also Oshima et al. 1982, 92). Meanwhile, dependence on oil from the Middle East fell from 78.1 percent in 1973 to 68.2 percent in 1983 (Fujime 1997, 176; see also Chrisstoffels 2007, 12). In 1986, 7.1 percent of Japanese oil imports came from China (Bromley 1991, 187).

LIMITATIONS

Despite these noteworthy improvements, Japan's energy security situation still left much to be desired. Japan remained dependent on imports to meet nearly 85 percent of its energy needs, even when nuclear power is excluded. Virtually all oil and natural gas and about 85 percent of coal came from overseas. And even the decline in the share of oil originating in the Middle East offered little comfort, since such a high percentage still came from the region. Japan was less successful in increasing the share of imports produced by Japanese oil companies, which rose only from 8.5 percent in 1973 to 11 percent in 1984 (IEA 1986, 321).

Even the bilateral deals struck with various oil-producing states did not necessarily spare Japan from supply disruptions. In the mid-1970s, Iran accounted for as much as 20 percent of Japan's imports, much of which was lost during the Iranian Revolution (Yergin 1991, 688), and further disruptions occurred during the subsequent Iran-Iraq War. These unintentional interruptions in the flow of oil suggested that "the search for oil security based on bilateral interdependence might have become illusory" (Yorke 1981, 446; see also Krapels 1982, 59). "Japan was still vulnerable to oil cutoffs and increased prices despite its policy of accommodation" (Morse 1981a, 41).

In the meantime, this dimension of Japan's policy response to the first oil shock had generated not insubstantial political costs. The bilateral deals with national oil companies were at odds with IEA policies, and the government's efforts to cater to producing nation interests continued to strain relations with Japan's allies, especially the United States (Morse 1981a, 41; Morse 1982, 263). In particular, Japanese reluctance to go along with sanctions against Iran in 1979 and its insistence on buying Iranian oil despite the taking of U.S. diplomats as hostages prompted the United States to criticize Japan for its "insensitive" action (Morse 1981a, 42; Yorke 1981, 444).

As impressive as the buildup of nuclear power may have been, moreover, the actual results were far less than the government had hoped. The original (1970) nuclear program called for the creation of 60 gigawatts (GW) of installed nuclear capacity by 1985. Over time, however, this goal was repeatedly revised downward, first to 49 GW in 1975, then to 33 GW in 1977, and finally to only 30 GW in 1979 (Eguchi 1980, 269; IEA 1981, 185). Even then, in 1985, the actual amount of installed capacity stood at just 25 GW, and the government was facing growing public opposition to the nuclear program (McKean 1985, 336–37; EDMC 2010, 186).

CONTRIBUTIONS OF JAPANESE POLICY

Finally, some questioned how much credit for the progress that was achieved could be attributed to government policies. Some observers pointed to the generally modest nature of the government's response to the oil shocks. The government never developed a comprehensive energy plan (Eguchi 1980, 275), and in the view of one critic, "Japanese policies tended to be less than forceful and often remained mere declarations of intent, suggestions of alternatives, and unenforceable guidelines" (Shibata 1983, 139). In particular, the government was criticized for relying heavily on voluntary energy savings efforts by individuals and companies (IEA 1980, 145; Shibata 1983, 143).

Such criticisms, however, underestimated the important role that market forces alone could play in modifying behavior. And after some initial hesitation, the government decided to let prices rise as high as the market would take them (IEA 1981, 176; McKean 1985, 335). In addition, these criticisms overlooked the many concrete steps that the government took at home to increase Japan's energy security. It played a key role in the creation of petroleum stockpiles. It raised taxes on petroleum products. It banned the construction of new oil-fired power plants and provided support for the substitution of coal. And it smoothed the way for the nuclear power program by promoting public support. Finally, the critics failed to appreciate the enormous informal leverage that the government could exercise over the major industries through its system of administrative guidance (McKean 1985, 335).

Somewhat paradoxically, given its recent history of aggression, the state played an even greater role in the international realm, although the benefits of these efforts were more questionable. It struck out on its own diplomatically for the first time since World War II, at the risk of straining ties with its principal ally. It engaged actively in resource diplomacy with countries around the world. And it provided substantial financial support for Japanese energy companies engaged in exploration and production abroad. Perhaps all that was missing from Japan's external policies, though understandably so, was a military component to back up its efforts to secure overseas energy supplies.

Japanese Responses to Energy Insecurity in the 2000s

During much of the 1980s and the 1990s, energy security receded as an immediate driver of Japanese policy. Instead, energy market liberalization and environmental concerns came to the fore. In the mid-2000s, however, this situation was reversed and energy security once again became a central preoccupation of policymakers. As one observer noted, "New realities are pushing energy security to the top of the agenda in a way that has not been seen in more than two decades" (Evans 2006, 1).

This shift was most clearly manifested by the release in May 2006 by the recently (2001) created Ministry of Economics, Trade, and Industry (METI) of the *New National Energy Strategy* (NNES). The NNES described the new risks that Japan now faced, making the case that the focus of national energy strategy should be on energy security, even while acknowledging that environmental issues could not be neglected (METI 2006c, 10–11). It then established, for the first time, ambitious numerical targets to be obtained by 2030 for the purpose of promoting

Japan's energy security. Finally, it laid out eight specific programs for achieving those targets that ranged across nearly the entire scope of energy policy.

Despite the fanfare, Japan's response to these revived concerns about energy security unfolded along familiar lines. The government pursued a comprehensive approach that included additional emergency preparations, renewed efforts at energy conservation and efficiency, the promotion of domestic alternatives to fossil fuel imports, resource diplomacy, and increased support for Japanese companies engaged in developing energy sources abroad. The main innovations were an unprecedented level of support for renewable sources of energy and a new emphasis on cooperation with other Asian countries to reduce energy demand and increase regional supplies.

Over the following years, however, much of the government's attention shifted back to the problem of climate change. This rebalancing of goals was reflected in the government's 2010 Basic Energy Plan (BEP), which included even more ambitious targets for reductions in CO_2 emissions, renewable sources of energy, and especially, nuclear energy. Nevertheless, if achieved, these targets would have gone far toward improving Japan's energy security. But there were reasons to doubt their feasibility even before the disaster at Fukushima Daiichi the following year undermined the BEP's assumptions about nuclear power and forced the government to undertake an agonizing reappraisal of its energy strategy.

Background

As the new millennium dawned, Japan's energy security remained much improved over the early 1970s. Oil's share in the national energy mix had continued to decline, reaching around 50 percent in 2000. Oil had been replaced by nuclear energy and natural gas, consumption of which had both doubled since 1985. Nuclear power in particular now accounted for 30 percent of electricity production, and the amount of installed nuclear capacity had increased from under 25 to more than 45 GW, or just slightly less than in France (Fujii 2000, 67; EDMC 2010, 36 and 186; BP 2013).

Japan could also now boast the largest petroleum stockpile among the industrialized countries in terms of days of consumption and the second largest overall in absolute terms. In the late 1980s, the government had decided to increase its own stocks from 30 to 50 million kiloliters, a goal that was achieved in the late 1990s, although it simultaneously allowed private companies to reduce their required holdings from 90 to 70 days of supply. Thus in 2000, the country held more than 160 days of supply in both government and private stocks (Fujime 1997, 185; Kurumada 2002; EDMC 2010).

The news was not all good, however. Improvements in energy efficiency had stalled since the mid-1980s, contributing to an overall rise in primary energy consumption from 370 to 515 mtoe (BP 2013). Even oil consumption had risen in absolute terms, from 206 to 269 mtoe in 1996, before beginning a very gradual decline. Despite the much increased contribution from nuclear power, Japan also remained about 80 percent dependent on energy imports, with most oil, gas, and coal coming from abroad. Thus insofar as oil had been replaced by other fossil fuels, Japan's import dependence was not reduced, and the share of oil originating in the Middle East had steadily risen since the mid-1980s, reaching 87 percent in 2000 (EDMC 2010, 154; BP 2013).

In addition, the government's efforts to assist Japanese energy companies with exploration and development projects had borne little fruit. According to Japan energy expert Peter C. Evans, most government investments in Japanese oil development companies were failures. By the late 1990s, JNOC had accumulated $9.7 billion in bad debts, and most of the more than 100 Japanese oil development companies in which JNOC had invested were operating in the red (Evans 2006, 21). To top it all off, in 2000, the Japanese Arabian Oil Company lost its concession in Saudi Arabia, which had been the single largest source of oil produced by Japanese companies (Manning 2000, 151; IEA 2003, 63; Evans 2006, 14). Thus by 2001, so-called Japanese "equity" oil amounted to just 470,000 barrels per day, or the equivalent of only 11.5 percent of Japan's crude oil imports, well below the goal of 30 percent, despite some three decades of effort and tens of billions of dollars in outlays (IEA 2003, 61; see also Manning 2000, 152; Herberg 2004, 356).

Finally, there were three general energy policy developments in the 1990s and early 2000s that would constrain subsequent government efforts to promote Japan's energy security. In the 1990s, the government began to liberalize and deregulate the domestic energy markets. In 1996, it repealed the law restricting the import of refined petroleum products, and by 2002, when the 1962 Petroleum Industry Law was abolished, the refining industry and gasoline markets had been completely opened (Fujime 1997, 183; IEA 2003, 69–70; Eastcott 2004). Thus, according to one analyst, "the Western belief that as long as enough oil flowed toward the market place, security of supply would be guaranteed, became established in Japan" (Chrisstoffels 2007, 14). Liberalization of the natural gas market began in 1995 and that of the electricity market in 2000 (IEA 2003, 9–10). This process culminated in the early 2000s under the government of Prime Minister Junichiro Koizumi (2001–6), which sought to reduce state involvement in the economy and, among other things, decided to dissolve JNOC (Chrisstoffels 2007, 17–18; Kohalyk 2008, 76).

Second, protecting the environment assumed a high priority in Japanese energy policy during the 1990s (Fujii 2000, 61). In particular, climate change became a major concern, and some 80 percent of Japanese greenhouse gas (GHG) emissions (and 90 percent of CO2 emissions) originated from energy use (ECCJ 2009, 4). Under the 1997 Kyoto protocol, Japan committed itself to reducing its GHG emissions by 6 percent below the 1990 level (Arima 2001, 1–2).

To help achieve this goal, the government substantially revised the Energy Conservation Act in 1998. In the industrial sector, the law was extended to cover all factories with annual energy consumption of more than 1,500 kiloliters of oil equivalent, which roughly doubled the number of factories that were covered. In addition, the law was broadened to include passenger cars and other types of equipment, such as air conditioning units, that consumed large amounts of energy through the establishment of the Top Runner Program, which was introduced in 1999. The program, which initially covered 11 products, set energy efficiency standards to be met by a target year, usually four to six years in the future, that were higher than the performance of the current "top runner" in the same category. Of particular importance was the target it set for gasoline powered passenger cars of 15.1 kilometers per liter by 2010. This was the first time the government had established a binding fuel economy standard, although it was only done after consultation with and with the consent of the auto manufacturers.[2] The program also provided for the imposition of fines in the event that a manufacturer did not meet the standards (Arima 2000; Arima 2008).

Finally, the second half of the 1990s and early 2000s witnessed a sharp decline in public trust in nuclear power. To be sure, public concern had never been far below the surface and dated back at least to the Three Mile Island accident of 1979. A 1980 atomic energy white paper reported that the biggest obstacle to the construction of new power plants was fear by local residents about the adequacy of safety measures (Morse 1981b, 15).

But a series of accidents and scandals involving nuclear safety brought these concerns once again to the fore, resulting in "a sea-change in Japanese public attitudes about nuclear power" (Manning 2000, 157). In 1995, a sodium leak resulted in the indefinite shut down of the prototype fast breeder reactor (FBR) at Monju. Then a small fuel preparation plant suffered an accident in 1997 followed by an uncontrolled nuclear reaction two years later, which was described as the world's worst nuclear accident since Chernobyl (Kono 1997, 201; Jain 2007, 33). It resulted in a serious radiation leak that killed two employees and exposed many other workers and local residents to radiation. These alarming events were closely followed by revelations, in 1999, that the technical records of mixed plutonium-uranium fuel produced in Britain for use in Japan and then, in 2002, that the testing records for 17 Japanese nuclear reactors had been falsified (IEA 2003, 106; Herberg 2004, 355). Thus as the 2000s began, public opposition to the construction and operation of nuclear power facilities had reached its highest levels in decades (Fujii 2000, 69; Jain 2007, 33; Chrisstoffels 2007, 16).

Renewed Japanese Concerns about Energy Security

Japan's energy policy objectives have long been summarized as the "3 Es": energy security, economic development, and environmental sustainability (IEA 2003, 22). Nevertheless, concerns about energy security remained relatively muted during the 1990s, but they grew steadily during the early 2000s, reaching a crescendo in the middle of the decade. Several interrelated sets of developments contributed to the reemergence of these concerns (ANRE/METI 2006, 13). The first was a steady rise in the price of crude oil beginning in 2003. By the end of 2005, the price had more than doubled, and there seemed to be no end in sight. As the NNES noted, "It is highly possible that the current high price level of crude oil will continue for the medium- and long-term" (METI 2006c, 1).

One reason for this conclusion was a general tightening of the global structure of supply and demand. On the one hand, the demand for oil in China and other developing countries was growing rapidly. On the other hand, the previous era of low oil prices and restrictions on foreign investment in many oil rich areas had meant low levels of investment, resulting in less than optimal oil production capacity (ESSG 2006, 4).

To make matters worse, the potential for disruptions to Japan's oil supply and price shocks more generally seemed higher than it had been in many years. A combination of developments, including Islamic terrorism, the Arab-Israeli conflict, the Iraq war, and conflicts over Iran, raised concerns about the stability of the Middle East, whose problems were viewed as posing the greatest immediate threat to Japanese energy security (ESSG 2006, 3; see also JFIR 2006, 1; Toichi 2006, 4). But there were also worries about the vulnerability of oil shipments from the region, which passed through multiple choke points, to attacks by terrorists or pirates (Bustelo 2008, 9). And the recent influx of speculative money into the oil futures markets had added another potential source of price volatility (Toichi 2006, 2).

A second but related set of concerns stemmed from a resurgence of resource nationalism among energy suppliers. The early 2000s saw strengthening state control over energy resources and restrictions on foreign capital in oil- and gas-producing countries (METI 2006c, 4). This trend posed a direct challenge to

Japan's traditional policy of attempting to secure resources through direct investments in overseas energy development projects (Chrisstoffels 2007, 1). The year 2006 began and ended with particular stark examples of this trend. First, the Russian gas monopoly Gazprom cut off natural gas deliveries to Ukraine, which affected supplies in parts of Western Europe, and then the Russian government pressured the Japanese companies Mitsui and Mitsubishi as well as Shell to sell a majority of their shares in the Sakhalin 2 oil and gas project to Gazprom (Evans, 2006, 16; Bustelo 2008, 9).

Finally, Japanese officials were concerned about growing regional competition and conflict, especially with China, over energy resources. During the first part of the decade, Japan and China had both courted Russia aggressively, seeking to influence the route of a new oil pipeline to be built from Siberia (Evans 2006, 15–16). In addition, private Japanese energy companies were facing increasingly stiff competition from the state-owned Chinese oil companies in the Caspian and elsewhere (Evans 2006, 17–18). And Japan was engaged in territorial disputes with China and South Korea over underseas energy resources. Thus the managing director of the influential Institute of Energy Economics of Japan (IEEJ), Tsutomu Toichi, noted, "A tense relationship has already arisen between Japan and China due to competition for oil resources in East Siberia of Russia and gas resources in the East China Sea" (Toichi 2006, 4).

Moreover, Japanese officials feared that, in the competition for scarce energy resources, Japan would increasingly be at a disadvantage. With the rapid growth of China, India, and other Asian countries, Japan would "constitute a smaller and smaller share of Asia's supply and demand mix" (Evans 2006, 10). In particular, the government projected that Japan's share of the world LNG market would fall from 50 percent in 2002 to less than 20 percent in 2020. And as its share of the market declined, so would its buying power (METI 2006c, 7; Evans 2006, 11).

Overview of Japanese Policy Responses

These renewed concerns about energy security prompted a sweeping review of Japanese energy policy in the mid-2000s. As a study by the independent Japan Forum on International Relations concluded, "There has never been a time when a comprehensive energy strategy has been more sorely needed for a country as poor in energy resources as Japan" (JFIR 2006, 5). In June 2002, the Diet had passed a Basic Energy Act that called for the adoption by the cabinet of a basic energy plan that would be reviewed at least every three years. The first BEP had been duly prepared and adopted in 2003. Consistent with recent Japanese policy, it had placed roughly equal emphasis on the three general goals of energy policy.

Rather than wait until 2006 to revise the BEP, however, METI initiated a sep-arate ad hoc process outside the recently established formal channels for review-ing energy policy to address the growing concerns about energy security. In late 2005, its Agency for Natural Resources and Energy (ANRE) established two advisory committees to spearhead the process. A General Advisory Panel on Re-sources and Energy was tasked with drafting a new energy strategy while an En-ergy Security Study Group (ESSG) provided an independent evaluation of policies related to Japan's future energy security (ESSG 2006, 1; Chrisstoffels 2007, 43).

These efforts culminated in the publication in May 2006 of the NNES by METI. (The scheduled revision of the BEP was completed in October 2006 and approved by the cabinet in March 2007.) In contrast to the more balanced 2003 BEP, the NNES placed primary emphasis on the goal of energy security. As the document clearly stated, "It is essential for our country to establish the new na-tional energy strategy with focus on the energy security" (METI 2006c, 10; see also Evans 2006, 19; Sudo 2008, 151–52; Toichi 2008, 1; Fujita 2009).

The NNES laid out three general approaches for securing a stable energy sup-ply for Japan. The first was to establish a state-of-the-art energy supply-demand structure by improving energy efficiency and diversifying Japan's energy sources. The second was to strengthen Japan's resource diplomacy as well as international cooperation on energy issues. The third was to enhance the country's emergency response capabilities and measures (METI 2006c, 12).

Going further, the NNES established five specific targets "as common long-term goals to be achieved jointly by the government and private entities" by 2030 (METI 2006c, 14):

1. a further 30 percent improvement in energy efficiency (over the 2003 level)
2. a reduction in Japan's oil dependence from nearly 50 percent to less than 40 percent of the total energy mix
3. a reduction in the oil dependence of the transportation sector from nearly 100 percent to around 80 percent
4. the maintenance of nuclear power's share of electricity generation at 30 per-cent or its increase to 40 percent or more
5. an increase in the amount of oil produced by Japanese energy companies from 15 percent to around 40 percent of total oil consumption

In addition to their ambitious nature, these targets were remarkable in two re-spects. It was the first time in decades that the government had provided such numerical targets for the energy industry (Corcoran and Hosoe 2006). And they offered a much longer-term perspective than had the first BEP in 2003 and the triannual supply and demand forecasts previously prepared by the government, which typically looked ahead only 10 years.[3]

How were these ambitious targets to be achieved? The NNES went on to elaborate eight specific programs covering a wide range of actions for implementing the strategy. Most external observers concluded that, overall, the new strategy called for a greater role for the government and less reliance on the market in energy policy than before (Evans 2006, 2; Chrisstofells 2007, 47). Noted one analyst, the opinion that "the traditional position regarding energy policy which was based on market mechanisms should be transformed into policy approaches that are based on national strategic thinking" seems to have won a wide basis of support within the Diet and the Japanese civil service (Atsumi 2007, 30). And as the analysis of the ESSG concluded, "Energy security cannot be ensured only through the use of this [market] mechanism" (ESSG 2006, 3). The NNES contained frequent references to public-private partnerships and cooperation, and it stated that the government would "promote the creation of powerful energy companies with outstanding funding ability, technical capacity, and management ability" (METI 2006c, 32). As we shall see, however, the actual roles to be played by the government remained highly circumscribed. In particular, the government would continue to rely primarily on the use of taxes, spending, and regulation "rather than directly inserting itself in the market" (Hughes 2006).

Domestic Policy Responses

With few exceptions, Japan's responses to energy security in the 2000s largely followed and built upon the major tracks laid down in the 1970s: emergency preparations, energy conservation and efficiency, promotion of substitutes, especially nuclear power, resource diplomacy, and support for the overseas activities of Japanese energy companies. The principal departures from the past were an unprecedented level of support for renewable sources of energy and a new emphasis on cooperation with other Asian countries.

EMERGENCY PREPARATIONS

One specific program contained in the NNES concerned "Enhancement of the Emergency Response" (METI 2006c, 30–31). During the second half of the decade, the government began to make several improvements in its strategic stockpile system. The process leading up to most if not all of these steps, however, had begun even before the publication of the NNES.

As noted above, Japan had already accumulated a substantial petroleum stockpile, which stood at approximately 170 days of supply in 2006 (Toichi 2006, 7;

EDMC 2010). Despite its large size, this stockpile still left Japan vulnerable in a couple of areas. One of these was liquefied petroleum gas (LPG), which is distinct from natural gas. LPG accounted for about 4 percent of Japan's primary energy supply. It was used widely in homes and automobiles and could not be easily substituted for. About three-quarters of the LPG used in Japan was imported, and most of that came from the Persian Gulf. During the 1990–91 Gulf War, Japan's imports of LPG were disrupted, and the government immediately decided to establish a national stockpile of 1.5 million tons, or a little less than 10 percent of annual consumption. (The private sector was already required to stockpile 50 days of supply.) It took more than a decade to construct the first LPG stockpiling sites, but these finally began to fill in 2005, and by 2008 the stockpile was already nearly half full. The government planned to complete the LPG stockpile by 2012 (JOG-MEC 2009, 18–20; JOGMEC 2010, 7–8).

Another potential gap in the stockpile system concerned natural gas. Although virtually all of the natural gas used in Japan was imported as LNG, the government had established no natural gas stockpiles. One reason is that the sources of Japan's LNG were much more diverse, with less than one-quarter coming from the Persian Gulf. Nevertheless, some supplies had been disrupted in the early 2000s, and the NNES called for an assessment of the feasibility of creating an emergency response system for natural gas. Although discussions within the government began, as of mid-2010, no decision had been taken, in part because of a lack of resources; other stockpiling activities were accorded higher priority.[4]

The oil stockpile itself had other limits that the government sought to address. Less than one quarter of the combined government and private sector stockpiles consisted of petroleum products, such as gasoline; the remainder consisted of crude oil. In 2005, however, Hurricane Katrina disrupted U.S. refining operations, resulting in shortages of gasoline. Thus, in May 2006, an ANRE advisory committee recommended that the government establish its own stockpile for refined products, especially gasoline, diesel, and kerosene (PAJ 2009, 23). And in 2009, after three years of deliberations, the government decided to move ahead. Nevertheless, the program began very modestly, with the goal of accumulating just one day's worth of consumption of the designated products, beginning with kerosene (JOGMEC 2009, 18; PAJ 2009, 20).

ENERGY CONSERVATION AND EFFICIENCY

Several other programs outlined in the NNES addressed the target of increasing energy efficiency by 30 percent. This target seemed highly ambitious. Japan's energy intensity (PEC divided by GDP) had already declined some 37 percent since the first oil shock, and virtually all of this decline had occurred before the late 1980s. In addition, Japan's energy intensity was already just half that in the United States and the European Union (Arima 2008). Thus, presumably, there were few easy gains to be made.

One step that the government did not take this time, in contrast to the 1970s, was to raise energy taxes substantially. According to the Petroleum Association of Japan, total petroleum-related taxes were already equivalent to about $44 per barrel (PAJ 2009, 59). Instead, the government's approach was to build on successful existing policies that were explicitly aimed at increasing energy efficiency: the 1979 Energy Conservation Act and the 1999 Top Runner Program.

Since the introduction of the Top Runner Program, the Energy Conservation Act had been further amended in 2002 and 2005 in order to help Japan achieve its GHG reduction targets under the Kyoto Protocol. For example, it had been extended to cover factories in all industries (not just the original five), added several additional products to the Top Runner Program, and imposed obligations on cargo and passenger carriers (ECCJ 2009, 16–17). In addition, a target of 1 percent annual reductions in energy intensity was added in 2005.[5] But the law was revised even more extensively in 2008, at least in part to help achieve the targets contained in the NNES.

A major limitation of the original Energy Conservation Act was that it did relatively little to promote energy efficiency in the commercial, residential, and transportation sectors, in comparison with industry. For example, approximately only 10 percent of energy consumption in the commercial sector was covered, in comparison with about 90 percent in industry. And while energy consumption in the industrial sector had stayed roughly constant since 1973, it had more than doubled in the other sectors. To begin to address this limitation, the law was amended to cover all businesses, including service companies, chains, and convenience stores, that consumed more than 1500 kiloliters of oil equivalent per year. This modification was expected to bring approximately half of all energy consumption in the commercial sector within the ambit of the law. More than 14,000 factories and businesses would henceforth be covered.[6]

The other major policy initiative for the purpose of increasing energy conservation was a strengthening of the Top Runner Program. The program was extended to cover a total of 23 different mass-produced products, including 16 of the 17 products that were responsible for the most energy consumption in Japan (ECCJ 2009, 88). And the all-important target for passenger vehicles, which accounted for more than one-third of all energy consumption by such products, was raised. The original target of 15.1 kilometers per liter was achieved six years early, in 2004, so in 2006, a new target of 18.5 km/l by 2015 was established (Arima 2008; ANRE/METI 2009, 31).

PROMOTING SUBSTITUTES

Just as in the 1970s, the government also undertook measures to promote the use of alternatives to fossil fuels. As before, one of these alternatives was nuclear power. But in contrast to the 1970s, the government now also put substantial emphasis on so-called "new," or renewable, sources of energy.

As noted above, one of the five numerical targets established in the NNES concerned nuclear power, and the NNES contained a so-called "Nuclear Power Nation Plan" to achieve that target. The nuclear plan set a number of more specific goals (see also METI 2006a), the most important of which were

- increasing the number of nuclear power plants while replacing old reactors
- increasing the capacity utilization rate of existing nuclear power plants
- establishing a complete nuclear fuel cycle, including enrichment, reprocessing, and fuel fabrication, and beginning the use of mixed plutonium-uranium oxide (MOX) fuel in existing nuclear power plants
- making progress toward the commercialization of fast breeder reactors

These goals were reiterated in the "Nuclear Energy National Plan," which was prepared by the Nuclear Energy Subcommittee of the METI Advisory Committee in August 2006 and formed part of the revised BEP adopted by the cabinet in March 2007. Although the NNES did not specify any numbers, the IEEJ estimated that Japan would have to construct 10 new nuclear power plants and raise the average plant utilization rate to 88 percent by 2030 (Toichi 2006, 17).

The government viewed maintaining a substantial contribution from nuclear power as vital for several reasons (METI 2006a, 11–19). It would increase Japan's energy self-sufficiency and reduce the country's dependence on foreign oil in particular. It would reduce competition with China and India over resources. It would help Japan reduce CO_2 emissions. And it would provide greater stability and certainty to the electricity supply than renewable forms of energy. As the NNES concluded, "It is especially essential to maintain a certain level of dependence on nuclear energy" (METI 2006c, 12).

In 2006, Japan's fifty-fifth nuclear power plant had begun operation, giving Japan nearly 50 GW of generating capacity (IEA 2008, 162). Because of accidents, scandals, and earthquakes, however, the overall utilization rate was down to about 70 percent. Thus Japan was actually generating less nuclear energy than it had in the late 1990s and the first two years of the decade. And the nuclear power program was about to suffer a further setback the following year, when a major earthquake necessitated the shutdown of the seven reactors with nearly 8 GW of capacity at Tokyo Electric Power Company's (TEPCO) Kashiwazaki-Kariwa power plant.

Apart from such acts of nature, the government faced two major obstacles to achieving its nuclear power goals. The first was continuing low levels of public confidence in the nuclear reactor program. The 2002 scandal, also involving TEPCO plants, had been followed by an accident at another power plant in 2004 that resulted in the deaths of five workers and further revelations of serious deficiencies in inspection procedures (Buckley 2006). The lack of public trust in turn meant lengthy delays in obtaining approval to begin building new plants and in reopening plants that had been closed for safety inspections (IEA 2008, 175–76).

The second and related obstacle was reluctance on the part of the power companies to invest in the nuclear industry, given the high costs of construction.[7] Especially in an era of deregulation in which nuclear energy had to compete with other sources of power, delays in the licensing process and prolonged shutdowns because of public opposition made nuclear power a less attractive option. Beginning in the mid-1990s, the number of power plants under construction at any one time had varied between just two and four (METI 2006a, 42). And the shutdown of the Monju prototype FBR had prompted power companies to withdraw from participation in a project to build a demonstration model.[8]

The government proposed a number of measures to overcome these obstacles (METI 2006a). To restore public trust, it promised greater transparency and communication, especially with local communities where nuclear facilities were or would be located. It also would continue to provide substantial grants—of up to 6 billion yen—to localities hosting different types of nuclear facilities (METI 2006b, 4). To encourage greater private sector investment, the government would take a number of steps to reduce the costs and risks. It would streamline the inspection process in order to reduce the frequency and length of reactor shutdowns. It would seek to restart the prototype FBR as soon as possible and subsidize the costs of building a demonstration FBR that exceeded those of regular power reactors. For the longer term, it would seek to reduce the costs of decommissioning old reactors and intensify its efforts to develop a long-term solution for nuclear waste disposal. And it would continue to devote substantial sums to research and development (METI 2006a; METI 2006b; METI 2006c, 23–24).

Although the NNES set no numerical target for the introduction of new forms of renewable energy, it did contain two programs for promoting their use. The "New Energy Innovation Plan" in the NNES called for bringing down the cost of solar energy generation while promoting the production of solar, wind, and biomass energy. Both that and the "Transport Energy for the Next Generation Plan" targeted the increased use and production of biofuels as well as the introduction of vehicles that run on electricity and fuel cells.[9]

The government had already taken several steps to promote the use of new energies mainly due to concerns about climate change. Following the passage of the 1997 New Energy Promotion Act, the government set a new energy target (in 2001 and again in 2005) of 19.1 million kiloliters of oil equivalent (or 3 percent of PEC) by 2010 (IEA 2008, 152). Previously, it had established subsidies and tax deductions to encourage the installation of solar photovoltaic (PV) cells on residences and of all forms of new energy by other institutions. For example, the government would pay 100,000 yen ($7,000), or approximately 10 percent of the cost, for every kilowatt of PV installed on a home, and it would cover one-half to one-third the installation cost for businesses, local governments, and nonprofit organizations. (Somewhat puzzlingly, the government stopped the PV subsidy for a few years in the mid- to late 2000s before resuming it at a slightly lower level.) In 2010, these subsidies amounted to nearly 100 billion yen ($1 billion).[10] Of potentially greatest significance in the long term was the government's introduction in 2003 of a renewables obligation, or renewable portfolio standard (RPS), which would require electric power retailers to include an increasing share of energy from new renewable sources (not including hydroelectric power) in their sales volume. Under the original RPS, however, they would only have to reach the very modest target of 1.35 percent in 2010 (IEA 2008, 154–55).

Despite this modest start, by 2009, the government's goal was to increase the total share of renewable energy, including large-scale hydroelectric and geothermal energy, in the primary energy supply from 6 percent (2005) to 9 percent in 2020 and to 11.6 percent in 2030. To achieve this goal, the government sought to encourage in particular the installation of PV, with a target of increasing the amount of installed PV capacity more than twentyfold—from 2.1 GW in 2008 to 28 GW—by 2020. In late 2009, it established a buyback program for surplus PV electricity generated by residences and other entities, offering to purchase residential electricity at 48 yen per kilowatt-hour, or approximately two times the household cost of electricity (Ito 2010).[11] And in 2010, the government was considering extending the program, in the form of a feed-in tariff, to all small sources of electricity.[12] According to one estimate, a comprehensive feed-in tariff could increase electricity production from new sources by 40 to 50 billion kilowatt-hours or more (roughly 4–5 percent of Japan's current electricity output) in 10 years.[13]

External Policy Responses

The Japanese government's efforts to promote energy security in the 2000s also had a substantial international dimension, which consisted of three main components. The government sought to strengthen its efforts at resource diplomacy. It increased its financial support for Japanese energy companies engaged in upstream business activities, such as exploration and production. And it engaged in wide-ranging cooperative efforts with Asian countries broadly aimed at reducing their demand for fossil fuel imports.

RESOURCE DIPLOMACY REDUX

The NNES included a "Comprehensive Strategy for Security Resources" that called for extensive cooperation that was not limited to the energy sector with energy rich countries as a way of strengthening Japan's overall relationships with them. It also called for formulating a policy for supporting the acquisition of energy development rights by Japanese companies by, among other things, using financial and economic assistance to strengthen strategic ties with energy rich countries (METI 2006c, 26–27; see also Toichi 2006, 18).

In March 2008, in response to this call, the cabinet approved a set of *Guidelines for Securing Natural Resources*. The guidelines declared that "the government will support key resource acquisition projects by promoting active diplomacy and helping these projects to be strategically connected to economic cooperation measures, such as official development assistance (ODA), policy finance, and trade insurance." Thus Japan would use bilateral and multilateral diplomacy as well as various forms of foreign assistance to promote its energy security (METI 2008).

Not surprisingly, much of Japan's recent resource diplomacy has been focused on the Persian Gulf. Japan has established high-level bilateral and multilateral strategic dialogues with a number of Middle Eastern states. For example, in March 2006, Japan launched an initiative to establish a corridor for peace and prosperity, and the following spring, Prime Minister Shinzo Abe visited the region (Niquet 2007, 22). In addition, it has provided, through the Japan Bank for International Cooperation (JBIC), substantial loans and other forms of financial assistance to countries in the region, such as Qatar and the United Arab Emirates, for energy-related projects. One particular loan, to the Abu Dhabi National Oil Company, resulted in a five-year oil contract for 120,000 barrels a day.[14] At the same time, the government has encouraged investment by oil-producing states in Japan's downstream industries as a way of securing access to foreign oil. In the mid-2000s, for example, Saudi Aramco purchased a 15 percent stake in Showa Shell Sekiyu, and it later bought oil-storage facilities in Okinawa in return for preferential access in the event of an emergency (Hosoe 2005; Kohalyk 2008, 81)

The targets of Japan's new resource diplomacy have not been limited to the Middle East, however. In 2006, for example, Prime Minister Koizumi visited Kazakhstan, followed by the Minister of Economy, Trade, and Industry the following year. They offered substantial assistance and obtained in return an agreement on uranium supplies (ANRE/METI 2007; Bustelo 2008, 12). And in 2009, the Japan Oil, Gas, and Metals National Corporation (JOGMEC) signed a memorandum of understanding to engage in comprehensive cooperation with the Venezuelan state oil company, Petróleos de Venezuela, S.A. (PDVSA) (JOGMEC 2009, 7).

RENEWED SUPPORT FOR JAPANESE ENERGY COMPANIES

A second major thrust of Japan's recent international energy security policy has been to provide even greater financial assistance to Japanese energy companies engaged in overseas oil and gas exploration and development projects. The government had long provided equity investment, loans, and loan guarantees for this purpose. But the "Comprehensive Strategy for Security Resources" contained in the NNES called for increased levels of support (METI 2006c, 27; see also Toichi 2006, 18; Evans 2006, 21).

Various governmental organs have contributed to this effort. The most important of these has been the Japan Oil, Gas and Metals National Corporation (JOGMEC), which assumed JNOC's functions in 2004 as part of a broader rationalization process undertaken by Prime Minister Koizumi. JOGMEC has provided equity capital for exploration projects and asset acquisition, and liability (loan) guarantees for development projects (although unlike JNOC, it could not provide loans), and in 2007, the upper limits of what JOGMEC could offer were raised from 50 to 75 percent of total project costs (ANRE/METI 2007; JOGMEC 2009, 6–7). As of 2008, JOGMEC had invested a total of 66.9 billion yen in equity and had outstanding loan guarantees of 237 billion yen (JOGMEC 2009, 7–8).

JOGMEC was not the only official entity involved in these efforts. JBIC, Nippon Export and Investment Insurance (NEXI), and Japan External Trade Organization (JETRO) made contributions as well. JBIC offered loans in amounts ranging from hundreds of millions to billions of dollars for uranium mining projects in Kazakhstan as well as oil and gas projects in locations as diverse as Australia, Brazil, the Caspian Sea, and Sakhalin Island.[15] In addition, the government established a new type of trade insurance scheme to encourage businesses to venture into high-risk exploration projects. Under the program, the government would cover possible losses, up to the full value of the investment, incurred by Japanese companies due to improper interference by host governments or public organizations, and premiums were lowered by 50 to 70 percent (ANRE/METI 2007). Thanks in part to this assistance, the industry group Petroleum Association of Japan could boast in 2009 that Japanese firms were involved in 139 oil and gas development projects around the world, 73 of which had performed well in commercial production (PAJ 2009, 26).

REGIONAL COOPERATION ON ENERGY SECURITY

Finally, a separate program in the NNES was devoted to an "Asia Energy and Environment Cooperation Strategy" (Evans 2006, 20; METI 2006c, 29–30). This strategy was intended to contribute to Japan's energy security in two ways. First, by promoting energy conservation, renewable sources of energy, nuclear power, and clean energy technologies, especially for the use of coal, it would reduce competing demand for oil and gas in the region, but especially in China and India (Chrisstoffels 2007, 46). And by helping to build effective stockpiling systems throughout Asia, it would reduce the impact of future supply disruptions.

To achieve these goals, the government has engaged in a wide range of bilateral and multilateral cooperative activities. In this regard, China has been regarded as a particularly important partner, given its low energy efficiency (about one-tenth that of Japan), and since 2006, Japan and China have held a high-level annual energy cooperation forum. Japan has also pursued these goals in the annual energy minister meetings of 13 member "ASEAN + 3" (since 2004) and the 16 member East Asia Summit (EAS) (since 2007) (ANRE/METI 2010, 44). At the January 2007 EAS meeting, Prime Minister Abe proposed that each Asian country set energy-savings targets and establish action plans to achieve them, which was reflected in the Cebu Declaration on East Asian Energy Security, and he presented his idea of a Japanese "energy assistance initiative" (ANRE/METI 2007).[16]

In terms of concrete forms of assistance, since the mid-2000s, the Energy Conservation Center of Japan (ECCJ) has run two programs to promote energy conservation in the region. One is the dispatch of Japanese energy experts to conduct energy audits of factories and buildings and to provide on-the-spot training to local officials. This program currently involves about 80–90 visits of one to two weeks per year. In addition, the ECCJ offers training programs in Japan for policymakers and government officials in order to build capacity in other countries. This program currently involves several hundred visitors per year.[17] Finally, the government has been eager to help other Asian countries improve their emergency response systems (Hosoe 2005). In 2009, at Japan's initiative, the "ASEAN + 3" energy ministers agreed to start to formulate a roadmap to establish an oil stockpiling system (JOGMEC 2009, 19).

Evaluation of Japanese Policy Responses in the 2000s
SUBSEQUENT DEVELOPMENTS IN JAPANESE POLICY

During the years following the issuance of the NNES, more of a balance was re-stored in Japanese energy policy. Concerns about security of supply abated some-what, while those about environmental sustainability, especially climate change, returned to the fore, as occurred in Germany. In May 2007, Prime Minister Shinzo Abe announced an initiative, "Cool Earth 50," to reduce greenhouse gas emissions in Japan and globally.[18] In July 2008, the cabinet adopted a detailed "Action Plan for Achieving a Low-carbon Society" (Anonymous 2008). And shortly after taking power in September 2009, the new government led by the Democratic Party of Ja-pan announced an ambitious goal of reducing greenhouse gas emissions by 25 percent below the 1990 level by 2020 and then prepared a detailed bill on "Global Warming Countermeasures" that it submitted to the Diet the following March.[19]

At the same time, government officials began to fret about the international competitiveness of the Japanese energy industry. For example, Japan's solar cell industry, which had been the largest in the world, was surpassed in 2008 by those of Germany and China.[20] Then, in late 2009, a Japanese nuclear power plant man-ufacturer was outbid for a contract to build four nuclear reactors in the United Arab Emirates by a Korean-consortium that had never held an international con-tract (Coker 2009).

These shifts in emphasis were reflected in the revision of the BEP adopted by the cabinet in June 2010.[21] The new BEP laid out seven general goals, only one of which concerned security of supply. Likewise, only one of the five targets for 2030 contained in the BEP—raising Japan's "energy independence ratio" from the current 38 percent to about 70 percent—was directly related to energy security. Instead, the emphasis of the new policy was on fighting climate change, especially by reducing Japan's CO2 emissions.

Nevertheless, the 2010 BEP did contain a number of specific measures and tar-gets that, if implemented and achieved, would have resulted in a significant im-provement in Japan's energy security. On the supply side, it called for more than doubling the shares of nuclear power and renewable energy sources in the energy mix, to 24 and 13 percent, respectively, while oil's share would fall to just 28 per-cent. The shift would be particularly marked in the power sector, where nuclear energy and renewables would account for more than 50 percent and 19 percent, respectively, of all electricity generated. The former figure represented an increase in the share of nuclear-generated electricity of at least 10–20 percent over that contained in the NNES. To achieve these ambitious targets, Japan would have to more than double the amount of renewable generating capacity, build at least 14 new nuclear reactors, and increase the overall operating capacity of the nuclear sector to 90 percent. Since fossil fuels would still constitute more than 60 percent of PEC, the government would also continue to strengthen bilateral ties with resource-rich countries and to increase financial support for Japanese companies seeking to acquire overseas energy concessions, with the goal of raising the "self-developed fossil fuel supply ratio" to about 50 percent.

On the demand side, Japan would seek to reduce CO_2 emissions by more than half in the residential and commercial sectors and by 25 percent in the industrial sector, mainly by increasing energy efficiency. Specific measures included making net-zero-energy houses the norm by 2030 and promoting the widespread use of high-efficiency water heaters and lighting. In the transportation sector, the government would mobilize all possible policy measures to increase the share of sales held by low emission vehicles, such as hybrids, electric vehicles, and those that run on fuel cells, to as much as 50 percent by 2020 and 70 percent by 2030, thereby greatly reducing the demand for oil.

THE PROSPECTS FOR ACHIEVING JAPAN'S ENERGY GOALS AND TARGETS

Both the NNES and the 2010 revision of the BEP contained a number of targets that, if achieved, would result in a significant improvement in Japan's energy security. From the outset, however, it was clear that doing so would not be easy. In the words of a senior official in the authoritative IIEJ, "These [NNES] targets are major challenges for Japan and the achievement thereof will require serious efforts" (Toichi 2006, 17; see also Bustelo 2008, 10).

First, substantial questions loomed over the ability of the government to engineer a substantial increase in the amount of oil produced by Japanese companies. Although the 2010 BEP sought to broaden the focus to include all fossil fuels, Japan's principal concern has traditionally been with access to oil. Coal and natural gas may be ready substitutes in electric power generation and, to a lesser extent, industrial applications, but the transportation sector remained almost entirely dependent on oil. As noted above, however, past efforts to increase the level of so-called "equity oil" had met with little success, and most of the world's oil remained under the control of national oil companies and thus off limits to private investors. The Japanese government and companies, moreover, now had to compete with Chinese counterparts that operated under fewer constraints. For example, noted one observer, "as a democracy, Japan must naturally maintain transparency and provide a proper rationale for all ODA projects." Thus, he concluded, "The actual contribution of oil fields developed with Japanese participation will probably remain limited" (Atsumi 2007, 35 and 37; see also Chrisstoffels 2007, 49–51).

Other questions concerned the targets related to increasing energy efficiency. Here part of the difficulty lay with the fact that Japan's overall energy efficiency, defined by the ratio of PEC over GDP, was already the world's lowest, and was even significantly lower—by approximately 50 percent—than that of the EU or the United States (Masaki 2006). Most of the drop in Japan's energy intensity, moreover, had occurred by the mid-1980s. In fact, between 1990 and 2005, it declined by less than 3 percent (EDMC 2010, 32). Thus most of the easy savings had already been exploited (see also Niquet 2007, 8).

This conclusion was especially true for the industrial sector. To be sure, industry remained the largest energy consuming sector, at nearly 46 percent of energy use in 2005, and still accounted for almost 37 percent of oil consumption (EDMC 2010, 38 and 166). But it had also been the principal target of government efforts to increase energy efficiency since the 1970s—approximately 90 percent of the energy consumption in the sector had long been covered by the Energy Conservation Act, and partly as a result, the share of energy consumption attributable to the industrial sector has steadily declined, from nearly two-thirds in 1973 (ECCJ 2009, 3; EDMC 2010, 38).[22] After decades of efforts to make industry more energy efficient and to reduce its reliance on oil, there would not seem to be much further potential there.

Likewise, although there might be many efficiency gains to be made in the residential and commercial sectors, they accounted for just 14 percent of oil consumption. Instead, reducing Japan's overall oil dependence hinged on cutting that of the transportation sector, which was responsible for 44 percent of all oil use in 2005. Achieving the NNES transportation target of 80 percent dependence would have been sufficient to bring overall oil consumption below 40 percent of PEC, but this would not be easy. Indeed, Toichi described it as "the most difficult target to achieve" (Toichi 2006, 17).

Turning to the supply side, much depended on the buildup of renewable sources of energy, which also faced substantial obstacles. Despite rapid growth in solar and wind power after 1998, hydroelectric plants still accounted for more than 90 percent of Japan's renewable generating capacity ten years later. And because Japan's hydroelectric potential was already largely exploited, virtually all of the additional renewable generating capacity called for in the BEP, some 67 GW, would have to come from other, generally intermittent, sources, especially solar and wind. Yet concerns remained about the ability of the grid to handle more than a certain amount of electricity from such sources.[23] According to some experts, the existing power system could accommodate enough photovoltaic generating capacity to provide only about 6 to 8 percent of the electricity supply.[24] Thus greater penetration by renewables might depend on the development of cost-effective, large-scale electric storage capacity.[25] In addition, the most productive sites for wind power tended to be located far from where the electricity is needed, necessitating the construction of expensive new power lines often in the face of local resistance.[26] Thus a 2010 METI electricity supply plan projected that total power generation by hydroelectric and "new-energy" plants in 2019 would be just 29 percent higher than the 2007 level, well short of the eventual 142 percent increase called for in the BEP.[27]

As challenging as the targets for renewable energy might be, however, even more substantial obstacles appeared to stand in the way of realizing the targets for nuclear power, which was ideal for reducing both fossil fuel imports and CO2 emissions, even before the March 2011 disaster at Fukushima Daiichi. Here, two distinct issues were involved: increasing the amount of electricity generating capacity, chiefly by building more power plants, and raising the capacity utilization (utility factor) of the existing ones. In both cases, at least the short- to medium-term outlook was not encouraging. The construction of new reactors had slowed greatly in the previous decade because of safety concerns and local opposition. The 2006 NNES had effectively called for a significant increase in the number of nuclear facilities, but as of early 2010, only one more reactor had been completed, and all of the reactors planned in 2006 were as many as three to five years further behind schedule.[28] Thus, the Japan Atomic Energy Commission concluded in 2009, "No considerable growth is expected for the present regarding activities to construct new or additional plants in Japan" (JAEC 2009, 21).

Increasing nuclear capacity utilization in Japan was not likely to be much easier. From the mid-1990s to the early 2000s, it had hovered around 80 percent, and during the mid- to late 2000s, it had been consistently below 70 percent and fallen as low as 58 percent. In contrast, the nuclear utility factor in the United States, South Korea, and Finland had fluctuated between 90 and 95 percent in recent years (Nagatomi et al. 2010). The reasons for the relatively low percentage in Japan included shorter operational cycles between routine inspections, longer outage times for maintenance and repairs, and extensive unplanned outages due to accidents and other safety concerns. In addition, local governments continued to have a say in the length of the operational cycle as well as when plants could resume operation after planned and, especially, unplanned outages.[29]

THE IMPLICATIONS OF FUKUSHIMA DAIICHI

These obstacles were greatly compounded by the tragic events of March 2011, when a historic earthquake and tsunami struck the northeast coast of Japan. The resulting loss of cooling at the Fukushima Daiichi nuclear power plant led to the destruction of three nuclear reactors and the loss of three others at the site. The government soon requested that operations be suspended at another power plant because of safety concerns (Fackler and Tabuchi 2011). And over the following year, all of Japan's remaining active nuclear reactors were shut down for required routine maintenance and not restarted out of deference to local sensitivities. By May 2012, not a single reactor was generating electricity (Fackler 2012).[30]

The government initially resisted calling for a permanent phase out of nuclear energy. But the disaster had clearly blown a huge hole in Japan's approach to promoting energy security as well as fighting climate change. Henceforth Japan's nuclear options would be highly circumscribed. Many of the existing plants might never re-open, and it was hard to imagine when any new reactors would be built. Thus government officials set about the difficult task of devising an entirely new energy policy that would inevitably have to place even more emphasis on renewables and energy savings (Pollack 2011; Vivoda 2011), and as 2013 came to an end, a consensus on the role that nuclear power should play remained elusive. In the meantime, the overtaxed power system flirted with blackouts, and Japan was forced to increase imports of fossil fuels to use for electric power generation, at a cost of tens of billions of dollars per year (Tabuchi 2011; Hayashi and Hughes 2013).

One of the few bright spots was the impetus that the disaster gave to the deployment of renewable energy sources. In August 2011, the Diet approved a comprehensive feed-in-tariff (FIT) scheme that offered generous incentives, especially for the deployment of solar PV. As a result, during the first year of the program alone, the government approved almost 19 GW of new PV capacity, and by late 2013, more than 6 GW of that had been installed (ANRE/METI 2014).

Still, renewables were not likely to be a panacea. The growth of other renewable power sources, especially wind, lagged well behind that of solar PV. Not only were tariffs under the FIT less favorable, but wind farms had to pass more complex environmental impact assessments (ten Hoedt 2013). As early as mid-2013, moreover, the incorporation of new PV capacity into the power system was beginning to face challenges, as some power grids were reportedly already reaching their capacity to absorb renewable sources (Watanabe 2013). More fundamentally, Japan lacked clear regulations defining grid access for renewables, including purchase volumes and costs, leaving decisions on such critical matters largely to the discretion of the utilities (Japan Times 2013).

Explaining Japanese Responses to Energy Insecurity

How might we best explain the patterns of Japanese policies to promote energy security in the 1970s and 2000s? Clearly, material factors have played an important role. The principal threats to Japan's energy security have stemmed from the country's extremely limited energy resource endowments and its resulting high-level of dependence on energy imports. Certainly, the overall emphases of its policy responses have been consistent with its paucity of domestic fossil fuels, especially oil: reducing energy consumption, creating stockpiles, promoting alternative energy sources, and seeking to diversify and gain greater control over the foreign sources required to meet its residual energy needs.

Material factors alone, however, can account for only part of the story. As the other cases suggest, within the broad policy thrust dictated by Japan's lack of energy resources, the country has still enjoyed a range of choices. These have concerned how exactly to reduce energy consumption, which specific alternatives to promote (e.g., natural gas, nuclear, renewables, and others), what policy mechanisms to use, and so on. Thus to explain the precise measures that the government has adopted, we must also consider domestic factors.

Societal Factors

At the domestic level, a potentially fruitful place to start is with broad societal attitudes and values, or political culture. In what is perhaps the most thorough analysis to date of the impact of political culture on Japanese energy policy, Chad Kohalyk has argued that postwar Japanese society has been suffused with two norms in particular that have done much to shape how the country has addressed its sources of energy insecurity. One of these is antimilitarism, or what Kohalyk defines as "doubt in military measures as a means of enhancing national security and general distrust of the military establishment" (Kohalyk 2008, 28). This aspect of Japanese political culture has tended to rule out a role for the military in Japanese energy security policy and, in particular, the use of military force to ensure energy security (Kohalyk 2008, 20–21). Over time, moreover, antimilitarist attitudes have been institutionalized in constitutional and legal constraints on the use of force, which in turn have left Japan with little military capacity even if there were a desire to use it. Thus even though the Japanese Self-Defense Forces have been used in a growing range of roles since the 1990–91 Persian Gulf War, these still fall well short of traditional combat operations, and the foreign deployment of Japanese forces remains sharply restricted by the 1992 International Peace Cooperation Law (Kohalyk 2008, 53).

A second important norm of relevance to this analysis is what Kohalyk has termed economism, or a tendency to give priority to economic power over military power (Kohalyk 2008, 2). As Japan expert Ronald Morse observed some three decades ago, "the Japanese leadership still finds it hard to see the world in anything but economic terms," a tendency that he regarded as a legacy of an era in which Japan assumed virtually no international political or military responsibilities (Morse 1981a, 38). There is less consensus, however, on whether this norm extends to favoring a particular role for the government in the economy. While Kohalyk sees it as justifying a high degree of cooperation between government and industry and government intervention (Kohalyk 2008, 2; see also Sudo 2008, 156), Yujiro Eguchi previously identified a traditional Japanese tendency to rely on the strength of the private sector: "Private business may be informed, encouraged, and shown the way, but it is not usually interfered with" (Eguchi 1980, 276).

Although somewhat more specific and transitory than political culture, public attitudes about nuclear power also bear mentioning once more as an important potential constraint on policy. As early as 1979, the Three Mile Island incident in the United States made the Japanese public much more wary of nuclear power, and doubts about nuclear safety began to slow the momentum of the nuclear program (Suttmeier 1981, 117 and 120). As noted above, these public concerns have only intensified in the last 15 years as a result of a series of accidents, scandals, and related cover-ups, posing a major impediment to the realization of the government's targets for increasing the amount of nuclear-generated electricity. Unique to Japan, however, the anxiety generated by these mishaps has been magnified by the citizenry's "nuclear allergy" as a result of the atomic bombings of Hiroshima and Nagasaki in 1945 (Berger 1998).

Often at odds with these broad public attitudes and societal norms have been the goals of powerful private interest groups in the energy sector. The oil industry in Japan has been highly fragmented. Not so, however, the power industry, which has been dominated by 10 vertically integrated regional electric utilities plus one large wholesale supplier. In 2005, the six largest producers generated more than 70 percent of Japan's electricity (IEA 2008, 131). Also to be reckoned with since the 1970s have been the major corporations involved in manufacturing nuclear reactors and other aspects of the nuclear fuel cycle. Thus, as Richard Samuels has noted, "The capacity of utilities and vendors consistently to pressure the state contrasts markedly with what obtained in petroleum" (Samuels 1987, 254). Indeed, these industries have allegedly used their ample resources to co-opt politicians, government officials, regulators, academics, and members of the media. The existence of this so-called "nuclear village" may help to explain the considerable emphasis that nuclear power has received in Japanese energy policy (Kingston 2012; Samuels 2013, 118–122).

The Japanese State
DECISION-MAKING AUTONOMY

Like material factors, societal forces leave many aspects of Japanese policy to promote energy security unexplained or underspecified. This book argues that much of the remaining variance can be understood in terms of three faces of state strength. As for the first face, in the case of Japan, the government has enjoyed intermediate to high levels of autonomy in setting policy. Here, though, it is important to distinguish between elected officials and the permanent bureaucracy. Members of the parliament and of the cabinet generally have tended to have small staffs and thus to rely heavily on the accumulated expertise of the career officials in the ministries. Likewise, Sven Steinmo has written, "The structure of the electoral system contributed to a clientelistic system that allowed for the centralization of economic power into the hands of the bureaucratic officials" (Steinmo 2010, 91). Thus many of "the details of policy making have often reverted to administrators in the central government" (Steinmo 2010, 100). And in the case of energy policy, this has usually meant MITI and later METI.

Especially in the 1970s, MITI/METI and the state more generally exercised a high degree of policymaking autonomy and adopted policies to promote energy security that were not favored or were opposed by industry. An early example was the requirement that refiners and retailers maintain substantial stocks. Similarly, the deregulation of the petroleum refining and retail markets and the electric power industry were not popular in the affected industries. Broad public opinion, where it exists on particular policies, exercised even fewer constraints. Hence the government's support for nuclear power, despite the limited amount of popular support.

In more recent years, the record on autonomy has been more mixed, because of close ties between the bureaucracy and the business community. As Peter Evans has argued, "External networks connecting the state and civil society are even more important [than the internal coherence and corporate identity of the bureaucracy]. . . . Japanese industrial policy depends fundamentally on the maze of ties that connect ministries and major industrialists" (Evans 1995, 49–50).

Likewise, Miranda Schreurs has noted a tradition of close government consultation with industry (Schreurs 2002, 11). For example, ANRE has had an elaborate structure of advisory committees and subcommittees, most of whose members come from industry or are academics with close ties to industry.[31] "By the time a policy paper reaches the top decision makers," noted Ronald Morse, "a government and industry wide deliberative and consultative process has already taken place" (Morse 1982, 257–58). In addition, officials reaching the end of their government careers have commonly received lucrative jobs in the private sector, often with companies they have regulated, a practice known as *amakudari*, or descent from heaven (Fackler and Tabuchi 2011). Whatever the precise reasons, the bureaucracy has been careful to take the views of industry into account when developing policy.

Not surprisingly, perhaps the clearest examples of such influence have involved the electric utilities and nuclear industry (Pollack 2011). Not only has the government been a consistently strong supporter of nuclear power, but the goals it has established for renewable electricity have been rather modest, especially in comparison with countries like Britain and Germany, reflecting the opposition of the utilities. More seriously, in view of recent events, one can point to the lack of effective oversight of the nuclear industry, despite long-standing calls for nuclear regulatory bodies that are more independent and capable (Vivoda 2011; Samuels 2013, 118–22).

Such influence has not been limited to the power companies and reactor builders; other commercial interests have exerted influence as well. For example, where the government has promoted renewable electricity, it has privileged photovoltaic technology over wind power in deference to Japan's powerful semiconductor industry.[32] Although the government continued to offer subsidies for the installation of small-scale wind generation capacity by individuals, businesses, and local governments, its initial feed-in tariff/buyback program was limited to PV. Likewise, both automakers and petroleum retailers have long opposed any change in the restrictive 3 percent upper limit for the ethanol content in gasoline (E3) (IEA 2008, 155).[33] And even the ambitious targets for the Top Runner program were adopted only with the consent of the affected consumer product manufacturing industries.[34]

DOMESTIC CAPACITY

Even where the government has enjoyed autonomy from society and interest groups in determining energy policy, the formal tools at its disposal for achieving its goals have been limited. As a general rule, Japanese policy instruments have fallen in the middle of the range between primary reliance on market forces (like Britain in the 2000s), at one extreme, and forceful direct state intervention in the energy economy (like France, especially in the 1970s), at the other. Instead, the government has typically used a combination of regulations, taxes, and subsidies as well as exhortation to shape the behavior of companies and individuals. Examples are legion, but include the increase in taxes on oil products in the 1970s, the mandatory targets contained in the Top Runner program, and the subsidies that have been used to increase acceptance of nuclear power plants and the installation of renewable electricity generating capacity. In addition, the state has supplemented these formal methods with the strong informal tool of administrative guidance, which has been defined as "an informal, extralegal form of persuasion developed and used principally by MITI. Technically unenforceable, it was backed up by MITI's assorted legal powers" over licensing and permitting, rate setting, and the allocation of materials (McKean 1985, 335).

To be sure, there have been exceptions to this middle path. At one end of the spectrum, the government has assumed a large share of the responsibility for maintaining strategic stockpiles, first of crude oil and more recently of LPG and petroleum products. In addition, it has taken a substantial equity stake in many upstream projects undertaken by Japanese companies, although it has tended not to exercise control commensurate with its financial involvement. But the involvement of the Japanese state has been nowhere near as great as that of France. In particular, it has not been a direct commercial participant in energy markets through state-owned or controlled corporations (Samuels 1987, 1–2).

At the other end of the spectrum, the government relied especially heavily on market forces, in the form of high oil prices, to promote adjustment in energy consumption patterns in the 1970s and early 1980s. Indeed, in most cases, the state has ultimately depended on private actors to take the actions, such as building new power plants or cutting energy consumption, needed to achieve its goals, and it has not been able to force Japanese companies to invest in projects that they did not expect to be profitable (Chrisstoffels 2007, 49–53).

A further important set of constraints on the domestic capacity of the Japanese state has been evidenced in the area of nuclear energy policy. Local governments have wielded effective veto power over decisions to build new nuclear power plants and to reopen existing facilities that had been temporarily shut down for maintenance or out of safety considerations.[35] Although the government was able to overcome this obstacle in the past through the heavy use of subsidies to local communities, it has loomed as a major constraint on Japanese policy since the March 2011 events at Fukushima Daiichi. Conversely, when the government sought the closure of a dangerously sited power plant following the Fukushima Daiichi disaster, it had to rely on the grudging consent of the affected power company (Fackler and Tabuchi 2011).

INTERNATIONAL CAPACITY

Turning finally to the external face of state strength, we find that, here too, Japan has had significant but still limited means for pursuing its energy security objectives. Its most substantial tools have been economic in nature. Japan has been able to offer, variously, lucrative trade agreements, financial and technical assistance, and development aid to countries that are actual or potential energy producers. In this way, it has been able to gain some additional, but not absolute, certainty over access to oil supplies in the Persian Gulf and to diversify both the types and sources of its energy imports, especially by promoting the creation of an LNG market in Asia.

In contrast, Japan has lacked the military instruments that have often been available to the other major energy consumers, although this limitation has domestic roots in Japan's postwar antimilitarism. Most obviously, Japan has lacked a power projection capability that could be used, even if only in a purely defensive manner, to help ensure access to foreign energy supplies in extreme circumstances, for example, by providing a defensive shield to threatened energy producers. Even if the Japanese public had been willing to countenance overseas deployments, moreover, other foreign policy considerations, especially the sensitivities of former victim countries, have militated against acquiring a military capability substantial enough to be of any use in defending distant foreign energy supplies.

To be sure, there have been few if any occasions when a Japanese military contribution would have been necessary for the successful defense of energy supplies or even the transit routes on which shipments to Japan depend. Instead, Japan has generally been able to rely on the United States to play that role (Kohalyk 2008, 54). Thus equally if not more important, as a practical matter, has been the absence of a substantial domestic arms industry. As a result, Japan has not been able to curry favor or otherwise gain influence with energy producers by exporting modern weapons either in the form of military sales or assistance, as other major consumer countries have often done (Eguchi 1980, 273; Morse 1982, 265; Chrisstoffels 2007, 22 and 51).

Policy Legacies and Path Dependence

It is difficult to put much emphasis on the role of policy legacies in shaping Japanese policy in later years, as Japan has pursued to an important extent just about every possible avenue available for reducing its energy insecurity. Thus one cannot attribute the energy security concerns of 2000s to anything in particular that Japan did or did not do in earlier years. The renewed concerns largely reflected the inherent vulnerability of Japan's position. Instead, previous policy efforts, especially in the areas of energy efficiency and nuclear power, provided a broad foundation on which to base new efforts to increase the country's energy security. The principal exception was the lack of much previous experience with the promotion renewable sources of energy, which became especially problematic when the disaster at Fukushima Daiichi forced Japan to reevaluate its plans to place greater reliance on nuclear energy.

Perhaps the clearest example of path dependence is the contribution that previous policy decisions made to the interest group structures that shaped policy in the 2000s. In particular, the organization of the electricity sector into powerful regional monopolies and the emphasis placed on nuclear power in responses to the oil shocks laid the groundwork for the formation of the influential "nuclear village" noted above. In this case, however, the success of these interests in promoting nuclear power may have laid the groundwork for subsequent limits insofar as the disaster at Fukushima Daiichi could have been avoided by more effective oversight of the industry.

Conclusion

When it comes to energy security, Japan has faced difficult circumstances. Lacking much in the way of indigenous fossil fuels, it has been forced to meet most of its energy needs with imports. The risks of this dependence were driven home by the first oil shock, but they have been a steady source of motivation for Japanese energy policy ever since. Concerns about energy security have never been far below the surface.

In response to this high level of foreign energy dependence, Japan has pursued a comprehensive set of policy measures. On the domestic front, it has engaged in a wide range of actions to build up strategic reserves of imported energy sources, to reduce energy consumption, and to develop substitutes first for oil and later for all fossil fuel imports. In the 1970s, it emphasized nuclear power, but in more recent years, it has begun to give a more prominent role to renewable sources of electricity. Externally, it has taken a number of steps to diversify its sources of energy imports and to gain greater control of them.

As a result of these efforts, Japan has been able to reduce the level of energy insecurity somewhat, but an irreducible amount remains. Japan remains heavily dependent on fossil fuels, almost all of which must still be imported, and the lion's share of oil still comes from the Persian Gulf. In addition, the disaster at Fukushima Daiichi appears to have placed significant limits on the degree to which Japan can rely on nuclear power to increase its energy security in the future. Instead, much will depend on its ability to increase its energy efficiency above what are already high levels and to deploy renewable sources of energy in a physical environment that has not been regarded as particularly suitable for the purpose.

Throughout this process, the Japanese state has played an important but still limited role. With the exception of the creation of the stockpile system, it has rarely intervened directly to achieve its goals. Instead, it has relied mainly on private actors to take the necessary steps, using a combination of taxes, regulations, subsidies, and even exhortation to help bring about the desired results. The Japanese state has generally taken a cooperative rather than a confrontational approach with industry and the general public, even when doing so might have frustrated the achievement of its goals. Even then, it has sometimes found itself buffeted, on the one side, by deeply ingrained cultural values and public opinion and, on the other, by the strong private sector interest groups, especially the electric utilities and the nuclear power industry.

CHAPTER NINE

The United States

Plus ça change . . .

You could never implement the energy policy as a purely economic matter. It has been a foreign policy since the beginning.

—Henry Kissinger, quoted in Nau, "The Evolution of U.S. Foreign Policy on Energy"

For too long, our nation has been dependent on foreign oil. And this dependence leaves us more vulnerable to hostile regimes and to terrorists who could cause huge disruptions of oil shipments and raise the price of oil and do great harm to our economy.

—George W. Bush, 2007 State of the Union address

Of the five countries examined in this study, the energy security concerns—and policy responses—of the United States have changed the least over the years. In the 1970s, American energy security concerns, like those in the other countries, revolved primarily around the price and availability of oil. In the 2000s, such oil-related worries, although not absent elsewhere, remained most prominent in the United States. More than in any other major developed democracy, energy security has continued to mean primarily oil security in the United States.

One reason for this state of affairs is that the United States made the least effort to reduce its oil dependence and thus its vulnerability to oil price and supply shocks, or was the least successful in doing so, in response to the oil shocks. In the 1970s and early 1980s, the United States initiated the creation of a substantial crude oil reserve that could be drawn on in a crisis. It also took a number of steps to reduce domestic oil consumption, most notably the introduction of fuel economy standards for cars and light trucks, and to increase domestic oil production. But cumulatively, these measures resulted in the smallest decline in oil as a share of primary energy consumption among the major developed democracies, even as domestic oil production later stagnated once again and then resumed its previous decline. Somewhat paradoxically, moreover, successes in reducing oil consumption in some sectors, especially for electric power generation, resulted in greater inflexibility of demand as oil use became increasingly concentrated in the almost entirely oil-dependent transportation sector.

Meanwhile, the United States placed heavy emphasis on external policy actions in its response to the energy insecurity of the 1970s. It orchestrated the collective responses of the major consumer countries to the Arab oil embargo. And, more consequentially, it substantially deepened its political and military involvement in the Persian Gulf as a means of stabilizing world oil supplies, culminating in a commitment to defend the countries of the region against external aggression.

As a result, the principal U.S. efforts to augment energy security in the 2000s looked strikingly similar to those of the earlier period. Leading measures included further increasing the size of the Strategic Petroleum Reserve (SPR), further raising automotive fuel economy standards, requiring the inclusion of a growing amount of alternative fuels, especially ethanol, in the motor fuel supply, and increasing domestic oil production. In addition, the United States became even more deeply embroiled in the Persian Gulf, with the invasion and occupation of Iraq. Although few would argue that the war was primarily about controlling or obtaining access to the region's oil supplies, it was hard to separate the war from the continuing heavy U.S. dependence on oil and its resulting vulnerability to oil supply disruptions.

The 1970s: U.S. Responses to the Oil Shocks

Of the major developed democracies, the United States had been by far the most self-sufficient in oil—and energy more generally—in the years immediately prior to 1973. Thus, although some experts had anticipated the problems that the United States was to face in the 1970s as a result of declining domestic production and growing imports of oil, the first oil shock came as a surprise to most Americans. The fact that the U.S. oil supply and, as a result, the U.S. economy could be subject to disruptions originating on the other side of the world was difficult to accept.

Nevertheless, over the next eight years, successive administrations attempted to fashion policy responses to this new reality. Presidents Gerald Ford and Jimmy Carter in particular presented comprehensive energy plans that were largely intended to address the issue of U.S. energy security. The results of these efforts were mixed. One important success was the creation of the SPR, which would greatly enhance the U.S. ability to cope with a future oil supply disruption. Another was the establishment of mandatory fuel economy standards for most vehicles, which promised to slow, if not stop and reverse, the growing appetite of the transportation sector for petroleum products. And thanks in particular to the construction of the trans-Alaska pipeline, the decline in domestic oil production that had begun in 1970 received a temporary reprieve. On the other hand, no administration was able to impose substantial consumption taxes on oil or petroleum products, and it took until 1981 to fully lift the price controls that had been established as a temporary measure a full decade earlier, before the first oil shock.

The United States was equally if not more active on the international front during this period. Its initial response in its external relations focused on organizing cooperation among the consumer countries, ideally to form a common front in dealing with the oil producers but, failing that, to improve their collective abilities to deal with future supply disruptions and to lower their dependence on oil imports. These efforts led to the creation of the International Energy Agency and its emergency oil sharing system. Over time, however, the emphasis of U.S. external efforts shifted to the oil producers themselves, especially in the Persian Gulf. The United States steadily deepened its involvement in the region as a means of ensuring the steady flow of adequate amounts of oil at affordable prices from that region. What had begun as massive arms sales to U.S. allies in the gulf, especially Iran and Saudi Arabia, came to include other forms of military assistance and culminated in an unprecedented formal commitment to defend the region's oil supplies against external aggression and the beginning of a significant buildup of U.S. military power projection capability.

By the early to mid-1980s, U.S. energy security had much improved. Both oil consumption and imports were below the levels of 1973, and the capacity of the SPR reached the equivalent of three months of imports. In addition, the United States had made substantial progress toward the acquisition of the forces and facilities required to implement its new commitment to the defense of its oil interests in the Persian Gulf. But, other than the buildup of the SPR, it was not clear how much of this improvement could be attributed to government policy responses, rather than market forces, and the dividends of the new level of engagement in the Middle East remained to be seen. Absent stronger policies to encourage conservation, production, and the substitution of other fuels for oil, moreover, the United States remained vulnerable to lapsing once again into a dangerous degree of oil dependence.

Background

On the surface, at least, the United States should have been the best prepared of the five countries examined in this book to weather the oil shocks of the 1970s.

Thanks to its vast reserves of coal and natural gas as well as oil, it was the least dependent on oil to meet its energy needs in 1973, and it was still able to produce the majority of the oil that it consumed. As a share of primary energy consumption (PEC), U.S. oil consumption had risen in the late 1940s and early 1950s, but it held remarkably steady between the mid-1950s and the early 1970s, fluctuating narrowly between about 43 and 44.5 percent. Although coal consumption declined over the same period, it was largely replaced by natural gas, whose share of PEC doubled between 1949 and 1970, to more than 32 percent (EIA 2010, 9).

Nevertheless, the total amount of oil consumed in the United States grew substantially, more than doubling between 1950 and 1970. Although the United States became a net oil importer in the late 1940s, for most of the period leading up to the oil shocks, domestic production was able to keep up with this growing demand. Rather than insufficient supplies, the main political problem faced by the United States, as production increased in the Middle East, Venezuela, and elsewhere after World War II, was too much oil in the form of cheap imports that undercut domestic prices and took market share from the more expensive oil produced on U.S. territory (EIA 2012, 129).

The solution to this problem, announced by the Eisenhower administration 1959, was to impose mandatory quotas on oil imports, which were initially set at 9 percent of total U.S. consumption (Yergin 1991, 538). Although exceptions were made for oil from neighboring countries and the quotas were gradually relaxed, they were generally successful at protecting domestic producers, holding imports below 20 percent of total consumption until the very end of the 1960s. Even with import quotas, moreover, the United States enjoyed significant spare production capacity until the late 1960s. This capacity was prominently on display in 1967, when Arab oil producers first attempted to impose an oil embargo—on the United States, Britain, and West Germany—in response to the 1967 war between Israel and its Arab neighbors. With the help of increased output from Iran and Venezuela, the United States was able to neutralize the production cuts, and this first Arab effort to exert political pressure failed.

Over the next several years, however, the picture changed dramatically. United States consumption continued its inexorable rise, but in 1970, domestic production peaked and then started to decline. This turn of events had two important implications. First, it meant that the United States would have to rely increasingly on imports to meet demand. As a result, the import quotas were further relaxed, and in April 1973, they were abolished altogether. Imported oil flooded the domestic market, nearly doubling between 1970 and 1973 from just over 3 MBD to 6 MBD. As a share of total oil consumption, they grew from under 23 percent to nearly 36 percent over the same period, and it was widely accepted that half of U.S. oil needs would have to be met by imports in 1980 (de Marchi 1981b, 476; EIA 2010, 129).

The second implication of the peak in domestic oil output was that the United States no longer possessed any meaningful spare production capacity. Through the early 1960s and perhaps as late as 1968, surplus U.S. production capacity had stood as high as 4 MBD. By 1971, however, domestic oil producers were producing all out. Thus there was nothing to draw on in the event of a future supply disruption elsewhere (Vietor 1984, 198–99; Beaubouef 2007, 8).

One other domestic policy would have important implications for how the United States responded to the first oil shock. In the late 1960s and early 1970s, the United States experienced levels of inflation not seen since the immediate postwar years. In 1971, President Richard Nixon announced a temporary freeze on all wages and prices, including those for domestically produced crude oil and petroleum products, which were subsequently extended. At the time, domestic oil prices were nearly 30 percent above the world market price, but by early 1973 the delivered cost of imports had caught up (Vietor 1984, 238–39). The Nixon administration made several modifications to the oil price controls, and recognizing that they had begun to inhibit domestic oil production, it introduced a two-tier pricing system for crude oil in August 1973. So-called "new" oil, which include included production from new properties, production from oil properties in excess of pre-1973 levels, and "stripper" oil from extremely low volume wells, was de-controlled, while the remaining "old" oil was subject to a ceiling of $4.25 per barrel (de Marchi 1981a, 456–57; de Marchi 1981b, 497; Kalt 1983, 99; Vietor 1984, 242–43; Ikenberry 1988, 169).

Abroad, the United States had not been particularly concerned about promoting energy security. The main thrust of American policy had been to support the activities of U.S.-based international oil companies. This goal had become increasingly problematic as various oil-producing countries sought to gain greater control over the operations on their territories, but the trend toward nationalization was not generally seen as threatening the availability of world oil supplies.

In the early 1970s, however, one important change occurred. After World War II, Britain had played the leading role in maintaining the stability of what was becoming the world's key oil-producing region, the Persian Gulf. In 1968, however, the British government announced that it would withdraw all of its forces from "East of Suez" by 1971, and because of its continued engagement in Vietnam and declining public support for foreign engagements, the Nixon administration was unwilling to assume the British mantle. Instead, it turned to Saudi

Arabia and, especially, Iran to fill the power vacuum left by the British departure. The administration increased the sale of arms to Iran and, in 1972, lifted virtually all restrictions on its ally's purchase of advanced weaponry, but it continued to eschew any direct involvement in the security of the region (Duffield 2008, 105–6).

Impact of the Oil Shocks

The first oil shock generated two principal sets of concerns in the United States. The first, which was relatively transitory in nature, was that the United States might suffer a shortage of oil. In early November, Nixon warned that oil supplies would fall at least 10 percent—and as much as 17 percent—short of anticipated demand, and indeed for several months, imports fell by approximately that amount, contributing to shortages of gasoline, diesel, and aviation fuel (Davis 1982, 104 and 107; Vietor 1984, 244; Beaubouef 2007, 17; Hakes 2008, 33).

As the initial panic receded, however, attention shifted to the consequences of the jump in world oil prices. Even with price controls in place, the U.S. economy was not immune. According to one estimate, real U.S. gross national product (GNP), after growing between 5 and 6 percent in 1972 and 1973, fell by 0.6 percent in 1974 and again the following year before recovering. Inflation nearly doubled from 3.3 percent in 1972 to 6.2 percent in 1973 and then again to 11 percent in 1974 before declining. Meanwhile, the unemployment rate jumped from an annual average of 4.9 percent in 1973 to 8.5 percent two years later, a postwar record, and real wages did not increase for the first time since World War II. Thus not only did the United States suffer its most severe recession since the 1930s, but it experienced its first bout of stagflation (Mork 1982, 85; Schneider 1983, 283; Beaubouef 2007, 23).[1] A final concern was the growing transfer of wealth to the oil-producing states. The bill for oil imports jumped from about $4 billion in 1972 to more than $15 billion in 1974 (in current dollars) and continued to rise thereafter, with much of the proceeds going to OPEC countries (Hakes 2008, 36; EIA 2010, 173).

The second oil shock raised similar concerns. During the first half of 1979, crude supplies fell between 2 and 4 percent below the level of demand, and some parts of the country experienced even greater shortages of gasoline. Long gas lines appeared in California and then spread to the East Coast and other urban areas, prompting President Carter to declare a national energy supply shortage (Davis 1982, 122; Schneider 1983, 443–45; Beaubouef 2007, 96; Hakes 2008, 56–58). The price of gasoline nearly doubled in nominal terms from 1978 to 1980, exceeding a dollar per gallon for the first time ever (EIA 2010, 181). Economic growth did not slow as much as during the previous oil shock, although the United States did slip into recession in 1980, and the rate of inflation skyrocketed, reaching more than 13 percent in 1980 (Beaubouef 2007, 95).

The second oil shock had not even subsided when the December 1979 Soviet invasion of Afghanistan raised an entirely different type of concern. The controversial action was widely regarded as an attempt by the Soviets to gain influence, if not outright control, over the oil fields of the Persian Gulf. In particular, with forces now arrayed along much of Iran's borders, the Soviets were better poised to exploit the postrevolutionary turmoil in that critical oil producer (Schneider 1983, 490). In Carter's words, the invasion posed "a grave threat to the free movement of Middle East oil" (Hakes 2008, 63).

Finally, between the oil shocks, during the early years of the Carter administration, U.S. policy was briefly animated by yet another concern: that world oil supplies would begin to run out in the 1980s. According to a CIA report published in 1977, projected world demand for oil would substantially exceed production capacity by 1985, resulting in a serious crisis. Even the Soviet Union, which had rivaled the United States for the title of world's largest oil producer, and its allies would be substantial net importers by then (CIA 1977; Nau 1980, 54–55; Cochrane 1981, 558; Hakes 2008, 46). But even before he took office, Carter held a deep belief in the impending exhaustion of fossil fuels (Cochrane 1981, 552).

Overview of U.S. Policy Responses

How did the United States attempt to address the energy security concerns of the 1970s and early 1980s? It is not easy to summarize. The U.S. response was spread out over eight years, four administrations, two national elections resulting in changes in the party in control of the White House, and one presidential resignation. As a result, it went through multiple phases characterized by evolving goals as well as changes in the desired means. The last major components did not fall into place until the beginning of the Reagan administration.

THE NIXON ADMINISTRATION

On November 7, 1973, several weeks after the beginning of the oil embargo, Nixon gave a televised address, in which he announced a number of steps and proposals for dealing with the immediate crisis, such as reducing highway speed limits, lowering thermostats, and relaxing emission controls on the use of coal. To deal with the underlying problems, however, the president also proclaimed an ambitious long-term objective: "Let us set as our national goal, in the spirit of Apollo, with the determination of the Manhattan Project, that by the end of this decade we will have developed the potential to meet our own energy needs without depending on any foreign energy sources. Let us pledge that by 1980, under Project Independence, we shall be able to meet America's energy needs from America's own energy resources" (Nixon 1973; see also Schneider, 1983, 326; Hakes 2008, 26).[2]

In a January 1974 energy message, Nixon described the project as entailing three concurrent tasks: (1) rapidly increasing domestic energy supplies, (2) conserving energy by eliminating nonessential uses and improving the efficiency of energy utilization, and (3) developing new technologies through a massive new energy research and development program (Bupp 1977, 286; Schneider 1983, 326). Both of the announcements, however, were short on actionable items. Rather, the principal initiative was a wide-ranging analytical study of the nation's energy goals and options that would take most of 1974 to complete (Ikenberry 1988, 106).

During the following months, the administration was increasingly distracted by the Watergate scandal (Yergin 1991, 619). Thus the task of developing a detailed set of domestic measures to increase U.S. energy security was left to Nixon's successors. In the short term, moreover, Nixon's top priority was to mitigate the impact on consumers of higher oil prices, so there was no talk of lifting price controls.

With the sudden jump in world prices, however, the two-tier pricing system introduced just two months before the beginning of the oil shock created regional price disparities and shortages, since the mix of imported, old, and new oil used by refiners in different parts of the country varied. Rather than scrap the controls, however, Nixon sought to address the problem by requesting authority to allocate crude oil and petroleum products, which Congress promptly granted him in the form of the Emergency Petroleum Allocation Act (EPAA). In particular, the EPAA mandated the reallocation of crude oil from the larger, vertically integrated oil companies to small and independent domestic refiners (de Marchi 1981a, 451–54; Plummer 1982b, 122; Kalt 1983, 104; Vietor 1984, 244; Ikenberry 1988, 169–70).

By itself, however, the EPAA, could not eliminate large disparities in refiners' average crude oil costs. To address this further problem, federal regulators then created the Old Oil Entitlements Program, announced in November 1974, which was intended to equalize feedstock costs to domestic refiners without requiring the actual transshipment of oil. Each month, entitlements equal to the number of barrels of old oil produced were issued to all refiners in proportion to their refining capacities. Refiners with fewer entitlements than the amount of old oil they wished to process had to buy more from refiners with a surplus. Thus companies with cheap domestic oil were to subsidize their crude-short competitors, all in the interest of preserving competition (de Marchi 1981a, 472–73; Kalt 1983, 106–7; Vietor 1984, 246).

The Nixon administration's other principal response was on the international front. Most important, it sought to fashion a collective response to OPEC on the part of the consumer countries. In December 1973, Secretary of State Henry Kissinger called for the formation of an Energy Action Group, composed of the United States, Western Europe, and Japan that would collaborate on conserving energy, developing new sources of oil, and giving oil-producing countries incentives to increase supply. In January, Nixon invited representatives from the European Community and several other countries to a conference in Washington the following month where U.S. officials hoped to hammer out detailed plans for cooperation (Lieber 1976, 20–23; Schneider 1983, 257–60; Ikenberry 1988, 87). Meanwhile, they also opposed efforts by other states, especially France and Japan, to forge bilateral deals with OPEC producers, fearing such actions would undermine their efforts to create a united front (Ikenberry 1988, 86).

THE FORD ADMINISTRATION

Gerald Ford, who was sworn in as president on August 9, 1974, quickly went about fashioning a comprehensive energy program. In October, he pledged to reduce U.S. oil imports, then running at about 6 MBD, by 1 MBD by the end of 1975 and another 1 MBD over the following two years (Schneider 1983, 327; Hakes 2008 37). And the following January, he presented a detailed Energy Independence Act to Congress that would, among other things, assure the United States of a "reliable and adequate" supply of energy and make the country "invulnerable to cutoffs of foreign oil." The most important proposed measures for increasing U.S. energy security were

- decontrol of domestic crude oil prices beginning in April coupled with a windfall tax on oil company profits and tax rebates to ease the burden of higher energy prices on consumers
- standby authority to impose tariffs and quotas on oil imports as well as a general oil floor price should prices decline sufficiently to threaten domestic production
- opening up the Outer Continental Shelf to oil exploration and production
- the creation of strategic oil storage of 1 billion barrels for domestic needs and 300 million barrels for national defense purposes
- a program to produce 1 MBD of synthetic fuels from coal and oil shale by 1985

- tax incentives and regulations to increase the substitution of coal for oil in electric power generation

In the meantime, while waiting for Congress to act and to encourage it to do so, Ford would use his authority to impose a temporary fee of up to $3 per barrel on imported oil and petroleum products (de Marchi 1981b, 487–89 and 499; Schneider 1983, 327 and 347; Vietor 1984, 249; Ikenberry 1988, 176–77; Beaubouef 2007, 28–29; Hakes 2008, 38).

Later in the year, in October, Ford proposed the creation of a government corporation, the Energy Independence Authority, to encourage the development of new energy sources by promoting the flow of capital to promising forms of energy production where private-sector financing was inadequate. It would be authorized to provide up to $100 billion in loans, loan guarantees, price guarantees, and other forms of financial assistance to private sector energy projects over a 10-year period. Funds would be raised through the sale of up to $25 billion in securities and the issuance of up to $75 billion in government guaranteed obligations (Bupp 1977, 291; de Marchi 1981b, 520; Schneider 1983, 349; Ikenberry 1988, 118).

As will be discussed in greater detail later, Ford's ambitious proposals encountered a mixed fate. Although in January the president had urged Congress to act within 90 days, it was not until December that it passed and Ford was able to sign a 250-page omnibus energy bill, the Energy Policy and Conservation Act (EPCA). The resulting legislation, moreover, "bore little resemblance to the president's proposed Energy Independence Act" (Beaubouef 2007, 35). The EPCA mandated higher fuel efficiency standards for a large number of products, including automobiles and electrical appliances, authorized the president to require power plants to use coal rather than oil and to order mandatory conservation measures, and established the SPR. But it extended and further complicated oil price controls rather than removing them, and it explicitly denied the president authority to impose tariffs on oil imports (Beaubouef 2007, 35–36; see also Davis 1982, 113). For its part, Congress quickly killed the proposed Energy Independence Authority (de Marchi 1981b, 520; Schneider 1983, 349).

THE CARTER ADMINISTRATION

Like Ford, Jimmy Carter made energy one of his top priorities after taking office. According to one detailed assessment, the new administration approached the energy crisis as *the* major problem facing the country (Cochrane 1981, 578). Indeed, on his inauguration day, Carter promised to send Congress a comprehensive energy plan in three months (Cochrane 1981, 551). True to his word, in April, he presented a National Energy Plan containing more than 100 specific proposals. The plan reflected heightened concerns about U.S. dependence on imported oil, especially in the face of the anticipated peaking of world production. Rather than declining to around 4 MBD, as Ford had pledged, imports were rapidly approaching 9 MBD, and the new administration expected this number to increase to between 12 and 16 MBD by 1985. Thus Carter proposed to reduce imports to less than 6 MBD by 1985 and to reduce gasoline consumption by 10 percent below the current level over the same period. He also reiterated the goal of establishing a strategic reserve of 1 billion barrels (Carter 1977; Cochrane 1981, 561; Schneider 1983, 330).[3]

To achieve these goals, the plan placed primary emphasis on reducing demand (Cochrane 1981, 553; Davis 1982, 117; Schneider 1983, 332). As Carter argued, "Conservation is the quickest, cheapest, most practical source of energy" (Carter 1977). In addition, the president was determined to raise the domestic price of oil to the international level while not allowing the oil companies to reap the full benefit of the higher price (Yager 1981, 611). To do so, however, he would not eliminate price controls, which he argued "should be retained as long as world oil prices remain subject to arbitrary control" (Vietor 1984, 260), although he proposed to modify them in a way that would raise the average price per barrel by approximately 16 percent by 1980.[4]

Instead, Carter emphasized the phased imposition of a crude oil equalization tax (COET), which would raise the price of gasoline and other petroleum products to world levels while capturing for the government some of the economic rents created by OPEC. The administration estimated that the COET would reduce demand by 800,000 barrels per day in 1980 and 3.9 MBD in 1985, and it would raise $38 billion in government revenue over five years. To reduce the impact on consumers, however, all proceeds of the tax would be rebated to consumers on a per capita basis. Other proposed measures included

- a heavy and rising tax on the use of oil by industry and electric utilities, and the prohibition oil use in new boilers
- graduated taxes on fuel-inefficient automobiles and light-duty trucks
- a standby gasoline tax of 5 cents per gallon each year that total U.S. consumption exceeded targets set by the government, with the proceeds being rebated back to taxpayers (Cochrane 1981, 566–75; Davis 1982, 117, 198, and 260; Schneider 1983, 331–32; Vietor 1984, 260–61; Hakes 2008, 45–48)[5]

Then in 1979, in the throes of the second oil shock, Carter took several other significant steps intended to halt and reverse U.S. dependence on foreign oil. In

April, he announced that he would use his authority to phase out oil price controls over the next 30 months, beginning June 1, and he called for a windfall profits tax of 50 percent on the additional revenues that the oil companies would receive as a result. The revenues from the tax would be deposited in an Energy Security Trust Fund, which would be used for low-income assistance, subsidies for mass transit, and the development of alternative energy resources (Yager 1981, 612–14; Vietor 1984, 265–66). And in June, Carter proclaimed a goal of cutting U.S. foreign oil dependence in half by 1990, a savings of more than 4.5 MBD. To that end, he proposed a 50 percent cut in the use of oil by utilities, the creation of an Energy Security Corporation financed largely by the windfall profits tax to lead an effort to develop 2.5 MBD of oil substitutes by 1990, and the establishment an Energy Mobilization Board empowered to expedite the construction of critical energy facilities (Yager 1981, 612–13 and 625; Ikenberry 1988, 126–27; Beaubouef 2007, 80; Hakes 2008, 62).

Like Ford, Carter's initiatives met with only mixed success. After rapid passage in the House of Representatives, the National Energy Plan bogged down in the Senate, where it became hostage to the debate over deregulating natural gas prices. It was not until November 1978 that Carter was able to sign the National Energy Act, which contained only about half of his original program and lacked the COET, which had been the centerpiece of the plan (Cochrane 1981, 578–84; Schneider 1983, 333–35; Vietor 1984, 259 and 262). Then, it took Congress almost a year to enact a crude oil windfall profits tax, and a similar amount of time transpired before Carter's June 1979 proposals were translated into the 1980 Energy Security Act, which created a Synthetic Fuels Corporation, among other things (Vietor 1984, 270).

THE REAGAN ADMINISTRATION

Ronald Reagan took an entirely different approach to promoting U.S. energy security from that of his predecessors. His administration sought to deregulate the energy sector and reduce government involvement, preferring to rely instead on markets to the greatest possible extent. Thus one of Reagan's first acts as president was to lift immediately the remaining oil price controls. He also sought to dismantle the Department of Energy, which had only been established in 1977, although he placed considerable value on the growing SPR.

Domestic Policy Responses

What was accomplished by all this governmental activity, especially under presidents Ford and Carter? What significant domestic policy measures to increase

U.S. energy security were adopted? One can point to three principal achievements. In the area of emergency preparations for a future oil supply disruption, a major step forward was taken with the creation of the SPR. Domestic oil production received at least a temporary shot in the arm with the approval and construction of the trans-Alaska oil pipeline. And the adoption of fuel economy standards made a potentially significant contribution to reducing future oil consumption, though it would take years before the benefits would be felt.

These achievements, however, were roughly balanced by an equal number of important limitations in the U.S. response. Other than the substitution of coal and, to a lesser extent, nuclear energy for electric power generation, there was little progress toward the development of alternatives for oil, especially in the form of liquid fuels. No significant taxes were imposed on oil or petroleum products as a means of discouraging consumption. And it took more than seven years to remove oil price controls, which greatly inhibited the adjustment of domestic supply and demand to the new circumstances of the world oil market.

EMERGENCY PREPAREDNESS

One of the biggest achievements of U.S. policy was in the area of emergency preparedness. The 1975 EPCA authorized the creation of a SPR containing up to 1 million barrels of crude oil. The bill also established a short-term goal of 150 million barrels (the early storage reserve) in three years and a long-term goal of about 500 million barrels by the end of 1982. Nevertheless, the EPCA provided only broad guidelines for developing the SPR; detailed implementation plans were left to the executive branch to develop (Krapels 1980, 60–89; Schneider 1983, 328; Beaubouef 2007, 36–37).

In 1978, at the urging of the Carter administration, Congress increased the stockpiling goal for 1985 to 1 billion barrels (Schneider 1983, 332–35; Beaubouef 2007, 81–82). The actual creation of the SPR, however, proceeded much more slowly than had been hoped. Because of technical problems, the stockpile contained less than 70 million barrels by the end of 1978, and in early 1979, when supplies grew tight and the price of oil skyrocketed, the government suspended oil purchases. Additions to the SPR did not resume until late 1980 under the terms of the Energy Security Act, which specified an average fill rate of at least 100 thousand barrels per day. In 1981, the Reagan administration greatly accelerated the fill rate, which averaged 600 thousand barrels per day that year, and the original goal of 500 million barrels was reached in 1985 (Krapels 1980, 62; Plummer 1982b, 115–16; Bull-Berg 1987, 66; Beaubouef 2007, 93, 106–8, 131, 146; EIA 2010, 167).

The United States was much less successful at developing rationing plans for a future emergency. The EPAA of late 1973 contained authority to move to gasoline rationing, if necessary (de Marchi 1981a, 451), and the 1975 EPCA requested the president to submit a gasoline rationing plan to Congress for approval. It was not until March 1979, however, that Carter submitted sent such a plan to Congress, where it quickly died in the House. Congress then passed a new procedure for developing a plan, but it refused to give the president much authority to implement a future plan without its approval (Yager 1981, 606–8 and 628). Finally, the market-oriented Reagan administration put an end to the discussion, vetoing a bill giving the president authority to allocate oil in any future supply emergency and even going so far as to destroy rationing coupons that had been printed during the Carter years (Schneider 1983, 469; Stagliano 2001, 43).

REDUCING OIL CONSUMPTION

One of the first steps taken to reduce oil consumption following the first oil shock was to restrict the speed at which people could drive. In early 1974, the Nixon administration imposed a 55 mile per hour speed limit, which Congress made permanent later in the year (Hakes 2008, 37). Of potentially much greater long-term significance, however, were the fuel economy standards established by the EPCA. The Corporate Average Fuel Economy (CAFE) program required automakers to increase the average fuel efficiency for new passenger cars and light-duty trucks. Congress itself set the initial standards for passenger cars, which rose from 18 miles per gallon (mpg) in mile year (MY) 1978 to 27.5 mpg in MY 1985, while the Department of Transportation set the rules for light trucks, which began at 17.2 mpg in MY 1979 and increased to 20.2 mpg in MY 1987. The 1985 standard implied a doubling in the overall fuel economy for U.S.-made automobiles, which had averaged only about 14 mpg between 1965 and 1975 (Duffield 2008, 67–68).

Less remarked were new regulations limiting the use of oil to generate electricity. In 1973, oil constituted more than 20 percent of the fossil fuel used in power generation (Beaubouef 2007, 17; EIA 2010, 230). The 1975 EPCA expanded the federal government's authority to order power generators to switch from oil to coal, and the 1978 National Energy Act prohibited the use of oil as fuel in new electrical generating plants and industrial plants (Cochrane 1981, 585; Davis 1982, 198–99; Schneider 1983, 335; Hakes 2008, 43 and 52).

On the other hand, Congress refused to authorize most of the taxes proposed by Ford and Carter. It rejected in particular the centerpiece of the Carter program, the COET, and taxes on industrial and utility users of oil and gas, which the administration had argued would reduce imports by 2.3 MBD in 1985 (Cochrane 1981, 586–87; Schneider 1983, 334). Nor did Congress approve any other taxes or fees on petroleum products, crude oil, or imports during the 1970s and early 1980s in order to discourage consumption. The Ford administration dropped the oil import fee it had imposed when Congress passed the EPCA in late 1975, and when Carter imposed a $4.62 per barrel oil import fee aimed at raising gas prices by 10 cents per gallon, Congress voted overwhelmingly to repeal it (Schneider 1983, 468).

The principal exception to Congress' aversion to taxes was the inclusion of the so-called "gas-guzzler" tax in the 1978 Energy Tax Act, although the final version was milder than what Carter had proposed (Cochrane 1981, 585). It first applied to cars manufactured in MY 1980, which were potentially subject to fines ranging from $200 to $550, and was gradually phased in over the following decade (Davis and Diegel 2004, table 4.21; Duffield 2008, 66).

INCREASING DOMESTIC PRODUCTION

Much less was done to promote domestic oil production. The principal achievement in this area was the narrow passage (by one vote) of the Trans-Alaska Pipeline Authorization Act in November 1973, just one month after the beginning of the Arab oil embargo. This piece of legislation allowed construction to begin on a controversial pipeline that would connect the substantial oil discoveries on Alaska's North Slope with a shipping terminal in Valdez on Prince William Sound. The pipeline was completed in May 1977, allowing oil to begin flowing the following month (Duffield 2008, 74).

In contrast, the government offered few new incentives to promote oil exploration and production in the lower 48 states and offshore. Indeed, a fundamental criticism of Carter's National Energy Plan was that it failed to provide adequate drilling incentives (Cochrane 1981, 592–93). For its part, Congress eliminated the long-standing oil depletion allowance and other tax breaks that the oil industry had enjoyed. And when the government finally moved to decontrol oil prices at the end of the decade, Congress passed a windfall profits tax on domestic crude production ranging from 50 to 70 percent that neutralized much of the incentive that higher prices would provide. According to estimates at the time, the tax would raise $227 billion in revenues by 1988 (Vietor 1984, 270).

PROMOTING ALTERNATIVES TO OIL

As noted above, some measures were taken to foster the substitution of coal for oil in electric power generation. In contrast, relatively little effort was made to promote nuclear power as an alternative to oil. This neglect was somewhat ironic, given that the United States had been a leader in the development of civilian nuclear power, and nuclear power was widely regarded as cleaner than coal. By the end of 1973, 42 nuclear plants with an installed capacity of 23 gigawatts (GW) were in operation, generating nearly 5 percent of all U.S. electricity, and dozens of more were under construction (EIA 2010, 275 and 277). The Project Independence Report issued in November 1974 argued for a total of 240 GW of installed capacity by 1985, and in January 1975, Ford called for adding 200 nuclear power plants by that date (Bupp 1977, 297; Schneider 1983, 341).

Well before the nuclear accident at the Three Mile Island in March 1979, however, the nuclear power industry was in trouble. Since the mid-1960s, the cost of new nuclear power plants had risen faster than the rate of inflation. Orders for new reactors, which had peaked at 34 in 1973, averaged less than 4 per year between 1975 and 1978, and cancellations averaged about 9 per year over the same period. Thus the 1977 National Energy Plan estimated only 138 plants would be operating in 1985, 100 less than Ford had envisioned just two years before (Bupp 1977, 297; Schneider 1983, 470; Ahearne 1983, 355–57).

The Carter administration introduced another constraint on the development of civilian nuclear power. Until then, the industry was looking forward to the introduction of the nuclear fuel cycle, involving the recovery of plutonium from spent nuclear fuel for use as fuel in a new generation of reactors. Carter, however, was extremely concerned about the proliferation risk that the widespread use of plutonium would pose, and he quickly decided to defer indefinitely commercial reprocessing and recycling of spent fuel as well as the construction of a demonstration fast breeder reactor that would produce more fissile material than it consumed (Cochrane 1981, 548–49 and 576).

Then, Three Mile Island sounded the death knell for the U.S. nuclear industry. The Nuclear Regulatory Commission temporarily suspended issuing operating licenses for new nuclear power plants and mandated improvements in reactor safety that were expected to raise the cost of reactors by tens of millions of dollars. The issuance of construction permits also ground to a halt, and some 45 permitted units were never built (Schneider 1983, 470; Yager 1981, 635). In this environment, there was little the government could do to promote nuclear power, even if it wanted to.

The government did somewhat more to promote the development of liquid fuel substitutes for oil. Although Ford's proposed Energy Independence Authority was defeated in Congress, Carter's proposal for a synthetic fuels program eventually met with some success. In 1980, Congress created an autonomous Synthetic

Fuels Corporation (SFC) to provide financial assistance for the rapid development of a major synfuels production capacity using the extensive coal, tar sands, and oil shale resources of the United States. Departing from the traditional model of government funding for research and development, the SFC could use price guarantees, purchase agreements, loans and loan guarantees, and even support for joint ventures. The legislation set specific production goals of 500,000 barrels per day by 1987 and 2 MBD by 1992, and Congress authorized $20 billion for the first four years. In 1984, however, funding for the SFC was cut in half, and at the end of 1985, Congress voted to abolish it (Davis 1982, 256–57; Schneider 1983, 467–68; Bull-Berg 1987, 43–44, 54; Duffield 2008, 73–74).

Longer-lived but more modest was government support for alcohol fuels, especially ethanol. The 1978 energy legislation established a full exemption to the 4-cent federal gasoline tax for alcohol fuels, including gasohol, a blend of 90 percent gasoline and 10 percent ethanol. This effectively created a subsidy of 40 cents per gallon of ethanol. When the gasoline tax was raised to nine cents per gallon in 1983, the gasohol exemption was increased to 5 cents, and then to 6 cents in 1984 (Duffield 2008, 74).

LIFTING OIL PRICE CONTROLS

Perhaps the most significant step that the government could have taken to increase U.S. energy security was to eliminate the price controls on oil and petroleum products imposed in the early 1970s and the allocation and entitlements schemes that developed around them. To be sure, price controls helped to cushion consumers from the sudden jump in world oil prices. In fact, the real price of gasoline increased by only 42 percent between 1973 and 1979 (EIA 2010, 181). But these programs stimulated oil consumption and imports, discouraged conservation, and inhibited the development of new domestic oil resources (Kalt 1983; Vietor 1984, 236–71). It was estimated that the benefits to consumers amounted to an effective annual subsidy of $23 billion in the mid- to late 1970s (Stobaugh and Yergin 1979, 3, cited in Bull-Berg 1987, 37).

While the market effects of artificially low prices on consumption, production, and imports could have been anticipated, the entitlements program had the further pernicious effect of subsidizing the importation of foreign crude oil by refiners by ensuring that such oil would end up costing no more per barrel than the equalized cost of all crude refined in the United States. This effective subsidy consistently ranged between 10 and 20 percent of the price of each barrel of imported oil over 1975–80 (de Marchi 1981a, 473; Kalt 1983, 107–8). According to one estimate, the associated growth in crude imports used to satisfy the subsidized demand was in the range of 0.8 to 1.3 MBD, which was in addition to the increase caused by the depressing effect of price controls on domestic crude production (Kalt 1983, 108). On top of all this, these programs distorted the mix of refined products, created a number of other economic inefficiencies, and imposed a substantial regulatory burden (de Marchi 1981a, 453–54; Kalt 1983, 112; Vietor 1984, 257 and 270–71).

Despite the potential benefits of eliminating them and their attendant allocation and entitlements programs, however, price controls remained fully in place until mid-1979 and were not completely removed until early 1981, more than seven years after the first oil shock. One reason this proved so difficult is that the 1973 EPAA codified the price controls in law, making it difficult for any president to end them without congressional cooperation (Hakes 2008, 28). In particular, it stipulated that amendments regarding allocation or price controls would require a finding by the president that continued regulation would be unnecessary, among other things, and that Congress must concur with the president's judgment (de Marchi 1981a, 469). Thus, although Ford called for eliminating the price controls just over a year later, he was ultimately forced to compromise with Congress in order to obtain some of his other goals. Indeed, the resulting EPCA not only maintained the price of old oil at $5.25, but it placed a cap of $11.28 on the price of new oil, bringing down the weighted average price of domestic crude from $8.75 to $7.66. As a result, the new law further discouraged domestic production. Not only did the lower tier price foster the neglect and abandonment of existing wells, but the upper tier price was allegedly too low to justify the costs of new wildcat exploration, deep offshore drilling, or enhanced tertiary recovery (Vietor 1984, 254).

The EPCA did, however, allow the president to increase the average price by as much as 10 percent per year in order to compensate for inflation and to provide a production incentive. After 40 months, moreover, the president could take positive action to end the controls, subject to congressional review (de Marchi 1981b, 504 and 540–41; Yager 1981, 612; Davis 1982, 113; Schneider, 1983, 328; Vietor 1984, 251–52). But Congress subsequently took no action on Carter's 1977 proposals to modify the price controls. Thus it was not until mid-1979, following Carter's April announcement, that the price controls began to be lifted. On June 1, they were removed from all newly discovered oil. And at the beginning of 1980, the remaining controls began increasing in monthly installments, with the goal of eliminating them completely by October 1981. Reagan completed the process at the beginning of his presidency by abolishing all remaining controls in one fell swoop (Yager 1981, 612–13; Schneider 1983, 465–67).

External Policy Responses

In contrast to the limited steps taken at home to reduce oil consumption and imports, the United States made extensive use of external policy instruments to promote its energy security in response to the oil shocks. As Susan Strange has argued, because the United States was unable to restrain domestic demand sufficiently or to build a big enough strategic stockpile, it had "to look more to its defence and foreign policies to achieve the security it wanted" (Strange 1988, 202; see also Ikenberry 1988, 80). To this end, the United States pursued a two-pronged approach. On the one hand, it sought to ensure the steady flow of adequate amounts of oil at reasonable prices from the Persian Gulf. On the other hand, it worked with other consumer countries to improve their ability to coordinate their response to a future oil supply disruption while reducing their dependence on oil imports.[6]

U.S. POLICY TOWARD OIL PRODUCERS

During the 1970s and early 1980s, the United States became increasingly involved in the Persian Gulf for reasons largely having to do with its pursuit of greater energy security. The specifics of U.S. policy evolved along with the changing nature of the principal threats to the flow of oil from the region. These ranged from the embargo and intentional production cuts to internal sources of instability (e.g., the Iranian revolution) to regional interstate conflicts (e.g., the Iran-Iraq War) to threats emanating from outside the region (e.g., the Soviet invasion of Afghanistan). Rather than follow all the twists and turns of U.S. policy, however, it can be summarized as follows.

The goals of U.S. policy fell into two broad categories. First, successive administrations sought to influence the production decisions of the Persian Gulf states. More specifically, they sought to dissuade the oil producers from engaging in further embargoes or production cuts and, conversely, to encourage them to produce at levels that would result in moderate prices and to increase output whenever necessary to compensate for unexpected supply disruptions.

Second, U.S. policymakers sought to protect the Persian Gulf states from threats that could result in unintended disruptions of their oil production and exports. This meant strengthening friendly producers so they could more effectively deal with various internal and external threats on their own. But it could also mean, as a last resort, playing a direct role in the defense of the region's oil supplies and transit routes.

How did the United States go about trying to realize these ambitious goals? Simply put, it employed a wide range of policy tools. Indeed, it arguably devoted more resources to these efforts than it had directed toward any region other than Western Europe and Northeast and Southeast Asia since World War II.

In response to the Arab oil embargo and production cuts, the United States initially contemplated using coercive methods in order to get the participating oil producers to relent. In the 1974 Trade Act, for example, the United States specifically excluded OPEC members that withheld oil supplies or raised oil prices from eligibility for trade preferences granted to developing countries (Campbell 1976, 688–89). More seriously, top U.S. officials occasionally hinted at the possibility of military intervention to ensure the flow of oil. In September 1974, Secretary of Defense James Schlesinger warned that reprisals were possible if the situation did not improve. And at the end of the year, then Secretary of State Henry Kissinger offered the following much cited statement: "I am not saying that there's no circumstance where we would not use force. But it is one thing to use it in the case of a dispute over price; it's another where there is some actual strangulation of the industrialized world" (Kissinger 1982, 689). Behind the scenes, some contingency planning took place, and the prospects for alternative military missions were evaluated in several congressional studies (Bull-Berg 1987, 112; see also Nau 1980, 45; Davis 1982, 109–10).

Such threats were seen as being of limited use, however, and the United States instead placed primary emphasis on providing a variety of inducements and forms of assistance. Initially, it pursued a strategy of creating greater economic linkage and interdependence with the oil producers. In the case of Saudi Arabia, this approach culminated in a June agreement on economic and military cooperation (Nau 1980, 43; Schneider 1983, 262; Bull-Berg 1987, 58 and 91–93).

Even more important, however, were the growing military ties between the United States and the gulf states, especially Iran and Saudi Arabia. We have already noted the Nixon administration's earlier decision to rely on Iran to protect U.S. interests in the region. Following the first oil shock, this relationship only intensified. Between 1973 and 1978, Iran ordered some $16 billion in military equipment, including some of the most advanced U.S. military aircraft. Total sales of arms and military services to Saudi Arabia were even greater, averaging about $4 billion per year, roughly half of which consisted of military construction projects. The United States also agreed to equip and train the Saudi Arabian National Guard for internal security purposes.[7]

Finally, the United States provided more general forms of political and diplomatic support. It offered strong and largely unconditional backing for the Shah of Iran, even in the face of widespread human rights abuses and growing opposition and protest. Then after the Shah fell, it dispatched forces to the region at least twice as a show of support for the Saudis in the face of growing regional turmoil.

The most dramatic American gesture, however, was the articulation of the so-called Carter Doctrine in January 1980. In his state of the union address that year, shortly after the Soviet invasion of Afghanistan, President Carter made the following statement: "Let our position be absolutely clear: An attempt by any outside force to gain control of the Persian Gulf region will be regarded as an assault on the vital interests of the United States of America, and such an assault will be repelled by any means necessary, including military force."

Over the following years, the United States developed a special regional military planning and command structure, which in 1983 became the U.S. Central Command (CENTCOM), and it steadily improved its ability to intervene militarily by increasing the U.S. naval presence in the gulf and nearby waters and acquiring additional strategic mobility forces and prepositioned equipment.[8] Although the European allies agreed to assume increased responsibility for their own defense if American forces were committed to the Persian Gulf, the initial Western efforts to defend the region's oil supplies were conducted almost entirely by the United States (Bull-Berg 1987, 111).

EFFORTS TO PROMOTE COOPERATION WITH OTHER CONSUMER COUNTRIES

At the same time, the United States made the most extensive efforts to promote cooperation among the advanced industrialized consumer countries in response to the oil shocks. In particular, it played the leading role in the creation of the International Energy Agency (IEA) and its subsequent activities.

Initially, the United States, under the Nixon administration, hoped to coordinate the energy policies of the consumer countries in such a way as to induce the OPEC members to moderate oil prices. The goal was to create a unified consumer bloc that could bargain effectively with the oil producers. This goal turned out to be unattainable, as many Europeans and the Japanese feared antagonizing the oil producers. Thus U.S. attention shifted to less controversial measures.

In February 1974, the United States hosted an energy conference in Washington. There it proposed the adoption of a set of emergency measures that could be implemented in the event of a future supply disruption. The final communiqué called for the creation of such a scheme and established a working group to develop a plan for a comprehensive action program, with only France dissenting. These efforts culminated in November 1974, with the creation of the IEA and the adoption of an International Energy Program (IEP). The IEP required members to maintain reserves equivalent to 60 (later raised to 90) days of oil imports and to plan and implement, if necessary, measures to reduce oil consumption during an interruption. It also provided for the equitable sharing of oil supplies in an emergency, the Emergency Sharing System (ESS).[9]

Immediately following the creation of the IEA, the United States advocated for further cooperative efforts to promote energy security. In late 1974, Kissinger called on the membership to reduce its oil imports by 20 percent and asked for conservation measures that would achieve a 10 percent cut in consumption by the end of 1975. He also recommended a full-scale program of research and development on alternative energy sources. And to promote domestic production of oil and its substitutes, the United States proposed the establishment of a floor for the cost of imported oil, the so-called Minimum Safeguard Price (MSP), which was adopted in 1976. During subsequent years, the United States continued to press for reductions in oil imports and, in response to the second oil shock, it sought to obtain an agreement establishing individual country import quotas with the possibility of sanctions against those countries that exceeded their quotas.[10]

Evaluation of U.S. Policy Responses to the Oil Shocks

How much more secure was the United States a decade after the first oil shock, and why? In particular, to what degree were any improvements in U.S. energy security the result of policy responses to the oil shocks?

In many respects, the United States appeared more secure than it had been in 1973. The country was still far from self-sufficient in energy, but the situation had improved. After rising for several years in the mid-1970s, overall U.S. oil consumption had dropped steadily and reached just 15.7 MBD in 1985, or 10 percent less than at the time of the first oil shock. Likewise, oil's share of primary energy consumption, which stood at nearly 46 percent in 1973, had fallen to under 41 percent (EIA 2010, 9; BP 2013). Meanwhile, domestic petroleum production, after declining for several years, stabilized and then even grew slightly, reaching 10.6 MBD in 1985. As a result, net oil imports started to drop in 1977 and reached an average of only 4.3 MBD, less than the figure for 1972, and the share of oil consumption provided by imports declined to just over 27 percent in 1985, lower than any time since before the oil embargo (figure 9.1) (EIA 2010, 129). Finally,

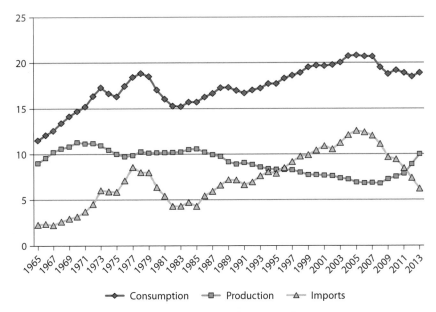

Figure 9.1 U.S. petroleum consumption, production, and imports, 1965–2013 (millions of barrels per day). Note: Petroleum production includes crude oil and natural gas plant liquids. *Source*: Energy Information Administration, "Petroleum Overview," www.eia.gov/totalenergy/data/browser/xls.cfm?tbl=T03.01.

whereas the United States possessed virtually no spare production capacity in the early 1970s, the government now disposed of a SPR of nearly 500 million barrels, or the equivalent of more than 100 days of net imports (figure 9.2) (EIA 2010, 165–67). At the macro-level, the United States was now much better prepared to deal with a future oil supply disruption than it had been in 1973.

Oil consumption had fallen in almost every sector. Most dramatically, it had dropped by more than two-thirds in the electric power sector and by 44 percent in the residential sector. But even the commercial sector and industry had recorded declines of 32 percent and 9 percent, respectively. The principal exception to these trends, and source of concern, was transportation, where oil consumption had actually increased by 9 percent between 1973 and 1985. As a result, the share of U.S. oil consumption attributable to the sector had risen from 52.3 to 62.6 percent, while transportation remained almost entirely dependent on petroleum products. Thus oil use had become even more concentrated in the sector where ready substitutes were least available (EIA 2010, 44 and 154–57). Nevertheless, the fuel economy of new cars and light trucks had risen substantially, to an average of more than 25 mpg in 1985 (Davis and Diegel 2004, table 4-20). Thus oil

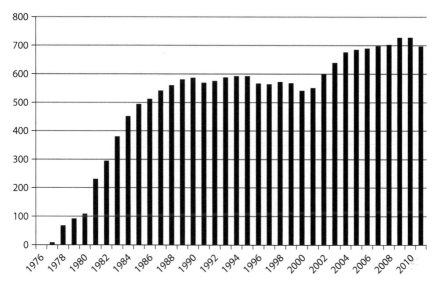

Figure 9.2 U.S. Strategic Petroleum Reserve, 1976–2011 (billions of barrels). *Source*: EIA 2012, 159, table 5.17.

consumption in the transportation sector might level off or even decline as the more efficient vehicles constituted an ever larger share of the fleet (figure 9.3).

To what degree did U.S. policy responses contribute to these trends, positive or otherwise? Clearly, the government played an indispensable role in some areas, such as the creation of the SPR. Likewise, the largest contribution to halting and at least temporarily reversing the decline in U.S. domestic oil production was the legislation that made possible the construction of the trans-Alaska pipeline, through which roughly 20 percent of U.S. crude oil was flowing in 1985. Government policies also contributed to the declining share of oil in electricity production, from around 17 percent in 1973 to just 4 percent in 1985 (EIA 2010, 129 and 230).

Arguably, though, the improvements in patterns of oil consumption, production, and imports had more to do with market forces than with government policies. First, it is important to note that oil consumption and imports did not peak until 1978 or 1979, when the second oil shock saw world prices more than double and the lifting of price controls finally began. One can only speculate how much further consumption and imports would have dropped—and domestic production would have risen—if price controls had been removed as early as 1973. Although U.S. energy intensity had declined by 18 percent between 1973 and 1981, federal programs and tax credits probably accounted for less than 5 percent, and

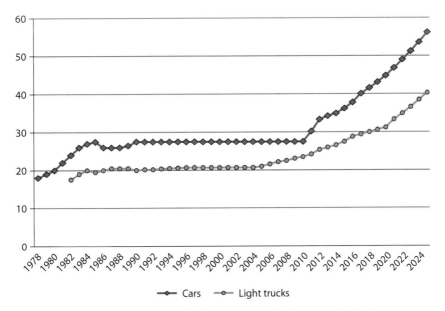

Figure 9.3 U.S. fuel economy standards, 1978–2025 (miles per gallon). *Source*: Transportation Energy Data Book, tables 4.19, 4.21, and 4.22, http://cta.ornl.gov /data/index.shtml.

perhaps as little as 2 percent, of that improvement, according to estimates by the DOE (Hirst et al. 1983, 193 and 202–3). And even the role of the CAFE program in bringing about the increases in light vehicle efficiency has been questioned. As a 2002 National Research Council study concluded, "High fuel prices and a desire on the part of automakers to reduce costs by reducing the weight of vehicles contributed to improved fuel economy" (Duffield 2008, 70).

With perhaps the principal exception of the CAFE program, moreover, there were few policies in place to prevent renewed dependence on oil and imports, should prices fall substantially. The government had imposed no significant taxes on crude oil, oil imports, or petroleum products, and the principal initiative to develop alternative fuels was canceled in 1985. Other than the SPR, the U.S. government had no plan for handling a future oil cutoff (Schneider 1983, 469). It may be that the level of peacetime federal government activism in the energy field had been unprecedented (Beaubouef 2007, 6), but it was still quite limited.

We see a similar mixed pattern of success in the international realm. The United States took by far the most active role of any developed democracy in attempting to ensure the steady flow of oil from the gulf, and its increased involvement arguably exerted some positive influence on production decisions in the region. There was no second Arab oil embargo, and the principal U.S. allies, Saudi Arabia and, until 1979, Iran, maintained output at sufficiently high levels as to help bring down gradually the real cost of crude oil. Indeed, Saudi Arabia actively resisted further OPEC price increases on multiple occasions and raised its production at least twice to help compensate for oil supply disruptions elsewhere in the gulf, resisting the temptation to profit from higher world prices. As one analysis concluded, "It seems likely that Saudi Arabia may be producing more oil than is warranted by its financial interests. . . . If this is true, it can be attributed principally to a tacit agreement with the United States that protection will be provided to the Saudi regime in return for increased oil production" (Plummer and Weyant 1982, 259).

Overall, however, it is not clear that U.S. external policy made the Persian Gulf and thus the world oil market generally more stable. The United States was unable to prevent a second oil price shock in 1979, even though the net loss of output was less than that of the Arab oil embargo. Indeed, U.S. policy may have helped to precipitate the crisis by exacerbating the unpopularity of the Shah and thus setting the stage for the Iranian revolution, which saw Iran go from being one of America's most important allies to one of its most implacable foes.

Heightened American involvement in the Persian Gulf had other costs as well. Especially after 1979, there was the financial cost of the growing military commitment and the increased risk of being drawn into a regional conflict. American ties to Iran and Saudi Arabia also limited U.S. freedom of action and frequently entailed compromising and even sacrificing other important U.S. foreign policy objectives. For example, U.S. support for the Shah conflicted with the goals of promoting human rights and limiting foreign arms transfers. By the same token, U.S. military sales to Saudi Arabia raised alarms about the security of Israel (Duffield 2008).

Likewise, U.S. efforts to promote cooperation among the consumer countries encountered mixed success. On the one hand, the United States did spearhead the formation of the IEA and the organization's emergency oil-sharing system, including the requirement that members maintain strategic stocks equivalent to 60, and later 90, days of imports. But the ESS had important limitations, which were prominently on display during the second oil crisis in 1979. The IEA refused to activate the system in response to a Swedish request, and it could do little more than exhort its members to cut their oil imports (Ikenberry 1988, 99; Duffield 2008, 88).

Moreover, the United States failed to achieve its other goals with regard to consumer countries. During the first oil shock, it was unable to forge a united front that could articulate a common bargaining position in negotiations with OPEC on oil supply and pricing. And during the following years, its efforts to obtain reductions in IEA member oil imports were largely unsuccessful. United States proposals for national targets for import cuts were successfully resisted, and the MSP was set at too low a level to stimulate domestic production of oil and its substitutes (Ikenberry 1988, 80–96 passim; Duffield 2008, 91–93).

U.S. Responses to Energy Insecurity in the 2000s

The U.S. energy security concerns of the 2000s were quite similar to those of the 1970s, in part because the United States had done comparatively little to reduce its dependence on oil. As during the earlier period, these concerns revolved primarily around growing import dependence and the rising cost of oil. Although the United States experienced nothing comparable to the oil shocks of the 1970s, the price of oil—and automotive gasoline in particular—rose inexorably over the course of the decade, eventually reaching record highs in mid-2008. These price concerns were compounded by the negative consequences of importing so much oil, which reached 60 percent of consumption in the middle of the decade.

Consequently, U.S. policy responses during this period focused on reducing U.S. oil consumption and promoting the production and export of oil in other parts of the world. At home, the government approved the first major increases in fuel economy standards in more than two decades, and it established a mandate for the inclusion of ever great volumes of renewables in the nation's transportation fuel supply. Taken together, these measures held out the promise of eventually reducing U.S. oil consumption by as much as one quarter. In addition, it made efforts to increase the size of the SPR so that the nation was better prepared to deal with a future oil supply disruption.

At the same time, as in the 1970s, the United States actively sought to promote its energy security in the international realm. The Bush administration maintained and, in some regions, intensified policies initiated during the Clinton administration to promote the diversification of world oil supplies. And U.S. involvement in the Persian Gulf to safeguard the region's oil supplies, which had been growing ever deeper since the 1970s, culminated in the invasion and subsequent occupation of Iraq.

Background

In 2000, 39 percent of U.S. primary energy consumption (PEC) was attributable to petroleum. This represented a not insignificant decrease from 1973, when the comparable figure was 46 percent. Nevertheless, the United States continued to rely much more heavily on oil than any other energy source. The shares provided by natural gas and coal stood at 24 and 23 percent, respectively. Although nuclear power had grown substantially since 1973, it still accounted for just 7 percent of U.S. PEC, with renewable sources of energy providing the remaining 6 percent (EIA 2010, 9).

Not only did the United States continue to rely most heavily on oil, but its dependence on petroleum imports had risen and was continuing to grow. In 1985, domestic crude oil production had returned to 93 percent of its all-time peak but then began a steady and seemingly irreversible decline (EIA 2010, 131). Conversely, net petroleum imports had bottomed out in the early to mid-1980s, at 4.3 MBD. But after that, they had grown more or less steadily, reaching 10.4 MBD in 2000. As a share of total petroleum products supplied, moreover, net imports had also grown, from 27.3 percent in 1985 to 52.9 percent in 2000, and these figures were expected only to increase (EIA 2010, 9).

A third development of significance for U.S. energy security was the growing concentration of petroleum consumption in the transportation sector. The amount of oil used to produce electric power and for residential and commercial applications had dropped in both relative and absolute terms since 1973. The industrial sector had seen an absolute increase in petroleum use, but its share of total oil consumption had declined slightly, to just under 25 percent. In contrast, that attributable to transportation had grown from 52.3 percent in 1973 to 66.0 percent in 2000 and was continuing to rise (EIA 2010, 154–57). What made this trend particularly significant was that the sector itself was almost entirely dependent (96.7 percent) on petroleum products in 2000 (EIA 2010, 44). There were few or no alternatives to oil for most important means of transportation, making this sector particularly vulnerable to a future supply or price shock.

An important underlying cause of these trends was the fact that world oil prices had dropped substantially in the mid-1980s and remained well below post-oil shock prices through the 1990s. But these market conditions that promoted oil consumption and imports and inhibited U.S. domestic production were reinforced by U.S. policies. As discussed above, government responses to the oil shocks ultimately culminated in the almost complete deregulation of the oil market in 1981. Thus, in contrast to the 1960s and early 1970s, there were no constraints on petroleum imports. In addition, restrictions on oil exploration and production in sensitive areas, including substantial offshore areas and important parts of Alaska, suppressed domestic oil output, though by how much is difficult to estimate.

Not least significant in contributing to these trends were U.S. fuel economy standards. As petroleum consumption became increasingly concentrated in the transportation sector, regulation of fuel economy became an increasingly important determinant of overall consumption. As noted above, the CAFE standards had resulted in a significant increase in fuel economy of new vehicles by the mid-1980s. During the following years, however, they were subverted by the increasing use of light trucks in the form of minivans and sport utility vehicles (SUVs), which were held to a lower standard than passenger vehicles. As a result, the overall fuel economy of the U.S. vehicle fleet stagnated and even dipped as the 1990s came to a close (EIA 2010, 59). And in the late 1990s, the Congress prevented the transportation department from even studying possible changes (Duffield 2008, 71).

The one bright spot in the U.S. energy security panorama was the SPR, which had reached nearly 600 million barrels in the mid-1990s. Nevertheless, this amount still stood well short of the authorized volume of 1 billion barrels. And in terms of one key measure—its equivalence in days of net petroleum imports—the effective size of the SPR was actually declining steadily as oil imports grew.

The Reemergence of U.S. Concerns about Energy Security

During the first part of the decade, domestic energy supplies were disrupted on several occasions. These included electricity shortages in California in 2000 and 2001, an extensive power outage in the Northeast in 2003, and Hurricanes Katrina and Rita in 2005, which temporarily halted import and refining operations in the Gulf of Mexico. In addition, concerns were expressed over the rising share of natural gas that had to be imported, although virtually all of those imports continued to come from Canada, which posed little risk of a supply disruption.

Instead, the energy security issues that captured the most sustained attention in the United States during the early 2000s once again revolved around oil. These concerns had several dimensions. First, there was the country's growing dependence on oil imports. The share of oil consumption that had to be met by imports passed the 50 percent mark in the late 1990s and continued to grow, reaching more than 60 percent in 2005 (EIA 2012, 120). Official projection suggested even higher levels of import dependence in the future. In 2004, the Department of Energy forecast that it would reach nearly two-thirds in 2020 and 70 percent in 2025, assuming no major changes in policy (EIA 2004, 150; see also Abraham 2004).

At the same time, the prices of oil and petroleum products were rising rapidly, at least by recent historical standards. In late 2000, the cost of a barrel oil reached $30 for the first time since the 1990–91 Gulf War and for only the second time since the price collapse of the mid-1980s. Then, after dropping briefly during the following two years, it began a more or less steady rise that ultimately led to an all-time high of nearly $150 per barrel in mid-2008, before temporarily dropping sharply.[11] The rising cost of crude oil was reflected in the all-important U.S. gasoline prices. After hovering between $1 and $1.20 a gallon for most of the 1990s, they jumped to around $1.50 a gallon in 2000 and 2001. Then, after dipping in the wake of 9/11, they too began a fairly steady rise that set record after record and culminated in gas at over $4.00 a gallon in 2008.

The underlying cause of the higher prices was a growing mismatch between supply and demand in world markets. Global consumption was rising rapidly—by nearly 10 percent between 1995 and 2000 and again between 2000 and 2005—largely due to increasing demand in China, India, and elsewhere in the developing world. Meanwhile, investment in new production capacity had lagged in the late 1980s and 1990s because of low oil prices. As a result, the market grew ever tighter, and the world's surplus production capacity dropped to its lowest level in three decades, just 1 MBD in 2004 (Morse and Jaffe 2001, 10; Clawson and Henderson 2005, 4).

In this context of tight markets and the price inelasticity of oil demand, prices were poised to go even higher in the event of a major supply disruption, a prospect that seemed increasingly likely (Morse and Jaffe 2001, 4 and 9; Clawson and Henderson 2005; see also Duffield 2008, 34–38). Of particular concern was the potential for political turmoil and conflict in the Persian Gulf, where so much of the world's oil production and remaining spare capacity were concentrated. Analysts pointed to a number of possible events in the region that could lead to a significant restriction of the global oil supply: contested leadership transitions in countries such as Saudi Arabia, terrorist attacks on oil facilities, a possible confrontation with Iraq or Iran, and following the prolonged U.S. invasion and occupation of the former, the spread of domestic instability to neighboring oil-producing states. Nor were such concerns limited to the Persian Gulf. During the early years of the decade, both Venezuela and Nigeria both saw brief but substantial declines in their oil output because of internal upheavals.

Finally, the combination of a large percentage of oil imports and high oil prices meant that Americans were sending a large and growing share of their wealth abroad. After averaging about $50 billion per year during the 1990s, the net cost of petroleum imports surged past the $100 billion mark in 2000. Then, beginning in 2004, it grew rapidly until 2008, when it reached nearly $400 billion and accounted for almost half of the United States' ballooning trade deficit.[12]

Beyond the economic consequences, this vast transfer of wealth undermined U.S. national security in several important respects. Increased oil revenues tended to foster corruption and slow political reform in many oil-producing states.

Especially following the attacks of September 11, 2001, concerns grew that money sent abroad to pay for oil imports was being used to finance anti-American terrorist activity. And substantial oil revenues helped to empower regimes, such as those in Venezuela, Iran, and increasingly Russia, that were hostile to American values and interests. As one prominent study concluded, "Because of their oil wealth, these and other producer countries are free to ignore U.S. policies and to pursue interests inimical to our national security" (Deutch and Schlesinger 2006, 25). Thus U.S. import dependence translated into a loss of foreign policy influence (Bush 2006, 28–29; Kohl 2007, 13).

Overview of U.S. Policy Responses

The U.S. responses to these renewed concerns about energy security unfolded over a number of years. The Bush administration took the initiative in 2001, but it was dependent on a much more slowly moving Congress to enact the most important domestic aspects of U.S. policy. Thus it was not until the end of 2007 that all the main elements of the U.S. response were in place.

Less than two weeks after taking office in January 2001, President George W. Bush established a National Energy Policy Development Group (NEPDG) consisting of a number of members of his cabinet and chaired by the vice president. In May, the group issued a 170-page "National Energy Policy" report that identified the twin problems of high energy prices and growing imports. Despite its length, however, the report contained few concrete proposals for enhancing U.S. energy security. It called for opening up a portion of the Arctic National Wildlife Refuge (ANWR) in Alaska for exploration and oil and gas production, but the principal emphasis was on promoting market liberalization and foreign investment, especially by U.S. companies, in oil-producing countries (NEPDG 2001).

In June, the administration delivered its proposals requiring legislative enactment to Congress. But for the next four years, its role was largely limited to exhorting Congress to produce meaningful energy legislation, although President Bush did direct the government to fill the SPR to its full capacity of 727 million barrels following the September 11 attacks. In both 2002 and 2003, Congress came close to passing a broad energy bill. Each time, however, a final deal remained elusive. As one account described the latter efforts, "Lawmakers from both parties condemned the proposal, developed mainly by pro-industry Republicans, for its $31 billion price tag, its subsidies for power companies, a plan to provide legal immunity to producers of a gasoline additive blamed for water pollution, and its failure to promote alternative energy savings plans like better fuel efficiency" (Hulse 2003b).

Thus it was not until after the next national election that Congress finally took action. The Energy Policy Act of 2005 (EPACT) was the first comprehensive energy legislation since the early 1990s. With regard to energy security, its most notable elements were the introduction of a renewable fuel standard (RFS) to promote the consumption of biofuels, tax credits for the purchase of vehicles that used little or no petroleum products, and financial incentives for deepwater offshore oil production in the Gulf of Mexico. It also provided for expanding the capacity of the SPR to 1 billion barrels of oil (Holt and Glover 2006; Lazzari 2008).

As oil prices continued to rise, the Bush administration called for further action. In his January 2006 State of the Union address, President Bush enunciated the goal of replacing more than 75 percent of U.S. oil imports from the Middle East by 2025 and proposed an Advanced Energy Initiative involving increased research in alternative transportation fuels and technologies, such as hybrids, electric cars, and hydrogen fuel cells. The following year, he set an even more ambitious target: cutting U.S. gasoline use by 20 percent over the next 10 years, or "Twenty in Ten." To achieve this goal, he called for aggressively expanding the supply of alternative fuels, to 35 billion gallons by 2017, increasing the CAFE standards by roughly 4 percent per year beginning in 2010, and authorizing oil and gas exploration in ANWR. He also asked Congress to double the capacity of the SPR (White House 2007).

This time, Congress responded much more quickly, passing the 2007 Energy Independence and Security Act (EISA) by the end of the year. In some respects, the 2007 bill was much more far reaching than EPACT, although it contained almost no tax provisions. With regard to energy security, it raised the CAFE standards for the first time since they were established in 1975, it greatly expanded the RFS adopted in 2005, and it provided additional incentives and support for the development and purchase of advanced batteries, plug-in hybrids, and electric vehicles. More symbolically, it made energy security a core mission of the Department of State and added the Secretary of Energy to the National Security Council (Sissine 2007). According to one early estimate, the legislation would cut U.S. oil consumption by more than 4 MBD by 2030 (Pelosi 2007).

Initially, U.S. oil dependence and high oil prices were prominent issues in the 2008 presidential campaign. Candidate Barack Obama put forward a detailed proposal for saving more oil than the United States currently imported from the Middle East and Venezuela combined (Duffield 2008). And upon taking office, the new Obama administration moved quickly to accelerate the increase in the CAFE standards. Because of the sharp decline in oil prices that occurred in late 2008, the financial crisis, and enduring concerns about climate change, however, political attention quickly shifted away from the issue of energy security, and subsequent legislative efforts focused on limiting greenhouse gas emissions. The principal bill passed by the House of Representatives, the American Clean Energy and Security Act of 2009 (HR 2454), sought to establish a cap and trade system for carbon emissions and, despite its title, contained few if any provisions primarily intended to promote U.S. energy security.

Domestic Policy Responses

Over the course of the decade, then, the U.S. government took a handful of important steps at home intended to increase U.S. energy security. These covered familiar terrain, all having to do with America's oil dependence in general and its growing reliance on oil imports in particular. And they covered the full range of approaches, including efforts to reduce oil consumption, promote substitutes for petroleum products, stimulate domestic oil production, and increase the size of the SPR.[13]

REDUCING OIL CONSUMPTION

As noted above, one of the most important elements of U.S. policy during this period was the first legislated increase in fuel economy standards in more than 30 years. With only slight variations, the standard for passenger cars had stood at 27.5 mpg and that for light trucks, including SUVs and minivans, at just over 20 mpg since the late 1980s, and during the second half of the 1990s, Congress had prohibited the Department of Transportation from even studying possible changes.

Early in the Bush administration, Congress lifted this restriction, and in 2003, the administration issued a rule that would boost the fuel economy of light trucks by 1.5 mpg, or a total of 22.2 mpg, by 2007 (Bamberger 2004, 11). The administration was developing a further modest increase in the standard for light trucks when the Congress finally acted. The 2007 EISA mandated an effective 40 percent increase in fuel economy for all light-duty vehicles (LDV), from an average 25 mpg to 35 mpg, by 2020. It also established for the first time a fuel economy program for medium and heavy-duty trucks and created a separate standard for work trucks (Sissine 2007; Hakes 2008, 87–88). According to various estimates, the higher standard would reduce U.S. oil consumption by 1.1 to 1.2 MBD by 2020 and even greater amounts thereafter as the American vehicle fleet turned over (Pelosi 2007; Andrews 2007).

After taking office in 2009, the Obama administration accelerated the introduction of the new standards and slightly raised them, setting a new target of 35.5

mpg by 2016. And in 2012, after intensive negotiations with automakers, the administration announced an even more dramatic increase in fuel economy to 54.5 mpg by 2025, although various credits were expected to reduce the actual mileage of new vehicles to about 49 mpg (Vlasic 2012).

The 2005 EPACT contained a further noteworthy measure designed to reduce fuel consumption. This was a consumer tax credit for vehicles with lean-burn engines, hybrid engines, and fuel cells. The size of the credit varied from $250 to $3,400, depending on the vehicle's fuel economy. But once a manufacturer had sold 60,000 vehicles, the credit would phase out over the following year, and the entire program ended in 2010. Congress passed a similar tax credit for plug-in hybrid and battery powered vehicles in 2008.

DEVELOPING SUBSTITUTES FOR OIL

A second important element of the U.S. policy response to oil and import dependence was the big push to develop alternative transportation fuels through the establishment of a Renewable Fuel Standard (RFS). The 2005 EPACT mandated that a minimum of 4 billion gallons of ethanol and biodiesel be included in the nation's fuel supply in 2006 and that this minimum usage volume rise to 7.5 billion gallons by 2012, after which the share of renewables would be held constant. The 2007 EISA then greatly accelerated and expanded the buildup of renewable fuels. It established a modified standard of 9 billion gallons in 2008, rising to 36 billion gallons by 2022. It also capped the amount of ethanol that could be derived from corn starch at 15 billion gallons, ensuring that a growing share—and eventually the majority—would consist of advanced biofuels, especially cellulosic ethanol (derived from cellulose) (Sissine 2007; Schnepf and Yacobucci 2012). When fully implemented, the RFS would provide the equivalent of about 1.6 MBD of gasoline.[14]

The 2005 EPACT also contained nearly $4 billion for research, demonstration projects, and transition programs involving hydrogen and fuel cells. But these were regarded as much longer-term potential solutions to the dependence of the U.S. transportation fleet on petroleum.

INCREASING DOMESTIC OIL PRODUCTION

A third important theme of U.S. policy efforts during this period was increasing domestic oil production. As noted above, an early goal of the Bush administration was to open up the ANWR for exploration and drilling, and it made reducing federal restrictions on domestic oil production more generally a high priority. The policy achievements in this area were less dramatic, but over the course of the decade, the administration and its allies in Congress were able to register a number of successes. The 2005 EPACT prohibited the Environmental Protection Agency from regulating hydraulic fracturing (fracking) under the Safe Drinking Water Act, it offered the oil industry billions of dollars in tax breaks to help independent producers recoup some drilling costs even when a well came up dry, and it provided royalty relief for oil production in water deeper than 400 meters in the Gulf of Mexico. Separately, the Interior Department was granted the power to issue drilling permits on millions of acres of federal lands without extensive environmental impact studies for individual projects, a power that was used thousands of times and accounted for a quarter of all permits issued on federal land in the following six years. And the Bush administration opened up large tracts of the Gulf of Mexico and the waters off Alaska to exploration, granting lease deals that required companies to pay only a small share of their profits to the government (Krauss and Lipton 2012a). Even the Obama administration initially proposed opening substantial additional areas offshore to exploration and drilling (Broder 2010).

The Bush administration, however, was never able to achieve its top priority of opening up ANWR, which was thought to contain one of the largest concentrations of untapped petroleum reserves. Republican members of Congress repeatedly introduced bills to that end without success. Indeed, the original House version of the 2005 EPACT contained provisions to allow drilling there, but they were removed from the final version. In addition, the 2007 EISA repealed two tax subsidies for oil and gas, although efforts to impose $31 billion in new taxes on oil and gas producers were blocked.

EMERGENCY PREPARATIONS: INCREASING THE SIZE OF THE SPR

A final sets of efforts concerned improving the capacity of the United States to respond to a future oil supply disruption by increasing the size of the SPR. In the mid-1990s, the SPR had reached nearly 600 million barrels, but had then shrunk to just over 540 million barrels through a series of sales and exchanges (EIA 2012, 159). Following the terrorist attacks of September 11, 2001, President Bush directed that the SPR be filled to 700 million barrels, or nearly its total physical capacity at the time of 727 million barrels (Beaubouef 2007, 46). Then, in the 2005 EPACT, Congress directed the government to expand the SPR to its authorized capacity of 1 billion barrels, which would require not only topping off the existing storage sites but also enlarging them and/or adding a new facility. Finally, in his 2007 State of the Union address, President Bush called for doubling the size of the SPR, to 1.5 billion barrels by 2027. This proposal, however, was not included in that year's energy bill, and in 2011, the process of adding new capacity was canceled.[15]

External Policy Responses

While taking these steps at home, the United States under the Bush administration was also very active on the international front in its efforts to promote American energy security. As in the 1970s, these effort involved relations both with actual and potential oil-producing states and, to a lesser extent, with other oil-dependent countries and regions. With regard to the former, U.S. policy had two general goals. One was to diversify world oil supplies by promoting production in new areas. The other was to reduce the risk of a disruption of existing oil supplies, especially in the Persian Gulf (see also Abraham 2004).

As noted above, the Bush administration's 2001 National Energy Policy placed considerable emphasis on promoting foreign investment and market liberalization in oil-producing countries. As one administration official put the matter, "We intend to engage intensively with energy partners all over the world to diversify supplies, improve investment opportunities and assure that market forces work as transparently and efficiently as possible" (Larson 2003). Indeed, by one count, one-third of all the recommendations in the NEP concerned obtaining access to oil sources abroad (Klare 2004b, 5).

This goal took on added urgency following the terrorist attacks of September 2001, which raised questions about the reliability of Persian Gulf oil supplies. Thus the new National Security Strategy issued by the Bush administration in October 2002 called for expanding "the sources and types of global energy supplied, especially in the Western Hemisphere, Africa, Central Asia, and the Caspian region" (Bush 2002, 20).

Precisely what actions the Bush administration took to promote the diversification of world oil supplies, however, is difficult to establish in detail. Some, such as economic assistance, may have been intended to serve multiple purposes and thus cannot be easily attributed to just the goal of increasing U.S. energy security. In addition, many efforts took place behind the scenes and went unreported in the press.[16]

In some cases, moreover, making progress toward this goal involved continuing policies begun during the Clinton administration. Thus, for example, the creation of an East-West energy corridor from the Caspian region to the Mediterranean, which had been initiated in the 1990s, remained a major priority. In particular, the Bush administration emphasized the completion of the BTC pipeline connecting Baku on the Caspian Sea to the Turkish port of Ceyhan (Larson 2003; Klare 2004b, 8).

In other cases, diversifying world oil supplies required innovations in policy, reflecting new challenges and opportunities. Thus, for example, the pace of U.S. energy diplomacy toward the Gulf of Guinea accelerated greatly during the Bush administration. After 2001, American leaders engaged in a number of high-level contacts with their counterparts in the oil-producing states of the region. Also during the early 2000s, U.S. economic assistance to key oil producers Nigeria and Angola grew substantially. And the region witnessed strengthening military ties and an unprecedented level of military contacts with the United States (Duffield 2008, 147–48).

The other prong of U.S. policy toward oil-producing countries and regions concerned reducing the risk of another major supply disruption, by military means if necessary. As the Clinton administration's final national security strategy, issued just one month before Bush took office, noted, "The United States will continue to have a vital interest in ensuring access to foreign oil sources. We must continue to be mindful of the need for regional stability and security in key producing areas, as well as our ability to use our naval power, if necessary, to ensure our access to, and the free flow of, these resources" (Clinton 2000, 44). And the most logical geographical focus of this component of U.S. policy was the Persian Gulf, which remained the world's single largest source of oil by far.

Such considerations lay behind the long-standing U.S. policy of containing Iran. Certainly, one goal of containment was to prevent the Islamic republic from asserting influence or control over its oil-rich neighbors. Likewise, the single most consequential expression of U.S. policy toward the Persian Gulf during this period, the 2003 invasion and subsequent occupation of Iraq, cannot be divorced from considerations of energy security.

At the time and over the following years, numerous reasons have been given or hypothesized for the Iraq war. The Bush administration itself justified its decision in terms of Iraq's possession of chemical and biological weapons, its effort to acquire a nuclear capability, Saddam Hussein's ties to terrorist groups, and his brutal repression of the Iraqi people. Critical outside observers have emphasized such factors as a desire to dominate the Middle East, the interests of U.S. oil companies, Israeli security concerns, and President Bush's psychology.[17]

Lying beneath many of these explanations, however, has been the importance to the health of the world and the U.S. economies of ensuring a steady and substantial flow of oil from the region. Many people, including a good number of critics of the war, agreed that Iraq under the rule of Saddam Hussein posed a significant potential threat to the stability of the Persian Gulf's oil supplies. After all, Iraq had twice invaded oil rich neighbors in the previous quarter century—Iran in 1980 and Kuwait in 1990; absent UN sanctions, it could once again possess the most powerful conventional armed forces in the region; it had long sought—or seemed to seek—weapons of mass destruction that could provide even greater leverage over its neighbors; and intelligence reports concluded that it continued to harbor aspirations to regional hegemony. Thus, Vice President Dick Cheney warned in an August 2002 speech, "Armed with an arsenal of these weapons of terror, and seated atop 10 percent of the world's oil reserves, Saddam Hussein could then be expected to seek domination of the entire Middle East, take control of a great portion of the world's energy supplies, directly threaten America's friends throughout the region, and subject the United States or any other nation to nuclear blackmail."

In addition, Iraq's own contribution to world oil supplies was well below its long-term potential. According to most estimates, Iraq possessed the world's second largest oil reserves, and much of the country had not yet been explored. Yet because of UN sanctions and Saddam Hussein's own efforts to manipulate output and exports for political reasons, Iraq did not even rank among the world's top 10 producers (BP 2013). Thus regime change promised to eliminate these threats to and restrictions on the region's oil supply in one fell swoop (Duffield 2005; Duffield 2008, 179–81; Duffield 2012a).

In contrast to the 1970s, the United States did much less to promote cooperation among oil-consuming countries during this period, although it was not entirely inactive in this realm. The Bush administration sponsored a number of initiatives, but none was on par with the establishment of the IEA and the ESS in the 1970s. Indeed, it took little action of note with regard to energy security within the IEA. Likewise, although the idea of having NATO play a greater role in the provision of energy security was relatively popular in the United States, most of the concrete proposals emanated from outside of the administration, with Senator Richard Lugar being perhaps the most prominent proponent. The principal exception to this low level of activity in the multilateral realm has been strong U.S. support for the Energy Security Initiative of the APEC Energy Working Group, which was established in late 2001 (GAO 2006, 29).

Instead, U.S. policy seemed to focus much more on bilateral cooperation with major energy partners. The 2006 European Union–United States summit placed considerable focus on energy issues, and a U.S. proposal led to the creation of an EU-US Energy Council in 2009. On the other side of the world, the United States established energy dialogues with China and India in the mid-2000s followed by a framework for cooperation on energy and the environment with China in 2008 (GAO 2006, 45; DOE 2011). Few if any of these and other bilateral activities, however, were primarily concerned with energy security, and, as a result, they tended to promote U.S. energy security at best at the margin, if at all.

Evaluation of U.S. Policy Responses in the 2000s

By 2013, U.S. energy security appeared to be much improved. U.S. oil consumption had declined by some 10 percent since the peak of 2005, to levels not seen since the 1990s, and the EIA projected that it would remain roughly at the same level for the next several decades. Even more dramatically, U.S. crude oil production had arrested its previous slide and had grown by nearly half. The EIA projected that total domestic petroleum output would continue to rise until about 2020 before beginning a slow decline (EIA 2014, 37).

As a result of these positive trends in consumption and production, net U.S. petroleum imports, which had been growing steadily through the mid-2000s and had been expected to continue to rise, dropped dramatically. By 2013, they had fallen by roughly one-half in absolute terms and, as a share of consumption, from a peak of nearly 60 percent in 2005 to only one-third (figure 9.1). In 2014, the EIA projected that net imports would constitute just 25 percent of U.S. liquid fuel consumption later in the decade before slowly rising again (EIA 2014, A-27).

Nevertheless, the United States still remained vulnerable to the effects of a major oil supply disruption. Given the global nature of the oil market, a price rise triggered by a shortage anywhere in the world would quickly propagate. The U.S. ability to mitigate the impact of a supply disruption, moreover, remained limited, as the SPR had reached its full capacity of 727 million barrels in 2009 and then had actually declined to under 700 million barrels in 2011 as a result of a release to compensate for the loss of Libyan oil (figure 9.2) (EIA 2012, 159).

It would also be difficult to attribute much of the recent improvements to the new policies adopted in the 2000s. The growth in petroleum output was largely due to technological advances that enabled—and the higher prices that incentivized—drilling ever deeper offshore, enhanced recovery from conventional oil fields, and especially, the widespread introduction of hydraulic fracturing, which resulted in both a dramatic increase in the exploitation of so-called tight oil and a rise in natural gas plant liquids that accompanied the rapid increase in shale gas production. Likewise, the decline in consumption owed primarily to generally high world oil prices and the sharp economic downturn in the United States that began in 2007.

Although the higher fuel economy standards might eventually reduce oil consumption by millions of barrels per day, their impact was only just beginning to be felt. Because of the slow turnover of the LDV fleet—about 6 percent per year—its overall actual fuel economy remained just over 20 mpg (figure 9.3) (Davis et al. 2013, 4-1). The RFS had made a bigger difference, with ethanol output reaching 14 billion gallons in 2011. But biofuels still comprised less than 6 percent of total U.S. transportation fuel consumption, and total production had leveled off because of difficulties with the large-scale introduction of biodiesel and advanced biofuels such as cellulosic ethanol (Schnepf and Yacobucci 2012, 1). Indeed, the EIA projected that ethanol consumption would reach only 16.4 billion gallons in 2022 and then decline because of increased fuel economy and limited sales of FFVs (EIA 2013a, 83).

Just as noteworthy as these measures, moreover, was what the new energy policy legislation did not attempt to do in order to reduce U.S. oil consumption and imports. Perhaps most notably, it provided for no increase in the traditionally low U.S. taxes on motor fuels, which have made American consumers uniquely sensitive to oil price spikes. Although economists argue that higher fuel taxes would be the most efficient way to reduce oil consumption (for example, CBO 2002, ix), the federal gasoline tax had remained frozen at 18.4 cents per gallon since 1993, and it was now lower in real terms than it was before the first oil shock. And, as noted above, little progress was made on opening up protected areas, such as the Arctic National Wildlife Refuge, to drilling. Beginning in 2009, moreover, U.S. energy policy legislative efforts shifted to focus on the creation of a cap-and-trade system for carbon emissions. Although such a system might help to limit climate change, its implications for U.S. energy security were unclear and potentially negligible. Indeed, the bill passed by the House of Representatives in 2009 contained no provisions explicitly aimed at reducing oil consumption (Duffield 2012b).

Finally, we must ask what contributions U.S. external policy actions may have made to improving U.S. energy security during this period. United States policy may have created a more favorable environment for oil exploration and development in other parts of the world. But other than the 2005 opening of the U.S.-backed BTC pipeline, which allowed oil from the Caspian region to reach Western markets without passing through Russia, it would be difficult to attribute any particular increases in oil production and exports outside the Persian Gulf directly to U.S. efforts.

Within the Persian Gulf itself, the impact of U.S. policy is potentially more discernible. Certainly, the region has not witnessed another major oil supply disruption, other than perhaps the temporary loss of Iraqi output during the first years of the war there. One would be hard pressed, however, to argue that the region had become much more stable and thus less prone to oil supply disruptions than before. Although the war removed the long-standing threat posed by Iraq to its neighbors, it also introduced new tensions and unleashed other potentially destabilizing forces. And while the generally higher world oil prices since 2003 have had numerous causes, the dislocations and uncertainties generated by the Iraq war were certainly important contributing factors.

As for Iraq, the hope that it might once again join the ranks of the world's largest oil producers had yet to be realized. Indeed, oil production did not pass its prewar peak of 2.5 MBD until 2011. In 2012, the IEA projected that Iraqi output would increase to more than 6 MBD in 2020 (IEA 2012c, 11). But earlier predictions of a similar nature had proved wrong, and significant domestic and international obstacles remained to be overcome before Iraq could achieve its full potential as an oil exporter (Dombrowski and Duffield 2009, 169–71; EIA 2013b, 29–30).

At the same time, one must acknowledge the tremendous costs incurred by recent U.S. policy in the Persian Gulf, and especially of the Iraq war. As argued above, even if energy security was not the main reason for the war, it was an important, if unacknowledged, one. And the war took thousands of American (and untold Iraqi) lives and disrupted tens of thousands of others, while the ultimate price tag is likely to number in the trillions of dollars. More generally, the overall costs of the war to U.S. national security arguably outweighed the benefits. At the same time, U.S. policy toward other states in the region continued to constrain American freedom of action, sometimes entailing the compromise and even the sacrifice of other important foreign policy objectives such as promoting democracy, protecting human rights, and limiting arms sales.[18]

Explaining U.S. Responses to Energy Insecurity

How can we best explain the pattern of U.S. policy responses to energy insecurity, first in the 1970s and then in the 2000s? In particular, what accounts for the relatively limited measures taken at home, especially to reduce oil consumption, and relatively extensive action taken abroad, especially to promote stability in the Persian Gulf?

Material Factors

As elsewhere, a useful place to begin the analysis is with a consideration of material factors. In contrast to France, Germany, and Japan, the United States has been a major oil producer with the potential to produce more. Thus in the 1970s, congressional authorization of the trans-Alaska pipeline resulted in a significant increase in output, and throughout the 2000s, a major focus of debate was whether or not to lift restrictions on drilling in ANWR and parts of the outer continental shelf. In general, the presence of this production potential gave successive administrations more leeway in responding to concerns about energy security, and it probably had the effect of reducing pressure to limit oil consumption, or at least provided an excuse for not doing so. This situation of relative complaisance was compounded by the presence of substantial amounts of oil in generally friendly neighboring (Canada and Mexico) or nearby (Venezuela) countries, to which access was virtually guaranteed, which meant that after the late 1970s, the United States never received more than one quarter—and often much less—of its imports from the Persian Gulf.

Broad Societal Dispositions

Also shaping U.S. policy responses to some extent were broad societal dispositions. These could be both a constraint on and a fillip to government action, depending on the issue in question. In the 1970s, public attitudes tended to have the former effect. By then, that the price of petroleum products such as gasoline should be low was taken as an article of faith, and much skepticism attended the idea that the United States now faced a fundamentally different energy situation rather than a transitory problem. Instead, the first oil crisis was blamed first and foremost on the oil companies, which were seen as conspiring to raise the price of oil in order to increase their profits, and secondly on the federal government. Consequently, there was much public opposition to lifting price controls and little support for a major government role in meeting the country's energy needs (Bupp 1977, 285; de Marchi 1981b, 543–44; Vietor 1984, 202).

In the second period, the role of the public was somewhat reversed. Although Americans remained deeply opposed to higher energy taxes, as oil prices rose while Congress dithered, pressure grew on the government to take action. As one senator noted just before the passage of the EISA in 2007, "There's a general perception outside of Washington that we haven't done near what we could to move the country to a more acceptable energy mix" (Broder 2007).

State Strength

Notwithstanding the importance of material factors and societal dispositions, in the case of the United States, this study finds that many aspects of U.S. policy responses can be best understood in terms of variations in the strength of the state.

And in this respect, the United States represents something of a paradox, one which was recognized more than three decades ago by Stephen Krasner. At home, the United States has generally been regarded as having a weak state, with little policymaking autonomy and capacity. Externally, however, the government has enjoyed relatively high autonomy in decision making and considerable capacity to pursue its goals (Krasner 1978a, 260).

This imbalance has fostered a further paradox. At times, domestic limitations on U.S. energy policy have encouraged policymakers to rely heavily on international strategies to solve their problems (Ikenberry 1988, x). Yet a principal constraint on external U.S. policy responses has been the state's weaknesses on the domestic front. As a result, Krasner has noted, "The differences between the potential and actual international power of the state is probably larger for the United States than for any other advanced industrial society" (1978b, 53).

The weakness of the U.S. state at home has stemmed from several sources. One has been the fragmentation or decentralization of political authority, both within the executive and between the executive and legislative branches (Krasner 1978b, 53 and 61). As Charles Jones noted in a 1979 analysis, "Ours is a pluralistic, relatively high access, decentralized, multicentered, and incremental policy-making system featuring bargaining and compromise" (Jones 1979, 100). Until the creation of the Department of Energy, four years after the first oil shock, there was no centralized administrative body charged with energy policy making, and even since then, a number of other departments and agencies—State, Transportation, and Agriculture, to name just a few—have continued to play important roles in the process. At the same time, the executive branch has limited power to make energy policy by itself and must often rely on the Congress to pass the necessary enabling legislation. Yet the Congress itself has been a notoriously fragmented policymaking institution, with its authority over energy matters parceled out among a number of committees. Indeed, until 1977, nearly two dozen committees and more than 50 subcommittees dealt with some aspect of energy policy or another. Thus, one analyst observed, "Bargaining within the executive branch, within the legislative, and between the two branches of government was the order of the day. Coalitions were always able to block proposals that altered the status quo" (Bull-Berg 1987, 50). As Krasner has also noted, "The Constitution is more concerned with limiting than enhancing the power of the state. . . . This dispersion of power is even more striking in the American legislature. Bills can be blocked at any one of a number of decision making nodes" (1978b, 62).

This decentralization of authority has greatly limited the types of policies that the government has been able to adopt, especially where policies were opposed by the broader public or special interests. As a general rule, moreover, domestic policy making within the United States has been highly susceptible to the influence of public opinion and outside groups, and energy policy has been no exception. Indeed, the U.S. energy sector has been characterized by the presence of a large number of often powerful interest groups. The oil and gas industry has been more powerful in the United States than any other advanced industrialized country, but it has plenty of company from the electric power industry, the auto industry and its associated labor unions, the coal and agricultural industries, and increasingly, environmental groups, among others (Beaubouef 2007, 26). Thus, Krasner concluded, "It has been difficult for the executive to implement a coherent and decisive plan because so many specific interest groups are affected by energy and the dispersion of power has made it possible for them to block policy at a large number of decision making nodules" (1978a, 247). Likewise, Robert Keohane has argued with regard to oil policy that "in the United States, the influence of powerful societal interests often prevents the formulation and execution of strong and consistent state policies" (Keohane 1982, 167).

Another reason for the "weak state" characterization of the United States is that the government has had a relatively restricted set of policy tools at its disposal. In principle, it has been able to tax, spend, and regulate the energy sectors. But, as a general rule, its ability to extract domestic resources or to alter the behavior of private sector actors has been very limited. The same has been even more true of the state's opportunities for direct involvement in the energy sector, which have been typically confined to funding research and development, financing demonstration projects, and making small investments. Thus, as John Ikenberry concluded in his study of U.S. responses to the oil shocks, "institutional constraints left the state with few instruments or capacities within the energy sector" (Ikenberry 1988, 104; see also Krasner 1978a, 270, and 1978b, 53 and 61). Paradoxically, this situation of weakness has meant that the U.S. government has sometimes been most effective when its preferred policy has been to take no action.

These characteristics of the American state have been prominently on display in a number of energy policies. One example is the difficulty that successive administrations had in lifting price controls on petroleum products, which would arguably have enhanced U.S. energy security by promoting a more rapid adjustment to higher oil prices. The petroleum industry itself was deeply divided on the issue, with domestic producers demanding an immediate lifting of the controls and domestic refiners favoring continued regulation. In this case, consumer interests carried the day, as they were well represented in the then

Democratic-controlled Congress, which maintained that any gains would not justify the burdens higher costs would place on consumers (Schneider 1983, 327; Vietor 1984, 243–48; Ikenberry 1988, 168–72). Indeed, congressional efforts to finesse the problems caused by price controls by establishing new allocation and entitlement programs may have only made the situation worse by creating new constituencies for the extension of price controls (de Marchi 1981a, 452 and 473).

A similar fate met proposals to raise taxes on gasoline and crude oil. As a spur to congressional action, Ford imposed a fee on imported crude oil, but this measure was absent from the final legislation (EPCA). Carter proposed a gradual increase in the gasoline tax, up to a total of 50 cents per gallon, and a tax on domestically produced crude oil that would bring its cost up to the level of oil from OPEC. In this case, however, both consumers and the oil industry joined forces to have both measures killed in Congress (Davis 1982, 112 and 117; Vietor 1984, 259–62; Hakes 2008, 38–39 and 47–50).

At first glance, the creation of the SPR might appear to be an example of state strength, but in its details, it too reflects the limited powers of the government. The oil industry successfully opposed the imposition of a mandatory inventory requirement, an approach that was used with success in some other countries. Instead, the government would have to bear the entire burden for maintaining a strategic reserve. And the government was unable to compel the industry or consumers to pay for even part of the program through taxes and fees, having to rely instead entirely on general revenues (Plummer 1982b, 126–27; Beaubouef 2007, 25–26, 38–39, 48–50, and 147).

More recent examples of these dynamics can be found in the unsuccessful energy legislative efforts of the early 2000s. The first attempts to translate the Bush administrations' NEP into legislation resulted in what one senator described as "a grab-bag of goodies for special interests." The 2003 energy bill came to 1,200 pages and was weighed down with more than $20 billion in new tax breaks, prompting Senator John McCain to call it "a leave-no-lobbyist-behind bill" while others termed it a "porkfolio" of special interest spending (Borenstein and Chatterjee 2003; Hulse 2003a; Revkin 2003).

Through the mid-2000s, moreover, the auto industry and its associated labor unions had, with the help of sympathetic members of Congress, successfully opposed any significant increase in the CAFE standards. In this case, however, rising oil prices eventually generated public pressure sufficient to overcome this resistance, especially when traditional proponents of higher fuel economy standards were joined by national security interest groups. Nevertheless, the oil industry was able to block the imposition of higher taxes on it in order to provide tax breaks for alternative fuels and renewable energy (Maynard 2007; Andrews 2007).

In contrast, the United States has enjoyed considerable strength on the international front. Especially since World War II, the executive branch has been accorded much more, although far from absolute, freedom to determine policy on foreign versus domestic issues, especially when national security interests were thought to be at stake. Likewise, the U.S. government has had a substantial, if not unlimited, array of policy tools at its disposal for use in its external relations, ranging from economic assistance to arms sales to the use of military force on a large scale. This external strength has compensated in part for the limits of what could be achieved at home. Indeed, in some cases, as John Ikenberry has suggested, domestic weakness has motivated the United States to seek solutions to its energy security problems abroad rather than at home (Ikenberry 1988, 81).

We can find evidence of this relatively great strength on display in U.S. dealings with both energy exporters and other consumer countries. During the 1970s and early 1980s, the level of American involvement in the Persian Gulf was unmatched. The United States allowed the sale of tens of billions of dollars in advanced weaponry to Iran and Saudi Arabia and eventually made a commitment to defend the states of the region against external threats that was backed up by a steadily growing military capability. And in the 2000s, it took the unprecedented step of invading a major oil-producing country in the region largely by itself, at least in part for reasons having to do with ensuring the free flow of oil from the gulf. The United States clearly had much more to offer to the Persian Gulf states than did other developed democracies, even if this capacity had its limits and did not always—or even often—translate into clear foreign policy successes.

We find a similar pattern in U.S. policy toward other oil-consuming countries. The United States led the way in fashioning the consumer response to the oil shocks, and it was able to use its strength to gain the cooperation of sometimes reluctant partners. At the Washington Energy Conference, U.S. leaders explicitly tied agreement on the oil issue to broader security issues, hinting that the United States might reconsider its commitment to the defense of its European allies if they were not forthcoming. As President Nixon told the assembled leaders, "Security and economic considerations are inevitably linked and energy cannot be separated from either." Similarly, the United States was able to overcome resistance to the ESS by promising to make its own oil supplies available. Thus, concluded one analysis, "The most significant factor in the shift [in the European position] was the pressure exerted by the United States" (Schneider 1983, 260; see also Lieber 1976, 23; Nau 1980, 41; Ikenberry 1988, 89).

At the same time, as noted above, constraints on state strength in the domestic sphere limited what the United States could achieve internationally. For example, the government's inability to reduce U.S. oil consumption by lifting price controls undercut the credibility of its bargaining position on the issue of establishing a MSP for oil (Ikenberry 1988, 94). More recently, the prosecution of the Iraq war was constrained by the level of effort that U.S. leaders believed the public would tolerate in terms of the expenditure of lives and resources.

Policy Legacies and Path Dependence

In the U.S. case, we also see evidence of policy legacies. At home, the relatively limited efforts undertaken in the 1970s to reduce U.S. oil consumption contributed to the enduring centrality of oil prices and imports to U.S. energy security concerns. Even the most ambitious measures, the CAFE standards, were undermined by what in retrospect appears to be inevitable changes in the composition of the American LDV fleet. Thus oil's share of U.S. PEC, which stood at 46 percent in 1973, never dropped below 38 percent during the following three decades and was rising again as the twenty-first century began.

A similar pattern characterizes the external dimension of U.S. efforts to promote energy security. The initial commitment to defend the Persian Gulf undertaken at the end of the first period led to an ever-deepening political and military involvement in the region that set the stage for the invasion and occupation of Iraq. As I have written elsewhere, even if oil-related considerations played no conscious role in the Bush administration's decision to invade Iraq, it is difficult not to view the war as the logical culmination of a series of prior steps that were taken largely, if not exclusively, because of the region's oil resources (Duffield 2008, 179–81).

Conclusion

Of the five countries examined in this study, the United States represents perhaps the most paradoxical case. Its efforts at home to reduce its vulnerability to oil shocks in the wake of the oil crises of the 1970s, if not the least ambitious, were arguably the least successful. Although U.S. energy security appeared to be improving in the mid-1980s, by the early 2000s, the United States was only slightly less dependent on oil than it had been in 1973, and the share of total energy consumption represented by imported oil was at an all-time high, even as world prices were reaching sustained levels not seen since the early 1980s.

These relatively modest efforts at home stand in contrast to what was the most assertive and ambitious set of responses to energy insecurity in the international realm. Not only did the United States take the lead in organizing the response of the consumer countries to the oil shocks, but it also became progressively—and largely by itself—enmeshed in the politics of the Persian Gulf largely out of an attempt to ensure the free flow of oil from the region. In other words, the United States attempted to an unmatched extent to manage its energy security concerns via external policy tools.

This overall pattern of U.S. responses to energy insecurity largely reflects the paradoxical nature of the American state. At home, the state has been one of the weakest, characterized by sharply circumscribed autonomy to determine policy and a generally limited set of policy instruments. Thus it took successive governments the better part of a decade to reduce price controls following the first oil shock, and the main tool adopted for reducing oil consumption, the CAFE standards, was riddled with loopholes that reduced its effectiveness over time. In contrast, on the international front, the United States was able to pursue a much more ambitious agenda, and not just because of its relatively greater material and financial resources. Also important were the relatively greater freedom of action afforded to government officials to devise policy in the external realm and the ability of the state to extract resources from society, up to a point, in the pursuit of its foreign policy objectives, as exemplified most dramatically by the Iraq war.

CHAPTER TEN

The Quest for Energy Security

Findings and Implications

The meaning of the "energy crisis" is different from country to country, and from specific policy area to specific policy area. . . . Each country used a different mix of institutions and policies to achieve their [sic] national purposes.

—Paul Kemezis and Ernest Wilson, *The Decade of Energy Policy*

Energy insecurity can assume a variety of guises, and states typically have a range of policy options at their disposal for addressing it. The experience of even so uniform a group of countries as the major developed democracies since World War II underscores this reality. Although they faced similar energy security concerns in the 1970s, mainly revolving around the price and availability of oil, these countries responded to those concerns in distinctly different ways. By the 2000s, moreover, their energy situations, and the principal challenges that they faced, had diverged markedly, setting the stage for an even more diverse set of policy responses.

This final chapter has four purposes. The first is to summarize in comparative perspective the energy security concerns of the major developed democracies reviewed in this book, both in the 1970s and again during the past decade, and the policies that they adopted in response to those concerns. The second aim is to review the possible explanations for these patterns. The chapter examines in particular the utility of the concepts of state strength and policy legacies for understanding the policy responses of the major developed democracies. Then the chapter explores the theoretical and practical implications of the findings for the scholarly study of public policy in comparative perspective and for the prospects for international cooperation to promote collective energy security, respectively. Finally, it considers the implications of recent advances in the production and distribution of energy, particularly the fracking revolution, for energy security in the developed democracies and beyond.

Energy Security Concerns and State Responses

This first section summarizes the principal energy security concerns of the five countries reviewed in this study and how they have responded to those concerns. As in the individual chapters, it makes sense to divide this summary into two parts, corresponding to the two time periods examined in the country chapters: the 1970s and the 2000s.

The 1970s

In the 1970s, the primary energy security challenges faced by the major developed democracies were very similar in nature, stemming as they did from high levels of dependence on oil. By 1973, oil accounted for 46 to nearly 80 percent of primary energy consumption in those five countries, and in all but the United States, most of the oil was imported (table 10.1). Thus the principal concern revolved around the possibility of a major disruption of oil supplies that could trigger a sharp increase in oil prices and possibly even fuel shortages. Such a disruption might be intentional, as exemplified by the first oil shock. Or it might be the unintended consequence of an internal upheaval, as represented by the Iranian Revolution, or of a regional conflict, a possibility raised in 1980 by the outbreak of the Iran-Iraq War.

In view of the common nature of their energy security concerns, it is not surprising that the policy responses of the developed democracies to the oil shocks bore a number of broad similarities (table 10.2). At home, each country sought to reduce its oil consumption through a variety of measures, including efforts at conservation and improving energy efficiency, and each promoted the substitution of other energy sources for oil, especially nuclear power, natural gas, and coal. The period also saw major attempts to prepare for future emergencies through

Table 10.1. Levels of dependence on oil and other principal energy sources (percentage of primary energy consumption)

		1973	1985	2000
Britain	Oil	50.0	38.3	35.2
	Natural gas	11.1	23.0	38.9
France	Oil	68.1	43.1	37.3
	Nuclear power	1.8	25.9	37.0
Germany	Oil	56.5	42.2	39.4
	Natural gas	10.2	15.4	21.5
	Nuclear power	1.1	10.8	11.6
Japan	Oil	77.5	55.8	49.6
	Natural gas	1.5	9.6	13.1
	Nuclear power	0.6	9.3	14.1
United States	Oil	46.0	40.5	38.2
	Natural gas	31.3	25.4	25.9
	Nuclear power	1.1	5.2	7.8

Source: BP 2013.

Table 10.2. Primary policy responses to energy insecurity

		Domestic	International
Britain	1970s	North Sea oil and gas production Support for coal and nuclear power	Obstruction of EC energy policy initiatives
	2000s	Promotion of renewable and nuclear electricity, LNG terminals, and gas pipelines Simplification of planning and licensing processes	Engagement with gas-exporting countries Promotion of EU energy market liberalization, common external energy policy, and emissions trading scheme
France	1970s	Reduction of oil consumption and imports Major nuclear power program	Bilateral deals with producers Support for EC ties with Arab states Opposition to U.S. initiatives
	2000s	Renewed commitment to nuclear power program Support for renewables Energy conservation (white certificates)	Promotion of EU policies (except market liberalization)
Germany	1970s	Taxes and restrictions on oil use Support for coal industry Conservation and efficiency programs	Support for foreign gas contracts and new gas import routes Support for U.S. initiatives
	2000s	Promotion of energy efficiency Support for renewable power Extension of nuclear phaseout	"Energy foreign policy": promotion of energy dialogues, support for EU external energy policy Support for German companies Resistance to EU market liberalization
Japan	1970s	Oil stockpiling Higher petroleum taxes Industry energy management program Support for coal and nuclear power	"Resource diplomacy": bilateral agreements with oil producers Support for Japanese energy companies overseas
	2000s	Increased energy efficiency Increased nuclear power Support for renewable energy	Renewed resource diplomacy Renewed support for Japanese energy companies Regional energy cooperation
United States	1970s	Fuel economy standards Strategic Petroleum Reserve	Arms sales and military assistance to Iran and Saudi Arabia Carter Doctrine and increased military intervention capability in Persian Gulf
	2000s	Increased fuel economy standards Renewable fuel standard	Global promotion of oil production Intervention in the Persian Gulf/Iraq War

the buildup of strategic stockpiles of crude oil and petroleum products, as exemplified by the U.S. Strategic Petroleum Reserve.

At least as noteworthy as these similarities, however, were the differences in how these five highly similar states responded to their energy security concerns. Important differences can be observed in every dimension of energy security policy. Most obviously, those that were able, mainly the United States and Great Britain thanks to recent discoveries on Alaska's North Slope and in the North Sea, respectively, sought to increase domestic oil production. Indeed, British oil output surpassed domestic demand at the beginning of 1980s.

But significant variation also characterized the ways in which and the degree to which governments sought to reduce oil consumption and energy use more generally. Perhaps the greatest efforts were made by Japan, which raised taxes on most petroleum products and took a number of steps to promote conservation in the energy-intensive industrial sector. And partly as a result of these efforts, Japan was able to reduce its energy intensity by one-third between 1973 and 1985. France and Germany also undertook rather comprehensive and far-reaching programs that resulted in energy savings of 20 to 25 percent. In contrast, the U.S. government was slow to lift price controls on domestically produced oil, which artificially stimulated consumption, and it continued to maintain very low taxes on petroleum products. Instead, U.S. efforts to reduce oil consumption in the United States focused mainly on the introduction of fuel economy standards for passenger cars and light trucks, which would take years to achieve their full effect.

Important differences also occurred in the development and promotion of alternatives to oil. All five countries experienced an upsurge of interest in nuclear power, for example, but the degree of emphasis varied considerably. France began an all-out program to generate electricity at nuclear plants, while the United States and Britain did relatively little to promote nuclear energy, and the Japanese and German efforts fell somewhere in between. The first oil shock also prompted efforts to halt at least temporarily coal's slide as a share of PEC in Western Europe and Japan, but only in the United States did coal see a significant increase. In contrast, natural gas consumption as a share of PEC in the United States continued the decline that had begun in 1970, while it exploded in Britain, more than doubling between 1973 and 1985, and grew steadily in Japan, thanks to government support for liquefied natural gas (LNG), and in West Germany, which had just begun to import gas from the Soviet Union and approved additional long-term import contracts in the following years.

Thus, although overall energy use in 1985 in all five countries was roughly the same as it had been at the time of the first oil shock, they had reduced their oil consumption by widely varying degrees and had diversified their energy mixes in distinct ways. The most dramatic change occurred in France, which saw oil use decline from 68 percent to 43 percent of PEC, while the share attributable to nuclear power surged from less than 2 percent to more than a quarter. In both Japan and West Germany, oil consumption fell by more than 25 percent as a share of PEC, being replaced principally by a combination of nuclear energy and natural gas in both countries. Britain recorded a slightly smaller percentage decline in oil consumption as a share of PEC, from 50 to 38 percent, reflecting in part the country's lower initial level of oil dependence, and that oil was replaced primarily by North Sea gas. Bringing up the rear was the United States, which reduced oil consumption by just over 5 percentage points of PEC, from 46 to 40.5 percent.

Equal if not even greater variation characterized these states' international efforts to promote their energy security. France and Japan in particular went to great lengths to secure access to foreign oil supplies, employing varying forms of resource diplomacy and support for state-owned and private companies. As the focus of concern shifted from the intentional withholding of oil from the market by oil producers to unintentional disruptions, especially as a result of interstate conflict and external aggression, however, the United States increasingly assumed the leading role through arms sales to and then direct involvement in the defense of oil-producing states in the Persian Gulf.

Nor did these five states make similar efforts to foster cooperation among themselves and other consumer countries in order to promote their collective energy security. Here, too, the United States led the way as "the most persistent and forceful advocate of a cooperative response by the industrial consumer nations to rising oil prices" (Ikenberry 1988, 84). It called the first meeting of major consumer countries following the Arab oil embargo and played the key role in establishing the International Energy Agency (IEA) and forging an agreement to share oil stocks in an emergency. Although the other countries generally went along with these U.S. proposals, they were less supportive of other American initiatives, such as forming a common front in negotiations with the oil producers, setting binding targets for oil imports, and establishing a minimum oil price in order to promote conservation and substitution. And France refused to join the IEA altogether. Its preference was instead for greater cooperation within the European Community on energy issues, but proposals for that body to develop a common energy policy were frustrated by Britain and others.

Finally, these states used strikingly different methods to build up their strategic stockpiles, which saw significant variation in the degree of state involvement.

The United States relied entirely on government held reserves, while France and Japan initially put the entire burden on private companies to maintain the necessary petroleum stocks see (Krapels 1980).

The 2000s

In the 2000s, in contrast to the earlier period, there was no common starting point for state action. The energy security concerns of the major developed democracies were much more diverse than they had been in the 1970s. Only in the United States did the primary worries still revolve around the price and availability of oil. Elsewhere, these concerns reflected the changes that had occurred in the national energy mix and the sources of energy supplies. In France, attention now focused on the need to replace the country's large investment in aging nuclear power plants. Britain, in contrast, faced the challenge of replacing rather quickly natural gas from the North Sea, which began to decline rapidly around 2000. In Germany, energy security moved even more rapidly to the fore when commercial conflicts between Russia and Ukraine raised concerns about the reliability of Germany's natural gas supply, a growing percentage of which came from Russia. And Japan faced a comprehensive set of worries stemming from its continued high degree of reliance on energy imports, although these now included a more diverse mix of oil, natural gas, and coal.

The principal policy responses of these five countries reflected these differences in energy security concerns. The French government sought to create a political foundation for renewing the country's commitment to nuclear power, which would eventually involve extending the lifetimes of existing power plants and building the first of a new generation of reactors, while also, for the first time, providing support for renewable energy sources. In Germany, efforts centered on improving energy efficiency and further increasing reliance on renewable forms of energy, especially wind and solar power for electric power generation, which were already receiving significant support in the form of feed-in tariffs. Britain, in contrast, focused on creating new capacity to import natural gas and on developing alternative means of electric power generation. The latter involved not only promoting wind power but also reversing decades of neglect of nuclear energy, which now became a centerpiece of government policy. At home, Japan too sought to address its energy security concerns by redoubling its efforts to improve energy efficiency, greatly increasing its commitment to nuclear power, and investing for the first time in renewable sources of energy. Only, again, in the United States did domestic policy efforts revolve almost entirely around measures intended to reduce the role of oil in the energy economy, and especially the transportation sector, both by further increasing light vehicle fuel efficiency and by greatly expanding the amount of biofuels in the nation's fuel supply.

There was also considerable variation in the degree to which efforts to promote energy security had an external dimension. France, in contrast to its actions in the 1970s, was the most inwardly focused, reflecting the importance of nuclear power to the country's energy security. Although Germany did more to promote international dialogue and cooperation on energy issues, its policy also tended to emphasize what it could do at home. Britain, in contrast, strongly promoted developments in the European Union that would increase its access to natural gas supplies as well as bilateral relations with Norway and other potential sources of natural gas. Japan renewed its previous efforts to secure control over foreign energy resources through diplomacy and support for Japanese energy companies engaged in overseas exploration and production. But once again, the most dramatic actions were taken by the United States, which intervened forcefully in the Persian Gulf to address a major threat to the stability of the region's oil supplies.

Explaining State Responses to Energy Insecurity

How are we best to explain these patterns of policy responses to energy insecurity? What accounts in particular for their differences, especially the contrasting choices made in the 1970s that sent states on increasingly divergent energy trajectories in subsequent years?

There is no simple answer to these questions. As discussed in chapter 3, energy security policy is complicated and multidimensional. And as the cases have confirmed, there are many different ways in which even the major developed democracies can respond to similar concerns about energy insecurity. Correspondingly, a number of factors are likely to have a bearing on the choices states make among these many options.

In chapter 4, I identified some of the factors thought likely to be important in shaping state responses to energy insecurity. The case studies provided some evidence of the impact of each of these factors, although they were not all equally influential in all cases or at all times. This section summarizes the principal findings with regard to each factor, but pays particular attention to the roles played by state strength and policy legacies.

Initial Conditions

Clearly, an important starting point for understanding the policies pursued by these five states is the nature of their energy security concerns. Especially in the 2000s, as noted above, they faced a rather varied set of energy security challenges, which set the stage for often quite different responses. But even in the 1970s, when worries mainly revolved around the price and availability of oil, there was some variation in the magnitude of their concerns. Indeed, as noted in the 1973 edition of the influential annual *Strategic Survey*, "Energy interests and dependence provided the most concrete area of divergence in outlook and policy among [the United States and its] allies" (quoted in Krapels 1980, 33). At one end of the spectrum stood Japan, which relied on oil from abroad to meet nearly four-fifths of its energy needs in 1973. Not far behind was France, where oil accounted for more than two-thirds of PEC and was almost entirely imported. At the other end was the United States, where less than half of PEC was provided by oil and domestic oil production still met nearly two-thirds of demand. Britain and West Germany fell in between. Thus the urgency to reduce dependence on oil in general and imports in particular was not equally shared (see, for example, Rustow 1982, 163).

In some cases, moreover, state responses to energy insecurity were notably constrained by other important national policy goals and existing policies to achieve them. In the 1970s, for example, U.S. energy policy had to contend with the desire to fight inflation by limiting price rises. In the 2000s, Germany was in the process of phasing out its nuclear power plants, and Britain, Germany, and Japan were deeply committed to reducing carbon emissions.

Material Factors

Within the context of existing energy policies and the nature and magnitude of energy security concerns, material factors, especially the presence or absence of energy resource endowments, also played an important role in conditioning state responses. The ready availability of substantial oil, gas, and coal supplies, either within a state's territorial boundaries or nearby, typically exerted considerable influence over how that state addressed its energy security concerns.

Perhaps the most obvious example of the impact of resource abundance was Britain in the 1970s, where the response to the first oil shock largely revolved around the expeditious exploitation of the oil and gas recently discovered in the North Sea. A similar, if less striking, development occurred in the United States, where the Arab oil embargo dissolved political opposition to opening up Alaska's North Slope for oil production. West Germany and, to a lesser extent, France possessed substantial reserves of coal that they could use to arrest quickly the previous seemingly inexorable growth in their dependence on foreign oil even as they took other steps to reduce it. Although not a large gas producer itself, West Germany was also well positioned geographically to benefit from the presence of substantial regional gas supplies, especially in the Netherlands, Norway, and the Soviet Union, that could be easily transported by pipeline. Only Japan was almost entirely bereft of significant energy resources at home or nearby on which it could draw.

In the 2000s, as a general rule, these five countries seemed to have fewer fossil fuel resources at their immediate disposal, at least prior to the widespread deployment of hydraulic fracturing technology in the United States. Partly as a result, and thanks to technological progress since the 1970s as well as disillusionment with nuclear power, there was much more interest in renewable forms of energy. Here too we can identify some variation in each country's potential. By virtue of its vast geographical expanse, agricultural output, and southerly location, the United States clearly possessed the greatest potential for the production of biofuels and solar and wind power, although the latter were of little use in addressing its principal oil-related energy security concerns. As the case of Germany demonstrates, however, limited territory and sunshine are not absolute constraints on the amount of electricity that can be generated by renewable means. Aggressive policies could largely compensate for such shortcomings in natural endowments. Instead, the critical constraints turned out to be infrastructural in nature, especially adequate transmission systems and storage capacity.

Broad National Policy Dispositions

Another factor that has shaped state responses in some important respects has been broad societal policy dispositions in the form of political culture and elite ideology. France provides a good example of such forces at work. As I noted in chapter 6, postwar French political culture has been marked by a strong emphasis on attaining and maintaining national autonomy in all things, but certainly including energy. In addition, French attitudes have been supportive of a strong state role in directing the economy, or *dirigisme* (Berend 2005). These strands of French political thought greatly account for both the French preference for a substantial nuclear power program and how that program was pursued in the 1970s and, to a lesser extent, the continued support for nuclear energy in the 2000s.

An interesting contrast to France is provided by Britain, which saw a profound shift in views about the appropriate role of the state, at least among the political elite. During the 1970s, these attitudes were characterized by a strong *dirigiste* belief in need for state control of energy production and distribution. By the 2000s, however, even leaders of the center-left Labour Party had embraced pronounced neoliberal views about the benefits of relying to the greatest extent possible on market forces. These sharply contrasting orientations were on display in the disparate British responses to the country's growing dependence on imported oil in the 1970s and then imported gas in the 2000s.

German attitudes as well have generally been marked by a strong market orientation, which conditioned the West Germany response to the oil shocks. Nevertheless, the emphasis on market solutions has tended to moderate over time, being replaced by strong popular concerns about the dangers of nuclear power and, more recently, climate change. Hence public support and expectations have grown for a more interventionist government role in addressing such environmental concerns (see also Schreurs 2002, 4).

Antinuclear sentiments have also been strong in Japan, where they have increasingly hobbled government policy toward nuclear energy. Likewise, the external aspects of Japan's responses to energy insecurity have been constrained by the strong antimilitarist strain that has pervaded Japanese society since World War II. Thus the country has been limited to nonmilitary forms of diplomacy and assistance in its pursuit of access to energy resources.

The task of identifying distinct cultural or ideological forces that have left their mark on responses to energy insecurity is arguably most difficult in the case of the United States. The most distinctive of these is a broad aversion to the use of taxes, which has removed an important arrow from the government's quiver of potential policy instruments, and more generally, public expectations of low energy prices. Perhaps surprisingly, neither the American public nor political elites have embraced particularly strongly a market-based approached to addressing energy issues and instead have been willing to tolerate and even support considerable use of regulation and subsidies.

State Strength

Factors such as natural resource endowments and a society's political culture may dispose policy in certain general directions, but they rarely offer detailed guidance to policymakers or impose sharp constraints on policy options. Instead, this study has placed particular emphasis on evaluating the utility of the concepts of state strength and path dependence as determinants of state responses to energy insecurity in the developed democracies. In fact, the preceding chapters have provided numerous examples of the influence of state strength on the choices these countries have made among various policy options for promoting their energy security. Indeed, one could argue that the single most important key to understanding many aspects of the state responses documented above, and variations in them cross nationally and over time, is state strength. To an important extent, state strength has influenced the relative emphasis placed on external and internal policy responses and as well as among alternative domestic approaches to increasing energy security. Accordingly, this section seeks to summarize the evidence for the influence of state strength on state responses to energy insecurity as well as to evaluate in comparative perspective the impact of variations in state strength across the five cases and two time periods.

In chapter 4, I distinguished among three components, or "faces," of state strength: policymaking autonomy, domestic capacity, and international capacity. And in each of the five country chapters, we have attempted to identify how state strength along each of these dimensions has influenced the state's responses to energy insecurity. As noted in chapter 4, the degree of policymaking autonomy is not the same in all issue areas but can vary, especially across the domestic-international divide. In addition, as also argued in chapter 4, there can be a close relationship between what policymakers choose to do and the policy instruments at their disposal. Thus, for comparative purposes, it may be useful to organize the discussion of the influence of state strength into two categories: state strength in the domestic setting and in the international arena. Each encompasses both the degree of policymaking autonomy and the amount of state capacity in the respective realm.

DOMESTIC STRENGTH

It is difficult to pigeonhole each state in terms of its policymaking autonomy and capacity in the domestic realm. Energy security encompasses a number of policy areas, and the policymaking procedures as well as the available policy instruments may vary from issue to issue, even within a single state. Nevertheless, table 10.3 attempts to capture the central tendency for each state during each of the two time periods, recognizing that no case fits perfectly and that there will always be exceptions. And insofar as the table accurately captures these central tendencies, it suggests that there has been considerable variation in domestic strength across the five states and even over time within some individual states.

In the domestic realm, France, not surprisingly, emerges as having the strongest state overall, in terms of both policymaking autonomy and capacity. This strength greatly facilitated the quick adoption and implementation of what was the most ambitious nuclear energy program as well as the country's far-reaching efforts to curb oil consumption in the 1970s. Arguably, however, this domestic strength has waned somewhat over time, as evidenced by the difficulties the government faced in achieving its goals in the 2000s. The state still held substantial stakes in the country's major energy industries, but it was no longer

Table 10.3. Comparison of state strength in the domestic realm

	Domestic capacity		
State autonomy	Low (primary reliance on market forces)	Medium (R&D, regulation, subsidies, taxes, and other incentives)	High (direct state involvement in production and distribution)
Low		United States (1970s and 2000s)	
Medium	Britain (2000s) Germany (1970s)	Germany (2000s) Japan (2000s)	
High		France (2000s) Japan (1970s)	Britain (1970s) France (1970s)

the final arbiter of decisions about the operation and construction of nuclear power plants, nor could it bring about the development of renewable energy with the same alacrity that it had enjoyed with respect to nuclear energy in the 1970s.

Interestingly, perhaps the closest parallel to France was provided by Britain in the 1970s. Then the state played a major role in the development of North Sea oil, the distribution of natural gas, and the design and construction of nuclear power plants. But Britain also offers the example of the most dramatic shift in domestic strength. By the 2000s, the state had dispensed with many of its previous policy instruments, especially public ownership of energy companies. It was now largely limited to the use of light regulation and reforms of the planning process for energy infrastructure projects in its efforts to promote greater energy security and depended instead on private actors to make all the necessary investments in energy production, import, and distribution facilities.

Japan has sometimes been mentioned in the same breath as France when it comes to the categorization of strong states. And with respect to decision-making autonomy in the 1970s, this may have been true. But the Japanese state never possessed the panoply of policy instruments enjoyed by France. It could tax, regulate, and subsidize heavily, but it never played a direct role in the production and distribution of energy, and it often relied on more informal methods such as exhortation and administrative guidance to achieve its goals. By the 2000s, moreover, the ability of the state to make policy without the input and consent of the powerful energy industries had declined, and in the particularly sensitive area of nuclear power, the success of its policies was increasingly hostage to the approval of local authorities.

Germany provides an interesting counterpoint to France and Japan. The German state has traditionally enjoyed much less decision-making autonomy, especially when compared in the 1970s. Instead, policy making has been much more a process of consensus building, typically requiring cooperation across party lines in coalition governments and providing opportunities for the participation of affected interest groups. Germany's domestic capacity has tended to fall in the middle range. Like Japan, the government has generally had access to taxes, regulations, subsidies, and other market-based instruments but has not played a direct role in the energy economy. Thus it too has ultimately depended on the actions of the private sector to achieve its energy security goals and been unable to overcome determined opposition. Perhaps the most important difference that can be discerned between the two periods is the more aggressive use of policy instruments by Germany to promote renewable sources of electric power in the 2000s, although this too seemed to reach its limits when the impact on electricity prices became non-negligible.

The contrasting degrees of domestic strength in France, Germany, and Japan are evidenced in the disparate fates of their respective nuclear power programs. In the early 1970s, all three countries announced ambitious goals for the buildup of nuclear-generating capacity, but only France came close to realizing them. France's success followed directly from the direct role of the state in building nuclear power plants and the very limited ability of opponents to obstruct the program. In Japan and especially in Germany, in contrast, there was relatively little the government could do to overcome growing public opposition. Thus, by 1985, the latter two countries had approximately only half of the nuclear capacity that had been originally planned.

Finally, it is tempting to place the United States at the opposite end of the spectrum of domestic strength from France, as others have often done. To be sure, U.S. policy making has often exhibited the least degree of autonomy, seemingly hostage to public opinion and special interests, as on the issues of lifting price controls or raising energy taxes. And with the exception of strategic petroleum stockpiles, the government has not been directly involved in the production and distribution of energy. But when the state has taken action, it has on occasion been able to adopt relatively strong measures, such as fuel economy standards and the renewable fuel standard. Thus in this regard it lies closer to the center of the spectrum, and certainly ahead of Britain in the 2000s, with respect to domestic capacity.

The U.S. case also underscores one of the paradoxes of state strength. Precisely because of its weakness vis-à-vis societal interest groups, in this case the oil companies, the United States government had little choice but to play a central role in the construction of strategic oil reserves. In France, in contrast, the government was able to place the entire burden of maintaining stocks on oil importers. Japan and West Germany, which arguably enjoyed somewhat higher degrees of policymaking autonomy than did the United States but lacked the capacity of the French state, adopted mixed systems involving a combination of government and private holdings.

INTERNATIONAL STRENGTH

We also find considerable variation in the international strength of the five countries, with implications for the policies they pursued. Arguably, the greatest disparity in this component of state strength has existed between the United States and the other major developed democracies. To an important extent, this difference can be attributed to the much greater level of underlying national power, or the sum total of the material resources potentially available to the state, as defined in chapter 4. The United States has possessed more than twice the population and gross domestic product of Japan and several times those of the other three countries examined here.

These differences in national power would have meant little, however, if the U.S. government had not been able to translate them effectively into state power. And here we find that the U.S. government arguably enjoyed greater autonomy in decision making than in the domestic realm as well as an ability to extract and mobilize considerable national power resources in the pursuit of its external objectives. This strength has been most apparent with regard to the use of military instruments of external policy. In particular, the United States has uniquely been able to deploy substantial military forces in the Persian Gulf for prolonged periods of time. But it has also extended to other sources of external influence, such as diplomacy and military assistance. The availability of this relatively high degree of international strength has arguably contributed to a heavy reliance on external responses to concerns about the stability of world oil supplies.

At the same time, there have been important limitations to the international strength of the United States when it comes to the pursuit of energy security. For example, the U.S. government has never had state-controlled corporations that could negotiate supply arrangements with oil producers. And the domestic constraints on the state, such as those limiting its ability to curb American oil consumption, handcuffed the United States in its dealings with other consumer countries. But, overall, the United States has enjoyed a significantly greater degree of external strength than have the other major developed democracies.

Indeed, this disparity could have contributed to a reduced emphasis on external responses by the others through the phenomenon of free riding. As long as the United States took the lead in efforts to stabilize oil prices and secure the flow of oil from the Persian Gulf, there was less need for them to act, and it would be interesting to speculate what additional steps they would have taken if the United States had not been willing or able to play such an assertive role. Nevertheless, this tendency would have declined as the primary energy concerns of the others shifted away from oil.

Even among the other four countries, which have been much more similar to one another in terms of the dimensions of national power, there have been noteworthy differences in external strength. As in the domestic realm, France has stood out, especially in the 1970s. Here too, the French government enjoyed a high degree of policymaking autonomy, and it had at its disposal relatively strong state-controlled oil companies that could be used to secure supply agreements with oil producers. The state also played a major role in the production of advanced weaponry and nuclear facilities, which could be offered as additional inducements in such negotiations (Kolodziej 1980).

Britain in the 1970s might have possessed a degree of potential state strength in the international realm comparable that to France. In addition to the large state role in the energy economy, it still possessed a relatively large military and advanced arms industry, but it did not need to exercise that strength to promote its energy security. By the 2000s, in contrast, the government's principal tools were largely limited to traditional diplomacy and the prerogatives that came with its membership in the EU.

Arguably, Germany has exhibited the least degree of external state strength, especially in the 1970s. Because of postwar constraints on the German military, it lacked any significant military instruments and was reluctant to play a significant international role outside the Atlantic and European communities, especially if it involved any military dimension, such as arms sales (Duffield 1998). The government had created a national oil company, but it had difficulty competing with better established state-controlled enterprises. What Germany did possess was a large and growing domestic market as well as advanced technologies, although its ability to offer these in return for access to regional energy resources was limited by other international commitments.

Finally, Japan has occupied an intermediate position on this dimension of state strength. Like Germany, because of restrictions stemming from World War II, it has lacked a significant power projection capability and other military instruments of international influence. Nor has the government had the use of state-controlled energy companies to pursue its external energy security objectives. Notwithstanding these limitations, it has been able to engage in what has been the most aggressive and comprehensive program of resource diplomacy, using financial assistance, investments, technology sharing, and other means to cultivate close political and economic ties with energy producers. In addition, the government has been able to provide substantial subsidies, covering up to 75 percent of the costs, in support of Japanese energy companies engaged in overseas exploration and development projects.

In closing this section, it should be noted that state strength, while often beneficial in the pursuit of energy security, is not an unmitigated blessing. To the contrary, it can cause governments to overreach and ultimately result in excessively costly or counterproductive policies. In the domestic realm, one can point to France's nuclear program, which eventually produced substantial excess production capacity. In response, the French government promoted electricity use, however inefficient it might be, which later constrained the government's options in responding to the aging of the nuclear plant. On the international side, the most obvious example is the deepening U.S. involvement in the Persian Gulf, which ultimately culminated in the Iraq war. To be sure, this involvement was initially motivated at least in part by concerns about the security of the energy supplies of U.S. allies in Asia and Europe. But as the allies reduced their dependence on oil, the U.S. political and military commitment to the gulf took on a life of its own. One can only wonder about the degree to which the United States could have reduced its vulnerability to oil supply disruptions and high oil prices if it had invested to that end but a fraction of the resources that it has devoted to the region over the last four decades.

Policy Legacies and Path Dependence

The other principal theoretical focus of this study has concerned path dependence in the form of the longer-term legacies of policy choices. We are interested not only in the near-term impact of a state's responses on its energy security, but how those responses may shape the challenges that the state faces in the future as well as the opportunities for and constraints on how the state addresses them. And as with state strength, we can point to a number of examples of these policy legacies. Indeed, for most if not all of the cases, we find that, with regard to energy security, the 1970s served as a critical juncture when policy choices with consequential and long-lasting effects were made. In particular, some of the decisions of that period did much to set the stage for the energy security concerns of three decades later as well as to channel future state responses to them.

France, of course, provides a particularly stark example. The country was arguably the most successful in reducing its dependence on oil in the wake of the oil shocks. But the substantial and rapid investment in nuclear energy initiated in the 1970s presaged the principal challenge France would face in the 2000s, when it became necessary to begin to prepare for the replacement of the aging nuclear power plants. In contrast to the earlier period, however, the state now lacked the domestic strength to simply push through lifetime extensions of the existing reactors and the construction of a new generation of reactors.

A similar fate befell Britain, where oil was replaced primarily by natural gas. There, however, the transition largely took care of itself, thanks to the abundant reserves of gas that had been recently discovered in the North Sea. And in the 1990s, gas also began to displace coal, most of which had been mined at home. Instead, as domestic gas production began to decline, the energy security concerns of the 2000s grew largely out of the lack of previous investment in alternative means of securing gas supplies (i.e., pipelines and LNG terminals) and of generating electric power (e.g., nuclear, renewables, and even coal). The new challenges were compounded by the legacy of the decision to privatize and liberalize the energy sector starting in the early 1980s, which left the government with few tools to address them.

The relevant policy legacies in the case of Germany were more subtle. Germany never became as dependent on any single alternative source of energy as did France or Britain, where nuclear power and natural gas, respectively, came to constitute nearly 40 percent of PEC by 2000. Rather, the problem lay with the limited number of relatively inflexible sources of gas imports. By the mid-2000s, as much as 37 percent of the gas consumed in Germany came from a single source, Russia, by way of a very small number of pipelines, which, moreover, had to pass through countries with which Russia had less than ideal political relations. Germany's ability to respond to the new energy security concerns provoked by the conflicts over Russian gas were constrained by two more recent policies: the decision to phase out nuclear power and the commitment to reduce CO_2 emissions, which limited in particular how much Germany could rely on coal to meet its energy needs. At the same time, however, existing policies regarding energy conservation and the promotion of renewable sources of power facilitated the adoption of a response that would emphasis these two means of increasing energy security.

As in Britain, the domestic policy legacies that did the most to shape the U.S. energy security concerns of the 2000s took primarily the form of steps that were *not* taken in previous years. In particular, the failure of the United States to do more to reduce oil consumption left the country particularly sensitive to oil supply disruptions and price rises. The country that had been least dependent on oil as a share of PEC in 1973 was now more dependent than all but Japan, and thanks to low taxes, the percentage of the price of petroleum products attributable to the cost of crude oil was much higher in the United States than in the other major developed democracies, making those prices much more volatile. That said, the policy response following the oil shocks in the 1970s that, other than the eventual lifting of price controls, did the most to reduce oil consumption, the corporate fuel economy standards, also served as the basis for the strongest U.S. policy response in the 2000s, thereby providing another example of the significance of policy legacies.

The Unites States is also the source of the best example of policy legacies in the international sphere. Once initiated, the deepening U.S. political and military engagement in the Persian Gulf was difficult, if not impossible, to arrest, let alone reverse. It required the trauma of the Iraq war to break the trend toward ever greater involvement, and even then, the United States continued to maintain more bases and forces in the region than at any time before 1990.

It is more difficult to find clear evidence of policy legacies and path dependence in the case of Japan. Beginning in the 1970s, Japan sought to promote its energy security by taking action on multiple fronts: reducing oil consumption and energy use more generally; substituting coal, natural gas, and nuclear power for oil; establishing large petroleum stockpiles; and securing access to foreign oil supplies. And thanks to these efforts, it was able to reduce its oil dependence (measured as a percentage of PEC) by more than any country but France. Yet even all of this could not eliminate the inherent insecurity of Japan's energy situation. Almost no matter what Japan did, it would still be heavily dependent on energy imports that could be subject to disruption. And, ironically, had Japan invested even more heavily in nuclear power, without taking additional safety precautions, it might have found itself in an even more precarious situation following the disaster at Fukushima Daiichi.

Theoretical and Policy Implications

Next, we turn to the broader theoretical and practical implications of this study's findings about the nature of energy security in the major developed democracies and how they have responded to their energy security concerns.

The Utility of State Strength as an Analytic Concept

The first theoretical implication concerns the overall utility of the concept of state strength. Explaining state responses to energy insecurity is not a simple task.

A number of factors have influenced what the major developed democracies have done in this area. Nevertheless, as discussed above, it seems clear that state strength has served as an important determinant in each of the five cases.

It seems unlikely, moreover, that the usefulness of the concept will be limited to this narrow range of phenomena. The subject of state strength has fallen out of fashion in recent years in the study of comparative politics. But based on the analysis presented in this book, it would seem to continue to be relevant to the broader study of state behavior, especially where it concerns understanding variation across states and over time.

As a first step, we can imagine expanding the scope of application of state strength to the energy security policies of other developed democracies. The one difference to be expected is that the external dimensions of state strength are likely to be less relevant, given that the other developed democracies are likely to have less national power on which to draw. But, depending on a given state's energy mix, location, and proximity to energy resources, its efforts to secure supplies from abroad could constitute an important dimension of its energy security policy.

Another logical extension would be to the study of public policy in other issue areas, beginning with the full range of energy policies. Of particular relevance to the framework used in this study would be other policy problems that lend themselves to both domestic and international solutions. As the world becomes increasingly interdependent, it will become all the more important to understand how states choose among these two broad sets of policy options. But that should not preclude the application of the concept to the many policy areas that do not straddle the domestic-international divide to the same extent as does energy security, even if it means that some dimensions of state strength are likely to be less relevant than others to the analysis of a particular issue.

Ultimately, it would be interesting to explore the reach of the concept of state strength to a wider range of countries. To be sure, bringing in a variety of states that are either less developed or less democratic, or both, is likely to complicate any analysis, by further reducing the number of variables that can be effectively held constant. But at least within the narrow realm of energy security, it is increasingly difficult to justify a focus on the developed democracies from a practical standpoint. With the rise of China, India, Brazil, and other developing countries as important energy consumers and importers, we disregard their behavior only at the risk of not understanding the global dynamics of energy security.

At the same time, however, we must acknowledge the continuing limitations of state strength as an analytic concept. First, we still lack the ability to measure state strength systematically, and in a nontautological way that is independent of policy outcomes. This comparative analysis has had to rely on highly subjective and probably very imprecise characterizations of each country's strength.

Second, we must try to move away from monolithic characterizations of state strength, such as the strong state–weak state dichotomy (see also Samuels 1987, 6). Building on the work of Hollifield and others, this study has taken a further step in that direction by distinguishing between three components, or "faces," of state strength. Even this typology, however, may represent an excessive degree of aggregation. We have already suggested that the state's policymaking autonomy may vary depending on whether the policy concerns domestic or international affairs. But even within each of those broad policy realms, there may be important variation by specific policy area.

To be sure, adopting an ever more differentiated view of state strength may only complicate the empirical challenge of measuring it. But it could also open up potentially fruitful additional avenues of research on the determinants of state strength. Not only does state strength vary from country to country, but as the cases have shown, it can change over time, sometimes substantially. In the long run, state strength, or at least dimensions of it, is endogenous to the analysis and can even be the object of policy.

This is not the place to enter into an extensive analysis of state strength as a dependent variable, but the preceding chapters have shed some light on this important question. For example, the British case suggests the importance of widely shared beliefs about the appropriate role of the state in the political economy. In that case, we see a profound shift from an ideology that supported deep government involvement in the energy sector to equally deeply held elite views that the production and distribution of energy should be left to markets and the private sector. Thus broadly held sets of ideas, like ideology and political culture, can also have an indirect impact on responses to energy insecurity through the influence they exert on the characteristics of the state. The French case suggests a different pathway toward a reduction in state strength. There, while political leaders might have favored a continuation of largely unfettered *dirigisme*, the growing need to maintain public support for the nuclear program required the government to cede some control to an independent safety authority. Presumably, additional hypotheses could be gleaned from the cases.

Policy Legacies, Path Dependence, and Energy Policy

A second important finding concerns the implications of path dependence for energy policy. As noted above, policies adopted at one point have often done much to shape the energy security concerns of later years and the policy instruments available to governments for addressing those concerns. At a minimum, future studies of energy policy should be attentive to the impact of policy legacies. Likewise, in the real world, policymakers should bear in mind to the degree possible how choices made today might open up or foreclose other options in the future.

Taken together, these cases also shed some light on the underlying causes of path dependence and the conditions for the presence or absence of strong policy legacies, at least in the energy field. The most prominent theme is the lasting impact of investments in particular means of energy production and distribution. Much energy infrastructure, whether it be power plants, pipelines, LNG terminals, refineries, mines, offshore oil and gas fields, or power lines, is very costly to build, so investment in one type of energy system may limit what is available to spend on others. Not only that, but much energy infrastructure is highly specialized in nature and cannot be easily, if at all, moved or used for other purposes. Even fossil-fuel-fired power plants and pipeline systems are designed for a particular type of fuel and can only be modified to use or transport other fuels at some cost. Thus major investment decisions—or the lack thereof—at one point in time will greatly determine the potential sources of energy vulnerability a state will face and the tools available for addressing them for decades to come. For example, France's heavy investment in nuclear power set the stage for its energy security concerns of the 2000s, while the neglect of nuclear energy in Britain for more than two decades constrained the country's ability to respond to the problems created by declining gas production.

Another important theme is the impact of investment—or disinvestment—in particular sources of state capacity, which can shape the state's ability to respond to various forms of energy insecurity. Most obvious is the establishment or dismantlement of state-owned or -controlled enterprises that can participate directly in the production, acquisition, and distribution of energy. But it also includes the creation and precise forms of fiscal, regulatory, and credit programs related to energy policy that provide ready instruments for addressing new energy security concerns as they arise, however well or poorly tailored they may be to the new circumstances.

A third, less well-developed theme is the impact of such investment decisions on the constellation of interest groups in society, as emphasized by the pluralist approaches discussed in chapter 4. Other things being equal, the social, economic, and political beneficiaries of particular policies and investments will tend to prefer the continuation of existing arrangements and resist change. Not only that, but some, especially private sector actors, will tend to be financially empowered by the status quo and thus have greater resources at their disposal to maintain it. It is more difficult to point to clear examples of this phenomenon in the cases above, but they would include the resistance of the Japanese nuclear industry to supporting renewable sources of power and the opposition of the U.S. auto manufacturers and labor unions to increases in fuel economy standards.

International Cooperation to Promote Energy Security

The findings of this study regarding the energy security concerns of the major developed democracies and their policy responses also have practical implications.[1] Most obviously, they have an important bearing on the degree of energy security achieved by each of these countries. In some cases, they may also affect relations between these five states and energy-exporting countries. This section, however, will focus on their implications for international cooperation to promote energy security among both these and other import-dependent consumer countries. Just as in the 1970s, the recent reemergence of concerns about energy security has spawned a number of proposals for collective action. So far, however, these proposals have yielded even more modest results, in no small part because of the greater diversity of energy security concerns and policy preferences.

BACKGROUND: LIMITED COOPERATION IN THE 1970S

In order to put the recent period into perspective, it is worth briefly reviewing the experience of the 1970s, when concerns about energy security prompted new forms and unprecedented degrees of cooperation. At that time, as noted above, the primary energy security concerns of the major developed democracies were highly similar, revolving largely around the cost and availability of imported oil. In addition, cooperation was favored by the fact that the United States continued to exercise a degree of political hegemony over the others (Lieber 1976, 37). Even then, however, their policy responses were marked by important differences, and these differences were reflected in the limited degree of cooperation that ultimately took place among them.

The biggest achievement at the time was the creation by members of the Organisation for Economic Co-operation and Development (OECD) of the International Energy Agency (IEA) as a forum for coordinating their policies for dealing with oil supply disruptions and, in the longer term, reducing oil dependence. Headquartered in Paris near the OECD, the IEA did quickly establish an arrangement for sharing oil supplies in the event of an emergency. But its members were much less successful at developing meaningful measures for limiting oil consumption and imports. They agreed on long-term import targets but not on collective tools to implement them. The IEA also established a floor on oil prices as a means of stimulating domestic oil production and the development of alternative energy sources, but the price was set at too low a level, just seven dollars per barrel, to make any difference. Also France refused to join the organization, in part because it viewed the IEA as excessively confrontational toward the oil producers.[2]

Even the IEA's greatest achievement, the emergency oil sharing system, was revealed to have significant limitations when first put to the test during the second oil shock of 1978–79. The system's mandatory demand restraint and reallocation of oil supplies would only be activated if one or more IEA members suffered a supply reduction of at least 7 percent. Yet it soon became clear that smaller reductions could have negative economic consequences, especially if they generated substantial price increases. And when Sweden complained in 1979 of a much larger shortfall, the IEA declined to act, attributing the country's problems to special conditions (Scott 1994, 84–86 and 115–17).

RECENT EFFORTS AT INTERNATIONAL COOPERATION

The recent proposals for international cooperation to promote energy security have covered a broader range of possibilities. Some have concerned the IEA, but others have been addressed to the North Atlantic Treaty Organization (NATO) and the European Union (EU).[3] Thus far, however, progress has been slow and the results have been much more modest than they were in the 1970s. With the possible exception of the European Union, divergent national concerns and policy preferences have made—and are likely to continue to make—meaningful multilateral cooperation to promote energy security difficult, if not impossible, to orchestrate. The utility of the IEA has largely remained confined to addressing concerns about oil supply disruptions, and even there its capacity to respond effectively has been increasingly constrained by rising oil consumption in nonmember developing countries. NATO's role in promoting energy security has continued to be even more marginal because of differing member views about its relevance to addressing current energy security concerns. And even within the more homogenous EU, substantial obstacles have made it difficult for that body to respond in a unified way to the recent energy security challenges faced by its members.

COOPERATION IN THE INTERNATIONAL ENERGY AGENCY

The IEA has remained the principal international organization devoted exclusively to energy issues. Indeed, both its membership and its functions have expanded over the years. The organization now includes Britain, France (which finally joined in 1992), Germany, Japan, and the United States as well as 24 other advanced industrialized countries, and increasingly, it has played an important role in conducting research and analysis and publishing information on energy policies, markets, technologies, and other issues. Perhaps most important, however, the IEA has continued to promote the energy security of its members through a variety of provisions intended to minimize the impact of oil supply disruptions and to facilitate a collective response to them. In particular, it still requires members to maintain oil stocks equivalent to at least 90 days of imports as well as plans for releasing those stocks, restraining demand, fuel switching, increasing domestic production, and if necessary, sharing oil supplies in the event of a major oil supply disruption. Over the years, the organization has sought to increase the flexibility of these emergency response arrangements, and they have been used on several occasions to alleviate actual shortages and to reassure market actors that significant shortages would not develop. Thus one might expect the IEA to have been a logical and perhaps the most useful forum for the development of common approaches to the problem of energy insecurity. Yet, so far, the organization has seen little new activity in this regard.

In fact, the IEA's potential to address the recent energy security concerns of its members has remained quite limited. One reason has been the organization's traditional focus on the problems associated with dependence on oil, reflecting the circumstances of its birth. The IEA still maintains an emergency oil sharing system as well as an information system on the international oil market that can help to provide prompt warning of supply problems. But as the energy security concerns of its members have shifted from oil to other energy sources, such as natural gas and nuclear power, where the IEA has had much less of a formal role to play, the organization has become less relevant (see also Colgan 2009).

At the same time, the capacity of the IEA to blunt the negative consequences of even an oil supply disruption has declined due to the growth of demand in developing countries such as China and India. Although the number of IEA members has nearly doubled over the years, they now account for less than half of global oil consumption, as compared to more than 60 percent when the organization was created.[4]

To remedy this situation, some, including the IEA's executive director, have proposed bringing China, India, and perhaps other developing countries into the organization so that they can participate in the emergency oil sharing system (e.g., Colgan 2009; Habiby 2010; Hoyos 2010). At least two obstacles must be overcome before the IEA could be usefully expanded, however. First, membership in the organization has remained restricted to members of the OECD, who must be democracies with market-based economics. Thus it is likely to be some time before China, India, and perhaps other large developing countries are able to join. Second, China and India may in fact have little interest in joining the IEA. They and other developing countries are already able to benefit from the efforts of the current IEA members without having to bear any of the financial costs of membership. In addition, they may be unwilling to pay the sovereignty costs associated with meeting the IEA's information sharing and disclosure requirements. Thus unless the agreement establishing the IEA is amended to allow non-OECD members and new members are willing to release sensitive data regarding their stockpiles, meaningful participation in the Emergency Sharing System will be precluded (GAO 2006, 31; Colgan 2009).

ENERGY SECURITY AND THE NORTH ATLANTIC TREATY ORGANIZATION

Thus more prominent than anything that has occurred within the IEA have been recent proposals to assign NATO new responsibilities in the field of energy security. In early 2006, shortly after the first Russia-Ukraine gas conflict, Poland reportedly proposed that member countries be obliged to help each other during an energy crisis, and NATO secretary general Jaap de Hoop Scheffer called for putting the issue of energy security on the alliance's agenda (RFE/RL 2006). Later that year, U.S. senator Richard Lugar, at the time the foremost congressional authority on energy issues, argued that NATO should formally adopt energy security as one of its central missions and that the alliance must prepare for and respond to attempts to use the energy weapon against its members under Article Five of the North Atlantic Treaty.[5] Lugar also sponsored a Senate resolution that called on the president to raise the issue of establishing a NATO energy security strategy.[6] And at its Riga Summit in November 2006, the North Atlantic Council agreed to work toward defining "those areas where NATO may add value to safeguard the [energy] security interests of the Allies and, upon request, assist national and international efforts."[7]

Beyond resupplying a member threatened with or suffering from a cutoff of energy supplies, a number of other specific roles for NATO were suggested. Lugar, for example, proposed holding high level consultations between NATO and Russia on energy security, developing strategic partnerships with other energy exporters, and providing diplomatic and economic support for alternative energy routes from Central Asia and the Caucasus. Likewise, a high-level NATO official identified four possible areas of NATO involvement: monitoring and assessment of the energy security situation, the provision of security assistance to allies, maritime surveillance to deter attacks against important energy assets, and military operations to secure the supply of oil or gas in an actual crisis or conflict situation (Shea 2006).

Thus far, however, most of the ideas for using NATO to promote energy security have originated either in the United States or at the alliance's secretariat. In contrast, Britain, France, and Germany have exhibited little or no enthusiasm for the concept. France has traditionally been cool toward any proposals to expand the responsibilities of NATO. But even the more Atlanticist German government has preferred to address energy security in the context of EU-US relations or in the broader framework of the Organization for Cooperation and Security in Europe (OSCE) rather than through NATO (Steinmeier 2007a). And the British government, traditionally the most pro-NATO of the three, made no reference to the alliance in the series of major statements on energy policy that it has issued in recent years (e.g., DTI 2006; DTI 2007; BERR 2008; DECC 2012b).

There have been several overlapping reasons for the tepid European response. First, many of the proposals have not addressed the principal European energy security concerns, or at least have not offered much of a solution to them. NATO's comparative advantage lies in the area of ensuring the reliable delivery of oil and natural gas by sea from distant sources. In contrast, many European concerns have revolved around the adequacy and reliability of regional energy infrastructure (natural gas pipelines, import terminals, and storage facilities; nuclear power plants; and the like). Second, many Europeans would prefer to emphasize political and economic measures for enhancing energy security, whereas many of the proposals for using NATO have sought to exploit the alliance's military capabilities. By the same token, Europeans have feared that an increased role for NATO could be counterproductive, especially in dealing with Russia, given the alliance's strong association with the cold war and military approaches to security. Finally, some of the proposed functions, such as those involving intelligence and diplomacy, have already been handled or, in the view of many Europeans, might be better handled by other bodies (Gallis 2007; de Hoop Scheffer 2008; Rühle 2011).

Perhaps not surprisingly, in view of these European reactions, there have been no significant developments within NATO since the initial proposals were made. At an April 2008 summit in Bucharest, NATO leaders noted a report on "NATO's Role in Energy Security" that identified principles that would govern NATO's approach in this field and outlined options and recommendations for further activities. Based on these principles, the members agreed on five specific areas where further NATO engagement was deemed desirable: information and intelligence fusion and sharing; projecting stability; advancing international and regional cooperation; supporting consequence management; and supporting the protection of critical energy infrastructure. The alliance would also continue to consult on the most immediate risks in the field of energy security. Subsequently, work on implementing this decision went on quietly behind the scenes, as noted in semiannual declarations and communiques issued by the North Atlantic Council. But prominent public discussion of the issue within the alliance quickly died down, and there is no evidence that NATO has yet taken any important practical steps to enhance the energy security of its members. The subject received just two paragraphs and one very general recommendation in the 47-page report issued by the Group of Experts in May 2010, and the new strategic concept adopted in November 2010 simply stated that NATO would "develop the capacity to contribute to energy security, including protection of critical energy infrastructure and transit areas and lines, cooperation with partners, and consultations among Allies on the basis of strategic assessments and contingency planning."[8]

COOPERATION FOR ENERGY SECURITY IN THE EUROPEAN UNION

Instead, for the major European states, at least, the most promising forum for multilateral cooperation to promote energy security has been the EU. Energy policy per se was not a formal area of EU competence until the entry into force of the Lisbon Treaty in late 2009. Nevertheless, the organization has in recent years proposed or adopted a number of measures that, directly or indirectly, would enhance the energy security of its member states (Birchfield and Duffield 2011).

As early as 2000, the European Commission published a "green paper" that raised concerns about the security of the EU's energy supplies and suggested a general strategy for addressing the problems it identified. Although this initiative yielded no concrete results, the goal of energy security was a central element of subsequent efforts to fashion a more comprehensive energy policy. In early 2006, at the invitation of the national leaders, the commission prepared another green paper that laid out a general "European Strategy for Sustainable, Competitive and Secure Energy." The following year, the commission presented a more detailed action plan titled "Energy Policy for Europe" that was adopted by the heads of government that March. The action plan, like the green paper, placed equal emphasis on the goals of economic competitiveness, environmental sustainability, and security of energy supplies, but went beyond it to establish ambitious targets for reducing greenhouse gas emissions, increasing the share of renewable energy in the EU's overall energy mix, and raising overall energy efficiency in the EU all by 20 percent by 2020. Then based on the action plan, the commission developed an "energy and climate package" of more specific measures designed to achieve those goals (Commission 2000; Commission 2006; Commission 2007).

Some proposed measures have been specifically intended to increase the energy security of the EU. One set of measures would establish a coherent external energy policy whereby the EU could "speak with one voice" on international energy issues and integrate energy into other policies with an external dimension. Of particular interest here have been relations with Russia and other key energy producers and transit countries as well as support for the creation of new infrastructure for bringing energy to Europe, such as the proposed Nabucco pipeline from the Caspian Sea. Another set of steps, which have seemed especially urgent in the wake of the conflicts over natural gas between Russia and Ukraine, would create a more effective system for dealing with disruptions in natural gas supplies, including more gas storage, strategic stockpiles, and adequate pipeline capacity for moving gas wherever it might be needed in a crisis.

Other energy policy measures that have been proposed or adopted by the EU, even though intended primarily to promote low energy prices or fight climate change, would also contribute to greater energy security. For example, full liberalization and integration of the members' gas and electricity markets would add flexibility and increase the resilience of the EU energy system as a whole. Raising the share of renewable sources in the energy mix and increasing energy efficiency would reduce demand for imports of oil and gas.

Despite all this activity, progress toward the goal of increasing the energy security of the EU has been slow, and the prospects for significant advances in this area remain uncertain. One problem is that some important energy policy initiatives would do little to promote energy security or could even exacerbate the situation. For example, the much touted emissions trading system, by raising the cost of carbon emissions, could make natural gas relatively more attractive than coal and thus aggravate the region's import dependence (Henningsen 2011).

More fundamentally, even within the highly integrated EU, energy policy continues to be an area where national prerogatives are carefully guarded. The article on energy contained in the 2009 Lisbon Treaty concludes that measures to achieve common objectives "shall not affect a Member State's right to determine the conditions for exploiting its energy resources, its choice between different energy sources and the general structure of its energy supply."[9] This constraint might not be so problematic if the member states had similar policy preferences. But on many particular issues, the positions of Britain, France, and Germany, not to mention some other members, have often been far apart.[10]

One area of disagreement has been the completion of the internal electricity and gas markets. Britain has been a leading proponent, while France and Germany have resisted critical proposals, such as "unbundling" the ownership of energy supplies and transmission networks. Another point of contention has been the future role of nuclear power, which could greatly reduce the EU's dependence on imports of natural gas. Yet here the EU has lacked a common policy, with each country instead insisting on its unrestricted right to expand, reduce, or simply maintain its nuclear program at its current level regardless of the overall implications for the union.

Issues dealing more directly with energy security have been marked by no more comity. Britain has strongly endorsed the idea of establishing a common external energy policy, while Germany and France have continued to back bilateral agreements between their energy companies and foreign counterparts. Disagreement has also persisted over what common measures are needed to ensure security of gas supply. For example, Germany, which maintains substantial gas storage facilities, has been concerned lest countries that do not already stockpile gas seek to free ride on its emergency preparations (Westphal 2008).

Thus even within the highly integrated EU, substantial obstacles have stood in the way of collective efforts to increase energy security. Divergent policy preferences have made it difficult to create a united front. And even if the EU is able to make significant progress, its success will do relatively little to enhance the energy security of many other developed democracies, notably the United States and Japan, that lie outside its membership.

Notwithstanding these pessimistic findings, this analysis should not be construed to mean that nothing is to be gained from efforts to forge new cooperative relationships in the quest for greater energy security. Indeed, as noted, some progress has been made within the EU, and the IEA continues to serve a valuable purpose, while NATO remains vital to the overall security of its members. Rather, the purpose is to suggest that there are no simple and easily reached multilateral solutions to the contemporary problems of energy security. The energy security concerns and policy preferences of the countries examined in this study have tended to diverge over time. Thus meaningful advances in cooperation among them are likely to be very limited in nature and achieved only with considerable effort. Instead, significant improvements in their energy security are much more likely to be the result of technological advances.

Implications of the Energy Revolution: Fracking and Energy Security

Indeed, the past decade has seen important developments in many areas of energy production, distribution, and consumption. Among these are rapid declines in the cost of solar panels and wind turbines, nuclear reactor designs that promise substantial increases in safety, new technologies for fossil fuel production, and significant improvements in light vehicle fuel economy, including relatively low-cost hybrid electric vehicles. On the horizon are potential breakthroughs in the production of second-generation biofuels, inexpensive high capacity batteries for vehicles, smart grids, large-scale electricity storage, and possibly even high-volume carbon capture and sequestration, among other things. Together, these advances may ultimately constitute a veritable energy revolution.

In recent years, particular attention has been paid to developments in hydraulic fracturing, colloquially known as "fracking." This process actually combines advances in three different technologies—deep underground seismic imaging, directional drilling, and hydraulic fracturing of nonporous rock—to tap previously inaccessible sources of petroleum and natural gas. So far, fracking has been introduced on a large-scale only in the United States. But the potential for the use of fracking elsewhere is substantial, and the resulting impact on oil and especially gas production could eventually transform global energy markets. What are the implications of this development for the energy security of the major developed democracies and the world more generally?

Although fracking can be used to release oil and gas from a variety of low permeability ("tight") underground rock formations, is has been most often associated with the production of shale gas. The most comprehensive analysis of the world's shale gas potential was published by the EIA in 2013. It estimated the world's technically recoverable resources (TRR) of shale gas at over 200 trillion cubic meters (tcm). This figure represented nearly one-third of the EIA's estimate for total natural gas resources. A 2013 IEA report offered similar numbers. In contrast, the EIA's estimate for shale oil came to just over 10 percent of global TRR, although the share for the United States was more than 25 percent (EIA 2013c, 2–3; IEA 2013b, 108). What impact these massive resources will have, of course, depends on whether and how quickly they are exploited. As a practical matter, the impact is likely to vary from country to country and region to region.

The United States

The biggest contribution of fracking to energy security to this point has been in the United States. Even here, however, it is important to consider separately the impact in the oil and gas sectors, and arguably, fracking has had the biggest impact in the latter.

As noted in chapter 9, the introduction of fracking has contributed to a substantial increase in U.S. petroleum production. As recently as 2004, the EIA projected that U.S. crude oil production, which had been declining steadily since the mid-1980s, would continue to do so and drop below 5 MBD by 2020 (EIA 2004, 150). In 2008, however, this trend suddenly reversed course, and by 2013, production had jumped by half, to some 7.5 MBD. In early 2014, the EIA projected that crude oil production would peak at just under 10 MBD at the end of the decade before beginning a slow decline (EIA 2014, A23, table A11).

Thanks primarily to this rise in crude production, but also to increased output of renewable fuels and natural gas liquids as well as stagnant domestic petroleum consumption, petroleum imports dropped dramatically, both as a share of total consumption and in absolute terms. The former went from a peak of 60 percent in 2005 to just 40 percent in 2012 and was projected to fall to just over one-quarter of petroleum supply at the end of the decade before gradually rising again (EIA 2014, A23, table A11).

This sharp decline in petroleum imports had obvious economic benefits. It may also have contributed to U.S. energy security by reducing the risk of physical shortages of oil, although these had not been a serious concern for many years. Because of the global nature of the oil market, however, the United States remained vulnerable to oil price shocks triggered by supply disruptions elsewhere in the world. The main consolation, again an economic one, was that more of the revenues from higher oil prices would remain in the United States.

The energy security benefits of fracking for shale gas were clearer. By the early 1990s, the United States was meeting more than 10 percent of its gas needs with imports via pipeline from Canada (EIA 2012a, 183). Because of declining U.S. production, the EIA projected as recently as 2005 that the United States would become increasingly dependent on imports of liquefied natural gas (LNG) from more distant and less secure sources, and these would account for more than 20 percent of consumption in 2025 (EIA 2005, 159). Thanks to fracking, however, U.S. natural gas production began to rise again the following year, and the EIA now projects that domestic output in 2040 will be 1.1 tcm, or more than double its 2005 level. As a result, the United States will become a net exporter of gas before the end of this decade, and by the 2030s, shale gas will account for roughly half of all U.S. natural gas production (IEA 2012b, 104; EIA 2014, A-27, table A13).

The energy security benefits of the shale gas revolution have been greater than those of oil because the U.S. natural gas market is much more isolated from the world market. Gas can flow between the United States and its immediate neighbors via pipeline, but there has been very limited capacity to send gas further afield in the form of LNG. As discussed below, this situation will change as new LNG export facilities come online beginning in the second half of this decade. But the high cost of liquefying gas and transporting it from the United States to Europe and Asia will ensure that the market for gas remains somewhat segmented along regional lines.

Europe

Elsewhere in the world, the energy security benefits of fracking are less certain or likely to be longer in coming. EIA and other estimates of shale gas resources in Europe are comparable in magnitude to those for the United States, on the order of 17 tcm (Pearson et al. 2012, vi; EIA 2013c, 6). But the development of this resource is still in its infancy, and many obstacles stand in the way of its full exploitation, both under and above ground. Among these are more difficult geological conditions than those found in the United States; a significantly smaller and less experienced oil and gas service industry; more stringent environmental regulations, which limit the amount of land available for exploration and development; state ownership of subsoil mineral rights, which reduces the incentives for communities to accept shale gas activities; and a high population density, which increases the likelihood of local opposition (IEA 2012b, 122; Pearson et al. 2012, vii; IEA 2013b, 120–21; Goldthau 2013, 26 and 31; Spencer et al. 2014). Overall, the development of European shale gas has been and will continue to be much more controversial and contested than it has been in the United States.

We have already seen these factors at work in the three European countries examined in this study. Among them, France has been regarded as having the greatest shale gas potential. In 2013, the EIA pegged France's TRR at 3.8 tcm, or nearly 30 percent of the total shale gas resources of the EU (EIA 2013c, 6). Because of strong public opposition, however, hydraulic fracturing has been banned by law since 2011. Likewise, Germany imposed a moratorium on fracking for shale gas in 2013, and, in any case, its estimated resources are only a small fraction of those of France.

Of these three countries, then, the brightest prospects for shale gas production in the short to medium term are to be found in Britain. Indeed, as noted in chapter 5, estimates of Britain's shale gas resources were revised dramatically upward in 2013. The British Geological Survey then put the amount of shale gas in one large region—the Bowland Basin—alone at between 23 and 65 tcm, of which perhaps 10 percent might eventually be recovered. Nevertheless, exploration had only just begun, and although the government was supportive of shale gas development, opposition from local communities and environmental groups remained strong (Reed 2013a; Knowles and Farish 2014; White et al. 2014).

Whatever ultimately happens in Britain, France, and Germany, these three countries will also benefit from the exploitation of shale gas in other European countries as the EU gas market becomes more integrated through the liberalization of national gas markets and the construction of additional interconnecting pipeline capacity. By most accounts, the greatest potential within the EU lies in Poland, which has both the largest shale gas resources of any country west of Russia and relatively favorable conditions for developing them: a low population density, prior experience with oil and gas activities, and a government that is eager to reduce the country's near total dependence on Russian gas. A number of companies were already drilling test wells when the first successful frack was achieved in early 2014 (IEA 2012b, 123–25; Strzelecki and Swint 2014).

Next door and sharing a major shale gas region with Poland is Ukraine, whose estimated TRR are of the same magnitude even though the EIA lacked sufficient information to estimate the resources in large parts of the country (EIA 2013c, 6). Ukraine also has a comparable amount of coal-bed methane (CBM), a second important unconventional source of natural gas. Although not a member of the EU, Ukraine is deeply enmeshed in the European gas network as the traditional transit route for gas from Russia.

In view of the many obstacles, however, gas market expert Pierre Noël has written that the unconventional gas supply in Central and Eastern Europe "is unlikely to make a difference in the coming 10 to 15 years" (Noël 2013, 180). The most recent IEA projections for all unconventional gas production, including shale gas, in Poland and Ukraine, moreover, are very low, on the order of only 8 billion cubic meters (bcm) each by 2035. In late 2013, the IEA noted in particular that the prospects in Ukraine "are dampened by a generally difficult investment climate," which has been made only worse by the subsequent political turmoil in the country (IEA 2013b, 121).

All in all, then, shale gas production in Europe is likely to remain modest in both the medium and long term. In perhaps the most optimistic scenario published in recent years, EU unconventional gas production, after a slow start, eventually climbs to 77 bcm in 2035 and accounts for nearly half of all gas output. At the same time, consumption and imports continue to rise, with the latter reaching three-quarters of the former (IEA 2012b, 128–29). In the IEA's most recent estimate, however, EU unconventional gas production reaches only 20 bcm by 2035, and other scenarios fall between these projections (IEA 2013b, 121; Spencer et al. 2014). Thus even in the best case, shale gas will merely compensate for declining conventional gas production and not reduce the EU's import dependence (Pearson et al. 2012, xi; Goldthau 2013, 10).

Asia

Turning to Asia, Japan has little or no fracking potential, but its energy security could be affected by shale gas development in China. In recent years, China's natural gas imports have risen rapidly. To the extent that China can meet future demand from domestic sources, it will reduce competition for regional gas supplies.

China's shale gas potential is substantial. Recent EIA and IEA estimates put the country's TRR at between 31 and 36 tcm, or roughly 15 percent of the world total. And the government has ambitious plans for developing this resource, with a goal of 60 to 100 bcm of shale gas production by 2020 (IEA 2012b, 115–16; EIA 2013c, 6; Houser and Bao 2013, 24).

Most observers expect production to grow more slowly than that, since China's shale gas resources are likely to be more difficult and expensive to develop than those in the United States. Although development projects may face fewer environmental hurdles, most shale basins in China are technically complex. The largest shale basin is densely populated, and others lack gas pipelines or have limited water supplies. The regulatory environment may discourage the participation of experienced foreign companies. And the fact that gas production is dominated by state-owned enterprises may limit the type of competition that did so much to spur development in the United States (IEA 2012b, 115 and 117; Houser and Bao 2013, 25–28; Jaffe and Medlock 2013, 294).

In the longer term, however, the prospects for Chinese shale gas production are much brighter. Recent IEA projections for 2035 range between 120 bcm and 218 bcm, accounting for 23 to 37 percent of total natural gas output, respectively. Production at those levels would reduce China's import requirements by roughly one-third to one-half, thereby potentially freeing up substantial regional gas supplies for Japan (IEA 2012b, 118–20; IEA 2013b, 109, 118, and 121–22).

Global Implications of the U.S. Shale Gas Revolution

Of particular interest in recent years has been the potential for exports of natural gas by the United States to increase the energy security of its allies in Europe and Asia. In fact, fracking in the United States has already made a contribution to others' energy security by nearly eliminating American demand for LNG. Without shale gas, the United States might now be importing more than 100 bcm of LNG per year. (EIA 2005, 159; Krauss 2014). Thanks to the shale gas revolution, however, imports peaked at 22 bcm in 2007 and have since declined to almost nothing (EIA 2012a, 183). LNG shipments from the Atlantic basin that were originally destined for the United States have been free to go to Europe. At the same time, cheap natural gas in the United States has pushed down the price of coal. As a result, European countries have been importing more American coal to substitute for their relatively expensive natural gas in power generation. Both of these developments have in turn reduced European demand for LNG from the Persian Gulf, making more available for Asia and especially Japan, which has had to step up imports with the suspension of its nuclear power program.

Now, the United States is poised to become an LNG exporter. As of May 2014, the U.S. Department of Energy had granted authorization to seven LNG export terminals, with a total potential capacity of more than 100 bcm, and applications for another 30 were under review. It was unclear how many of those facilities would actually be built. But the first was scheduled to begin operation as early as 2016, and the EIA projected that U.S. LNG exports would pass the 50 bcm mark by 2020 and reach nearly 100 bcm in 2030, or approximately 10 percent of U.S. natural gas production, before leveling off (Johnson 2014; Krauss 2014; EIA 2014, A-27, table A13).

What impact will this export potential have? Much will depend on how much gas is actually available for export and at what price. And even if the EIA projections are borne out, U.S. LNG exports will amount to just over 1 percent of world supply in 2020 and just over 2 percent in the 2030s (IEA 2013b, 103). As American exports rise, putting upward pressure on U.S. gas prices, moreover, the price differential between the United States and other regions may diminish to the point where it no longer offsets the costs of liquefaction and transportation (Fesharaki 2013, 20–24; Ladislaw et al. 2014, 22).

Nevertheless, even small volumes of U.S. exports are likely to have a disproportionate influence on trade flows and pricing in other regions. As long as oil prices remain high, U.S. LNG will be able to compete with oil-indexed gas in both Europe and Asia, and its mere presence will play an important role in creating a more competitive international gas market. By providing an alternative supply, it will enable U.S. allies to diversify the geographical sources and pricing mechanisms of their imports, and it will provide them with additional leverage when negotiating with their traditional suppliers. Perhaps most important of all, U.S. LNG export capacity "will undermine the ability of major energy suppliers to use energy as a political weapon" (Cunningham 2013, 2). As a result, Japanese, South Korean, and European companies have been eager to sign agreements with potential U.S. LNG exporters (IEA 2012b, 86; Fesharaki 2013; Koyama 2013, 19–20; Ladislaw et al. 2014, 22).

Putting Fracking in Perspective

Overall, we should not exaggerate the potential contribution of fracking alone to energy security, however. Numerous obstacles stand in the way of the full development of the world's shale gas resources, so it is likely to be slow and uneven, notwithstanding its remarkable success in the United States. Moreover, the impact of fracking will be contingent on a number of other developments that will shape the supply and demand for gas. To begin with, the world's potential supplies of conventional gas, which is more easily tapped, remain massive. The proved reserves of just four countries—Russia, Turkmenistan, Iran, and Qatar—amount to more than half the EIA's estimates for total shale gas resources (BP 2013). Thus conventional gas production could continue to dwarf that of shale gas for many years to come, depending on conditions in those and other countries with substantial conventional reserves.

At the same time, shale gas may have to compete with other unconventional sources of gas. Brief reference has been made to coal-bed methane (CBM), which can often be more easily accessed and extracted than shale gas. Although the IEA puts CBM resources at less than a quarter of those for shale gas, it projects that CBM production will increase at a more rapid rate over the next two decades, accounting, for example, for most of the dramatic expected growth in Australia's natural gas output (IEA 2013b, 108, 117, and 121).

Garnering increasing attention are methane hydrates, which are found on and beneath the sea floor and in permafrost. Many estimates of their abundance fall between 1000 tcm and 5000 tcm, or 5 to 25 times the EIA's estimate of world shale gas resources. Fossil-fuel poor Japan has been particularly interested in developing this resource and has already extracted small amounts from the seabed off its coast (IEA 2013b, 119; Camus 2014).

Finally, one must consider substitutes for natural gas, especially for electric power generation. The world is still poised between a nuclear renaissance and a nuclear retreat, with some countries undertaking expansive construction programs and others phasing out nuclear power. Dramatic drops in the price of wind and solar power have made those increasingly attractive options, especially if their intermittency can be compensated for by advances in storage technology and demand management. And some still harbor hopes for the continued large-scale use of coal coupled with effective carbon capture and sequestration.

As I hope that this book has made clear, the sources of energy insecurity are too many and too diverse to be addressed by a single, dramatic technological advance. We have seen how the energy security concerns of a set of highly similar countries diverged to a marked extent after the oil shocks of the 1970s. Expanding our lens to include a wider array of countries should only add to the challenge of determining how best to promote energy security. At the same time, growing concern about the environmental impact of energy systems, especially in the form of climate change, will place ever greater constraints on what states can do. Thus progress will be needed on a number of fronts. The good news is that rarely, if ever, have the prospects for further energy revolutions seemed so promising.

Chapter 2 · What's the Problem?

1. In 2013, fuels accounted for more than 15 percent of world exports. See World Trade Organization, "Statistics Database," http://stat.wto.org/Home/WSDBHome .aspx.

2. Useful examples include Willrich (1975, 67), Bax (1981, 23), Kapstein (1990, 5), McFarlane (2004), Kalicki and Goldwyn (2005, 9), Deutch and Schlesinger (2006, 3), and Chrisstoffels (2007, 6).

3. For a similar discussion that is more narrowly focused on the problems of oil supplies, see Krapels (1980, 19–21). Likewise, Carlsnaes offers a typology of disruption risks in the Persian Gulf (1988, 13).

4. The following discussion draws on Krapels (1980, 1 and 20), Yager (1981, 603–6), Verleger (1982, 34–35), Rustow (1982, 183–84), Colglazier and Deese (1983, 416–20), Long (1985, 27–28), Ikenberry (1988, 97–98), Yergin (1991, 678–96), and Beaubouef (2007, 94–95).

5. Data on crude oil spot prices are available at Energy Information Administration, "Spot Prices," www.eia.gov/dnav/pet/pet_pri_spt_s1_d.htm.

Chapter 4 · Explaining State Responses
to Energy Insecurity

1. Peter Hall (1986, 160–61) has distinguished between four dimensions of what he calls "étatism": (1) the extent to which the state is a cohesive unit; (2) the extent to which the state is insulated from the demands of other social actors; (3) the capacity to implement policy, if necessary over the objections of key social groups; and (4) the political authority of the state. The three-part typology used here does not include cohesiveness as a dimension of state strength and incorporates state authority as an element of state capacity.

2. One of the few to do so is Hobson (2000, 5–9).

Chapter 5 · Britain

1. The 1972 Gas Act replaced the Gas Council with the British Gas Corporation, a fully integrated company that would build an integrated gas transmission and distribution system (Helm 2004, 39).

2. According to Schneider, the relatively small decline in the British petroleum supply "was a response by the oil companies to the emergency created by the British coal strike" (1983, 246–47).

3. DECC Energy and Emissions Projections are available at www.decc.gov.uk/en /content/cms/about/ec_social_res/analytic_projs/en_emis_projs/en_emis_projs .aspx.

4. "DECC Updated Energy and Emissions Projections—October 2011," http://we barchive.nationalarchives.gov.uk/20130106105028/www.decc.gov.uk/media/view file.ashx?filetype=4&filepath=11/about-us/economics-social-research/3124-annex -i-total-cumulative-new-capacity.xls.

Chapter 6 · France

1. Horst Menderhausen has argued that the embargo had less of an impact on France than other countries and offers a slightly lower figure of 5 percent, but it corresponds to the entire first half of 1974, not just the first three months when supplies were lower (1976, 69–71).

2. Energy intensity calculated from BP 2013 and Heston et al. 2012.

3. Interview with French government official, June 26, 2006, Paris.

4. Interview with French energy policy expert, June 26, 2006, Paris; interview with French energy policy expert, June 29, 2006, Paris.

5. Interview with French government official, June 29, 2006, Paris.

6. Interview with French government official, June 26, 2006, Paris.

7. See also letter from French Minister-Delegate for Industry François Loos to EU Energy Commissioner Andris Piebalgs, Jan. 10, 2007, www.industrie.gouv.fr/infopres /presse/lettre_commission-europeenne.pdf, and "Comments by France on the Proposals of the Green Paper 'A European Strategy for Sustainable, Competitive and Security Energy'," Oct. 17, 2006.

8. BBC, "Shale Gas Ban in France to Remain, says Hollande," (July 15, 2013), www .bbc.com/news/business-23311963.

9. Lucas has written of the "natural ease of the relationships between the administration and the heads of public enterprise" in the postwar years. "The nature of French public enterprise at the time therefore was akin to that of a branch of the administration" (Lucas 1985, 11).

10. Interview with French government official, June 29, 2006, Paris; interview with French energy policy expert, June 29, 2006, Paris.

Chapter 7 · Germany

1. Until 1990, Germany was divided and the Federal Republic was frequently referred to as West Germany.

2. Altogether, the nearly 3,000-mile pipeline would deliver more than 40 bcm per year to Western Europe, or about 10 percent of the region's gas consumption in 1978 (Deese and Miller 1981, 207).

3. This section draws on Duffield (2009) and approximately two dozen interviews conducted in Berlin in June 2006 and July 2007. Interviewees included members of parliament and/or members of their staffs from the CDU/CSU, SPD, and Green parties; officials in the Federal Ministry of Economics and Technology (BMWi), the Federal Ministry for the Environment, Nature Conservation, and Nuclear Safety (BMU), and the Foreign Office (Auswärtiges Amt); and independent experts.

4. "Russia Halts Oil Deliveries to Germany," Spiegel Online International (Jan. 8, 2007), www.spiegel.de/international/0,1518,458401,00.html.

5. "Energiegipfel: Energie für Deutschland - Startschuss für ein energiepolitisches Gesamtkonzept" (April 4, 2006), http://presseservice.pressrelations.de/standard/re sult_main.cfm?aktion=jour_pm&r=227776&quelle=0&pfach=1&n_firmanr_=103 124&sektor=pm&detail=1.

6. BMWi/AA, "Bericht der Arbeitsgruppe 1, Internationale Aspekte zum Energiegipfel am 9. Oktober 2006" (Sept. 25, 2006); BMWi/BMU, "Bericht der Arbeitsgruppe 2, Nationale Aspekte zum Energiegipfel am 9. Oktober 2006" (Sept. 25, 2006), www.bundesregierung.de/Content/DE/Archiv16/Artikel/2006/10/Anlagen/2006 -10-09-ag-2-nationale-aspekte.pdf?__blob=publicationFile&v=1; BMU/BMBF, "Be richt der Arbeitsgruppe 3, Forschung und Energieeffizienz zum Energiegipfel am 9. Oktober 2006" (Sept. 25, 2006).

7. "Ergebnisse des zweiten Energiegipfels—Vorschläge für die internationale Energiepolitik und ein Aktionsprogramm Energieeffizienz" (Oct. 9, 2006), www.bund esregierung.de/Content/DE/Archiv16/Artikel/2006/10/Anlagen/2006-10-10-ener giegipfel-papier.html.

8. The three reports are BMWi/AA, "Bericht der Arbeitsgruppe 1, Internationale Aspekte zum Energiegipfel am 3. Juli 2007" (June 22, 2007); BMWi/BMU, "Bericht der Arbeitsgruppe 2, Internationale Aspekte" (June 20, 2007); and "Bericht der Arbeitsgruppe 3, Forschung und Energieeffizienz" (June 20, 2007).

9. "Ergebnisse des dritten Energiegipfels: Grundlagen für ein integriertes Energie- und Klimaprogramm" (July 3, 2007), www.udo-leuschner.de/energie-chronik /070705d1.htm.

10. "Bundesregierung: Startschuß für Energie- und Klimaschutzkonzept" (July 3, 2007), www.enometrik.de/index.php?id=117&tx_ttnews[tt_news]=68&cHash=610 3f336acfa281c9efff571ba94a7c9.

11. "Eckpunkte für ein integriertes Energie- und Klimaprogramm" (n.d.), www .bmwi.de/BMWi/Redaktion/PDF/E/eckpunkt-fuer-ein-integriertes-energie-und -klimaprogramm,property=pdf,bereich=bmwi,sprache=de,rwb=true.pdf.

12. See "Klimaagenda 2020: Klimapolitik der Bundesregierung nach den Beschlüssen des Europäischen Rates" (April 26, 2007), www.bmu.de/reden/bundesum weltminister_sigmar_gabriel/doc/39239.php.

13. For the most detailed description, see BMWi/BMU, "Bericht der Arbeitsgruppe 2 "Internationale Aspekte"" (June 20, 2007), 2–3 and 11–16. See also Sander (2007).

14. The National Renewable Energy Action Plan, which was released just the month before, set 2020 solar and wind targets of nearly 52 GW and 46 GW, respectively (FRG 2010, 117).

Chapter 8 · Japan

1. Interview with NGO officials, Tokyo, May 21, 2010.

2. Ibid., May 21, 2010.

3. Interview with academic energy policy expert, Tokyo, May 31, 2010.

4. Interview with Japanese government official, Tokyo, May 28, 2010.

5. Interview with NGO officials, Tokyo, May 21, 2010.

6. See "Energy Efficiency Policies and Measures in Japan," unpublished document provided by METI officials, June 2010.

7. Interview with energy policy experts, Tokyo, May 25, 2010; interview with academic energy policy expert, Tokyo, May 31, 2010.

8. Interview with energy policy experts, Tokyo, May 25, 2010.

9. Hydroelectric power and geothermal energy were regarded as mature technologies that did not need government support (IEA 2003, 97).

10. See "Policies on New and Renewable Energy in Japan," unpublished document provided by METI officials, June 2010.

11. Ibid.

12. Interview with Japanese government officials, Tokyo, June 2, 2010; interview with energy policy experts, Tokyo, June 4, 2010.

13. See "Potential scenarios about feed-in tariff scheme of renewable energy," unpublished document provided by METI officials, June 2010.

14. See Japan Bank for International Cooperation, "JBIC Signs Loan Agreement with ADNOC" (Dec. 18, 2007), www.jbic.go.jp/en/information/press/press-2007/1218-7081.

15. See Japan Bank for International Cooperation, "Energy and Natural Resources: Diversifying Supply Sources," www.jbic.go.jp/en/special/resource/004/index.html.

16. Cebu Declaration available at www.asean.org/asean/external-relations/east-asia-summit-eas/item/cebu-declaration-on-east-asian-energy-security-cebu-philippines-15-january-2007-2.

17. Interview with NGO officials, Tokyo, May 21, 2010.

18. See "Invitation to 'Cool Earth 50': 3 Proposals, 3 Principles" (May 24, 2007), www.kantei.go.jp/foreign/abespeech/2007/05/24speech_e.html.

19. See "Overview of the Bill of the Basic Act on Global Warming Countermeasures" (n.d.), www.env.go.jp/en/earth/cc/bagwc/overview_bill.pdf.

20. See Earth Policy Institute, "Annual Solar Photovoltaics Production by Country, 1995–2012," www.earth-policy.org/datacenter/xls/indicator12_2013_2.xlsx.

21. The 2010 BEP, which is sometimes referred to as the "Strategic Energy Plan," is available at www.enecho.meti.go.jp/topics/kihonkeikaku/index.htm. See also the English-language summary METI, "The Strategic Energy Plan of Japan: Meeting Global Challenges and Securing Energy Futures (Revised in June 2010) [Summary]" (June 2010), www.meti.go.jp/english/press/data/pdf/20100618_08a.pdf, and the accompanying press release at www.meti.go.jp/english/press/data/20100618_08.html. For a detailed analysis of the BEP, see Duffield and Woodall (2011).

22. See also "Energy Efficiency Policies and Measures in Japan." For detailed descriptions of the extensive conservation measures that the government has taken in the industrial sector since the 1970s, see IEA (2008, 67–69) and ECCJ (2009, 72–86).

23. Interview with energy policy experts, Tokyo, June 4, 2010.

24. Interview with academic energy policy expert, Tokyo, May 31, 2010; interview with energy policy experts, Tokyo, June 4, 2010.

25. Interview with Japanese government official, Tokyo, May 27, 2010.

26. Interview with academic energy policy expert, Tokyo, May 31, 2010.

27. METI, "Outline of FY 2010 Electricity Supply Plan," cited in Koji Morita, "The Current Status of LNG: Uncertainty from Japan" (Sept. 29, 2010), http://eneken.ieej .or.jp/data/3469.pdf.

28. Based on a comparison of WNA (2010, 6) and METI (2006b, 26).

29. Interview with energy policy experts, Tokyo, May 25, 2010; interview with academic energy policy expert, Tokyo, May 31, 2010.

30. Two reactors were allowed to restart that summer in order to prevent power shortages but were required to shut down 13 months later. Thus as 2013 came to an end, all reactors remained off-line.

31. Interview with energy policy experts, Tokyo, May 25, 2010; interview with academic energy policy expert, Tokyo, May 31, 2010.

32. Interview with energy policy experts, Tokyo, June 4, 2010.

33. Interview with Japanese government officials, Tokyo, June 2, 2010.

34. Interview with NGO officials, Tokyo, May 21, 2010.

35. Interview with energy policy experts, Tokyo, May 25, 2010.

Chapter 9 · The United States

1. Data on U.S. GDP and inflation rates are available at www.bea.gov/national /Index.htm and http://inflationdata.com/inflation/Consumer_Price_Index/Histo ricalCPI.aspx, respectively.

2. Subsequently, in early 1974, Deputy Treasury Secretary William Simon interpreted self-sufficiency to mean not zero imports, but that imports should come from a sufficient range of sources and be sufficiently small in magnitude that a future embargo would not seriously disrupt the economy (de Marchi 1981a, 460–61; Schneider 1983, 326).

3. The lion's share of projected reductions in consumption and imports (3.0 of 4.6 MBD) was to be achieved by cutting industrial use, from 7 to 4 MBD, although industrial use would actual grow from 3.2 to 4.0 MBD (Cochrane 1981, 562–64).

4. For details, see Vietor (1984, 260) and Cochrane (1981, 571–72).

5. At the July 1978 Bonn summit meeting of major industrial countries, Carter pledged to raise the price of oil in the United States to the world level by the end of 1980 (Yager 1981, 612; Vietor 1984, 264).

6. This section draws on Duffield (2008).

7. In addition to Duffield (2008), see Schneider (1983, 262) and Bull-Berg (1987, 109–10).

8. For a detailed discussion, see Duffield (2008).

9. In addition to Duffield (2008), see Lieber (1976, 22), de Marchi (1981b, 527), Schneider (1983, 260), and Beaubouef (2007, 27).

10. In addition to Duffield (2008), see Schneider (1983, 266–67 and 336–37), Ikenberry (1988, 93–94), and Yager (1981).

11. Energy Information Administration, "Spot Prices," www.eia.doe.gov/dnav /pet/pet_pri_spt_s1_d.htm.

12. Energy Information Agency, "Monthly Energy Review" (Sept. 2012), table 1.5.

13. Both the 2005 EPACT and the 2007 EISA contained a number of other noteworthy energy policy measures, such as strong incentives for building new nuclear power plants, but none of these provisions bore directly on the central problem of U.S. energy security.

14. A gallon of ethanol yields only about 68 percent of the energy of a gallon of gasoline (Schnepf and Yacobucci 2012).

15. See Office of Fossil Energy, "Strategic Petroleum Reserve," http://energy.gov /fe/services/petroleum-reserves/strategic-petroleum-reserve.

16. The most thorough account through 2005 is Duffield (2008).

17. Two excellent overviews are Yetiv (2008) and Cramer and Thrall (2012).

18. For comprehensive discussions of the costs of U.S. policy toward the Persian Gulf in general and the Iraq War in particular, see Duffield (2008) and Duffield and Dombrowski (2009).

Chapter 10 · The Quest for Energy Security

1. This section is adopted from Duffield (2012b).

2. For further discussion of the limitations of the IEA, see Plummer and Weyant (1982, 264–65) and Carlsnaes (1988, 19–23).

3. This analysis is restricted to formal organizations whose members are primarily developed democracies, and thus where cooperation would seem to be more feasible than among a more diverse set of states and that are led by at least a subset of the five countries examined above.

4. The IEA's share of world oil consumption would have been approximately two-thirds in the 1970s but for the fact that France initially refused to join. Nevertheless, France maintained close ties to IEA members through its memberships in the OECD and the European Community (EC), and in 1980, the IEA and the EC adopted a formal interface arrangement to coordinate the operation of their oil emergency systems (Scott 1994, 98–99).

5. "27 Nov - Lugar Speech in Advance of NATO Summit at Opening gala dinner of the Riga Conference 2006" (Nov. 27, 2006), www.rigasummit.lv/en/id/speechin /nid/36/.

6. "Senate Clears Lugar's NATO Energy Security Resolution" (June 12, 2006), http://votesmart.org/public-statement/179913/senate-clears-lugars-nato-energy-se curity-resolution#.

7. "Riga Summit Declaration" (Nov. 29, 2006)," www.nato.int/cps/en/natolive /official_texts_37920.htm?selectedLocale=en.

8. "Bucharest Summit Declaration" (April 3, 2008), www.nato.int/cps/en/natol ive/official_texts_8443.htm; NATO 2020: Assured Security, Dynamic Engagement,

Analysis and Recommendations of the Group of Experts on a New Strategic Concept for NATO (May 17, 2010), www.nato.int/strategic-concept/expertsreport.pdf; and "Active Engagement, Modern Defense" (n.d.), www.nato.int/lisbon2010/strategic-concept-2010-eng.pdf.

9. The text is available at http://europa.eu/lisbon_treaty/full_text/index_en.htm.

10. For additional details on the British, French, and German positions, respectively, see McGowan (2011), Méritet (2011), and Duffield and Westphal (2011).

Abraham, Spencer. 2004. "U.S. National Energy Policy and Global Energy Security." *Economic Perspectives* 9 (2):6–9. www.ait.org.tw/infousa/zhtw/DOCS/ijee 0504.pdf.

Ackland, Len. 2009. "Can Germany Survive without Nuclear Power?" *Bulletin of the Atomic Scientists* 65 (4):41–52.

———. 2010. "Germany's Slowing Nuclear Phaseout." *Bulletin of the Atomic Scientists* (Jan. 22). www.thebulletin.org/web-edition/features/germanys-slowing-nuclear -phaseout.

Ahearne, John F. 1983. "Prospects for the U.S. Nuclear Reactor Industry." In *Annual Review of Energy*, vol. 8, edited by Jack M. Hollander and Harvey Brooks, 354–84. Palo Alto, CA: Annual Reviews.

Allison, Graham T. 1971. *Essence of Decision: Explaining the Cuban Missile Crisis.* Boston: Little, Brown.

Ambler, John S. 1988. "French Education and the Limits of State Autonomy." *Western Political Quarterly* 41 (3):469–88.

Anderson, Victor. 1993. *Energy Efficiency Policies.* London: Routledge.

Andrews, Edmund L. 2007. "Senate Adopts Energy Bill Raising Mileage for Cars." *New York Times*, June 22.

Anonymous. 2008. *Action Plan for Achieving a Low-Carbon Society* (July 29). www .kantei.go.jp/foreign/policy/ondanka/final080729.pdf.

ANRE/METI (Agency for Natural Resources and Energy / Ministry of Economy, Trade, and Industry). 2006. *Fiscal 2005 Annual Energy Report (Outline)* (June). www.meti.go.jp/english/report/downloadfiles/FY2005EnergyWP_outline.pdf.

———. 2007. *Fiscal 2006 Annual Energy Report (Outline)*. www.enecho.meti.go.jp /english/report/070802en.pdf.

———. 2009. *FY2008 Annual Energy Report (Outline)*. www.enecho.meti.go.jp/en glish/report/outline.pdf.

———. 2010. *Energy in Japan.* www.enecho.meti.go.jp/topics/energy-in-japan/eng lish2010.pdf.

———. 2014. "Announcement Regarding the Present Status of Introduction of Facilities Generating Renewable Energy as of November 30, 2013" (Nov. 18). www .meti.go.jp/english/press/2014/0221_01.html.

Arima, Jun. 2000. "Top Runner Program." Paper presented at the Workshop on Best Practices in Policies and Measures. Copenhagen, April 11–13. http://svmrev proxy01.unfccc.int/files/meetings/workshops/other_meetings/application/pdf /jpnja.pdf.

———. 2001. "Comprehensive Energy Policy Review: Simultaneous Achievement of the 3 'E'." Paper presented at the Workshop on Good Practices in Policies and Measures, Copenhagen, Oct. 8–10. https://unfccc.int/files/meetings/workshops/other _meetings/application/pdf/arima.pdf.

———. 2008. "Doing Energy Efficiency: The Japan Way" (Feb. 4). http://ebookbrow see.net/jun-arima-pdf-d43470540.

Ashworth, William. 1984. *The History of the British Coal Industry: 1946–1982: The Nationalized Industry*. Vol. 5. Oxford: Oxford University Press.

ASN (Autorité de sûreté nucléaire). 2011a. *Annual Report 2010*. Paris. www.asn.fr /annual_report/2010gb/download/annual-report-2010.html.

———. 2011b. *Complementary Safety Assessments of the French Nuclear Power Plants* (Dec.). www.french-nuclear-safety.fr/Media/Files/Complementary-safety -assessments-of-the-french-nuclear-power-plants-Report-by-the-french-nuclear -safety-authority-december-2011.

———. 2012a. "Nuclear Safety Authority (ASN) Opinion No. 2012-AV-0139" (Jan. 3). www.french-nuclear-safety.fr/Media/Files/00-Bulletin-officiel/Nuclear -Safety-Authority-ASN-opinion-n-2012-AV-0139-of-3rd-January-2012.

———. 2012b. "Publication of the ASN Report on the CSA." News release, Jan. 3. www.french-nuclear-safety.fr/Information/News-releases/ASN-Report-on-the -Complementary-Safety-Assessments-CSA.

Atkinson, Michael M., and William D. Coleman. 1989. "Strong States and Weak States: Sectoral Policy Networks in Advanced Capitalist Economies." *British Journal of Political Science* 19 (1):47–67.

Atsumi, Masahiro. 2007. "Japanese Energy Security Revisited." *Asia-Pacific Review* 14 (1):28–43.

Bahgat, Gawdat. 2003. *American Oil Diplomacy in the Persian Gulf and the Caspian Sea*. Gainesville: University of Florida Press.

———. 2011. *Energy Security: An Interdisciplinary Approach*. New York: Wiley.

Bamberger, Robert L. 2004. "Energy Policy: The Continuing Debate and Omnibus Energy Legislation" (Oct. 1). *CRS Issue Brief for Congress*. Washington, DC: Congressional Research Service.

Bataille, Christian, and Claude Birraux. 2003. "La durée de vie des centrales nucléaires et les nouveaux types de réacteurs." Office parlementaire d'évaluation des choix scientifiques et technologiques. Assemblée Nationale. www.assemblee -nationale.fr/12/pdf/rap-off/i0832.pdf.

Bax, Frans R. 1981. "Energy Security in the 1980s: The Response of US Allies." In *Energy and National Security: Proceedings of a Special Conference*, edited by Donald J. Goldstein, 23–58. Washington, DC: National Defense University Press.

BBC News. 2006. "Gas Shortage Sends Prices Soaring." March 13. http://news.bbc .co.uk/2/hi/business/4802786.stm.

Beaubouef, Bruce A. 2007. *The Strategic Petroleum Reserve: U.S. Energy Security and Oil Politics, 1975–2005*. College Station: Texas A&M University Press.

Bending, Richard, and Richard Eden. 1984. *UK Energy: Structure, Prospects and Policies*. Cambridge: Cambridge University Press.

Berend, Tibor Ivan. 2005. *An Economic History of Twentieth-Century Europe*. New York: Cambridge University Press.

Berger, Thomas U. 1998. *Cultures of Antimilitarism: National Security in Germany and Japan*. Baltimore: The Johns Hopkins University Press.

BERR (Department for Business Enterprise and Regulatory Reform). 2008. *Meeting the Energy Challenge: A White Paper on Nuclear Power* (Jan.). CM 7296. http://web archive.nationalarchives.gov.uk/+/www.berr.gov.uk/files/file43006.pdf.

Bhadrakumar, M. K. 2006. "Germany, Russia Redraw Europe's Frontiers." *Asia Times Online*, May 3. www.atimes.com/atimes/China/HE03Ad01.html.

Birchfield, Vicki, and John S. Duffield, eds. 2011. *Toward a Common EU Energy Policy: Progress, Problems, and Prospects*. New York: Palgrave Macmillan.

Blair, David. 2011. "Gas Storage: UK Suffers from Legacy of North Sea Abundance." *Financial Times*, March 21. www.ft.com/cms/s/0/084d21fc-50fa-11e0-8931-00144 feab49a.html.

Blair, Tony. 2005. "Transcript of speech given by the UK Prime Minister, Tony Blair, to the European Parliament in Strasbourg, 26 October 2006 (26/10/05)." www .astrid-online.it/eu/Documenti/Interventi/Blair_Speech_EP_26oct05.pdf.

BMU (Bundesministerium für Umwelt, Naturschutz und Reactorsicherheit). 2007a. *Das Integrierte Energie- und Klimaprogramm der Bundesregierung* (Dec.). www .bmu.de/files/pdfs/allgemein/application/pdf/hintergrund_meseberg.pdf.

———. 2007b. *The Integrated Energy and Climate Programme of the German Government* (Dec.). www.bmu.de/files/english/pdf/application/pdf/hintergrund _meseberg_en.pdf.

———. 2010. *National Renewable Energy Action Plan* (August). www.erneuerbare -energien.de/fileadmin/ee-import/files/pdfs/allgemein/application/pdf/nation aler_aktionsplan_ee.pdf.

BMWi (Bundesministerium für Wirtschaft und Technologie). 2001. *Energy Report: Sustainable Energy Policy to Meet the Needs of the Future* (June). Berlin: BMWi.

———. 2012. *Germany's New Energy Policy: Heading towards 2050 with Secure, Affordable and Environmentally Sound Energy* (April). Berlin: BMWi. www.bmwi .de/English/Redaktion/Pdf/germanys-new-energy-policy.

———. 2014. "Energiedaten: Gesamtausgabe" (April). http://bmwi.de/BMWi/Re daktion/Binaer/energie-daten-gesamt,property=blob,bereich=bmwi2012,sprache =de,rwb=true.xls.

BMWi/BMU. 2006. *Energieversorgung für Deutschland: Statusbericht für den Energiegipfel am 3. April 2006* (March). Berlin. www.erneuerbare-energien.de/fileadmin /ee-import/files/pdfs/allgemein/application/pdf/statusbericht_0603.pdf.

———. 2010. *Energy Concept for an Environmentally Sound, Reliable and Affordable Energy Supply* (Sept. 28). Berlin: BWMi and BMU. www.germany.info/content blob/3043402/Daten/1097719/BMUBMWi_Energy_Concept_DD.pdf.

Bohi, Douglas R. 1989. *Energy Price Shocks and Macroeconomic Performance*. Washington, DC: Resources for the Future.

Bohi, Douglas R., and Milton Russell. 1978. *Limiting Oil Imports: An Economic History and Analysis*. Baltimore: The Johns Hopkins University Press.

Borenstein, Seth, and Sumana Chatterjee. 2003. "Industry Tax Breaks Fill GOP Energy Bill." *The Seattle Times*, Nov. 15. http://seattletimes.com/html/nation world/2001791918_energy15.html.

Bosman, Rick. 2012. "How Germany's Powerful Renewables Advocacy Coalition Is Transforming the German (and European) Energy Market." *European Energy Review*, Feb. 27. http://europeanenergyreview.eu/site/pagina.php?id=3552.

Boxell, James. 2011. "EDF Alerted Over "Gaps" in Nuclear Plant." *Financial Times*, Aug. 24

———. 2012. "Nuclear Safety Work to Cost France Billions." *Financial Times*, Jan. 3.

BP. 2013. "Statistical Review of World Energy 2013." Historical Data Workbook. www .bp.com/content/dam/bp/excel/Energy-Economics/statistical_review_of_world _energy_2013_workbook.xlsx.

Broder, John M. 2007. "Voter Anger May Free Up Energy Bills." *New York Times*, Nov. 13.

———. 2010. "Obama to Open Offshore Areas to Oil Drilling for First Time." *New York Times*, March 31.

Bromley, Simon. 1991. *American Hegemony and World Oil: The Industry, the State System, and the World Economy*. University Park: The Pennsylvania State University Press.

Brown, Marilyn A., and Benjamin K. Sovacool. 2012. *Climate Change and Global Energy Security: Technology and Policy Options*. Cambridge, MA: The MIT Press.

Buchan, David. 2012. *The Energiewende—Germany's Gamble* (June). Oxford: Oxford Institute for Energy Studies. www.oxfordenergy.org/wpcms/wp-content/uploads /2012/07/SP-26.pdf.

———. 2014. *The French Disconnection: Reducing the Nuclear Share in France's Energy Mix* (Jan.). Oxford: Oxford Institute for Energy Studies. www.oxfordenergy .org/wpcms/wp-content/uploads/2014/01/SP-32.pdf.

Buckley, Sarah. 2006. "Japan's Shaky Nuclear Record." *BBC News Online*, March 24. http://news.bbc.co.uk/2/hi/asia-pacific/3548192.stm.

Bull-Berg, Hans-Jacob. 1987. *American International Oil Policy: Causal Factors and Effect*. New York: St. Martin's.

Bundesregierung. 1973. "Die Energiepolitik der Bundesregierung" (Oct. 3). Drucksache 7/1057 Bonn: Deutscher Bundestag.

———. 2005a. "Regierungserklärung von Bundeskanzlerin Angela Merkel" (Nov. 30). www.bundesregierung.de/Content/DE/Bulletin/2001_2007/2005/11/2005-11 -30-regierungserklaerung-von-bundeskanzlerin-dr-angela-merkel-vor-dem-de utschen-bundestag-.html.

———. 2005b. "Working Together for Germany—with Courage and Compassion. Coalition Agreement between the CDU, CSU and SPD" (Nov. 11). Berlin.

———. 2007. "Bericht zur Umsetzung der in der Kabinettsklausur am 23./24.08 .2007 in Meseberg beschlossenen Eckpunkte für ein Integriertes Energie- und Klimaprogramm" (Dec. 5). Berlin. www.bmub.bund.de/fileadmin/bmu-import /files/pdfs/allgemein/application/pdf/gesamtbericht_iekp.pdf.

Bupp, I. C. 1977. "Energy Policy Planning in the United States: Ideological BTU's." In *The Energy Syndrome: Comparing National Responses to the Energy Crisis*, edited by Leon Lindberg, 285–324. Lexington, MA: Lexington Books.

Bush, George W. 2002. *The National Security Strategy of the United States of America* (September). Washington, DC: The White House. www.globalsecurity.org /military/library/policy/national/nss-020920.pdf.

———. 2006. *The National Security Strategy of the United States* (March). Washington, DC: The White House. http://georgewbush-whitehouse.archives.gov/nsc /nss/2006/.

Bustelo, Pablo. 2008. "Energy Security with a High External Dependence: The Strategies of Japan and South Korea" (April 14). Working Paper 16/2008, Real Instituto Elcano, Madrid. http://papers.ssrn.com/sol3/Delivery.cfm/SSRN_ID112 2302_code202471.pdf?abstractid=1122302&mirid=1.

Butler, Declan. 2012. "France 'Imagines the Unimaginable.'" *Nature* 481 (7380): 121–22 (Jan. 12). www.nature.com/polopoly_fs/1.9780!/import/pdf/481121a.pdf.

Campbell, Robert M. 1976. "The Foreign Trade Aspects of the Trade Act of 1974, Part II." *Washington and Lee Law Review* 33 (3):639–99.

Camus, Gabriel. 2014. "A Story of Ice and Fire: How Methane Hydrates Could Change the World" (April 23). *Energy Post*. www.energypost.eu/story-ice-fire-methane -hydrates-change-world/.

Capoccia, Giovanni, and R. Daniel Keleman. 2007. "The Study of Critical Junctures: Theory, Narrative, and Counterfactuals in Historical Institutionalism." *World Politics* 59 (3):341–69.

Carlsnaes, Walter. 1988. *Energy Vulnerability and National Security: The Energy Crises, Domestic Policy Responses and the Logic of Swedish Neutrality*. London: Pinter.

Carter, Jimmy. 1977. "The President's Proposed Energy Policy" (May 1). *Vital Speeches of the Day* 43 (14): 418–20.

CBO (Congressional Budget Office). 2002. *Reducing Gasoline Consumption: Three Options*. Washington, DC: Congressional Budget Office.

Chen, Jie, and Bruce J. Dickson. 2010. *Allies of the State: China's Private Entrepreneurs and Democratic Change*. Cambridge, MA: Harvard University Press.

Chesshire, John. 1986. "An Energy-Efficient Future: A Strategy for the UK." *Energy Policy* 14 (5):395–412.

Chesshire, J. H., J. K. Friend, J. deB. Pollard, J. Stringer, and A. J. Surrey. 1977. "Energy Policy in Britain: A Case Study of Adaptation and Change in a Policy System." In *The Energy Syndrome: Comparing National Responses to the Energy Crisis*, edited by Leon Lindberg, 33–62. Lexington, MA: Lexington Books.

Chrisstoffels, Jan-Hein. 2007. "Getting to Grips Again with Dependency: Japan's Energy Strategy" (August). *Clingendael Energy Paper*. The Hague: Netherlands Institute of International Relations. www.relooney.info/SI_Oil-Politics/Energy -Security-Japan_1.pdf.

CIA (Central Intelligence Agency). 1977. "The International Energy Situation: Outlook to 1985" (April). Washington, DC. http://hdl.handle.net/2027/mdp.3901 5047406213.

Clawson, Patrick, and Simon Henderson. 2005. "Reducing Vulnerability to Middle East Energy Shocks: A Key Element in Strengthening U.S. Energy Security" (Nov.). *Policy Focus #49*. Washington, DC: Washington Institute for Near East

Policy. www.washingtoninstitute.org/uploads/Documents/pubs/PolicyFocus49 .pdf.

Clinton, William J. 2000. *A National Security Strategy for a Global Age* (Dec.). Washington, DC: The White House. www.globalsecurity.org/military/library/policy /national/nss-0012.pdf.

Cochrane, James L. 1981. "Carter Energy Policy and the Ninety-fifth Congress." In *Energy Policy in Perspective*, edited by Craufurd D. Goodwin, 547–600. Washington, DC: Brookings Institutions.

Cohen, Stephen S. 1982. "Informed Bewilderment: French Economic Strategy and the Crisis." In *France in the Troubled World Economy*, edited by Stephen S. Cohen and Peter A. Gourevitch. London: Butterworth Scientific.

Coker, Margaret. 2009. "Korean Team to Build U.A.E. Nuclear Plants." *Wall Street Journal*, December 28.

Colgan, Jeff. 2009. "The International Energy Agency: Challenges for the 21st Century." In *GPPi Policy Paper Series*. Berlin: Global Public Policy Institute.

Colglazier, E. William, Jr., and David A. Deese. 1983. "Energy and Security in the 1980s." In *Annual Review of Energy*, edited by J. M. Hollander and H. Brooks. Palo Alto, CA: Annual Reviews.

Commission (Commission of the European Communities / European Commission). 1982. *Review of Member States' Energy Policy Programmes and Progress Towards 1990 Objectives* (June 10). COM(82) 326 final. Brussels.

———. 1984. *Review of Member States' Energy Policies* (Feb. 29). COM(84) 88 final. Brussels.

———. 1988. *Review of Member States' Energy Policies* (May 3). COM(88) 174 final. Brussels.

———. 2000. *Green Paper: Towards a European Strategy for the Security of Energy Supply* (Nov. 29). COM(2000) 769 final. Luxembourg: Office for Official Publications of the European Communities.

———. 2006. *Green Paper: A European Strategy for Sustainable, Competitive and Secure Energy* (March 8). COM (2006) 105 final. Brussels.

———. 2007. *An Energy Policy for Europe* (Jan. 10). COM (2007) 1 final. Brussels.

Conant, Melvin A., and Fern R. Gold. 1978. *The Geopolitics of Energy*. Boulder, CO: Westview Press.

Corcoran, Tom, and Tomoko Hosoe. 2006. "Japan Govt to Assume More Aggressive Energy Role." *Reuters*, August 6.

Cowhey, Peter F. 1985. *The Problems of Plenty: Energy Policy and International Politics*. Berkeley: University of California Press.

Cramer, Jane K., and A. Trevor Thrall, eds. 2012. *Why Did the United States Invade Iraq?* New York: Routledge.

Cunningham, Nick. 2013. *The Geopolitical Implications of U.S. Natural Gas Exports* (March). American Security Project. www.americansecurityproject.org/ASP%20 Reports/Ref%200116%20-%20The%20Geopolitical%20Implications%20of%20 U.S.%20Natural%20Gas%20Exports.pdf.

Dam, Kenneth W. 1976. *Oil Resources: Who Gets What How?* Chicago: University of Chicago Press.

Davis, David Howard. 1982. *Energy Politics.* 3rd ed. New York: St. Martin's Press.

Davis, Stacy C., and Susan W. Diegel. 2004. *Transportation Energy Data Book: Edition 24* (Dec.). Oak Ridge, TN: Oak Ridge National Laboratory.

Davis, Stacy C., Susan W. Diegel, and Robert G. Boundy. 2013. *Transportation Energy Data Book: Edition 32* (July). Oak Ridge, TN: Oak Ridge National Laboratory.

de Carmoy, Guy. 1977. *Energy for Europe: Economic and Political Implications.* Washington, DC: American Enterprise Institute for Public Policy Research.

———. 1982. "French Energy Policy." In *After the Second Oil Crisis: Energy Policies in Europe, America, and Japan,* edited by Wilfrid L. Kohl, 113–135. Lexington, MA: Lexington Books.

DECC (Department of Energy and Climate Change). 2010a. *Gas Security of Supply: A Policy Statement from the Department of Energy and Climate Change* (April). https://ukccsrc.ac.uk/system/files/publications/ccs-reports/DECC_Gas_162.pdf.

———. 2010b. *Government Response to Malcolm Wick's Review of International Energy Security, 'Energy Security: National Challenges in a Changing World'* (April).

———. 2011a. *Digest of United Kingdom Energy Statistics 2011.* London: The Stationery Office. http://webarchive.nationalarchives.gov.uk/20130109092117/http://decc.gov.uk/assets/decc/11/stats/publications/dukes/2312-dukes-2011—full-document-excluding-cover-pages.pdf.

———. 2011b. *Overarching National Policy Statement for Energy (EN-1)* (July). London: The Stationery Office. www.gov.uk/government/uploads/system/uploads/attachment_data/file/37046/1938-overarching-nps-for-energy-en1.pdf.

———. 2011c. *UK Renewable Energy Roadmap* (July). London: DECC. www.gov.uk/government/uploads/system/uploads/attachment_data/file/48128/2167-uk-renewable-energy-roadmap.pdf.

———. 2012a. *Digest of United Kingdom Energy Statistics 2012: Long-Term Trends.* www.gov.uk/government/uploads/system/uploads/attachment_data/file/84178/5958-dukes-2012-long-term-trends.pdf

———. 2012b. *Energy Security Strategy* (Nov.) Cm 8466. London. www.gov.uk/government/uploads/system/uploads/attachment_data/file/65643/7101-energy-security-strategy.pdf.

DECC/Ofgem (Department of Energy and Climate Change and Office of Gas and Electricity Markets). 2011. *Statutory Security of Supply Report* (Nov.). HC 1604. London: The Stationery Office. www.gov.uk/government/uploads/system/uploads/attachment_data/file/247180/1604.pdf.

———. 2013. *Statutory Security of Supply Report 2013* (Oct.). HC 675. London: The Stationery Office. www.gov.uk/government/uploads/system/uploads/attachment_data/file/261604/HC_675_updated_accessible.pdf.

Deese, David A. 1979–80. "Energy: Economics, Politics, and Security." *International Security* 4 (3):140–53.

Deese, David A., and Linda B. Miller. 1981. "Western Europe." In *Energy and Security*, edited by David A. Deese and Joseph S. Nye, 181–209. Cambridge, MA: Ballinger.

Deese, David A., and Joseph S. Nye, eds. 1981. *Energy and Security*. Cambridge, MA: Ballinger.

de Hoop Scheffer, Jaap. 2008. "Energy Security in the 21st Century" (Oct. 23). www .nato.int/docu/speech/2008/s081023b.html.

de Marchi, Neil. 1981a. "Energy Policy under Nixon: Mainly Putting Out Fires." In *Energy Policy in Perspective*, edited by Craufurd D. Goodwin, 395–473. Washington, DC: Brookings Institution.

———. 1981b. "The Ford Administration: Energy as a Political Good." In *Energy Policy in Perspective: Today's Problems, Yesterday's Solutions*, edited by Craufurd D. Goodwin, 475–545. Washington, DC: Brookings Institution.

Department of Energy (UK). 1978. *Energy Policy: A Consultative Document*. Cmnd 1701. London: Her Majesty's Stationary Office.

Deutch, John, and James R. Schlesinger. 2006. *National Security Consequences of U.S. Oil Dependency: Report of an Independent Task Force*. New York: Council on Foreign Relations.

DGEMP (Direction Générale de l'Énergie et des Matières Premières). 2005. "La loi de programme du 13 juillet fixant les orientations de la politique énergétique" (July 21). www.vie-publique.fr/documents-vp/energie_2005/050713_lp_synthese.pdf.

———. 2006a. "Déclaration du premier ministre, Dominiqe de Villepin, sur la politique énergétique, le 15 mai 2006." www.industrie.gouv.fr/energie/politique/ville pin-mai-06.htm.

———. 2006b. *France's Energy Situation*. Paris: DGEMP.

DGEMP/OE (Direction Générale de l'Énergie et des Matières Premières and Observatoire de l'Énergie). 2004. *Energy Baseline Scenario for France to 2030* (June).

———. 2006. *Électricité et politique énergétique: spécificités françaises et enjeux dans le cadre européen* (Jan.). Paris. www.vie-publique.fr/documents-vp/regula tion_2006/dgemp_electricite_politique_energetique.pdf.

Dockrill, Michael. 1988. *British Defence since 1945*. Oxford and New York: Basil Blackwell.

DOE (U.S. Department of Energy). 1977. *The Role of Foreign Governments in the Energy Industries*. Washington, DC: Department of Energy, Office of International Affairs.

———. 2011. *U.S.-China Clean Energy Cooperation* (Jan.). Washington, DC: U.S. Department of Energy. www.us-china-cerc.org/pdfs/US_China_Clean_Energy _Progress_Report.pdf.

Dohmen, Frank, Alexander Jung, Michael Sauga, and Andreas Wassermann. 2012. "Germany Stalled on the Expressway to a Green Future." *Der Spiegel*, May 23. www.spiegel.de/international/germany/germany-s-energy-revolution-stalls-wit hout-decisiveness-and-incentives-a-834565-2.html.

Dombrowski, Peter J., and John S. Duffield. 2009. "Are We Safer Now?" In *Balance Sheet: The Iraq War and U.S. National Security*, edited by John S. Duffield and Peter J. Dombrowski, 158–202. Stanford, CA: Stanford University Press.

Doner, Richard F. 1992. "Limits of State Strength: Toward an Institutionalist View of Economic Development." *World Politics* 44 (3):398–431.

Doran, Charles. 2008. "Life After Easy Oil." *The American Interest* (July 1). www.the-american-interest.com/articles/2008/07/01/life-after-easy-oil/.

Dore, Ronald. 1983. "Energy Conservation in Japanese Industry." In *Energy: Two Decades of Crisis*, edited by Robert Belgrave, 91–156. Aldershot, Hamps., UK: Gower.

DTI (Department of Trade and Industry). 2003. *Our Energy Future: Creating a Low Carbon Economy* (Jan.). Energy White Paper. London: The Stationery Office.

———. 2005. *Creating a Low Carbon Economy: Second Annual Report on the Implementation of the Energy White Paper* (July). London: DTI.

———. 2006a. *The Energy Challenge: Energy Review Report 2006* (July). London: The Stationery Office.

———. 2006b. *Our Energy Challenge: Securing Clean, Affordable Energy for the Long Term* (Jan.) Energy Review Consultation Document. London: DTI.

———. 2006c. "UK Response to the Commission Green Paper: A European Strategy for Sustainable, Competitive and Secure Energy" (June 23). http://webarchive.nationalarchives.gov.uk/+/www.berr.gov.uk/files/file31659.pdf.

———. 2006d. "UK Supplementary Response to the European Commission's Green Paper 'A European Strategy for Sustainable, Competitive and Secure Energy'" (Oct. 2). London. http://webarchive.nationalarchives.gov.uk/+/www.berr.gov.uk/files/file34452.pdf.

———. 2007. *Meeting the Energy Challenge: A White Paper on Energy* (May). CM 7124. London: The Stationery Office.

Duffield, John S. 1998. *World Power Forsaken: Political Culture, International Institutions, and German Security Policy after Unification*. Stanford, CA: Stanford University Press.

———. 1999. "Political Culture and State Behavior: Why Germany Confounds Neorealism." *International Organization* 53 (4):765–803.

———. 2005. "Oil and the Iraq War: How the United States Could Have Expected to Benefit, and Might Still." *Middle East Review of International Affairs* 9 (3):109–41.

———. 2008. *Over a Barrel: The Costs of U.S. Foreign Oil Dependence*. Stanford, CA: Stanford University Press.

———. 2009. "Germany and Energy Security in the 2000s: Rise and Fall of a Policy Issue?" *Energy Policy* 37 (11):4284–92.

———. 2012a. "Oil and the Decision to Invade Iraq." In *Why Did the United States Invade Iraq?* edited by Jane K. Cramer and A. Trevor Thrall, 145–66. London: Routledge.

———. 2012b. "The Return of Energy Insecurity in the Developed Democracies." *Contemporary Security Policy* 33 (1):1–26.

Duffield, John S., and Peter J. Dombrowski, eds. 2009. *Balance Sheet: The Iraq War and U.S. National Security*. Stanford, CA: Stanford University Press.

Duffield, John S., and Kirsten Westphal. 2011. "Germany and EU Energy Policy: Conflicted Champion of Integration?" In *Toward a Common European Union Energy*

Policy: Problems, Progress, and Prospects, edited by Vicki L. Birchfield and John S. Duffield, 169–86. New York: Palgrave Macmillan.

Duffield, John S., and Brian Woodall. 2011. "Japan's New Basic Energy Plan." *Energy Policy* 39 (6):3741–49.

Eastcott, James. 2004. "Japan's Downstream: Restructuring and Global Implications." *Middle East Economic Survey* 47 (30).

ECCJ (Energy Conservation Center Japan). 2009. "Japan Energy Conservation Handbook 2009." Tokyo: ECCJ.

Eckbo, Paul Leo. 1979. "Perspectives on North Sea Oil." In *Annual Review of Energy,* vol. 4, edited by Jack M. Hollander, Melvin K. Simmons and David O. Wood, 71–98. Palo Alto, CA: Annual Reviews.

Eddy, Melissa. 2012. "German Plan to Abandon Its Nuclear Energy Lags." *New York Times,* May 30.

EDMC (Energy Data Modelling Center). 2010. *EDMC Handbook of Energy & Economic Statistics in Japan.* Tokyo: The Energy Conservation Center.

Eguchi, Yujiro. 1980. "Japanese Energy Policy." *International Affairs* 56 (2):263–79.

EIA (U.S. Energy Information Administration). 2004. *Annual Energy Outlook 2004: With Projections to 2025* (Jan.). DOE/EIA-0383(2004). Washington, DC: EIA.

———. 2005. *Annual Energy Outlook 2005: With Projections to 2025* (Feb.) DOE/EIA-0383(2005). Washington, DC: EIA.

———. 2006a. *Annual Energy Outlook 2006: With Projections to 2030* (Feb.). DOE/EIA-0383(2006). Washington, DC: EIA

———. 2006b. "Germany." Country Analysis Briefs. Washington, DC: EIA.

———. 2010. *Annual Energy Review 2009* (Aug.). DOE/EIA-0384(2009). Washington, DC: EIA.

———. 2012. *Annual Energy Review 2011* (Sept.). DOE/EIA-0384(2011). Washington, DC: EIA.

———. 2013a. *Annual Energy Outlook 2013: With Projections to 2040* (April). DOE/EIA-0383(2013). Washington, DC: EIA.

———. 2013b. *International Energy Outlook 2013: With Projections to 2040* (July). DOE/EIA-0484(2013). Washington, DC: EIA.

———. 2013c. *Technically Recoverable Shale Oil and Shale Gas Resources: An Assessment of 137 Shale Formations in 41 Countries Outside the United States* (June). Washington, DC: EIA.

———. 2014. *Annual Energy Outlook 2014: With Projections to 2040* (April). DOE/EIA-0838(2014). Washington, DC: EIA.

ESSG (Energy Security Study Group). 2006. "Interim Report" (June). Tokyo. www.meti.go.jp/english/report/downloadfiles/060613interim_report.pdf.

EurActiv. 2011. "Wind Energy Fans Welcome Sarkozy Plans but Question Timing" (March 11). www.euractiv.com/climate-environment/wind-fans-welcome-sarkozy-plans-question-timing-news-501589.

———. 2012a. "Nuclear Phaseout Costs May Hurt Germany's Green Ambitions" (Aug. 29). www.euractiv.com/climate-environment/nuclear-phaseout-costs-may-crimp-news-514486.

———. 2012b. "UK Government Announces Biggest Energy Reforms in 20 Years" (May 23). www.euractiv.com/general/uk-government-announces-biggest-energy -reforms-20-years-news-512918.

Evans, Douglas. 1979. *Western Energy Policy: The Case for Competition.* New York: St. Martin's Press.

Evans, Peter. 1995. *Embedded Autonomy: States and Industrial Transformation.* Princeton, NJ: Princeton University Press.

Evans, Peter C. 2006. *Japan.* Brookings Foreign Policy Studies Energy Security Series. Washington, DC: Brookings Institution.

EWI/GWS/Prognos (Energiewirtschaftliches Institut an der Universität zu Köln, Gesellschaft für Wirtschaftliche Strukturforschung mbH, and Prognos AG). 2010. *Energieszenarien für ein Energiekonzept der Bundesregierung* (Aug. 27). Projekt Nr. 12/10 des Bundesministeriums für Wirtschaft und Technologie. www.bmwi .de/DE/Mediathek/publikationen,did=356294.html.

———. 2011. *Energieszenarien 2011* (July). Projekt Nr. 12/10 des Bundesministeriums für Wirtschaft und Technologie. www.prognos.com/fileadmin/pdf/publika tionsdatenbank/11_08_12_Energieszenarien_2011.pdf.

Fackler, Martin. 2012. "Last Reactor of 50 in Japan Is Shut Down." *New York Times,* May 5.

Fackler, Martin, and Hiroko Tabuchi. 2011. "Lag in Closing Plant Highlights Problems in Japan." *New York Times,* May 9.

Fagnani, Jeanne, and Jean-Paul Moatti. 1984. "The Politics of French Nuclear Development." *Journal of Policy Analysis and Management* 3 (2):264–75.

FCO/DTI/Defra (Foreign and Commonwealth Office, Department of Trade and Industry, and Department for Environment, Food, and Rural Affairs). 2004. *UK International Priorities: The Energy Strategy.* London.

FEI (Finnish Energy Industries). 2010. *Opportunities to Utilise Tendering as a Part of a Feed-in Tariff System* (Jan. 15). JR-100115-P&320-007. http://pda.ek.fi/www /fi/energia/liitteet/Tendering_as_a_part_of_a_feed-in_tariff_system__Final_ Report_201001115.pdf.

Feigenbaum, Harvey B. 1982. "France's Oil Policy: The Limits of Mercantilism." In *France in the Troubled World Economy,* edited by Stephen S. Cohen and Peter A. Gourevitch, 114–41. London: Butterworth Scientific.

Fells, Ian. 1977. "The Energy Future of West Germany." *Energy Policy* 5 (4): 341–44.

Fesharaki, Shahriar. 2013. "Implications of North American LNG Exports for Asia's Pricing Regime." 2013 Pacific Energy Summit Working Papers. www.nbr.org /downloads/pdfs/eta/PES_2013_summitpaper_Fesharaki.pdf.

Finon, Dominique. 1996. "French Energy Policy: The Effectiveness and Limitations of Colbertism." In *European Energy Policies in a Changing Environment,* edited by Francis McGowan, 21–56. Heidelberg: Physica-Verlag.

Fong, Glenn R. 1990. "State Strength, Industry Structure, and Industrial Policy: American and Japanese Experiences in Microelectronics." *Comparative Politics* 22 (3):273–99.

Fontaine, Nicole. 2003. *Livre blanc sur les énergies* (Nov. 7). www.ladocumentation francaise.fr/var/storage/rapports-publics//034000650/0000.pdf.

FRG (Federal Republic of Germany). 2010. *National Renewable Energy Action Plan.* Berlin: BMU. http://ec.europa.eu/energy/renewables/action_plan_en.htm.

Frieden, Jeff. 1988. "Sectoral Conflict and U.S. Foreign Economic Policy, 1914–1940." In *The State and American Foreign Economic Policy*, edited by G. John Ikenberry, David A. Lake and Michael Mastanduno, 59–90. Ithaca, NY: Cornell University Press.

Fujii, Hideaki. 2000. "Japan." In *Rethinking Energy Security in East Asia*, edited by Paul B. Stares, 59–78. Tokyo / New York: Japan Center for International Exchange.

Fujime, Kazuya. 1997. "Japan's Energy Policy: Current Status and Issues." *Japan Review of International Affairs* 11 (3):173–87.

Fujita, Toshihiko. 2009. "Overview of Japan's Energy Situation and Energy Conservation Measures." Paper read at the 22nd International Conference on Efficiency, Cost, Optimization Simulations and Environmental Impact of Energy Systems, Foz do Iguacu, Parana, Brazil, Aug. 31–Sept. 3. http://s3.amazonaws.com/zanran _storage/www.eventus.com.br/ContentPages/43235761.pdf.

Gallis, Paul. 2007. "NATO and Energy Security" (Aug. 15). *CRS Report to Congress.* Washington, DC: Congressional Research Service.

GAO (U.S. Government Accountability Office). 2006. *International Energy: International Forums Contribute to Energy Cooperation within Constraints* (Dec.). GAO-07-170. Washington, DC: GAO.

George, Alexander L., and Andrew Bennett. 2004. *Case Studies and Theory Development in the Social Sciences.* Cambridge, MA: MIT Press.

Gipe, Paul. 2006. "France Implements New Renewable Tariffs for Solar, Wind, and Biogas," July 26. www.wind-works.org/cms/index.php?id=189&tx_ttnews[tt_news] =646&cHash=7f6d985e6c799e346da7f4caf7d58e6f.

———. 2008. "Higher Solar Feed-in Tariffs Part of Aggressive New French PV Program," Nov. 17. www.wind-works.org/cms/index.php?id=189&tx_ttnews[tt_news] =643&cHash=5f8365ce74958b0f0f2d178bd14960ec.

Giraud, André L. 1983. "Energy in France." In *Annual Review of Energy*, vol. 8, edited by Jack M. Hollander and Harvey Brooks, 165–91. Palo Alto, CA: Annual Reviews.

Goldthau, Andreas. 2012. "A Public Policy Perspective on Global Energy Security." *International Studies Perspectives* 12 (4): 65–84.

———. 2013. "The Politics of Natural Gas Development in the European Union" (Oct. 23). James A. Baker III Institute for Public Policy, Rice University. http://bak erinstitute.org/media/files/Research/b7b96328/CES-pub-GeoGasEU-102513. pdf.

Goodwin, Craufurd D., ed. 1981. *Energy Policy in Perspective: Today's Problems, Yesterday's Solutions.* Washington, DC: Brookings Institution.

Götz, Roland. 2005. "The North European Pipeline: Increasing Energy Security or Political Pressure" (Sept.) *SWP Comments 42.* Berlin: Stiftung Wissenschaft und Politik.

Greene, David L., Donald W. Jones, and Paul N. Leiby. 1998. "The Outlook for Oil Dependence." *Energy Policy* 26 (1): 55–60.

Griffin, James M. 2009. *A Smart Energy Policy: An Economist's Rx for Balancing Cheap, Clean, and Secure Energy*. New Haven: Yale University Press.

Habiby, Margo. 2010. "Oil Demand Not Keeping Pace With Economy, Tanaka Says." *Business Week*, March 12.

Hakes, Jay. 2008. *A Declaration of Energy Independence: How Freedom from Foreign Oil Can Improve National Security, Our Economy, and the Environment*. Hoboken, NJ: John Wiley & Sons.

Hall, John A., and G. John Ikenberry. 1989. *The State*. Minneapolis: University of Minnesota Press.

Hall, Peter A. 1986. *Governing the Economy: The Politics of State Intervention in Britain and France*. New York: Oxford University Press.

———. 1993. "Policy Paradigms, Social Learning, and the State: The Case of Economic Policymaking in Britain." *Comparative Politics* 25 (3):275–96.

Halperin, Morton H. 1974. *Bureaucratic Politics and Foreign Policy*. Washington, DC: Brookings Institution.

Hatch, Michael T. 1986. *Politics and Nuclear Power: Energy Policy in Western Europe*. Lexington: University of Kentucky Press.

Hayashi, Masatsugu, and Larry Hughes. 2013. "The Policy Responses to the Fukushima Nuclear Accident and Their Effect on Japanese Energy Policy." *Energy Policy* 59 (August):86–101.

Helm, Dieter. 2004. *Energy, the State, and the Market: British Energy Policy since 1979*. Revised ed. Oxford: Oxford University Press.

———. 2005. *A New British Energy Policy*. London: The Social Market Foundation.

———. 2007a. "British Energy Policy" (Aug. 15). www.dieterhelm.co.uk/sites/default/files/British_EP_150808.pdf.

———. 2007b. "Labour's Third Energy White Paper" (Dec. 21). www.dieterhelm.co.uk/sites/default/files/Commentary_May07.pdf.

———. 2008. *Credible Energy Policy: Meeting the Challenges of Security of Supply and Climate Change*. London: Policy Exchange.

Henningsen, Jørgen. 2011. "Energy Savings and Efficiency." In *Toward a Common European Union Energy Policy: Problems, Progress, and Prospects*, edited by Vicki L. Birchfield and John S. Duffield, 131–41. New York: Palgrave Macmillan.

Herberg, Mikkal E. 2004. "Asia's Energy Insecurity: Cooperation or Conflict?" In *Strategic Asia 2004–05: Confronting Terrorism in the Pursuit of Power*, edited by Ashley J. Tellis and Michael Wills. Seattle: National Bureau of Asia Research.

Hirst, Eric, Robert Marlay, David Greene, and Richard Barnes. 1983. "Recent Changes in U.S. Energy Consumption: What Happened and Why?" In *Annual Review of Energy*, vol. 8, edited by Jack M. Hollander and Harvey Brooks, 193–245. Palo Alto, CA: Annual Reviews.

HL (House of Lords, European Union Committee). 2004. *Gas: Liberalised Markets and Security of Supply: Report with Evidence* (June 24). HL Paper 105. London: The

Stationery Office. www.publications.parliament.uk/pa/ld200304/ldselect/ldeu com/105/105.pdf.

HMG (HM Government). 2009a. *The UK Low Carbon Transition Plan: National Strategy for Climate and Energy* (July 15). London: The Stationery Office. www .gov.uk/government/uploads/system/uploads/attachment_data/file/228752 /9780108508394.pdf.

———. 2009b. *The UK Renewable Energy Strategy* (July). Cm 7686. London. www .gov.uk/government/uploads/system/uploads/attachment_data/file/2288 66/7686.pdf.

Hobson, John M. 2000. *The State and International Relations.* Cambridge: Cambridge University Press.

Hockenos, Paul. 2012. "Germany's Stalled Energy Transition: Waiting for the Master Plan." *European Energy Review,* April 19.

Hollifield, James F. 1990. "Immigration and the French State." *Comparative Political Studies* 23 (1):56–79.

Holt, Mark, and Carol Glover. 2006. "Energy Policy Act of 2005: Summary and Analysis of Enacted Provisions" (March 8). *CRS Report for Congress.* Washington, DC: Congressional Research Service.

Hoshi, Hisashi. 2013. "Trade-off between Renewable Energies and Thermal Power: Closure of Thermal Power Stations Increasing in Germany." *IEEJ e-Newsletter* no. 19 (Aug. 16). http://eneken.ieej.or.jp/en/jeb/130816.pdf.

Hosker, Edmund. 2013. "UK Energy Security." Speech at the Institute of Energy Economics Japan (July). http://eneken.ieej.or.jp/data/4992.pdf.

Hosoe, Tomoko. 2005. "Japan's Energy Policy and Energy Security." *Middle East Economic Survey* 48 (3).

Houser, Trevor, and Beibei Bao. 2013. "Charting China's Natural Gas Future" (Oct. 31). James A. Baker III Institute for Public Policy, Rice University. http://baker institute.org/media/files/Research/07a18d60/CES-pub-GeoGasChina2-103113. pdf.

Hoyos, Carola. 2010. "China Invited to Join IEA as Oil Demand Shifts." *Financial Times,* March 30.

Hughes, Llewelyn. 2006. "Japan's New National Energy Strategy." *The Diplomat,* Sept. 25.

Hulse, Carl. 2003a. "A Final Push in Congress: Energy Bill." *New York Times,* Nov. 26.

———. 2003b. "Senate Blocks Energy Bill; Backers Vow to Try Again." *New York Times,* Nov. 22.

IEA (International Energy Agency). 1979. *Energy Policies and Programs of IEA Countries: 1978 Review.* Paris: OECD.

———. 1980. *Energy Policies and Programs of IEA Countries: 1979 Review.* Paris: OECD.

———. 1981. *Energy Policies and Programs of IEA Countries: 1980 Review.* Paris: OECD.

———. 1982. *Energy Policies and Programmes of IEA Countries: 1981 Review.* Paris: OECD.

———. 1983. *Energy Policies and Programmes of IEA Countries: 1982 Review.* Paris: OECD.

———. 1984. *Fuel Efficiency of Passenger Cars: An IEA Study.* Paris: OECD.

———. 1985. *Energy Policies and Programmes of IEA Countries: 1984 Review.* Paris: OECD.

———. 1986. *Energy Policies and Programmes of IEA Countries: 1985 Review.* Paris: OECD.

———. 1987. *Energy Policies and Programmes of IEA Countries: 1986 Review.* Paris: OECD.

———. 1996. *The Role of IEA Governments in Energy: 1996 Update.* Paris: IEA.

———. 2002a. *Energy Policies of IEA Countries: Germany 2002 Review.* Paris: IEA.

———. 2002b. *Energy Policies of IEA Countries: The United Kingdom 2002 Review.* Paris: IEA.

———. 2003. *Energy Policies of IEA Countries: Japan 2003 Review.* Paris: IEA.

———. 2004. *Energy Policies of IEA Countries: France 2004 Review.* Paris: IEA.

———. 2007a. *Energy Policies of IEA Countries: Germany 2007 Review.* Paris: IEA.

———. 2007b. *Energy Policies of IEA Countries: United Kingdom 2006 Review.* Paris: IEA.

———. 2008. *Energy Policies of IEA Countries: Japan 2008 Review.* Paris: IEA.

———. 2010. *Energy Policies of IEA Countries: France 2009 Review.* Paris: IEA.

———. 2012a. *Energy Policies of IEA Countries: United Kingdom 2012 Review.* Paris: IEA.

———. 2012b. *Golden Rules for a Golden Age of Gas: World Energy Outlook Special Report on Unconventional Gas.* Paris: IEA.

———. 2012c. *Iraq Energy Outlook: World Energy Outlook Special Report* (Oct. 9). Paris: IEA.

———. 2013a. *Energy Policies of IEA Countries: Germany 20013 Review.* Paris: IEA.

———. 2013b. *World Energy Outlook 2013.* Paris: IEA.

Ikenberry, G. John. 1986a. "The Irony of State Strength: Comparative Responses to the Oil Shocks in the 1970s." *International Organization* 40 (1):105–37.

———. 1986b. "The State and Strategies of International Adjustment." *World Politics* 39 (1):53–77.

———. 1988. *Reasons of State: Oil Politics and the Capacities of American Government.* Ithaca, NY: Cornell University Press.

Ikenberry, G. John, David A. Lake, and Michael Mastanduno. 1988. "Introduction: Approaches to Explaining American Foreign Economic Policy." In *The State and American Foreign Economic Policy,* edited by G. John Ikenberry, David A. Lake, and Michael Mastanduno, 1–14. Ithaca, NY: Cornell University Press.

Ito, Yoko. 2010. "New Buyback Program for Photovoltaic Generation: Issues in the View of Electric Utilities Industrial Policy." Tokyo: Institute of Energy Economics, Japan.

JAEC (Japan Atomic Energy Commission). 2007. *White Paper on Nuclear Energy 2006* (*Summary*) (March). www.aec.go.jp/jicst/NC/about/hakusho/hakusho2006/wp_e .pdf.

———. 2009. *White Paper on Nuclear Energy 2008 (Summary)* (March). www.aec .go.jp/jicst/NC/about/hakusho/hakusho2008/wp_e.pdf.

Jaffe, Amy Myers, and Kenneth B. Medlock III. 2013. "China, India, and Asian Energy." In *Energy and Security: Strategies for a World in Transition*, edited by Jan H. Kalicki and David L. Goldwyn, 283–302. Washington, DC: Woodrow Wilson Center Press.

Jain, Purnendra. 2007. "Japan's Energy Security Policy in an Era of Emerging Competition in the Asia-Pacific." In *Energy Security in Asia*, edited by Michael Wesley, 28–41. London: Routledge.

Japan Times. 2013. "Renewable Energy Push Blunted as Ad-hoc Rules Stymie Private Upstarts" (Sept. 15). www.japantimes.co.jp/news/2013/09/15/national/renewable -energy-push-blunted-as-ad-hoc-rules-stymie-private-upstarts/.

Jentleson, Bruce W. 1986. *Pipeline Politics: The Complex Political Economy of East-West Energy Trade*. Ithaca, NY: Cornell University Press.

JESS (Joint Energy Security of Supply Working Group). 2002. *First Report* (June). London: DTI and Ofgem. http://webarchive.nationalarchives.gov.uk/+/www.berr .gov.uk/files/file10728.pdf.

———. 2006a. *Sixth Report* (April). London: DTI and Ofgem. http://webarchive. nationalarchives.gov.uk/20080906011456/www.berr.gov.uk/files/file28800.pdf.

———. 2006b. *Long-Term Security of Energy Supply: December 2006 Report*. http:// webarchive.nationalarchives.gov.uk/20081229170635/www.berr.gov.uk/files /file35989.pdf.

Jessop, Bob. 2006. "The State and State-Building." In *The Oxford Handbook of Political Institutions*, edited by R. A. W. Rhodes, Sarah A. Binder, and Bert A. Rockman, 111–30. Oxford: Oxford University Press.

JFIR (Japan Forum on International Relations). 2006. *The Establishment of an International Energy Security System* (May). Tokyo: Japan Forum on International Relations. www.jfir.or.jp/e/pr/pdf/27.pdf.

Jochem, Eberhard, Edelgard Gruber, and Wilhelm Mannsbart. 1996. "German Energy Policy in Transition." In *European Energy Policies in a Changing Environment*, edited by Francis McGowan, 57–87. Heidelberg: Physica-Verlag.

JOGMEC (Japan Oil, Gas and Metals National Corporation). 2009. *Reliable Partnership: Annual Report 2009*. www.jogmec.go.jp/content/300061131.pdf.

———. 2010. "Petroleum Stockpiling: A Tool for National Energy Security." Kawasaki, Japan.

Johnson, Keith. 2014. "The White House's Faulty Math on Gas Exports" (April 3). *Foreign Policy*. www.foreignpolicy.com/articles/2014/04/03/the_ white_houses_faulty_math_on_gas_exports.

Jones, Charles O. 1979. "American Politics and the Organization of Energy." In *Annual Review of Energy*, vol. 4, edited by Jack M. Hollander, Melvin K. Simmons and David O. Wood, 99–122. Palo Alto, CA: Annual Reviews.

Kalicki, Jan H., and David L. Goldwyn, eds. 2005. *Energy and Security: Toward a New Foreign Policy Strategy*. Washington, DC: Woodrow Wilson Center Press.

Kalt, Joseph P. 1983. "The Creation, Growth, and Entrenchment of Special Interests in Oil Price Policy." In *The Political Economy of Deregulation: Interest Groups in the Regulatory Process*, edited by Roger G. Noll, and Bruce M. Owen, 97–114. Washington, DC: American Enterprise Institute for Public Policy Research.

Kapstein, Ethan B. 1990. *The Insecure Alliance: Energy Crises and Western Politics since 1944*. New York: Oxford University Press.

Katakey, Rakteem, Rajesh Kumar Singh, and Rachel Morrison. 2012. "Europe Burns Coal Fastest Since 2006 in Boost for US." *Business Week*, July 12. www.business week.com/news/2012-07-02/europe-burns-coal-fastest-since-2006-in -boost-for-u-dot-s-dot-energy.

Katzenstein, Peter J. 1976. "International Relations and Domestic Politics: Foreign Economic Policies of Advanced Industrial States." *International Organization* 30 (1):1–45.

———. 1978. "Introduction: Domestic and International Forces and Strategies of Foreign Economic Policy." In *Between Power and Plenty: Foreign Economic Policies of Advanced Industrial States*, edited by Peter J. Katzenstein, 3–22. Madison: University of Wisconsin Press.

Kemezis, Paul, and Ernest J. Wilson, III. 1984. *The Decade of Energy Policy: Policy Analysis in Oil-Importing Countries*. New York: Praeger.

Kemfert, Claudia, and Friedemann Müller. 2007. "Die Energiepolitik zwischen Wettbewerbsfähigkeit, Versorgungssicherheit und Nachhaltigkeit—Chancen und Persecktiven für die Energieversorgung." *Vierteljahrshefte zur Witschaftsforschung* 76 (1):5–16.

Kempe, Iris. 2007. *A New Ostpolitik? Priorities and Realities of Germany's EU Council Presidency* (Aug.). CAP Policy Analysis No. 4. Center for Applied Policy Research, Munich. www.cap.lmu.de/download/2007/CAP-Policy-Analysis-2007-04 .pdf.

Keohane, Robert O. 1978. "The International Energy Agency: State Influence and Transgovernmental Politics." *International Organization* 32 (4):929–51.

———. 1982. "State Power and Industry Influence: American Foreign Oil Policy in the 1940s." *International Organization* 36 (1):165–83.

———. 1984. *After Hegemony: Cooperation and Discord in the World Political Economy*. Princeton, NJ: Princeton University Press.

Kingston, Jeff. 2012. "Japan's Nuclear Village." *The Asia-Pacific Journal* 10, issue 37, no. 1 (Sept. 10). www.japanfocus.org/-Jeff-Kingston/3822.

Kissinger, Henry. 1982. *Years of Upheaval*. New York: Little, Brown.

Klare, Michael T. 2004a. *Blood and Oil: The Dangers and Consequences of America's Growing Petroleum Dependency*. New York: Metropolitan Books.

———. 2004b. "Bush-Cheney Energy Strategy: Procuring the Rest of the World's Oil." *Foreign Policy in Focus* (Jan.). Washington, DC: Interhemispheric Resource Center / Institute for Policy Studies / SEEN.

Knorr, Klaus. 1975. *The Power of Nations: The Political Economy of International Relations*. New York: Basic Books.

Knowles, Michael, and Mike Farish. 2014. "Fracking in the UK: Engineers Say They Can Do It Safely" (April 22). *Energy Post*. www.energypost.eu/fracking-uk -engineers-say-can-safely/.

Kohalyk, Chad. 2008. "Energy Security and Strategic Culture: The Perspective of Japan." MA thesis, Royal Military College of Canada (April).

Kohl, Wilfrid L., ed. 1982. *After the Second Oil Shock*. Lexington, MA: Lexington Books.

———. 2007. "U.S. and German Approaches to the Energy Challenge: United States Energy Policy and Future Energy Security." *AICGS Policy Reports* 9: 5–29. Washington, DC: American Institute of Contemporary German Studies. www.aicgs .org/site/wp-content/uploads/2011/10/policyreport29.pdf.

Kolodziej, Edward. 1980. "France and the Arms Trade." *International Affairs* 56 (1):54–72.

———. 1992. "Renaissance in Security Studies? Caveat Lector!" *International Studies Quarterly* 36 (4):421–38.

Kono, Mitsuo. 1997. "The Future of Nuclear Power in Japan." *Japan Review of International Affairs* 11 (3):188–203.

Koyama, Ken. 2013. "The Changing LNG Situation in Japan after March 11" (Oct. 23). James A. Baker III Institute for Public Policy, Rice University. http://bakerin stitute.org/media/files/Research/d49d49a0/CES-pub-GeoGasJapan-103113.pdf.

Kramer, Andrew E. 2006. "Gazprom Signs Natural Gas Deal with Germans." *New York Times*, April 27.

Krapels, Edward N. 1980. *Oil Crisis Management: Strategic Stockpiling for International Security*. Baltimore: The Johns Hopkins University Press.

———. 1982. *Pricing Petroleum Products: Strategies of Eleven Industrial Nations*. New York: McGraw-Hill Inc.

Krasner, Stephen D. 1978a. *Defending the National Interest: Raw Materials Investments and U.S. Foreign Policy*. Princeton, NJ: Princeton University Press.

———. 1978b. "United States Commercial and Monetary Policy: Unravelling the Paradox of External Strength and Internal Weakness." In *Between Power and Plenty: Foreign Economic Policies of Advanced Industrial States*, edited by Peter J. Katzenstein, 51–87. Madison: University of Wisconsin Press.

Krauss, Clifford. 2014. "U.S. Gas Tantalizes Europe, but It's Not a Quick Fix." *New York Times*, April 7. www.nytimes.com/2014/04/08/business/energy-environment /us-gas-tantalizes-europe-but-its-not-a-quick-fix.html.

Krauss, Clifford, and Eric Lipton. 2012. "U.S. Inches toward Goal of Energy Independence." *New York Times*, March 23.

Kupchan, Charles A. 1987. *The Persian Gulf and the West: The Dilemmas of Security*. Boston: Allen and Unwin.

Kuzemko, Caroline. 2009. "Energy, Ideas and Institutions: A Contextual Analysis of UK Energy Policy, 1998–2008." Paper presented at the Annual Convention of the International Studies Association, New York (Feb.).

Ladislaw, Sarah O., Maren Leed, and Molly A. Walton. 2014. *New Energy, New Geopolitics: Balancing Stability and Leverage* (April). A Report of the CSIS Energy and

National Security Program and the Harold Brown Chair in Defense Studies. Center for Strategic and International Studies. http://csis.org/files/publication/140409 _Ladislaw_NewEnergyNewGeopolitics_WEB.pdf.

Lamborn, Alan C. 1983. "Power and the Politics of Extraction." *International Studies Quarterly* 27 (2):125–46.

Larson, Alan P. 2003. "International Aspects of U.S. Energy Security" (April 8). Testimony Before the Senate Foreign Relations Committee, Subcommittee on International Economic Policy, Export and Trade Promotion. Washington, DC. http://2001-2009.state.gov/e/rm/2003/19447.htm.

Lazzari, Salvatore. 2008. "Energy Tax Policy: History and Current Issues" (Oct. 30). *CRS Report for Congress*. RL33578. Washington, DC: Congressional Research Service.

Leinekugel le Cocq, Thibaut. 2011. "The French White Certificates Scheme: Second Target Period: Key Issues and Expectations" (Jan. 27). http://iet.jrc.ec.europa.eu /energyefficiency/sites/energyefficiency/files/files/documents/events/110127 _2nd_period_french_white_certificates_scheme.pdf.

Levi, Margaret 2002. "The State of the Study of the State." In *Political Science: The State of the Discipline*, edited by Ira Katznelson and Helen V. Milner, 33–55. New York: W. W. Norton.

Licklider, Roy. 1988. *Political Power and the Arab Oil Weapon: The Experience of Five Industrial Nations*. Berkeley: University of California Press.

Lieber, Robert J. 1976. *Oil and the Middle East War: Europe in the Energy Crisis*. Harvard Studies in International Affairs 35. Cambridge, MA: Harvard University.

———. 1980. "Energy, Economics and Security in Alliance Perspective." *International Security* 4 (4):139–63.

———. 1983. *The Oil Decade: Conflict and Cooperation in the West*. New York: Praeger.

Lindberg, Leon N., ed. 1977. *The Energy Syndrome: Comparing National Responses to the Energy Crisis*. Lexington, MA: Lexington Books.

Little, Douglas. 2002. *American Orientalism: The United States and the Middle East since 1945*. Chapel Hill: University of North Carolina Press.

Long, David E. 1985. *The United States and Saudi Arabia: Ambivalent Allies*. Boulder, CO: Westview Press.

LPOPE. 2005. *LOI n° 2005-781 du 13 juillet 2005 de programme fixant les orientations de la politique énergétique*. http://legifrance.gouv.fr/affichTexte.do?cidTexte=JO RFTEXT000000813253.

Lucas, Nigel. 1983. "Energy, the UK and the European Community." In *Energy: Two Decades of Crisis*, edited by Robert Belgrave, 217–78. Aldershot, Hampshire: Gower.

———. 1985. *Western European Energy Policies: A Comparative Study of the Influence of Institutional Structure on Technical Change*. Oxford: Oxford University Press.

Lucas, N. J. D. 1981. "The Influence of Existing Institutions on the European Transition from Oil." In *The European Transition from Oil: Societal Impacts and*

Constraints on Energy Policy, edited by Gordon T. Goodman, Lars A. Kristoferson and Jack M. Hollander, 173–89. London: Academic Press.

———. 1982. "British Energy Policy." In *After the Second Oil Crisis: Energy Policies in Europe, America, and Japan*, edited by Wilfrid L. Kohl, 91–112. Lexington, MA: Lexington Books.

Luft, Gal, and Anne Korin, eds. 2009a. *Energy Security Challenges in the 21st Century.* Santa Barbara, CA: ABC-CLIO.

———. 2009b. "Energy Security: In the Eyes of the Beholder." In *Energy Security Challenges for the 21st Century*, edited by Gal Luft and Anne Korin, 1–17. Santa Barbara, CA: ABC-CLIO.

Madelin, Henri. 1975. *Oil and Politics.* Translated by Margaret Totman. Lexington, MA: Lexington Books.

Mahoney, James. 2000. "Path Dependence in Historical Sociology." *Theory and Society* 29 (4):507–48.

Mancke, Richard B. 1976. *Squeaking By: U.S. Energy Policy since the Embargo.* New York: Columbia University Press.

Manning, Robert A. 2000. *The Asian Energy Factor: Myths and Dilemmas of Energy, Security and the Pacific Future.* New York: Palgrave.

Marquina, Antonio, ed. 2008. *Energy Security: Visions from Asia and Europe.* New York: Palgrave Macmillan.

Marsh, Alan. 1981. "Environmental Issues in Contemporary European Politics." In *The European Transition from Oil: Societal Impacts and Constraints on Energy Policy*, edited by Gordon T. Goodman, Lars A. Kristoferson, and Jack M. Hollander, 121–54. London: Academic Press.

Masaki, Hisane. 2006. "Japan's New Energy Strategy." *Japan Focus* (Jan. 18). www .japanfocus.org/-Hisane-MASAKI/1851.

Mastanduno, Michael, David A. Lake, and G. John Ikenberry. 1989. "Toward a Realist Theory of State Action." *International Studies Quarterly* 33:457–74.

Maull, Hanns W. 1981. "Time Wasted: The Politics of European Energy Transition." In *The European Transition from Oil: Societal Impacts and Constraints on Energy Policy*, edited by Gordon T. Goodman, Lars A. Kristoferson, and Jack M. Hollander, 271–305. London: Academic Press.

Maynard, Micheline. 2007. "Politics Forcing Detroit to Back New Fuel Rules." *New York Times*, June 20.

McFarlane, Robert. 2004. "A Declaration of Energy Dependence." *The Wall Street Journal*, Dec. 20, A15.

McGowan, Francis. 1996a. "Energy Policy in the EU - Diversity or Convergence?" In *European Energy Policies in a Changing Environment*, edited by Francis McGowan, 1–20. Heidelberg: Physica-Verlag.

———. 1996b. "Ideology and Expediency in British Energy Policy." In *European Energy Policies in a Changing Environment*, edited by Francis McGowan, 130–34. Heidelberg: Physica-Verlag.

———. 2011. "The UK and EU Energy Policy: From Awkward Partner to Active Protagonist?" In *Toward a Common European Union Energy Policy: Problems,*

Progress, and Prospects, edited by Vicki L. Birchfield and John S. Duffield, 187–213. New York: Palgrave Macmillan.

McKean, Margaret A. 1985. "Japan's Energy Policies." In *The Challenge of China and Japan: Politics and Development in East Asia*, edited by Susan L. Shirk, 331–38. New York: Praeger.

MEEDDAT (Ministère de l'Écologie de l'Énergie du Développement durable et de l'Aménagement du Territoire). 2008. *Grenelle Environnement: réussir la transition énergétique* (Nov. 17). Dossier de Presse. www.developpement-durable.gouv.fr /IMG/spipwwwmedad/pdf/DPfinal_energies_renouvelables_-_sans_photos _cle53a851.pdf.

——. 2009a. *Synthèse 2009: Programmations pluriannuelles des investissements de production d'électricité et de chaleur / Plan indicatif pluriannuel dans le domaine du gaz*. www.developpement-durable.gouv.fr/IMG/pdf/synthese_commune_2009 .pdf.

——. 2009b. *Rapport au Parliament: Programmation pluriannuelle des investissements de production d'électricité: Période 2009–2020* (July 11). www .developpement-durable.gouv.fr/IMG/pdf/ppi_elec_2009.pdf.

——. 2009c. *Plan Indicatif Pluriannuel des Investissements dans le secteur du gaz: Periode 2009–2020*. www.developpement-durable.gouv.fr/IMG/pdf/pipgaz_2009 .pdf.

MEEDDM (Ministère de l'Écologie de l'Énergie du Développement durable et de la Mer). 2010. *Plan d'action national en faveur des énergies renouvelables: Periode 2009–2020*. www.developpement-durable.gouv.fr/IMG/pdf/0825_plan_d_action _national_ENRversion_finale.pdf.

Menderhausen, Horst. 1976. *Coping with the Oil Crisis: French and German Experiences*. Baltimore: The Johns Hopkins University Press.

Méritet, Sophie. 2011. "French Energy Policy within the EU Framework: From Black Sheep to Model?" In *Toward a Common European Union Energy Policy: Problems, Progress, and Prospects*, edited by Vicki L. Birchfield and John S. Duffield, 145–67. New York: Palgrave Macmillan.

Merkel, Angela, Horst Seehofer, Guido Westerwelle, Volker Kauder, Peter Ramsauer, and Birgit Homburger. 2009. *Growth, Education, Unity: The Coalition Agreement between the CDU, CSU, and FDP* (Oct. 26). Berlin. www.cdu.de/sites /default/files/media/dokumente/091215-koalitionsvertrag-2009-2013-englisch _0.pdf.

METI (Ministry of Economy, Trade and Industry). 2006a. *The Challenges and Directions for Nuclear Energy Policy in Japan: Japan's Nuclear Energy National Plan* (Dec.). www.enecho.meti.go.jp/en/reports/pdf/rikkoku.pdf.

——. 2006b. *Main Points and Policy Package in "Japan's Nuclear Energy National Plan"* (Sept.). www.enecho.meti.go.jp/en/reports/pdf/rikkokugaiyou.pdf.

——. 2006c. *New National Energy Strategy (Digest)* (May). www.enecho.meti .go.jp/en/reports/pdf/newnationalenergystrategy2006.pdf.

——. 2008. *Guidelines for Securing Natural Resources*. www.meti.go.jp/english /newtopics/data/pdf/080328Guidelines.pdf.

Meyer-Abich, Klaus-Michael, and Robert A. Dickler. 1982. "Energy Issues and Policies in the Federal Republic of Germany." In *Annual Review of Energy*, vol. 7, edited by Jack M. Hollander, Harvey Brooks and M. K. Simons, 221–59. Palo Alto, CA: Annual Reviews.

Mikulcak, Katharina. 2012. "German Government Backtracks on the Energy Transition." *European Energy Review*, July 12.

MINEFI (Ministère de l'Économie, des Finances et de l'Industrie). 2007. *La facture énergétique extérieure provisoire de la France in 2006 et les émissions de CO2* (Jan. 11). http://archives.dgcis.gouv.fr/2012/www.industrie.gouv.fr/infopres/presse /facture-energie_2006.pdf.

Moran, Daniel, and James A. Russell, eds. 2008. *Energy Security and Global Politics: The Militarization of Resource Management*. New York: Routledge.

Moravcsik, Andrew. 1997. "Taking Preferences Seriously: A Liberal Theory of International Politics." *International Organization* 51 (4):513–53.

Mork, K. A. 1982. "The Economic Cost of Oil Supply Disruptions." In *Energy Vulnerability*, edited by James L. Plummer, 83–112. Cambridge, MA: Ballinger.

Morse, Edward L., and Amy Myers Jaffe. 2001. *Strategic Energy Policy: Challenges for the 21st Century*. New York: Council on Foreign Relations.

Morse, Ronald A., ed. 1981a. "Energy and Japan's National Security Strategy." In *The Politics of Japan's Energy Strategy: Resources, Diplomacy, Security*, edited by Ronald A. Morse. Berkeley, CA: Institute of East Asian Studies, University of California.

———. 1981b. "Japan's Energy Policies and Options." In *The Politics of Japan's Energy Strategy: Resources, Diplomacy, Security*, edited by Ronald A. Morse. Berkeley, CA: Institute of East Asian Studies, University of California.

———, ed. 1981c. *The Politics of Japan's Energy Strategy: Resources, Diplomacy, Security*. Berkeley: Institute of East Asian Studies, University of California.

———. 1982. "Japanese Energy Policy." In *After the Second Oil Crisis: Energy Policies in Europe, America, and Japan*, edited by Wilfrid L. Kohl. Lexington, MA: Lexington Books.

Müller, Friedemann. 2005. "German Energy and Security Policy: Technical versus Political Modes of Intervention." In *Germany's Uncertain Power: Foreign Policy of the Berlin Republic*, edited by Hanns W. Maull, 169–84. New York: Palgrave MacMillan.

———. 2007. "U.S. and German Approaches to the Energy Challenge: How to Secure Reliable Energy Sources in Germany." *AICGS Policy Report* 9: 27–46. Washington, DC: American Institute of Contemporary German Studies. www.aicgs .org/site/wp-content/uploads/2011/10/policyreport29.pdf.

Müller-Kraenner, Sascha. 2008. *Energy Security*. New York: Routledge.

Nagatomi, Yu, Yuji Matsuo, and Tomoko Murakami. 2010. *U.S., European and South Korean Efforts to Raise Nuclear Power Plant Utility Factors: What Japan Should Learn from These Efforts* (July). Tokyo: Institute for Energy Economic, Japan (IEEJ). http://eneken.ieej.or.jp/data/3285.pdf.

Nau, Henry R. 1980. "The Evolution of U.S. Foreign Policy on Energy: From Alliance Politics to Politics-as-Usual." In *International Energy Policy*, edited by Robert M. Lawrence and Martin O. Heisler, 37–64. Lexington, MA: Lexington Books.

NEPDG (National Energy Policy Development Group). 2001. *National Energy Policy: Report of the National Energy Policy Development Group*. Washington, DC. www.netl.doe.gov/publications/press/2001/nep/national_energy_policy .pdf.

Neubacher, Alexander, and Catalina Schröder. 2012. "Germany's Nuclear Phase-Out Brings Unexpected Costs." *Der Spiegel*, June 6. www.spiegel.de/international/ger many/germany-s-nuclear-phase-out-brings-unexpected-costs-to-consumers -a-837007-2.html.

Niquet, Valerie. 2007. *Energy Challenges in Asia* (Oct.) *Note de l'Ifri*. Paris: Ifri.

Nishiyama, Hidehiko. 2008. *Japan's Energy Policy against Climate Change* (June 6). www.jaea.go.jp/04/turuga/tief/tief6/pdf/SSe.pdf.

Nixon, Richard M. 1973. "Address to the Nation about Policies to Deal with the Energy Shortages" (November 7). www.presidency.ucsb.edu/ws/?pid=4034.

Noël, Pierre. 2013. "European Gas Supply Security: Unfinished Business." In *Energy and Security: Strategies for a World in Transition*, edited by Jan H. Kalicki and David L. Goldwyn, 169–86. Washington, DC: Woodrow Wilson Center Press.

Nordlinger, Eric A. 1981. *On the Autonomy of the Democratic State*. Cambridge, MA: Harvard University Press.

———. 1987. "Taking the State Seriously." In *Understanding Political Development*, edited by M. Weiner and S. P. Huntington. Boston: Little, Brown.

———. 1988. "The Return to the State: Critiques." *American Political Science Review* 82 (3):875–85.

Northedge, F. S. 1974. *Descent from Power: British Foreign Policy, 1945–1973*. London: George Allen & Unwin.

Ochs, Alexander, and Camille Serre. 2010. "An Analysis of France's Climate Bill: Green Deal or Great Disillusion?" www.worldwatch.org/analysis-france's-climate -bill-green-deal-or-great-disillusion.

Ofgem. 2013. *The Final Report of the Carbon Emissions Reduction Target (CERT) 2008–2012* (May). www.ofgem.gov.uk/ofgem-publications/58425/certfinalreport 2013300413.pdf.

Oshima, K., T. Suzuki, and T. Matsuno. 1982. "Energy Issues and Policies in Japan." In *Annual Review of Energy*, vol. 7, edited by Jack M. Hollander, Harvey Brooks and Melvin K. Simmons, 87–108. Palo Alto, CA: Annual Reviews.

OTA (Office of Technology Assessment). 1991. *U.S. Oil Import Vulnerability: The Technical Replacement Capability*. OTA-E-503. Washington, DC: U.S. Government Printing Office.

Page, Scott. 2006. "Path Dependence." *Quarterly Journal of Political Science* 1 (1): 87–115.

PAJ (Petroleum Association of Japan). 2009. *Petroleum Industry in Japan 2009* (Sept.). Tokyo: PAJ. www.paj.gr.jp/english/data/paj2009.pdf.

Pascual, Carlos, and Jonathan Elkind, eds. 2009. *Energy Security: Economics, Politics, Strategies, and Implications*. Washington, DC: Brookings Institution Press.

Pearson, Ivan, Peter Zeniewski, Francesco Gracceva, Pavel Zastera, Christophe McGlade, Steve Sorrell, Jamie Spiers, and Gerhard Thonhauser. 2012. "Unconventional Gas: Potential Energy Market Impacts in the European Union." JRC Scientific and Policy Reports. http://ec.europa.eu/dgs/jrc/downloads/jrc_report _2012_09_unconventional_gas.pdf.

Pelletiere, Stephen C. 2004. *America's Oil Wars*. Westport, CT: Praeger.

Pelosi, Nancy. 2007. "A New Direction for Energy Security: A Detailed Summary" (Dec. 6).

Pierson, Paul. 1993. "When Effect Becomes Cause: Policy Feedback and Political Change." *World Politics* 45 (4):595–628.

———. 2000. "Increasing Returns, Path Dependence, and the Study of Politics." *American Political Science Review* 94 (2):251–67.

———. 2004. *Politics in Time: History, Institutions, and Social Analysis*. Princeton, NJ: Princeton University Press.

Pirani, Simon, Jonathan P. Stern, and Katja Yafimava. 2009. *The Russo-Ukrainian Gas Dispute of January 2009: A Comprehensive Assessment* (Feb.). Oxford Institute for Energy Studies. www.oxfordenergy.org/wpcms/wp-content/uploads/2010/11 /NG27-TheRussoUkrainianGasDisputeofJanuary2009AComprehensiveAssess ment-JonathanSternSimonPiraniKatjaYafimava-2009.pdf.

PIU (Performance and Innovation Unit, Cabinet Office). 2002. *The Energy Review* (Feb.). London. www.gci.org.uk/Documents/TheEnergyReview.pdf.

Plummer, James L., ed. 1982a. *Energy Vulnerability*. Cambridge, MA: Ballinger.

———. 1982b. "U.S. Stockpiling Policy." In *Energy Vulnerability*, edited by James L. Plummer, 115–48. Cambridge, MA: Ballinger.

Plummer, James L., and John P. Weyant. 1982. "International Institutional Approaches to Energy Vulnerability Problems." In *Energy Vulnerability*, edited by James L. Plummer, 257–82. Cambridge, MA: Ballinger.

Poggi, Gianfranco. 1978. *The Development of the Modern State: A Sociological Introduction*. Stanford, CA: Stanford University Press.

Pollack, Andrew. 2011. "Japan's Nuclear Future in the Balance." *New York Times*, May 9.

Pollack, Josh. 2002. "Saudi Arabia and the Middle East, 1931–2002." *Middle East Review of International Affairs* 6 (3):77–102.

POST (Parliamentary Office of Science and Technology). 2004. *The Future of UK Gas Supplies* (Oct.). Postnote 320. London. www.parliament.uk/documents/post /postpn230.pdf.

Price, Terence. 1990. *Political Electricity: What Future for Nuclear Energy?* Oxford: Oxford University Press.

Prodi, Romano, and Alberto Clo. 1975. "Europe." *Daedalus* 104 (4):91–112.

Putnam, Robert D. 1988. "Diplomacy and Domestic Politics: The Logic of Two-Level Games." *International Organization* 42 (3):427–60.

Reed, Stanley. 2012. "With Controls, Britain Allows Hydraulic Fracturing to Explore for Gas." *New York Times*, Dec. 13.

———. 2013a. "Britain Looks to Fracking as North Sea Oil Dwindles," *New York Times*, Oct. 18. www.nytimes.com/2013/10/19/business/energy-environment /britain-looks-to-fracking-as-north-sea-oil-dwindles.html.

———. 2013b. "Britain Opens Door to More Shale Gas Drilling." *New York Times*, Dec. 17.

Revkin, Andrew. 2003. "No Crisis, No Bill? At 1,200 Pages, the Energy Plan Weighs Itself Down." *New York Times*, Nov. 23.

Revol, Henri. 1998. "Politique énergétique de la France." Rapport 439 (97–98), 1ère partie. www.senat.fr/rap/l97-4391/l97-4391_mono.html.

Revol, Henri, and Jacques Valade. 2001. "La sécurité d'approvisionnement en énergie de l'Union européenne" (Feb. 7). Rapport d'information n° 218 (2000–2001). www.senat.fr/rap/r00-218/r00-218.html.

RFE/RL (Radio Free Europe / Radio Liberty). 2006. "Energy: NATO Considers Role in Increasing Energy Security" (Feb. 24). www.rferl.org/content/article/1066136 .html.

Robinson, Colin, and Jon Morgan. 1978. *North Sea Oil in the Future: Economic Analysis and Government Policy*. London: Macmillan.

Rühle, Michael. 2011. "NATO and Energy Security." *NATO Review Magazine*. www .nato.int/docu/review/2011/climate-action/energy_security/EN/index.htm.

Rümler, Reinhard, Robert Senger, and Stefan Tenner. 2010. "Germany Leads Spectacular Growth in European Gas Storage Capacity." *European Energy Review*, Jan. 11.

Runci, Paul J. 2005. "Renewable Energy Policy in Germany: An Overview and Assessment" (Jan.). Pacific Northwest National Laboratory Technical Lab Report PNWD-3526. www.globalchange.umd.edu/energytrends/germany/.

Rustow, Dankwart A. 1982. *Oil and Turmoil: America Faces OPEC and the Middle East*. New York: W. W. Norton.

Rutledge, Ian. 2005. *Addicted to Oil: America's Relentless Drive for Energy Security*. New York: I. B. Tauris.

Samuels, Richard J. 1981. "The Politics of Alternative Energy Research and Development in Japan." In *The Politics of Japan's Energy Strategy: Resources, Diplomacy, Security*, edited by Ronald A. Morse, 134–63. Berkeley: Institute of East Asian Studies, University of California.

———. 1987. *The Business of the Japanese State: Energy Markets in Comparative and Historical Perspective*. Ithaca, NY: Cornell University Press.

———. 2013. *3.11: Disaster and Change in Japan*. Ithaca, NY: Cornell University Press.

Sandalow, David B. 2007. *Freedom from Oil: How the Next President Can End the United States' Oil Addiction*. New York: McGraw-Hill.

Sander, Michael. 2007. "A 'Strategic Relationship'? The German Policy of Energy Security within the EU and the Importance of Russia." *Foreign Policy in Dialogue* 8 (20):16–24.

Saumon, Dominique, and Louis Puiseux. 1977. "Actors and Decisions in French Energy Policy." In *The Energy Syndrome: Comparing National Responses to the Energy Crisis*, edited by Leon Lindberg, 119–72. Lexington, MA: Lexington Books.

Schaff, Christian. 1999/2000. "Die Kernenergie-Pläne der SPD in den 1970er Jahren." Hauptseminar in Neuere und Neueste Geschichte: Politik und Gesellschaft im Zeichen der Ölpreisekreise der 1970er Jahre. www.grin.com/de/e-book/97293/die -kernenergieplaene-der-spd-in-den-1970er-jahren.

Schmitt, Dieter. 1982. "West German Energy Policy." In *After the Second Oil Crisis: Energy Policies in Europe, America, and Japan*, edited by Wilfrid L. Kohl, 137–57. Lexington, MA: Lexington Books.

Schneider, Steven A. 1983. *The Oil Price Revolution*. Baltimore: The Johns Hopkins University Press.

Schnepf, Randy, and Brent D. Yacobucci. 2012. "Renewable Fuel Standard (RFS): Overview and Issues" (Jan. 23). *CRS Report for Congress*. R40155. Washington, DC: Congressional Research Service.

Schreurs, Miranda A. 2002. *Environmental Politics in Japan, Germany, and the United States*. Cambridge: Cambridge University Press.

Scott, Richard. 1994. *The History of the International Energy Agency*. Vol. 2, *Major Policies and Actions of the IEA*. Paris: International Energy Agency.

Secretariat-General. 2006. *French Memorandum for Revitalising European Energy Policy with a View to Sustainable Development* (Jan. 26). Council of the European Union 5724/06. http://register.consilium.europa.eu/doc/srv?l=EN&t=PDF&gc= true&sc=false&f=ST%205724%202006%20INIT.

Shea, Jamie. 2006. "Energy Security: NATO's Potential Role." *NATO Review* 3 (August). www.nato.int/docu/review/2006/issue3/english/special1.html.

Shibata, Hirofumi. 1983. "The Energy Crises and Japanese Response." *Resources and Energy* 5:129–54.

SIPRI (Stockholm International Peace Research Institute). 1974. *Oil and Security*. New York: Humanities Press.

Sissine, Fred. 2007. "Energy Independence and Security Act of 2007: A Summary of Major Provisions" (Dec. 21). *CRS Report for Congress*. RL34294. Washington, DC: Congressional Research Service.

Skocpol, Theda. 1985. "Bringing the State Back In: Strategies of Analysis in Current Research." In *Bringing the State Back In*, edited by Peter B. Evans, Dieter Rueschemeyer, and Theda Skocpol, 3–37. Cambridge: Cambridge University Press.

Skocpol, Theda, and Kenneth Finegold. 1982. "State Capacity and Economic Intervention in the Early New Deal." *Political Science Quarterly* 97 (2):255–78.

Sovacool, Benjamin K., ed. 2011. *The Routledge Handbook of Energy Security*. London: Routledge.

Spencer, Thomas, Oliver Sartor, and Mathilde Mathieu. 2014. "Unconventional Wisdom: An Economic Analysis of US Shale Gas and Implications for the EU." *IDDRI Policy Brief* no. 5 (Feb.). www.iddri.org/Publications/Collections/Syntheses /PB0514.pdf.

S/STI (Secretary of State for Trade and Industry). 2005. *First Annual Report to Parliament on the Security of Gas and Electricity Supply in Great Britain* (July 21). HC 346. London: The Stationery Office.

———. 2006a. *Energy Statement of Need for Additional Gas Supply Infrastructure* (May 16). http://webarchive.nationalarchives.gov.uk/+/www.berr.gov.uk/files /file28954.pdf.

———. 2006b. *Second Annual Report to Parliament on the Security of Gas and Electricity Supply in Great Britain* (July 11). HC 1370. London: The Stationery Office.

Stagliano, Vito. 2001. *A Policy of Discontent: The Making of a National Energy Strategy.* Tulsa: PennWell.

Steinmeier, Frank-Walter. 2006a. "Energie-Außenpolitik ist Friedenspolitik." *Handelsblatt*, March 23.

———. 2006b. "Energy Security: Avoiding Conflict Over Fuel." *International Herald Tribune*, March 23.

———. 2007a. "Die transatlantischen Beziehungen im 21. Jahrhundert: Rede des Bundesaußenminister Steinmeier anlässlich der 43. Münchner Konferenz für Sicherheitspolitik" (Feb 11). www.ag-friedensforschung.de/themen/Sicherheitskon ferenz/2007-steinmeier.html.

———. 2007b. "Rede von Bundesaußenminister Steinmeier anlässlich der Eröffnung der Reihe 'Energiesicherheit und internationale Beziehungen' " (Feb. 16). www.auswaertiges-amt.de/DE/Infoservice/Presse/Reden/2007/070216-Energie konferenz.html.

Steinmo, Sven. 2010. *The Evolution of Modern States: Sweden, Japan, and the United States.* New York: Cambridge University Press.

Stern, Jonathan P. 1983. "East European Energy and East West Trade in Energy." In *Energy: Two Decades of Crisis*, edited by Robert Belgrave. Aldershot, Hamps., UK: Gower.

Stobaugh, Robert, and Daniel Yergin, eds. 1979. *Energy Future: Report of the Energy Project at the Harvard Business School.* New York: Random House.

Stokes, Doug, and Sam Raphael. 2010. *Global Energy Security and American Hegemony.* Baltimore: The Johns Hopkins University Press.

Strange, Susan. 1988. *States and Markets.* New York: Basil Blackwell.

Strzelecki, Marek, and Brian Swint. 2014. "Europe Nears First Commercial Shale Gas Production in Poland." *Bloomberg*, Jan.23. www.bloomberg.com/news/2014-01 -23/europe-nears-first-commercial-shale-gas-production-in-poland-1-.html.

Sudo, Shigeru. 2008. "Energy Security Challenges to Asian Countries from Japan's Viewpoint." In *Energy Security: Visions from Asia and Europe*, edited by Antonio Marquina, 147–61. New York: Palgrave Macmillan.

Suleiman, Ezra N. 1974. *Politics, Power, and Bureaucracy in France: The Administrative Elite.* Princeton, NJ: Princeton University Press.

———. 1987. "State Structures and Clientelism: The French State versus the 'Notaires.' " *British Journal of Political Science* 17 (3):257–79.

Suttmeier, Richard P. 1981. "The Japanese Nuclear Power Option: Technological Promise and Social Limitations." In *The Politics of Japan's Energy Strategy:*

Resources, Diplomacy, Security, edited by Ronald A. Morse, 106–30. Berkeley: Institute of East Asian Studies, University of California.

Tabuchi, Hiroko. 2011. "Japan Quake Is Causing Costly Shift to Fossil Fuels." *New York Times*, Aug. 19.

Taylor, R. H., S. D. Probert, and P. D. Carmo. 1998. "French Energy Policy." *Applied Energy* 59 (1):39–61.

Teller, Edward, Hans Mark, and John S. Foster. 1976. *Power and Security*. Lexington, MA: Lexington Books.

Temkin, Benny. 1983. "State, Ecology and Independence: Policy Responses to the Energy Crisis in the United States." *British Journal of Political Science* 13 (4):441–62.

ten Hoedt, Rudolf. 2013. "Renewables in Japan at a Cross Roads. *European Energy Review*. July 18. www.europeanenergyreview.eu/site/pagina.php?id=4130.

Thelen, Kathleen. 1999. "Historical Institutionalism in Comparative Politics." *Annual Review of Political Science* 2 (June):369–404.

Togeby, Mikael, Kirsten Dyhr-Mikkelsen, and Edward James-Smith. 2007. *Design of White Certificates: Comparing UK, Italy, France, and Denmark* (Nov.). Copenhagen: Ea Energy Analyses. www.ea-energianalyse.dk/reports/710_White_certificates_report_19_Nov_07.pdf.

Toichi, Tsutomu. 2006. "International Energy Security and Japan's Strategy." Paper presented at the Conference on India's Energy Security. Goa, India, Sept. 29–30. http://eneken.ieej.or.jp/en/data/pdf/356.pdf.

———. 2008. "Japan's Energy Challenges and the Role of Gas." Speech addressed at Gastech 2008, Bangkok, March 10–13. http://eneken.ieej.or.jp/en/data/pdf/433.pdf.

Tsurumi, Yoshi. 1975. "Japan." *Daedalus* 104 (4):113–27.

Turner, Louis. 1983. "UK Interests and the International Energy Agency." In *Energy: Two Decades of Crisis*, edited by Robert Belgrave, 157–216. Aldershot, Hamps., UK: Gower.

Ullman, Richard H. 1983. "Redefining Security." *International Security* 8 (1):129–53.

Umbach, Frank. 2006. "Europas nächster Kalter Krieg." *Internationale Politik* 2 (Feb.):6–14.

———. 2007. "Towards a European Energy Foreign Policy?" *Foreign Policy in Dialogue* 8 (20):7–15.

Venn, Fiona. 1986. *Oil Diplomacy in the Twentieth Century*. New York: St. Martin's Press.

Verleger, Philip K. 1982. *Oil Markets in Turmoil: An Economic Analysis*. Cambridge, MA: Ballinger.

Vernon, Raymond, ed. 1975. *The Oil Crisis*. New York: Norton.

———. 1983. *Two Hungry Giants: The United States and Japan in the Quest for Oil and Ores*. Cambridge, MA: Harvard University Press.

Vietor, Richard H. K. 1984. *Energy Policy in America since 1945: A Study of Business-Government Relations*. Cambridge: Cambridge University Press.

Vivoda, Vlado. 2011. "Japan's Energy Security Predicament in the Aftermath of the Fukushima Disaster." *Journal of Energy Security*, Dec. www.ensec.org/index.php?option=com_content&view=article&id=335:japans-energy-security-predica

ment-in-the-aftermath-of-the-fukushima-disaster&catid=121:contentenergysec
urity1111&Itemid=386.

Vlasic, Bill. 2012. "U.S. Sets Higher Fuel Efficiency Standards." *New York Times*,
Aug. 28.

Wacket, Markus, and Hans-Edzard Busemann. 2013. "New German Govern-
ment Would Put Moratorium on Fracking, Cut Wind Energy Support." *Reuters*,
Nov. 8. http://uk.reuters.com/article/2013/11/08/uk-germany-energy-idUKBRE9A70
RL20131108.

Wagner, Hans. 2006. "Neue Ostpolitik: Wandel durch Verflechtung." *Eurasisches
Magazin*, Dec. 28. www.eurasischesmagazin.de/artikel/Wandel-durch-Verflech
tung/20061207.

Walt, Stephen M. 1991. "The Renaissance of Security Studies." *International Studies Quarterly* 35 (2):211–39.

Walton, Ann-Margaret. 1976. "Atlantic Bargaining over Energy." *International Affairs* 52 (2):180–96.

Watanabe, Chisaki. 2013. "Grid Congestion for Renewable Energy May Expand to
South Japan." *Bloomberg*, Aug. 28. www.bloomberg.com/news/2013-08-29/grid
-congestion-for-renewable-energy-may-expand-to-south-japan.html.

Weatherford, M. Stephen, and Haruhiro Fukui. 1989. "Domestic Adjustment to
International Shocks in Japan and the United States." *International Organization*
43 (4):585–623.

Weir, Margaret, and Theda Skocpol. 1985. "State Structures and the Possibilities
for 'Keynesian' Responses to the Great Depression in Sweden, Britain, and the
United States." In *Bringing the State Back In*, edited by Peter B. Evans, Dietrich
Rueschemeyer, and Theda Skocpol, 107–68. Cambridge: Cambridge University
Press.

Westphal, Kirsten. 2008. "Germany and the EU-Russia Energy Dialogue." In *The EU-
Russian Energy Dialogue: Europe's Future Energy Security*, edited by Pami Aalto,
93–118. Burlington, VT: Ashgate.

———. 2009. "Russian Gas, Ukrainian Pipelines, and European Supply Security:
Lessons of the 2009 Controversies" (Sept.). *SWP Research Paper* RP 11. Berlin: Stiftung Wissenschaft und Politik. www.swp-berlin.org/fileadmin/contents/products
/research_papers/2009_RP11_wep_ks.pdf.

White, Edward, Mike Fell, Louise Smith, and Matthew Keep. 2014. "Shale Gas and
Fracking." House of Commons Library Standard Note SN/SC/6073 (Jan. 22). www
.parliament.uk/briefing-papers/SN06073.pdf.

The White House. 2007. "Twenty in Ten: Strengthening America's Energy Security."
Washington, DC: The White House. http://georgewbush-whitehouse.archives.gov
/stateoftheunion/2007/initiatives/energy.html.

Wicks, Malcolm. 2009. *Energy Security: A National Challenge in a Changing World*
(Aug.). London: Department of Energy & Climate Change. http://130.88.20.21/uk
nuclear/pdfs/Energy_Security_Wicks_Review_August_2009.pdf.

Williams, Roger. 1980. *The Nuclear Power Decisions: British Policies, 1953–78*. London: Croom Helm.

Willrich, Mason. 1975. *Energy and World Politics*. New York: Free Press.

Willrich, Mason, and M. A. Conant. 1977. "The International Energy Agency: An Interpretation and Assessment." *American Journal of International Law* 71 (2): 199–223.

WNA (World Nuclear Association). 2010. "Nuclear Power in Japan" (April). www.world-nuclear.org/info/inf79.html.

———. 2011. "Nuclear Power in France" (Nov. 30). www.world-nuclear.org/info/inf40.html.

———. 2012a. "Nuclear Development in the United Kingdom" (June 12). www.world-nuclear.org/info/inf84a_nuclear_development_UK.html.

———. 2012b. "Nuclear Power in the United Kingdom" (Dec.). www.world-nuclear.org/info/inf84.html.

Wu, Yuan-Li. 1977. *Japan's Search for Oil: A Case Study on Economic Nationalism and International Security*. Stanford, CA: Hoover Institution Press.

Yager, Joseph A. 1981. "The Energy Battles of 1979." In *Energy Policy in Perspective*, edited by Craufurd D. Goodwin, 601–36. Washington, DC: Brookings Institution.

Yergin, Daniel. 1988. "Energy Security in the 1990s." *Foreign Affairs* 67 (1):111–32.

———. 1991. *The Prize: The Epic Quest for Oil, Money, and Power*. New York: Simon & Schuster.

———. 2006. "Ensuring Energy Security." *Foreign Affairs* 85 (2):69–82.

Yergin, Daniel, and Martin Hillenbrand, eds. 1982. *Global Insecurity: A Strategy for Energy and Economic Renewal*. New York: Houghton Mifflin.

Yetiv, Steve A. 2008. *The Absence of Grand Strategy: The United States in the Persian Gulf, 1972–2005*. Baltimore: The Johns Hopkins University Press.

Yorke, Valerie. 1981. "Oil, the Middle East and Japan's Search for Security." *International Affairs* 57 (3):428–48.

Zakaria, Fareed. 1998. *From Wealth to Power: The Unusual Origins of America's World Role*. Princeton, NJ: Princeton University Press.

Zubrin, Robert. 2007. *Energy Victory: Winning the War on Terror by Breaking Free of Oil*. Amherst, NY: Prometheus.

Zysman, John. 1977. *Political Strategies for Industrial Order: State, Market, and Industry in France*. Berkeley: University of California Press.

Abe, Shinzo, 224, 226, 227
administrative guidance, 236
advanced gas-cooled reactor (AGR), 70, 110
Agence française pour la maîtrise de l'énergie
(AFME), 125
Agence pour les économies d'énergie (AEE), 125
Agency for Natural Resources and Energy
(ANRE), 199, 217, 235
Algeria, 119, 129, 163
al Qaeda, 23
amakudari, 235
American Clean Energy and Security Act, 272
Anglo-Iranian Oil Company, 24
Angola, 276
Arabian Oil Company, 197, 213
Arctic National Wildlife Refuge (ANWR), 270,
271, 273, 274, 279

Baku–Tbilisi–Ceyhan (BTC) pipeline, 275–276,
279
balance of payments, 72, 74, 76, 111
Basic Energy Plan (BEP), 212, 216, 221, 227–228
biofuels, 99, 136, 141, 143, 147, 180, 273, 279.
See also ethanol; renewable transport fuels
Blair, Tony, 106; government of, 112
Britain, 1, 7, 29, 292–98, 300, 303, 308, 317, 321;
balance of payments, 72, 74, 76, 111; carbon
capture and storage, 100; Contracts for
Difference, 109; Electricity Market Reform,
109; electric power generation, 94–95, 108–9;
Emissions Trading Scheme, 89; energy review
(2006), 96; and EU energy policy, 9–10, 315–17;
and European Community, 80; and Iran, 80;
and Iraq, 105; natural gas infrastructure,
102–3; and the Netherlands, 104; and Norway,
91, 93, 104, 107, 205; and the Persian Gulf, 71,
80, 111, 115, 244; planning process, 95, 101–2,
103–4, 114; and Qatar, 105; renewable
transport fuels, 89, 99; and Russia, 105; and
Saudi Arabia, 80, 105
British Gas Corporation, 69n1, 86
British National Oil Company (BNOC), 75, 86,
113
Bureau de recherches de pétrole (BRP), 119

Bush, George W., 270, 271, 274; administration
of, 270, 271, 272, 273–74, 275, 276, 277

carbon capture and storage, 100
Carbon Emissions Reduction Target (CERT), 98
Carbon Reduction Commitment, 98
Carbon Trust, 89
Carlsnaes, Walter, 1, 33, 327
Carter, Jimmy, 245, 246, 249, 250, 250n5, 251,
253, 254, 255, 260, 284; administration of,
249–51, 252, 255
Carter Doctrine, 260
Central Command (CENTCOM), 260
Central Electricity Generating Board (CEGB),
69, 87
Charbonnage de France (CDF), 118
Cheney, Dick, 277
Chernobyl nuclear accident, 175, 214
China, 29, 215, 227, 269; and IEA, 312–13; and
Japan, 8, 206, 209, 216, 226; shale gas, 322; and
the U.S., 277–78
Climate Change Levy (CCL), 89
climate change policy: Britain, 88–89, 96–97, 111;
France, 133–34; Germany, 173–74, 179; Japan,
214, 223, 227
coal-bed methane (CBM), 321, 324
coal consumption: Britain, 68–69, 87, 94; France,
120–21, 125; Germany, 153, 157, 168; Japan,
196–97, 204; U.S., 243
coal industry: Britain, 70, 72; France, 120;
Germany, 155, 161–62; Japan, 197
coal production: Britain, 69, 70, 72, 76–77, 81,
88; France, 125–26; Germany, 153, 155;
Japan, 197
Commissariat à l'énergie atomique (CEA), 118
Compagnie française des pétroles (CFP), 119, 131
Congress, U.S., 247, 249, 251, 252, 253, 254, 256,
257, 268, 270, 271, 272, 273, 274, 282
conservation. See energy conservation
Contracts for Difference, 109
Corporate Average Fuel Economy (CAFE)
program, 253, 264, 268, 271, 284
critical junctures, 60, 62, 304
crude oil equalization tax (COET), 250, 253

de Carmoy, Guy, 148
Deese, David, 21
de Hoop Scheffer, Jaap, 313
DEMINEX, 154, 167, 170
Department of Energy (Britain), 75, 79, 113
Department of Energy, U.S., 251, 268, 282
Desertec Industrial Initiative, 181
de Villepin, Dominique, 135
Diet (Japan), 200, 205, 216, 231
diplomacy, resource, 206, 224–25
Dore, Ronald, 198

Eguchi, Yujiro, 233
Électricité de France (EDF), 118, 121, 134, 139,
   142–43, 148
Electricity Market Reform (EMR), 109
electric power generation, 94–95, 108–9
embargo, Arab oil: of 1967, 24–25, 243; of
   1973–74, 25–26
Emergency Petroleum Allocation Act (EPAA),
   247, 253, 257
Emergency Sharing System (ESS), 261, 265, 311
emissions. *See* greenhouse gas emissions
Emissions Trading Scheme (ETS), 89
Energiewende, 184
Energy Concept, 183, 187
energy conservation: Britain, 78–79, 83–84, 98;
   France, 124–25, 129–30, 137–38; Germany,
   158, 159, 165–66, 170, 174, 179–80, 186–87;
   Japan, 201–3, 213, 214, 219–21, 229; U.S., 250
Energy Conservation Act, 202, 203, 214, 220
Energy Conservation Center of Japan (ECCJ),
   226
energy efficiency: Britain, 83, 98, 106; France,
   129; Germany, 165–66, 169, 179–80, 186–87;
   Japan, 201–3, 219–21, 228, 229
energy foreign policy, 180–82
energy imports: France, 121, 129, 130, 135, 136;
   Germany, 153–54, 170; Japan, 197, 198, 209, 213
Energy Independence Act, 248
Energy Independence and Security Act (EISA),
   271, 272, 272n13, 273, 274
energy market liberalization: Britain, 86–87;
   France, 134; Japan, 213
energy mix: Britain, 68–69, 81–82, 87–88; France,
   120–21, 129, 133; Germany, 153–54, 168–69,
   173, 184; Japan, 196–97, 207–9, 212; U.S.,
   243–44, 268–69

Energy Policy Act (EPACT), 271, 272n13, 273, 274
Energy Policy and Conservation Act (EPCA),
   249, 252, 253, 257
energy security: definition of, 19–22; threats to,
   22–28
energy security, concerns about, 1–2, 28–30, 290,
   294, 295–96; Britain, 71–72, 90–95; France,
   122–23, 135; Germany, 155–57, 176–78; Japan,
   198–99, 215–16; U.S., 245–46, 268–70
energy summit, 178
energy taxes: Britain, 70, 78, 79; France, 120, 125;
   Germany, 155, 161, 162, 174; Japan, 201, 211,
   220; U.S., 250, 253–54, 256, 279, 284
Entreprise de recherches et d'activités pétrolières
   (ERAP), 119
equity oil, 213, 228
Erdölbeforratungsverband (EBV), 167
ethanol, 256, 273, 279. *See also* biofuels;
   renewable transport fuels
Euro-Arab dialogue, 128, 132
European Commission, 160, 315
European Community: and Britain, 80; and
   France, 128, 131–32
European Pressurized Water Reactor (EPR),
   139
European Union energy policy, 9–10, 315–17; and
   Britain, 89–90, 105–6, 317; and France, 141,
   371; and Germany, 181–82, 317
Evans, Peter, 234
Evans, Peter C., 213
exports: of liquefied natural gas, 320, 323–24;
   of natural gas, 171, 173, 176, 184, 294, 305

Federal Ministry of Economics (BMWi), 189, 192
Federal Ministry of the Environment (BMU),
   192
Federal Republic of Germany. *See* Germany
Feigenbaum, Harvey, 146
Finon, Dominique, 134, 144, 147
Ford, Gerald, 248, 249, 255, 257, 284; administration of, 248–49, 254
foreign policy, energy, 180–82
fracking. *See* hydraulic fracturing
France, 1, 7, 57, 59, 292–305, 308, 311, 314, 317,
   320; and EU energy policy, 141, 371; and the
   European Community, 128, 131–32; and Iran,
   131; and Iraq, 119, 128, 131; and Norway, 140;
   oil policy, 118–20; and oil-producing

countries, 127–28, 131, 149; and the Persian Gulf, 121; and Saudi Arabia, 128; Socialist government, 125, 126, 127, 145
fuel economy: Britain, 82, 83–84; Germany, 166; Japan, 203, 214; U.S., 253, 262, 267–68, 272–73, 279, 284. *See also* Corporate Average Fuel Economy program
fuels, 89, 99, 256, 273, 279. *See also* biofuels
Fukushima Daiichi nuclear accident, 108, 133, 142, 183, 231–32, 238

Gas Act: of 1965, 69; of 1972, 69n1; of 1986, 86
Gas Council, 69, 69n1
gas-guzzler tax, 254
Gaz de France (GDF), 118, 134
Gazprom, 172, 176, 177, 216
Generic Design Assessment (GDA), 102, 108
Germany, 1, 7, 29, 292–98, 301–3, 305, 314, 317, 320; Energiewende, 184; Energy Concept, 183, 187; energy foreign policy, 180–82; energy summit, 178; and EU energy policy, 181–82, 317; free market orientation, 154, 159, 170–71, 187–88; and Iraq, 205, 206; and the Nether-lands, 29, 163, 168, 173; and Norway, 29, 163, 169; nuclear phaseout, 171, 175, 180, 183, 193; and oil-producing countries, 191; and Russia, 171, 173, 176, 181–82, 184, 191, 294, 305; and Saudi Arabia, 167, 191; support for national oil companies, 154–55, 167; support for U.S. energy initiatives, 167–68, 191
Giscard d'Estaing, Valery, 128
Great Britain. *See* Britain
greenhouse gas emissions: Britain, 88–89; France, 111, 133–34; Germany, 173–74; Japan, 214, 228
Gulf of Guinea, 276
Gulf War, 28

Hakes, Jay, 11
Hall, Peter, 31, 52n1, 53, 146
Hatch, Michael, 118, 144
Heath, Edward, government of, 72
Helm, Dieter, 62, 72, 106, 111, 113
Hollande, Françoise, 143, 144
Hollifield, James, 51
hydraulic fracturing, 8, 318–25; Britain, 107–8, 321; France, 133–34, 320; Germany, 185, 320; U.S., 278, 319, 320

Ikenberry, John, 3, 33, 43, 54, 283
imports. *See* energy imports; natural gas imports; oil imports
India, 221, 226, 269, 277, 312–13
Indonesia, 25
Integrated Energy and Climate Program (IEKP), 178–80
interest groups, 48–49, 146, 188–89, 233, 238, 283–84, 309–10
International Energy Agency (IEA), 7, 54, 310–13; and Britain, 80–81; and China, 312–13; and France, 128–29, 131–32; and Germany, 167–68; and India, 312–13; and the U.S., 261, 265
international oil companies, 24, 26, 27, 73, 74, 119–20, 122, 154, 199
International Renewable Energy Agency (IRENA), 181
Iran, 163; and Britain, 80; and France, 131; and Japan, 206, 210; oil production, 24, 25, 26, 40, 243, 265; and the U.S., 242, 245, 259, 260, 265, 276, 285
Iranian revolution, 210, 265
Iran-Iraq War, 23, 27–28, 40, 128, 131, 210
Iraq, 71, 276–77, 280; and Britain, 105; and France, 119, 128, 131; and Japan, 205, 206
Iraq war, 23, 29, 241, 276–77, 280, 286, 304

Japan, 8, 29, 57, 292–98, 300–304, 306, 322, 324; administrative guidance, 236; amakudari, 235; and China, 206, 216, 226; Diet, 200, 205, 216, 231; Energy Conservation Act, 202, 203, 214, 220; equity oil, 213, 228; industrial energy consumption, 197, 202, 208, 229; and Iran, 206, 210; and Nigeria, 276; nuclear village, 233–34, 238; oil industry, 197, 198; and oil-producing countries, 205–6, 210; and the Persian Gulf, 205, 219, 224, 239; and Qatar, 206, 224; regional energy cooperation, 226–27; reliance on market forces, 201, 203, 211, 236; renewable portfolio standard, 223; resource diplomacy, 206, 224–25; and resource nationalism, 215–16; and Saudi Arabia, 206; support for Japanese energy companies, 206, 207, 213, 225; and the U.S., 206, 210
Japan Bank for International Cooperation (JBIC), 224, 225
Japanese Export-Import Bank, 206

Japan External Trade Organization (JETRO), 225–226

Japan National Oil Company (JNOC), 201, 207, 213

Japan Oil, Gas, and Metals National Corporation (JOGMEC), 225

Japan Petroleum Development Corporation (JPDC), 198, 207

Katzenstein, Peter, 31, 51

Kemezis, Paul, 32, 289

Keohane, Robert, 283

Kissinger, Henry, 240, 248, 259, 261

Knorr, Klaus, 56

Kohalyk, Chad, 232, 233

Koizumi, Junichiro, 213, 225

Kolodziej, Edward, 20

Korin, Anne, 19

Krasner, Stephen, 50, 51, 57, 282, 283

Large Combustion Plant Directive (LCPD), 94, 109

Lawson, Nigel, 86

Levi, Margaret, 49

Lieber, Robert, 122, 124, 126, 144

liquefied natural gas (LNG), 8, 29, 323–24; Britain, 93, 103, 105; Japan, 203, 207, 208, 216, 219; U.S. exports of, 320, 323–24

liquefied petroleum gas (LPG), 219

Lisbon Treaty, 315, 316

Loi de programme fixant les orientations de la politique énergétique (LPOPE), 136, 137

Low Carbon Transition Plan (LCTP), 96, 113

Lucas, Nigel, 42, 146n9

Luft, Gal, 19

Lugar, Richard, 277, 313

Magnox reactor, 70, 110

Manning, Robert, 195

market liberalization, energy: Britain, 86–87; France, 134; Japan, 213

Maull, Hanns, 130, 146–47, 190

McCain, John, 284

McGowan, Francis, 110

Menderhausen, Horst, 122n1

Méritet, Sophie, 134

Merkel, Angela, 177, 179

methane hydrates, 324

Minimum Safeguard Price (MSP), 261, 266

Ministry of Energy, Trade, and Industry (METI), 211, 217, 234

Ministry of International Trade and Industry (MITI), 198, 199, 234, 236

Monju fast breeder reactor, 214, 222

Morse, Ronald, 233, 235

Müller, Friedemann, 189

National Coal Board (NCB), 69, 76

National Energy Act, 251, 253

National Energy Plan, 250, 251, 254, 255

National Energy Policy, 270, 275, 284

National Energy Policy Development Group (NEPDG), 270

nationalism, resource, 215–16

natural gas consumption: Britain, 69, 87–88, 90, 91–92, 94; France, 121, 140; Germany, 153, 154, 157, 168, 184; U.S., 243

natural gas imports: Britain, 81–82, 90–93, 107; France, 140; Germany, 162–63, 168–69, 170, 173, 176, 177–78, 184; Japan, 203, 207, 208, 216, 219; liquefied, 8, 29, 105, 324; U.S., 319–23

natural gas infrastructure, 102–3

natural gas production: Britain, 70, 82, 90–91, 97–98, 107–8; France, 143–44; U.S., 319–20

natural gas storage: Britain, 80, 82, 91–92, 93, 103, 107; France, 140; Germany, 163, 185

Netherlands, the, 25; and Britain, 104; and Germany, 29, 163, 168, 173

New Energy Development Organization (NEDO), 205

New National Energy Strategy (NNES), 211–12, 217–18, 221

Nigeria, 23, 29, 30, 269, 276

Nippon Export and Investment Insurance (NEXI), 225

Nixon, Richard, 244, 245, 246, 247, 248, 285; administration of, 244, 248, 253, 260

Noël, Pierre, 321

Nordlinger, Eric, 53

Nord Stream pipeline, 176

North Atlantic Treaty Organization (NATO), 313–15; and Britain, 314; and France, 314

Norway: and Britain, 91, 93, 104, 107, 295; and France, 140; and Germany, 29, 163, 169

nuclear phaseout, 171, 175, 180, 183, 193

nuclear power, 292; Britain, 69–70, 73, 77–78, 81, 88, 94, 100–102, 108–9, 110; France, 118, 121,

126, 129, 131, 135, 138–39, 142–43, 145, 147,
148–49; Germany, 155, 156, 157, 158–59,
163–64, 168, 170, 190; Japan, 204–5, 210, 212,
221–22, 230–31, 236–37; public opposition to,
164, 175, 188, 214–15, 222, 233; U.S., 255
Nuclear Safety Authority (ASN), 133, 138,
142–43, 148
nuclear village, 233–34, 238

Obama, Barack, 271; administration of, 271, 272,
274
oil companies, international, 24, 26, 27, 73, 74,
119–20, 122, 154, 199
oil consumption: Britain, 69, 82, 87; France, 120,
129; Germany, 153, 168, 170; Japan, 197, 199,
207, 208–9, 212, 213; U.S., 243, 261, 262–63,
266–67, 278
oil imports: fees for, 249, 254, 284; France,
119–20, 121; Germany, 153–54, 173; Japan, 197,
209, 210; quotas for, 243; U.S., 243–44, 245,
250, 256–57, 261, 267, 268, 269–70, 278, 319
oil policy, 118–20
oil price controls, 244, 247, 251, 254, 256–57,
283–84
oil production: Britain, 71, 72–73, 74–76, 81, 88,
90, 97–98; U.S., 243, 257, 261, 267, 278, 319
oil shocks, 25–27; and Britain, 71–74; and France,
122–24; and Germany, 155–60; and Japan,
198–200; and the U.S., 245–51
oil stockpiles: Germany, 154, 166–67, 169, 173;
Japan, 200–201, 207, 212, 218–19. *See also*
Strategic Petroleum Reserve
Oil Taxation Act, 75–76
Organization of the Petroleum Exporting
Countries (OPEC), 25, 26

Page, Scott, 61
path dependence, 6–7, 60–63, 304–6, 308–10;
Britain, 115–16, 305; France, 149, 305;
Germany, 192–93, 305; Japan, 237–38,
306; U.S., 286, 305–6
Persian Gulf, 24, 27; and Britain, 71, 80, 111, 115,
244; and France, 121; and Japan, 205, 219, 224,
239; and the U.S., 241, 242, 258–60, 264–65,
276, 279–80, 285, 286
Petroleum and Submarine Pipelines Act
(PSPA), 75
Petroleum Association of Japan, 226

Petroleum Revenue Tax, 76
Pierson, Paul, 61
Plan for Coal, 76–77
planning process, 95, 101–2, 103–4, 114
Poggi, Gianfranco, 50
Poland, 313, 321
policy legacies. *See* path dependence
political culture, 47–48, 297–98; France, 144–45,
297; Japan, 232–33
Project Independence, 247

Qatar, 30, 105, 206, 224

Reagan, Ronald, 251, 257; administration of, 252,
253
regional energy cooperation in Asia, 226–27
renewable energy: Britain, 89, 98–100; France,
139–40; Germany, 164–65, 174, 180; Japan,
205, 222–23
Renewable Energy Law (EEG), 174–75, 185–86
renewable fuel standard (RFS), 271, 273, 279
Renewable portfolio standard (PRS), 223
renewable power: Britain, 89, 99, 108; France,
134, 140, 143; Germany, 174–75, 184, 185–86;
Japan, 223, 231–32
Renewables Obligation (RO), 89, 99
renewable transport fuels, 89, 99. *See also*
biofuels; ethanol
Renewable Transport Fuels Obligation (RTFO),
89, 99
Russia, 177–78, 216; and Britain, 105; natural gas
exports, 171, 173, 176, 184, 294, 305; relations
with Germany, 181–82, 191
Russia-Ukraine gas crises, 172, 177, 182, 216, 294

Samuels, Richard, 233
Saudi Arabia, 23, 265; and Britain, 80, 105; and
France, 128; and Germany, 167, 191; and Japan,
206; oil production, 27, 28; and the U.S., 24,
244–45, 259–60, 265, 285
Schlesinger, James, 259
Schreurs, Amanda, 53, 235
Schröder, Gerhard, 176
Shah of Iran, 26, 260, 265
shale gas, 318–24
Simon, William, 247n2
Skocpol, Theda, 53, 59
solar power, 140, 164, 174, 183, 184, 223, 229, 231

Soviet invasion of Afghanistan, 246, 260
state, definition of, 49–51
state strength, 5–6, 298–304, 306–8; Britain, 113–15, 300, 303; definition of, 51–60; France, 57, 59, 145–49, 299–300, 303; Germany, 188–91, 301, 303; Japan, 57, 234–37, 300, 303–4; U.S., 57, 59, 281–86, 301, 302–3
Steinmeier, Frank-Walter, 181
Steinmo, Sven, 234
Strange, Susan, 1, 258
Strategic Petroleum Reserve (SPR), 252, 262, 268, 270, 271, 274–75, 278, 284
Suez crisis (1956), 24, 70
Sulieman, Ezra, 146
Sweden, 311
Synthetic Fuels Corporation (SFC), 251, 255–56
Syria, 24, 27

tariff, feed-in: Germany, 174, 185; Japan, 223, 231, 235
taxes. *See* energy taxes; Oil Taxation Act; windfall profits tax
Thatcher, Margaret, government of, 74, 76, 77, 79, 84, 86
Thelen, Kathleen, 61
Three Mile Island nuclear accident, 145, 214, 233, 255
Toichi, Tutsomu, 216, 229
Top Runner Program, 214, 220, 235
Trans-Alaska pipeline, 254, 263

UK-Belgium interconnector, 88, 91
Ukraine, 321. *See also* Russia-Ukraine gas crises
Ullman, Richard, 20

United Arab Emirates (UAE), 224, 227
United Kingdom. *See* Britain
United States, 1, 6, 8, 13, 57, 59, 292–98, 301, 302, 304–6, 319–20, 323–24; and Angola, 276; and China, 277–78; and consumer countries, 260–61, 265–66, 277–78, 285, 292; crude oil equalization tax, 250, 253; gasoline rationing plan, 253; and Iran, 242, 245, 259, 260, 265, 276, 285; oil import fee, 249, 254, 284; oil import quotas, 243; oil price controls, 244, 247, 251, 254, 256–57, 283–84; and oil-producing countries, 258–60, 275–76; and the Persian Gulf, 241, 242, 258–60, 264–65, 276, 279–80, 285, 286; renewable fuel standard, 271, 273, 279; and Saudi Arabia, 24, 244–45, 259–60, 265, 285; spare oil production capacity, 243, 244; windfall profits tax, 251, 254

Venezuela, 23, 24, 25, 29, 243, 269

Walt, Stephen, 19
Washington Energy Conference, 128, 167, 206, 248, 260, 285
West Germany. *See* Germany
Wicks, Malcolm, 67
Willrich, Mason, 21, 32
Wilson, Ernest, 32, 289
Wilson, Harold, government of, 72
windfall profits tax, 251, 254

Yergin, Daniel, 21

Zakaria, Fareed, 56
Zysman, John, 145, 146